Pedagogy of Commerce

Pedagogy of Commerce

Rainu Gupta

SHIPRA

Rs. 595

ISBN: 978-93-91978-12-9

2025 Imp., PoD
First Published in India in 2023

Pedagogy of Commerce

Published by:
SHIPRA PUBLICATIONS
LG 18-19, Pankaj Central Market
I.P. Ext., Patparganj, Delhi 110092, India
+91 11 47322068; 9650028065, 9810522367
info@shiprapublication.com
www.shiprapublication.com

Preface

Teacher education is vital for creating a pool of teachers who will shape the future generation. We all are aware that the present scenario of education system is going to change by implementing New Education Policy 2020 in the coming years. The reason behind it is that the affective dimension of education has not given proper attention in our present day society.

Commerce is one of the major aspects of education system. It is highly important that every student should know about the business activities going on in the society and how they will make our nation 'aatm-nirbhar' in the coming years. For productive commerce education we need efficient and effective teachers. Certainly, a teacher needs to know his learners well in terms of their potential so that he/she can help in their process of development through his/her teaching.

An average student requires a book, which not only caters the course of study, but also presents the essentials in a compact, coherent and intelligible manner. What should a book on pedagogy of commerce try to do? First and most important, I believe, it should capture the interest of the students and demonstrate both the process and challenges of scientific observation and analysis of business environment in an interesting way. Second, it should seek to cultivate in the learners the habit of scientific analysis of society. Third, it should present the basic concepts and descriptive material clearly and intellectually. These should be illustrated so vividly that they 'come alive' and become part of the student's thinking vocabulary. Concepts should not be learned simply in definitions to be memorized, but as accurate, descriptive names for the ways people act and things people build.

In this book, the author has tried to do all these things. The present volume is a revised and enlarged edition of the well received book 'Teaching of Commerce' published in 2009 with numerous subsequent impressions. Here also, each chapter is presented in a systematic and vivid way and true exposition of various aspects of pedagogy of commerce. It provides information about the place of commerce as a discipline, its aims and objectives, Bloom's digital taxonomy, innovative methods and techniques of teaching and different approaches of lesson planning. The author's experience in working with student-teachers has shown her that the perusal of principles frequently does not leave the reader with clear concepts, he/she needs the assistance of specific examples. So, in an attempt to bring clarity and interest in the text repeated illustrations regarding skills, instructional material, developing portfolio, new trends in assessment etc. have been provided.

Teaching may appear easier and 'more natural' for some than to others, but there are no 'born teachers' who don't need to improve or others who can never improve regardless of effort. Good teachers work at being good and are constantly looking for ways to improve. The author is confident that this book will prove beneficial for both student-teachers and teacher-educators. She is grateful to all publishers and thinkers whose work has been consulted while preparing it. She would like to express her sincere gratitude to friends for their valuable suggestions. She is also thankful to Shipra Publications for bringing out this book in a good shape.

No doubt, I have taken care that the book should contain the maximum useful material yet it is for my valued readers to judge the true worth of my sincere efforts. You are welcome to e-mail me at rainugupta31@gmail.com with your thoughts and comments while reading this book or afterwards. I promise to get back to you promptly.

Rainu Gupta

Contents

1

Understanding Commerce

"Commerce is concerned with a group of activities, which directly and indirectly are involved in the distribution of goods between the place where they come into existence and the person who finally uses them."

— *Noel Branton*

The story of the development of human civilization is the story of its economic development. From the ancient period till now whatever the progress has been in every sector, the base of progress is money. Trade, commerce and industry constitute a vital part of our life's activities. Every woman/man works to earn money. In ancient period the form of commerce was easy. People who wanted to sell their commodity, would come to a local market and sit in the bazaar. The buyers would also come in that market and purchase the commodity by paying the price. The people doing this work were known as 'Vaish' and the job was known as commerce. With the passage of time the commercial process has become complex. The markets become wider i.e., from local to state, state to nation and then international. So the area of commerce becomes wider and wider. The need for efficiency in the field of trade arises and to fulfill that need education plays an important role. The increasing complexity of business and commerce organisation in the present day world would make it obligatory for the students to be conversant with the principles and practices of management and accounting. In the modern age, it can rightly be said that no man can live without knowledge of commerce. The invention and circulation of money make the relationship stronger between man and commerce because commerce relates with trade, money and economic activities and in present day material world money and economic activities are the fundamental bases of commerce.

Meaning of Commerce

All the activities which are undertaken in connection with the production of things and carrying them from the place of production to the place of consumption are called business. In short, the activities connected with the production are called **industry** and the activities connected with the transport of goods produced from the factories to the consumers are called **commerce**.

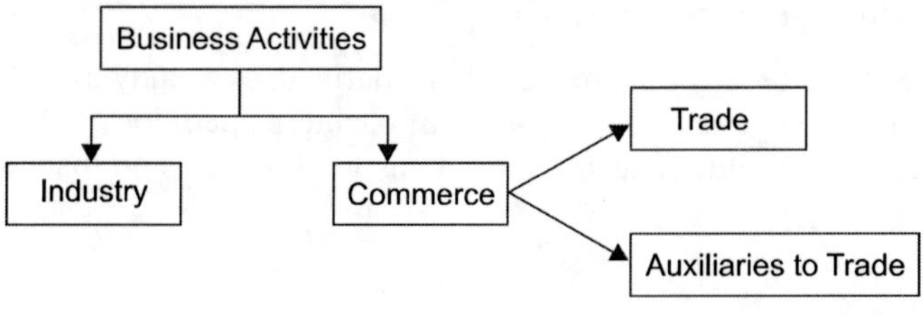

There is a long way which has to be covered in taking the finished products from the place of production to the place of consumption. It is a misconception that commerce is only the purchase and sale of goods. In commerce all those activities are included whose objective is to remove the obstacles in distribution of goods. This process begins in the following way.

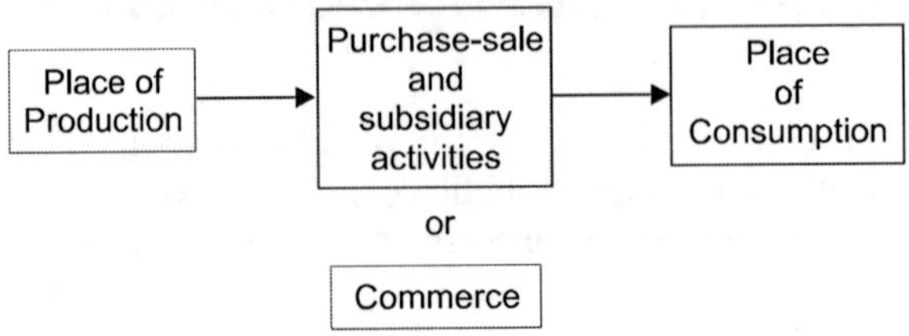

First of all, the wholesale dealer purchases the finished product from the factories. Later on the same product is purchased by the retailers. The last step in this process is the sale of this product to the consumer. But the process does not end with this. There are so many problems in sale-purchase or distribution of goods. For example, the means of transport are needed to take material from one place to another, insurance is needed for the safety of the material, sale-purchase of material need finance, godowns are needed for the stock of material, advertisement is needed for giving information about the material, etc. Thus, commerce is the sum total of all those activities which have to be undertaken in carrying things from the place of production to the place of consumption while removing the obstacles coming in the distribution of goods related to time, place, exchange and risk.

Definitions of Commerce

Various scholars have defined the concept in the following ways.

1. In the words of Evelyn Thomas, "Commercial occupations deal with the buying and selling of goods, the exchange of commodities and the distribution of the finished products."
2. In the words of James Stephenson, "Commerce is the sum total of those processes which are engaged in the removal of the hindrances of persons (trade), place (transport and insurance), and time (ware housing) in the exchange (banking) of commodities."
3. In the words of William R. Spreegal, "Commerce is mainly concerned with the transfer of goods. The activities related to classification, integration, storing, finance-management and transportation and insurance are to be performed in it."

Thus, whichever way commerce may be defined, as a study of distribution or as a study of exchange or even as a study of business operations, it has generally been divided into – Trade, Transport, Banking and Finance, and Insurance.

Characteristics of Commerce

On the basis of above definitions following are the characteristics of commerce:

1. Commerce is the distribution system of goods.
2. In commerce all the activities related to sale and purchase of goods and those which help in sales and purchase of goods are included.
3. Commerce creates the utility.
4. Commerce brings industry and consumer close to each other.
5. Commerce helps in providing the goods at relevant price, at proper time, at proper place, in proper form to the proper person.
6. It is a study of human beings as producers and consumers.
7. It is a study of distribution and exchange.

Components of Commerce

On the basis of the definition of commerce it can be divided into

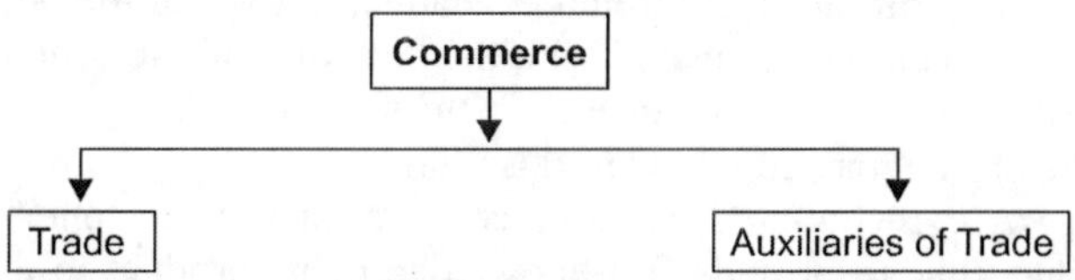

1. Trade: In general words, trade means buying and selling of goods with the purpose of getting profit. In other words, trade means exchange of goods and services for the purpose of material profit of both the buyer and the sellers. It can be carried on the smallest as well as largest scale. Trade can be classified in two categories:

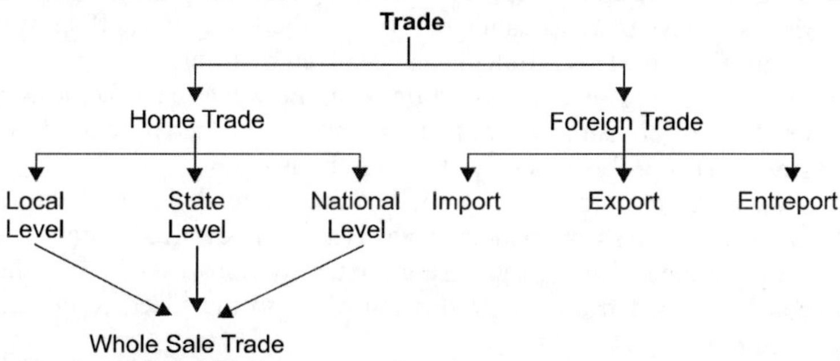

(*i*) *Home Trade:* Home trade means buying and selling of things within the national boundaries.

(*a*) *Local Trade*: It is limited to some village, town or district.

(*b*) *State Trade*: It is a trade among different districts of a state.

(*c*) *National Trade*: It is a trade among different states of the country.

(*ii*) *Foreign Trade:* When the trade crosses the national boundaries and reaches the foreign land then it is known as foreign trade.

Import Trade: When a businessman of a country buys some goods from the businessman of another country.

Export Trade: When the trader of one country sells something to the trader of another country.

Entreport Trade: When a country imports some goods from another country and then exports the same goods to some third country.

2. Auxiliaries to Trade: Commerce includes not only trade but also various other subsidiary activities which are undertaken to overcome the hurdle appearing in the way of trade. The following activities are included in it:

(*i*) *Middlemen*: There are less number of producers and a large number of consumers. Hence, it is not possible for all the consumers to purchase goods directly from the producers. So, there is a need of middlemen to establish contacts between producers and consumers. They consist of wholesaler, retailer etc. There is a chain from producer to consumer as: Producer → Wholesaler → Retailer → Consumer.

(*ii*) *Banking*: Money is required from the moment raw material is purchased till the sale of the finished product. Hurdles of finance in the form of cash, letter of credit, need of foreign exchange, to expand the business arises and these can be eliminated with the help of banking. The means other than the banks, namely finance companies, stock exchanges are also utilised in the present day economy to raise funds.

(*iii*) *Advertising*: Now-a-days a producer, to attract the customer towards his product, has to provide full knowledge of its product to the customer. Advertising helps in this activity. It enhances the knowledge of the customer and eliminates the hindrance of information.

(*iv*) *Insurance*: Whether goods are sold at small scale or large scale, at the time of storage and transporting of these goods from one place to another, risk is always there as damage of goods, theft of goods, effect of natural calamities, etc. This problem can be solved by insurance.

(*v*) *Warehousing*: There remains a time gap between manufacturing of any product and consumption of that product. So finished products have to be stored. This problem is solved by warehousing.

(*vi*) *Transportation*: Today, the trade has been extended from local level to national as well as international level. Hence, there is need of transportation. So hindrance of trade can be eliminated by transport i.e., commodities can be carried from the production place to the place where they are required.

(*vii*) *Communication*: There is large distance between the producers, middlemen and consumers. The means of communication like telephone, telegram, letter, telex, etc. help in finalising the business deals. Due to availability of modern means of communication as computer, internet, etc. business is performed on international basis.

(*viii*) *Packaging*: In present day economy the importance of packaging is increasing day by day. It is needed to maintain the quality of the product and to send it safely. It also provides an attractive look to the product.

(*ix*) *Stock and Produce Exchange*: Stock and produce exchange is known as the measure of economic growth of a country. These are the important activities of business. Stock exchange provides platform for sale and purchase of shares and debentures whereas produce exchange is an effective means of providing the goods. Stock exchange can have good impact on the disinvestment and providing proper environment for trade and industries but it can destroy it also.

Thus, it is clear that during the sale and purchase of goods, there arises many hindrances and these hindrances can be eliminated with the help of commerce.

Nature of Commerce

While discussing the nature of commerce we have to indicate whether it is a science or an art, a positive science or normative science, whether it can pass moral judgements in business. In order to decide whether commerce is a science or an art firstly we have to understand the meaning of 'science' and 'art'.

Science

The terms science has been defined as a systematised body of knowledge, which traces the relationship between cause and effect. A science is not a mere collection of facts, because a mere collection of facts can never constitute a science. To understand the meaning of science, we should know about the characteristics of science which are as follows:

1. The attitude of science is objective.
2. It has fixed explanation.
3. It has the power to predict.
4. The important characteristic is that it is systematic.

Commerce—A Science

In science facts should be systematically collected, classified and analysed. Applying these characteristics to our subject, we find that.

- The attitude of commerce is objective.
- Commerce can explain the events related to trade.
- The profit or losses can be predicted on the basis of accounts.

Thus, we find that commerce is that branch of knowledge where the various facts relevant to it have been systematically collected, classified and analyzed. Judged from this point of view, commerce is a full fledged science.

Some writers seem to imagine that commerce cannot be given the dignified status of a science because:

- Lack of exactness in commerce.
- Scientific laws are completely true and fixed, whereas in commerce there are no such type of laws because it is based on human efforts which change according to the given situations.
- The data on which scientific laws based are correct and true but the data in commerce cannot be so exact and true.
- There is inability to predict the future course of events as accurately as the physical sciences can.

It is, no doubt, true that commerce cannot predict the future course of events as accurately as natural sciences and it very often happens that business prophecies are falsified by subsequent events. But on the basis of this only, we can't deny the scientific nature of commerce studies. The only reason for this lack of predictability is that commerce deals with highly complex and various forces, some of which are not amenable to correct prediction. Commerce deals with men endowed with freedom of will and there is no guarantee that they will act in a preconceived manner.

An Art

An 'art', like science, is also a systematised body of knowledge. The object of art is the formulation of percepts immediately applicable to policy. The practical aspect of the art distinguishes it from science, which may be merely theoretical.

Commerce—An Art

Commerce, in certain respects, is an art as well. There are several branches of commerce, which offer us practical guidance in development of trade, in managing an institution. It provides the occupational training to the students like clerical, accountancy, etc. It develops human values in the students like patience, honesty, cooperation, brotherhood, etc. These human values help the students in later life as a businessman. It teaches how to accumulate the money and how to invest it.

Thus, we can say that commerce is both a science and an art because as a science, it formulates certain rules, principles and theories; while as an art, it gives them a practical shape. It is both an academic discipline and a vocational discipline. In the words of Prof. Cossa, "Science provides us theoretical knowledge whereas art provides training in practical practices."

Scope of Commerce

Commerce is the exchange of something of value between two entities. That "something" may be goods, services, information, money or anything else, the two entities consider and have value. Commerce is the central mechanism from which capitalism is derived.

By the term scope we mean the breadth, comprehensiveness, variety and the extent of the learning experience, the ability in real life situations provided through the teaching of commerce. The subject will be important for its subject matter as well as skills it develops among the students as a responsible citizen of the economy and thus it will ensure intelligibility and extension of experiences rather than mere verbal memorization of facts. In the period of globalization the world has became a small unit. It has been united in terms of communication, transportation and fear for the future. Obviously one cannot be a good citizen in today's world without general understanding of some of the major realities of the world as a whole.

Commerce today covers a vast field and comprises many branches of scholarship in its fold. Like the bee, it sucks honey from every flower. The subject matter of commerce is very wide because it includes all the commercial activities performed by man in the economy. Commerce is a body of organised knowledge and thoughts about trade affairs. It is a science of arts, trade and aids to trade; aids to trade are insurance, transport, communication, advertisement, etc. The scope of commerce has to be broad enough to acquaint the pupils with a wide range of trade activities that are meaningful to them. We generally study the following facts to have a knowledge of the scope of commerce.

1. Subject Matter of Commerce: Commerce has its own subject matter. Commerce area is both a knowledge subject and a skill subject. The objectives of the study of commerce are both preparatory to further studies in colleges and terminal to enter into the careers of middle level lives of employment. Its subject matter is very vast as shown in the diagram 1.1.

The subject matter of commerce includes the study of general commerce, economics, geography, commercial laws, book-keeping, business management, accountancy, advertising and salesmanship, office practices, etc. Most of the subject matter serves to introduce the students the activities of business enterprises.

According to University Education Commission 1948–49, professional business education should include mathematics, statistics, theory of organisation, business structure; finance, including management and budgeting of assets and of expenses; philosophy, history and theory of law; and organisation of work including economics; process analysis and procedures, standardisation of skills, cost analysis and the like.

***2. Form of Trade Organisation and Types of Trade*:** If we want to get organised knowledge about the problems of commerce, firstly we have to get knowledge about the nature and types of trade. When the trade is carried on within a country, it is known as internal trade. The scope of this type of trade limits to the country and its problems can be solved by keeping the situations of the county in mind. But the problems related to international or foreign trade are different. The problems related to it may be of transportation, exchange control, imperial preference, tax and toll tax, etc. Thus, internal and foreign trade are two different parts of commerce and there is need to think about the problems related to it from different angles.

It is necessary to understand the organisation of the trade to understand its problems. In ancient period when the field of exchange was limited, the trade was in the hands of individual traders. Now it has been changed into joint family firms. Today commerce involves a complex system of companies that try to maximise their profits by offering products and services to the market, which consists both of individuals and other companies at the lowest production cost. There is a system of world wide or foreign commerce, which some argue has gone too far.

Nature of trade is also the part of scope of commerce. Today there are two types of trade i.e. Wholesale Trade and Retail Trade. They exist in between the producers and consumers. So they are called intermediaries or middlemen. The price of the product increases due to these middlemen. So, in the present day economy, there is a planning to abolish the role of these middlemen, but their role is so specific and important that it is difficult to ignore or do away with their role completely.

The wholesaler buys the goods in large quantities from the producer or manufacturer or their authorised dealer and sells the same to the retailer in small quantities. Later on, the retailer sells these things to the customers as per their need.

3. Activities related to Commerce: The third important part of the scope of commerce is those activities related to commerce which are to be carried on at different levels of trade. These are mainly of two types:

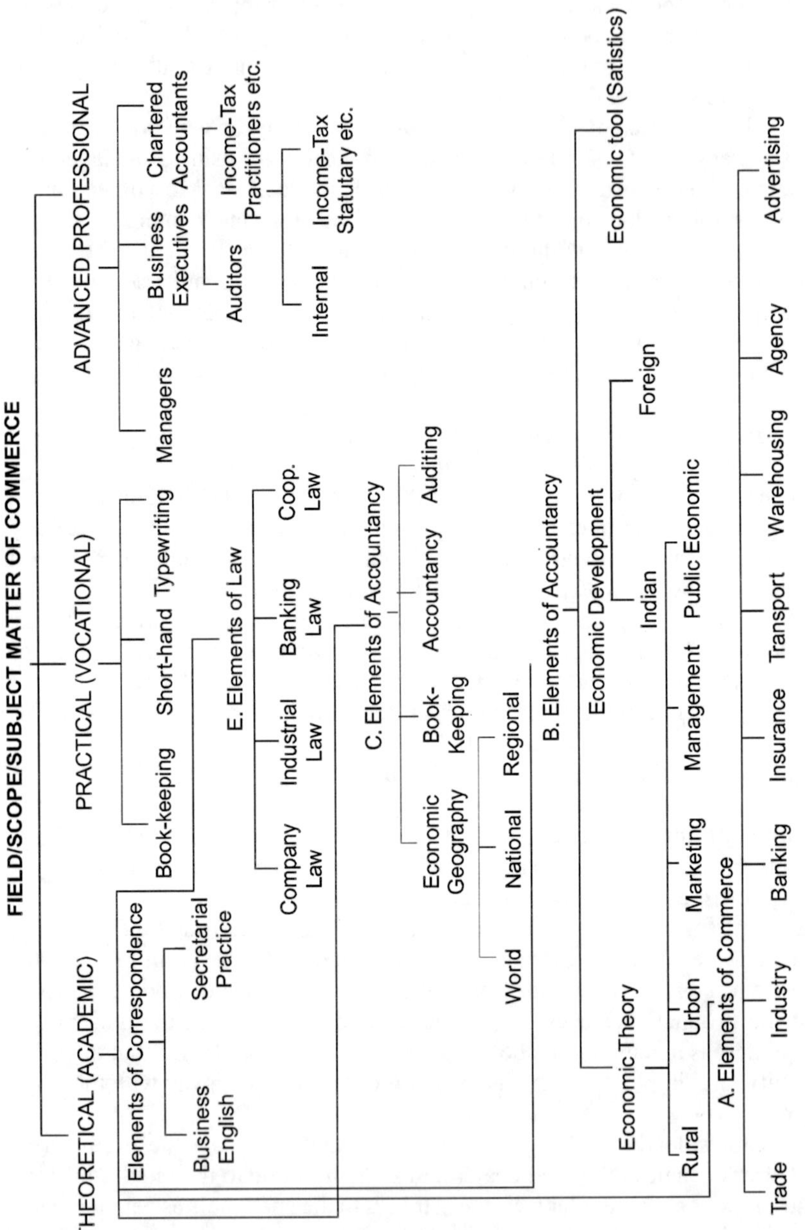

Fig. 1.1: Field/Scope/Subject Matter of Commerce

i. Primary Activities;
ii. Auxiliaries.

Commerce Activities

Primary | Auxillaries

(*i*) *Primary Activities:* It is the main part of commercial activities which includes buying and selling of things. These can be done on the smallest as well as the largest scale. For the larger scale activities there arises the need of credit facilities. that is why banks and other organisations came into being. In foreign trade, the buying of goods is based on mutual relationships between the two countries, international rules and guidlines, etc. In modern times there is so much competition in the market to sell the product that everybody is providing the easy payment facilities and options, as instalment system. Another is hire purchase system which also came in to practice. Industrialists and businessmen are also using different selling techniques and methods to sell their products in national and international markets.

(*ii*) *Auxiliaries:* Commerce includes not only primary activities but also the auxiliaries or subsidiary activities. Most important activities under it are sales promotion activities. When there are many producers of a thing, there is strong competition among them to sell the good. To attract customers towards his product, a producer provides full knowledge of his product to the customer through advertisement. He uses posters, cinema etc. for the advertisement. Sometimes the producers use different measures as reduction sales, clearance sales, and seasonal reduction to attract the customers.

Inquiry is also an important activity. When any bank or trader wants to provide loans to another trader then bank or trader should know about the other trader's economic condition. He takes the help of Inquiry Bureaus, business agencies, Chambers of commerce, accounts of that traders, etc. After getting complete information about that trader loan is given.

In subsidiary activities, the most important are the activities related to sales and distribution. These activities are of dual type. On one side, the traders provide information regarding the needs of the customers to the producers, and on the other hand, facilitate the consumer by providing different commodities from the producers at reasonable price.

Communication is another activity through which inquiries are made, orders are placed, complaints and suggestions are made and the trade transactions are finally settled.

4. Basic Institutions of Commerce: In the present economy, commerce field has become so vast that the produced goods are distributed throughout the world by different institutions / organisations. These institutions / organisations are of much importance to the field of business.

The most important in these are transport companies. Producers and consumers are far away from each other geographically and through transport it is possible to carry commodities from one place to another where they are required.

Another important system is means of communication like telephone, telegram, letter, telex etc. which help in finalizing the business deals. Due to availability of modern means of transportation and communication, business is performed on international basis.

The other agencies like produce exchange, stock exchange, etc. work as platform for sale and purchase of raw material, bullion, money, capital, exchange shares, stocks and government securities.

To fulfill the fund requirements there are indigenous banks, discount houses, acceptance houses, industrial banks, agricultural banks, investment banks cooperations etc.

Insurance companies provide many facilities for business to reduce the element of risk due to damage of goods, theft of goods and effect of other natural calamities. These can be life insurance, fire insurance, marine insurance, etc.

The other agencies as information bureaus, mercantile agencies, etc. provide reliable information regarding the borrowers of money. The agencies like chambers of commerce, trade associations and syndicates, etc. function for the welfare of the traders, to represent the trading in government, to solve the mutual differences, etc. Trade unions also play an important role in commerce.

Limitations of Commerce

While studying the scope of commerce, we come to know about the limitations too, as:

1. It studies only business activities.
2. Commerce is completely a positive science.
3. It includes the study of activities related to accountancy.
4. It studies the activities which are undertaken to overcome the hurdle appearing in the way of trade.

Thus, commerce is a vast discipline comprises of different branches of management. It can be summarised as:

1. Social intercourse.
2. To carry on trade.
3. The exchange or buying and selling of commodities, especially the exchange of merchandise, on a large scale, between different places and communities, extended trade or traffic.
4. It deals with goods and services.
5. Deals with creation of form, place and time utilities.
6. Deals with profit motive.

Thus, it can simply be stated that all the activities related to trade of the competitive business world may be included under the subject matter of commerce.

Place of Commerce in Secondary School Curriculum

Commerce is one of the most relevant subjects there is and has been since the dawn of time. Most of the scholars have divided school education of the child in the following stages on the basis of their mental level:

1. Pre-primary level – For children upto the age of 5 years.
2. Elementary level– For children in the age of 5–14 years.
3. Secondary level – For children in the age of 14–16 years.
4. Senior Secondary level – For children in the age of 16–18 years.

In the curriculum formulated by Indian Certificate of Secondary Education (ICSE), commerce has been introduced as a separate subject in class IX and X whereas the Central Board of Secondary Education and other state boards include courses of Business Studies and Accountancy in classes XI and XII. Incidentally, it does not mention the term 'Commerce'. Thus the subjects of commerce as business studies and others have been started at the senior secondary stage of education because it has been found that upto secondary level the main aim of education is to provide general knowledge and the students can learn more subjects at this level. It is a specialized discipline and the students will learn about it at senior secondary level.

Objectives of the commerce course prescribed for Indian Certificate of Secondary Education (ICSE).

1. To create an awareness of the environment with in which the business activity takes place.
2. To expose the students to certain technical terms in commerce.
3. To understand the way in which changes in the environment influence business activities.
4. To develop knowledge and understanding of the meaning and importance of commerce.
5. To understand the various hindrances of trade and to appreciate the aids that remove these hindrances.
6. To prepare students to cope with the stress and strain that occurs in the process of business activities.
7. To acquaint the students with the contemporary business problems.
8. To help students understand the various agencies of business sector and that all the agencies must work cooperatively to develop business sector.
9. To develop desirable attitudes and to become effective instruments of business change in future.
10. To become an effective citizen.
11. To develop an understanding about commercial activities.
12. To familiarise the students with basic terminology and elementary ideas of commerce.

At senior secondary stage, students have curious mind and the most important aim of education is to satisfy their curiosity. At this level they are to make their mind regarding the professional line they have to choose for their future. It is also desirable to light a new flame of knowledge among the students at this stage. This flame will also fill the young students with zeal for life. Commerce is introduced at the senior secondary level.

There are different angles for assessing the importance of a subject in the school curriculum. These angles are:

1. The utility of the subject in providing knowledge.
2. The utility of the subject in practical life.
3. The utility of the subject in developing balanced pattern of life.
4. The utility of the subject in the inculcation of the cultural values.

From the angles cited above, we judge the place of commerce in the school curriculum. Apart from these there are following reasons:

1. The students who have acquired knowledge of commerce, try to solve various problems in an independent manner. It will help in developing original thinking of the pupils.
2. It enables the students to choose further courses of study.
3. It provides the knowledge about flow of goods and services from the producer to the consumer.
4. The students get knowledge about the business situations of one's own country as well as of other countries with the study of internal trade, foreign trade, etc.
5. The study of commerce helps in development of socio-economic competency by assisting students to develop a clear understanding of the national economy. The nation needs people who are socially efficient and at the same time economically sound.
6. It enables the students to prepare for entry in a vocation.
7. It enables the students to understand how competition brings improvement in the quality of production of goods.
8. It enables the students to understand how advertisement helps in the selling of the product.
9. It enables the students to understand how prices of different products are determined.
10. The study of commerce helps the young pupils to become thoughtful. It makes them able to think about various social and national problems. They acquire the capacity and efficiency to play their role in the business life of the society.
11. It enable the students to fulfill their responsibility as a citizen of the whole world.
12. It enables the students to understand how a variety of consumer interests are developed.
13. Students learn how to lead a disciplined life.
14. Students learn how to adopt values as cultural values, moral values.
15. It provides knowledge of methods used in maintaining records of proprietary and partnership firms, companies and non-trading organisations.
16. It acquaints students with theoretical foundations and practice of organising, managing and handling routine operations of a business firm.
17. It enables students to prepare financial statements and interpret results for decision-making.
18. It acquaints the students with practice and procedure of determination of cost from the view-point of its elements.

Thus, we can say that commerce has an important place in the school curriculum. Education is a medium through which knowledge and intelligence required by an individual or society can be obtained or properly formulated. Commerce begins with functional aspects and then leads to liberal or ideological aspects. The individual and the society get goods and services at their doorsteps. The commerce system deals with every part of human life and thus commerce education becomes an education for better living. The increasing number of students in commerce rather than other subjects indicate its importance or place in the school curriculum. In the present scenario, it is very necessary that every citizen should have knowledge about the business world, so that he may be able to play the role as a responsible citizen. Commerce has an important place in the senior secondary curriculum because of developing different qualities related to theoretical as well as practical aspects. NEP 2020 aims at developing skills among the students and for that every student will have to do internship of 10 days with local trades or crafts from 6th grade.

Values of Teaching Commerce

Aims are considered as conscious purposes and goals. Values are the outcomes or results, achieved after teaching according to the prescribed aims and curriculum.

The subject of commerce is becoming very popular among the students in the present day education because of its utility. It has a practical approach to enrich business values among the pupils for their daily life as well as profession. Any subject is to be studied because of its utility in knowledge aspect as well as in practical life. Commerce has both kinds of values. It not only provides knowledge and information but it is a fruitful discipline also.

The values of study of commerce can be divided in two parts:

1. Theoretical values.
2. Practical values.

Theoretical Values

The study of commerce enhances the knowledge and knowledge in turn develops the mental level of the students.

1. *Enriched knowledge*: The subject of commerce is covered through content based on facts and informations related to trade, bookkeeping, insurance, financing, etc. It is helpful in enriching the knowledge of the students. They can be aware about most of the information regarding business terms, laws and principles. It helps in finding the answers of many questions as which type of market India have, what type of advertisement should be used, from where the goods can be purchased and sold etc. It will help in feeling the responsibility as a citizen of the country. It helps in knowing about the various plans of country drawn into bring about economic betterment. It helps in getting the knowledge about various concepts as organisation, management, banking, insurance etc. Commerce enriches the knowledge of the students with regard to business activities of their country as well as of other countries.

2. *Development of Logical Skills*: The rules and principles related to commerce education will help in developing the logical skills of the students. They can think of what type of changes are coming in business from the past until present day.

How the society is changing? What is the change is in the needs of the society? What changes are needed in the present age for the development of future? Now a days an individual does not accept anything without reason. In this way, commerce education helps in developing the logical power which is essential for the development of business world:

3. *Helpful in Providing Training in Co-operation*: For the development of the industry there is need of cooperation among its members. This can be developed with the help of teaching commerce. In it, pupils will learn that whenever there was a challenging situation before the business world, that was solved by the cooperation of all the members.

4. *Development of Scientific Attitude*: The pupils with the help of commerce acquire the knowledge of different areas *i.e.* Banking, communication, warehousing, partnership and cooperative society, company, internal and external trade, insurance, types of business enterprises, formation of company, etc. Modern age is the age of science. The knowledge of commerce helps in development of scientific attitude among the students.

5. *Development of Competence is Problem Solving*: Through commerce pupil receives training to solve the problems. It will lead to a sense of responsibility. It will help in developing the skill of self-reliance. With the help of the knowledge about facts and principles of business the young generation will begin to feel that they are capable of doing things themselves and they have got a personal responsibility in handling the situation. It will help in the development of competence in solving present day problems as well as in the near future also.

6. *Development of Skills of Tolerance and Openness*: In commerce there are various problems raised by the teacher before the students to give their views. The teacher respects the various views in areas having no certain answers. Students feel free to raise questions and explore various types of evidences. Pupils learn to listen to the views of others. These learning experiences provided by the teacher help in developing the skill of tolerance and openness.

7. *Development of Skills in Studying and Learning*: While studying commerce the students are to interpret the data, evaluate the information, organize the information, solve the cases related to real business world, distinguish facts from fictions, facts from opinions, summarize data, classify information and putting ideas and question in a clear manner. The skills in studying and learning various aspects of commerce help in development of personality.

8. *Knowledge of other Countries*: The study of commerce is helpful in acquiring the knowledge of one's own country. It also provides a lot of information about the business activities of other countries as well.

9. *Development of Character*: There is general accord, however, on certain fundamental ideas, attitudes, interests and appreciations are essential for high character. The background of our culture is responsible for right and wrong and for agreement upon certain virtues. Commerce education will help in inculcating high ideals and civic standards in preparing pupils to take their place as producer, consumer, trader, etc. in a democratic society.

10. *Relevant Understanding*: Commerce is not the mere transmission of

unrelated isolated facts but there is also a need of relevant understanding of facts and principles of business and trading. With the help of relevant experiences and activities inside and outside the classroom, there will be development of proper understanding of the subject matter and it will result in proper utilization of these in the development of business world on the bases of their applicability.

Practical Values

The practical values denotes that the acquisition of knowledge is not only for the development of skills, decision making power or development of scientific attitude, but also for the development of practical behaviour of human beings for their own and others' lives. The commerce system deals with every part of human life and thus commerce education becomes an education for better living. The close relationship between the functions of commerce and socio-economic development and cultural values has led to the increasing realisation of the importance of commerce.

In the study of commerce we are concerned with those activities which are mostly related with trade. It usually means all those activities that educate and train people at all levels who work in organisation that deal in the purchase of and sales of goods and services. We find a cut throat competition in every individual in every society and in every country to develop more and more in business activities. In the study of commerce we deal with that part of life in which we try to find out ways and means of leading a successful life by using limited resources. We find that practical aspect is more important than theoretical aspect. This is the reason A.B. Lowndes states that "the whole programme of commerce education aims at the provision of training for the whole of the commercial and administrative aspects of industry, and not only for the narrower aspects of buying, selling, banking, transportation, warehousing and recording".

Commerce education has the practical values as:

1. *Values to the Businessman*: The knowledge of commerce is very valuable for the businessman. In fact, commerce education plays a creative role for enabling the businessman to be efficient i.e. he can easily decide about – what form of business to be adopted, what means of transportation to be chosen and what auxiliary to trade be used, etc. He can also get the knowledge of good organizational behaviour to be adopted, different market conditions. He can make an estimate of demand and supply of various goods. He gets the knowledge about the warehousing facilities provided by the government and trading agencies. He can decide about– what type of insurance he needs for his business protection. Thus, it helps him in all activities related to business.

2. *Values to Labourers*: Commerce gives the concept of division of labour. Division of labour is the base of modern civilization. Economic life can't run smoothly without it. It helps in making the labour specialized in their field. It increases their capabilities, potentialities and abilities. Commerce education enables them to work efficiently in the business centres through transmitting the knowledge of new innovations in technology and the full knowledge of division of labour. Thus, we can say that commerce education enables the labour force to be efficient to work properly, which is the need of the present day Indian society. This is the efficiency only that leads to higher wages. An efficient labourer can get an opportunity of good job.

3. *Values to Consumers*: Commerce is important and useful for customers also. The consumers can get the useful and necessary things of daily use with the help of commerce. The study of commerce enables a consumer to appreciate that man is a social being and he must play an important role in bringing about social progress. Commerce provides knowledge of different commodities to the consumer. It also provides the knowledge about different taxes and the effect of advertisement on the sale of the commodity.

4. *Values to Politicians*: Commerce education is helpful for state administrators and politicians, because it fixes up certain targets and paves the ways for their accomplishment within the limit of available resources of State/Nation, through their optimum utilization.

5. *Values to Producers and Manufactures*: It is very important for every producer and manufacture to know the auxiliaries to their business or trade as Banking, insurance, advertising, warehousing, communication, transportation, packing, stock exchange, etc. Now manufactures can transport their products from one factory or company to the market easily at the lowest cost. Along with it, commerce education makes possible for manufacturers to forecast about the future trend of their products in the market.

6. *Values to Employment Seekers*: Now-a-days, value of commerce is increasing among the students, because it has vast employment opportunities for the youth in different spheres as banking, advertising, marketing, computer, insurance, management, finance and other fields also. Graduate in commerce can compete for Indian Economic Services (IES) and successful candidates are appointed in the various ministries to deal with business sector. Thus, it has much vocational value in the life of every individual of the society and helps in achieving the aim of education i.e. economic security.

7. *Value to Nation and Society*: It helps a lot in the development of nation and society, because commerce education provides better planning schemes for nation and society, as we know that good planning means a sharp looking into the future with hope and confidence. The proper planning process entails the process of assessment of resources and puts them to the result-oriented uses, so helps in procuring the pre-determined goal of nation/society easily. It is helpful for planning commission in making five year plans with the help of which India can move ahead in the business field. It is estimated that in the coming years, the problem of unemployment will be solved. There will be increase in per capita income as the increase in employment opportunities.

Thus, commerce is a valuable discipline for each country's development. It can help in solving various economic problems as unemployment, overproduction, unequal distribution of wealth, ineffective economic policies, low living standard, poverty and many other social evils. There is no aspect of human life, where the knowledge of commerce is not useful. Whether there may be statesmen, householders, businessmen, producers, labourers and manufacturers, they can't make progress without the knowledge of commerce education. Thus, looking at from every point of view, it is an extremely useful and important subject. The National Education Policy 2020 lays emphasis on practical knowledge and skill development which will begin from class 6th.

2

Understanding Business Studies and Accountancy

"Business is a human activity directed towards producing or acquiring wealth through buying and selling goods" — *Lewis H. Honey*

Meaning of Business Studies

Business Studies is the combination of two words i.e. Business + Studies. The etymology of 'Business' relates to the state of being busy either as an individual or society as a whole, doing commercially viable and profitable work. The term 'business' has at least three usages, depending on the scope: i) the singular usage to mean a particular *organisation*; ii) the generalised usage to refer to a particular *market sector*; 'the music business' and compound forms such as agrobusiness; and iii) the broadest meaning, which encompasses all activities by the community of suppliers of goods and services. The word 'studies' deals with the study. Thus, Business Studies is the subject which deals with the nature and purpose of business, forms of business organisation, business services, emerging modes of business, social responsibility of business and business ethics.

Any country's wealth and influence in the world are founded on its trade and industry, and the efficiency of the business community is vital in an every increasing competitive world.

- What makes a successful business?
- How ethical and environmentally friendly is big business?
- How are world business people meeting the challenges of globalisation and competition?
- How do we find a really good business idea?
- What difference is modern technology making to working pattern?

The students find answers to these and many other questions with the help of Business Studies. The Business Studies enable candidates to understand and appreciate the nature and scope of business, and the role business played in society. Business Studies students gain lifelong skills, including:

- Understanding different forms of business organisation, the environment in which businesses operate and business functions such as marketing, operation and finance.
- An appreciation of the critical role of people in business success.
- Confidence to calculate and interpret business data.

- Communication skills including the need to support arguments with reasons.
- Ability to analyse business situations and reach decisions or judgements.

Thus, business is a wide term. It includes all occupations in which people are busy in earning income.

Characteristics of Business Studies

1. It is the study of different types of human activities.
2. It is the study of different business activities.
3. It is the study of different forms of business organisations i.e. private, public and global enterprises.
4. It deals with the business services.
5. It is the study of e-business.
6. It tells about the social responsibilities of business and business ethics.
7. It provides information about the documents used in the formation of a company.
8. It provides knowledge about the sources from which finances can be arranged for business.
9. It deals with the provisions of government assistance and special schemes for industries in rural background and hilly areas.
10. It provides knowledge about different types of internal trade.
11. It deals with export and import procedures.

Classification of Business Activities

Business activities can be classified on various bases. The classification is on the basis of two functions, namely:

1. Industry
2. Commerce

1. Industry

Industry refers to an activity which converts raw material into useful products. It includes activities related to production and processing as well as activities related to rearing and reproduction of animals or other living species.

Industry may produce consumer goods or capital goods. Goods such as bread, butter, cloth, radio etc. are consumer goods. These goods are directly used by the consumer. Goods such as machinery, cement etc. are called capital goods as these are used further in the production process to make useful products.

Industry can be classified into two broad categories.

I. Primary Industry
II. Secondary Industry

I. Primary Industry

Primary industry includes all those industries which are concerned with extraction of natural resources and reproduction of living species. These industries can further be classified into two categories:

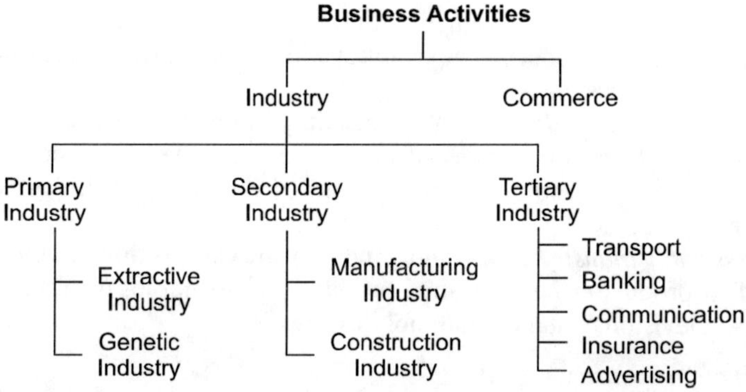

(i) *Extractive Industries*: Extractive industries are those which involve extraction of something from natural resources such as minerals from earth, fish from rivers and seas, timber from forest, etc. The products of extractive industry can be used directly or become the raw material for other industries.

(ii) *Genetic Industry*: The industries involved in the activities of rearing and breeding of living organisms i.e. birds, plants, animals, etc. are known as genetic industry. For example, rearing of cattle for milk, dairy farms, poultry farms, rearing of plants in nursery, growing fish in ponds (Pisciculture), etc. are included in genetic industry.

II. Secondary Industry

The secondary industry makes use of products which are extracted and produced by primary industry as their raw materials and produce finished products. For example, mining of iron ore is done in primary industry but steel manufacturing is done in secondary industry. There are two kinds of secondary industry:

1. Manufacturing Industries

These industries are engaged in the process of conversion of raw materials or semi-finished goods into finished goods. These industries create form utility by changing the form of raw materials into finished products. For example, timber is converted into furniture, iron into steel, sugarcane into sugar, cotton into cloth, etc. The manufacturing industries produce two types of goods:

(i) *Consumer goods*: The goods which can be directly consumed by the consumer are known as consumer goods. These goods are used for day-to-day consumption. For example, cloth, oil, soap, bread, etc.

(ii) *Industrial goods*: The goods which are produced for manufacturing consumer goods are known as industrial goods like machinery, equipment, and tools, etc. which are required to manufacture consumer goods.

Manufacturing industries are of the following types:

(i) *Analytical Industries*: In analytical industry the basic raw material is broken into different parts to produce finished products. For example, crude oil is processed and many finished products such as petroleum, diesel, kerosene oil, gasoline etc. are manufactured.

(ii) *Synthetic Industry*: In synthetic industry two or more materials are mixed to manufacture some new product. For example, various chemicals are mixed to produce soap, paints, cosmetics, etc.

(iii) *Processing Industry*: In processing industry the raw material is processed through various stages of production and then finished goods are manufactured. For example, Textile Industry, Iron and Steel Industry, Sugar Industry, etc.

(iv) *Assembly Industry*: In assembly industry the various finished products are combined to produce a new finished product. For example, manufacturing of computers, television, watches, automobiles, etc.

2. Construction Industry

These industries are concerned with the construction of buildings, dams, roads, etc. These industries use the products of manufacturing industries such as cement, iron and steel, lime, etc. The unique feature of these industries is that their products cannot be transferred or shifted to the market. They are constructed and remain at a fixed site only.

3. Tertiary or Service Industry

Tertiary industry is concerned with providing services which facilitate a smooth flow of goods and services. This industry helps in the activities of the primary and secondary industry. In other words, this industry provides services which support the activities of primary and secondary industry, that is why it is also known as service industry. The various types of services provided by tertiary industry are:

(i) *Transport*: It facilitates movement of goods from one place to another.
(ii) *Banking*: Provides credit facility to industries and trading firms.
(iii) *Insurance*: Provides coverage from various types of risks.
(iv) *Warehousing*: Provides storage place for goods produced by primary and secondary industry.
(v) *Advertising*: Provides information to consumer.

Scope of Business Studies

Business Studies is a vast subject, its scope is also very wide. Its scope includes:

1. *Study of human activities*: All human beings, wherever they are, are required to perform some or the other activity to satisfy their needs. Activities which human beings undertake are known as human activities. These can be classified into two categories:

- Economic Activities
- Non-economic Activities

2. *Study of business risk*: Business risk refers to the probability of losses or profits due to uncertainty or unexpected events, which are beyond control. The common causes of risk are:

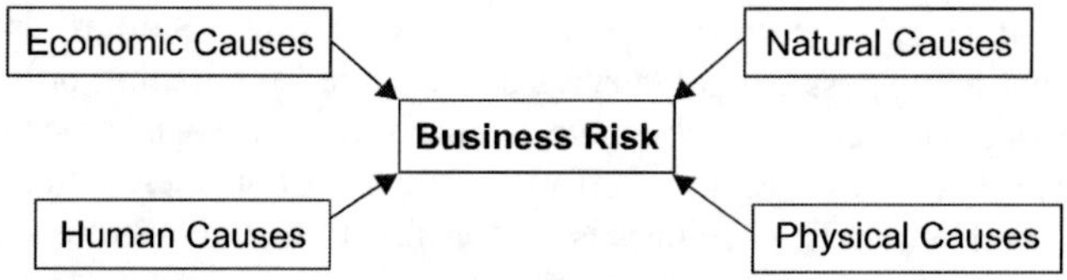

Natural calamities like earthquake, flood etc. affect a business a lot and can result in heavy losses. The dishonesty of employees can bring heavy losses for business. Price fluctuation, change in fashion, change in taste, change in degree of competition, change in demands of customers have direct impact on the earnings of the business. Use of old technology, mechanical defects may also result in damage of assets in the business. Business risk can also be classified as insurable risk and non-insurable risk.

3. *Study of business factors*: Business Studies deals with the study of business factors. In modern business world competition is very tough and risks are very high. Before starting a business various problems and factors associated with the business must be analysed and scanned properly as selecting the line of business, size of the business, choice of form of business organisation, location, financial requirements, competent and committed work force, etc.

4. *Study of forms of business organisations*: Business Studies provides knowledge about the forms of business organisation. It may be classified in three broad categories:

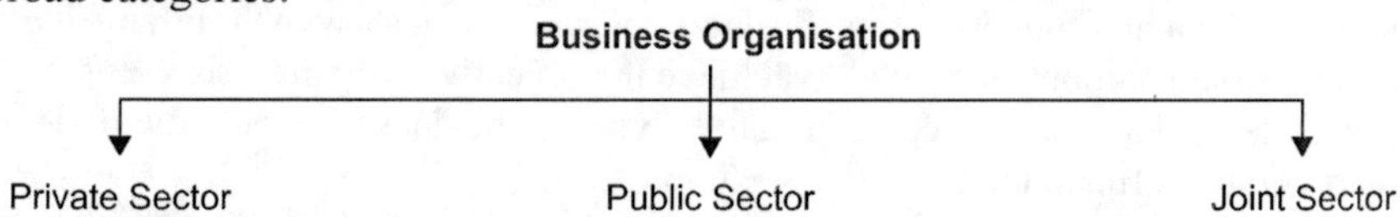

In private sector business organisation is owned, controlled and managed by private individuals. In public sector the business is owned, controlled and managed by central or state government whereas in joint sector the business enterprises are owned, controlled and managed jointly by private entrepreneur and government.

5. *Study of business services*: The service sector constitutes the basic infrastructure which is a must for smooth flow of business activities. The services can be broadly classified into three categories:

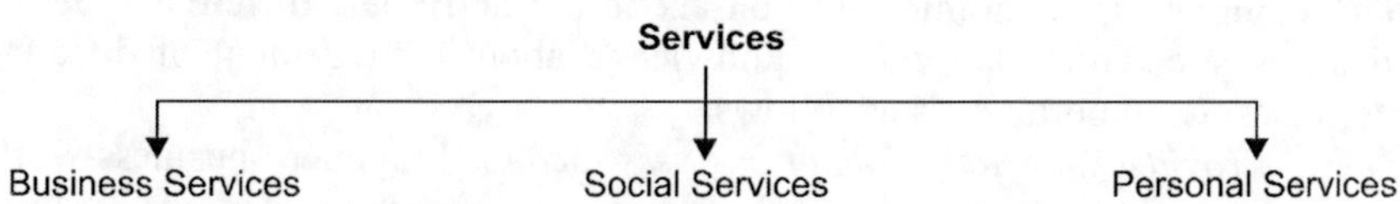

Business services are those which are used by the enterprise to carry on business activities more smoothly as banking, insurance, transportation, warehousing, communication, etc.

6. *Study of emerging modes of business*: Modern era is the era of globalisation, change and technology. In response to this, business throughout the world is changing its organisation, way of working and use of technology, business processes are being redesigned. The major change in mode of business is emergence of e-business, e-commerce and business processing outsourcing. E-business refers to 'carrying on business activities through internet'.

7. *Study of social responsibilities of business*: Business Studies also provides knowledge that a business cannot survive a long time by pursuing only economic objectives. Along with economic objective, it must have some social objectives. Social responsibility relates to the voluntary efforts on the part of businessmen to contribute to the social well being. The business is responsible to different groups as:

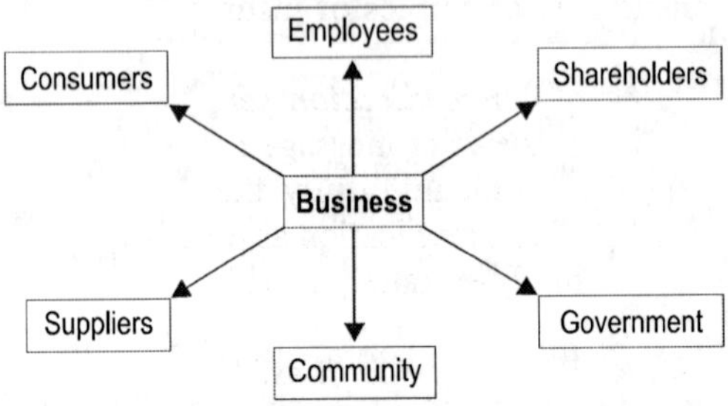

8. *Study of business ethics*: Business ethics refers to the set of moral values or standards or norms which govern the activities of a businessman. Ethics defines what is right and what is wrong. It involves critical analysis of human acts to determine whether these are right or wrong. The business ethics decides what is the expected conduct of businessman and what is not expected by the society.

9. *Study of finance*: Business finance refers to capital funds and credit funds invested in the business financing, means making money available when it is needed. Finance is the major function of any business enterprise. It deals with the arrangement of an adequate amount of capital to achieve the objectives of enterprise. Business Studies deals with the sources of finance, types of business finance, methods of raising finance, financial institutions, etc.

Thus, Business Studies has a vast scope which deals with all the activities to start a business, to run a business and to grow a business. It also deals with the management of a business.

Values of Business Study

The subject of Business Studies is an important subject for the students because through this subject, they get the knowledge about different types of business, about companies, economic and non-economic activities, different types of industries, etc. They also get the knowledge about management of different enterprises. Its importance is as follows:

1. *Provides knowledge about business factors*: In modern business world competition is very tough and risks are very high. Before starting a business various problems and factors associated with the business must be analysed and scanned properly, so Business Studies provides the knowledge about those business factors.
2. *Develops understanding about different forms of business organisations*. A business enterprise is an organisation which is engaged in some business or commercial activity. Business Studies helps in developing the understanding of different forms of business organisations i.e. private sector enterprises, public sector enterprises and joint sector enterprises.

3. *Provides knowledge about insurance.* **Insurance** has evolved as a process of safeguarding the interest of people from loss and uncertainty., as it is difficult for an individual or even a large business house to invest millions of rupees in the huge factory, building and equipment. etc. With the help of Business Studies the pupils get the knowledge about different types of insurance, principles of insurance and their uses for business enterprise.
4. *Understanding of communication services.* Communication refers to exchange of ideas, views or message between two or more persons. The students understand meaningfully the importance and drawbacks of different modes of communication as postal and telecom postal services, fax, internet, e-mail, extranet, world wide web, voice mail, unified messaging, etc.
5. *Understanding of storage facilities*: Generally goods are produced in anticipation of demand. Therefore, it becomes necessary to store the goods until the demand for them arises. Surplus goods are stored, preserved and made available whenever demanded. So the students understand the utility of warehousing services by studying Business Studies.
6. *Provides knowledge about emerging modes of business*: Modern era is the era of globalisation, change and technology. In response to this, business throughout the world is changing its organisation, way of working and use of technology. The major change in mode of business is emergence of e-business, e-commerce and business processing outsourcing. The students get the knowledge about the scope of e-business and opportunities or benefits of e-business in the present scenario.
7. *Development of business ethics*: Business ethics refers to the set of moral values or standards or norms which govern the activities of a businessman. Ethics define what is right and what is wrong. The students understand that the objective of business is not only to earn profit but to adopt business ethics also.
8. *Provides knowledge about the sources of business finance.* No one starts a business or run an enterprise without adequate funds. It must be available in an adequate amount at the right time for smooth functioning of an enterprise. In short, one can say that finance is the lifeblood of a business. The students get the knowledge that from which sources they can arrange the finance to start a business.
9. Develops understanding of general theory of management.
10. Provides knowledge of organisational behaviour and various important aspects related to industrial psychology.
11. Develops understanding to solve business disputes.
12. Acquaints with the concepts and utilisation of marketism.
13. Provides knowledge about the basic concepts, principles and working of commercial banks.
14. Provides knowledge about the organisation, management and working of cooperative banking system.

15. Provides knowledge about different labour laws.
16. Prepares students to choose their occupation in the future.
17. Helps in playing an active role in the proper utilisation of nation's resources.

Thus, Business Studies plays an important role in preparing the pupils for the business community. They not only learn to achieve business objective but also to achieve social and human objectives.

ACCOUNTANCY

Meaning

At the end of each year, all the businessmen want to know how much they have gained or lost during the year; how much capital is invested in the business at the end of the year; how much amount they are liable to pay and to whom they owe it; how much is owed to them and by whom, etc. In order to attain such information, it is essential to keep a complete and systematic record of each and every business transaction entered into during the year.

By keeping a complete and systematic record of every business dealing, the businessman can know how much is the amount of purchases; how much is the amount incurred during the year. Furthermore, he can ascertain the financial position of his business, such as, how much capital it has at the end of the year and how that capital stands invested in various assets; how much amount he has to take and from whom and how much amount he is liable to pay and to whom. Besides, the properly maintained accounts are helpful in the assessment of income-tax and sales-tax and are accepted as a proof in the court of law whenever needed.

Importance of accounting records is increasing day-by-day. Now-a-days, the properly maintained accounts give the answer of a number of questions, such as: What is the cost of production? Is such cost reasonable or not? Can it be reduced and if so, in what manner? What should be the selling price based on the cost of production? Thus, business owners can take important decisions with the help of the information provided by accounting data.

Definitions of Accounting

1. "Nearly every business enterprise has accounting system. It is a means of collecting, summarising, analysing and reporting in monetary terms information about business." — R.N. Anthony.
2. "Accounting is the art of recording, classifying and summarising in a significant manner and in terms of money, transactions and events, which are, in part at least, of in financial character, and interpreting the results thereof." — American Institute of Certified Public Accountants
3. "Accounting is the science of recording and classifying business transactions and events, primarily of a financial characters and the out of making significant summaries, analysis and interpretation of their transactions and communicating the results to persons who must make decisions from judgment." — Smith and Ashburn.

Characteristics of Accounting

An analysis of the above definitions brings out the following as characteristics of features or attributes of accounting:

(1) *Recording of financial transactions only*: Only those transactions and events are recorded in accounting which are of a financial character. There are so many transactions in the business which are very important for business but which cannot be measured and expressed in terms of money and hence such transactions will not be recorded. For example, the quarrel between the Production Manager and the Sales Manager, resignation by an able and experienced manager, strike by employees and starting of a new business by the other competitor etc. Though these events affect the earnings of the business adversely but as no one can measure the effect of such events in terms of money, these will not be recorded in the books of the business.

(2) *Recording*: Accounting is the art of recording business transactions according to some specified rules. In a small business where the number of transactions is quite small, all transactions are first recorded in a book called "Journal". But in a big business establishment, where the number of transactions is quite large, the Journal is further sub-divided into various subsidiary books such as: (i) 'Cash Book' for recording cash transactions; (ii) 'Purchase Book' for recording credit purchases of goods; (iii) 'Sale Book' for recording credit sale of goods; (iv) 'Purchases Return Book' for recording the return of credit purchase; (v) 'Sales Return Book' for recording the return of credit sales, etc. The number of subsidiary books to be maintained depends on the size and nature of the business.

(3) *Classifying*: After recording the transactions in Journal or subsidiary books the transactions are classified. Classification is the process of grouping the transactions of one nature at one place in a separate account. The book in which various accounts are opened is called "Ledger". Separate accounts are opened in the Ledger in the name of each person, whether customer or supplier. Likewise, separate accounts are opened for purchases, sales, assets, etc. Similarly, all expenses and incomes, which are already recorded in Journal, are again classified under separate heads in the Ledger, such as Wages Account, Salary Account, Advertisement Account, Commission Account, etc.

(4) *Summarising*: Summarising is the art of presenting the classified data in a manner which is understandable and useful to management and other users of such data. This involves the balancing of ledger accounts and the preparation of Trial Balance with the help of such balances. Final accounts are prepared with the help of Trial Balance which include Trading and Profit & Loss Account and a Balance Sheet. Trading account is prepared for calculating gross profit or gross loss during the year. Profit and Loss Account is prepared to ascertain the net profit or net loss during the year. Balance Sheet is prepared to present the financial position of the business.

The above mentioned characteristics of Accounting are also termed as 'Process of Accounting' or 'Accounting Cycle'.

Accounting Cycle

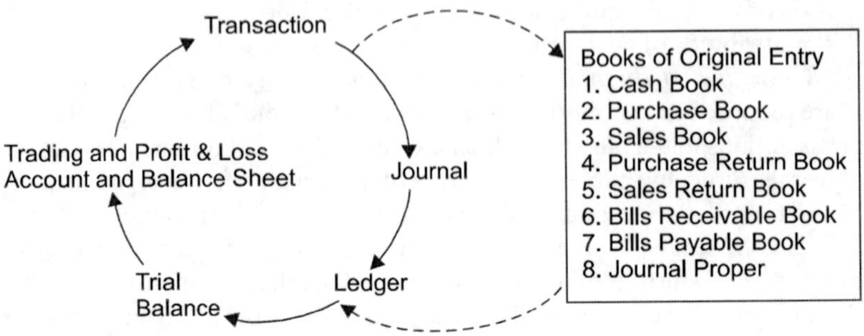

The above diagram shows the accounting cycle. This accounting cycle starts with the recording of business transactions in the Journal or Subsidiary Books and after passing through the Ledger and Trial Balance it results in the preparation of Final Accounts (i.e. Trading and Profit & Loss Account and Balance Sheet). This accounting cycle is generally completed in an accounting year and is again repeated in each subsequent year.

(5) *Recording in terms of money*. Each transaction is recorded in the books in terms of money only. For example, if a businessman purchases 200 chairs and 10 tables, their value in terms of money will be recorded in the books. Similarly, if a business possesses Rs.5,000 in Cash; Land Measuring 2,000 Metres; 5 Trucks; 5 Machines; 10 tons of raw material; 200 Chairs; 10 Tables, and so on, then in absence of money measurement concept these different types of assets cannot be added up and hence cannot give any useful information. But if they are expressed in terms of money, they will immediately provide useful information such as, Cash Rs.5,000; Land Rs.4,00,000; Trucks Rs.10,00,000; Machines Rs.2,00,000; Goods Rs.1,00,000; Chairs Rs.10,000 and Tables Rs.5,000.

(6) *Interpretation of the results*. In Accounting, the results of the business are presented in such a manner (i.e. by preparing Trading and Profit & Los Account and Balance Sheet) that the parties interested in the business such as proprietors, managers, banks, creditors, employees, etc. can have full information about the profitability and the financial position of the business.

Nature of Accountancy

Accountancy refers to a systematic knowledge of accounting concerned with the principles and techniques which are applied in accounting. It tells us how to prepare the books of accounts, how to summarise the accounting information and how to communicate it to the interested parties.

According to Kohler, "Accountancy refers to the entire body of the theory and practice of accounting."

Various transactions are made in a business every day such as purchase and sale of goods and services, receipt or payment of cash and so on. Each business transaction should be supported by documentary evidence such as cash memo, cash receipt, invoice or bill, debit and credit notes, pay-in-slip, cheque, etc. These business documents are called source documents and these are the first record about the details of business transactions. Such documents report the date, the amount, parties involved and the nature of transaction. Entries in the books are always made from the source documents. According to the verifiable objective principles of accounting, each transaction recorded in the books of accounts should have adequate proof to support it. These documents are the written and authentic proof of the correctness of the recorded transaction.

On the basis of this process based on principles and laws, accountancy is known as Science. As it has been already said that, "the practice and art of the science of accounting is known as accountancy."

Accounting process begins with the origin and identification of business transaction and is followed by recording, classification and summarisation of business transactions culminating in preparation of trial balance and financial statements i.e. Profit and Loss Account and Balance Sheet. Following steps are followed in accounting process:

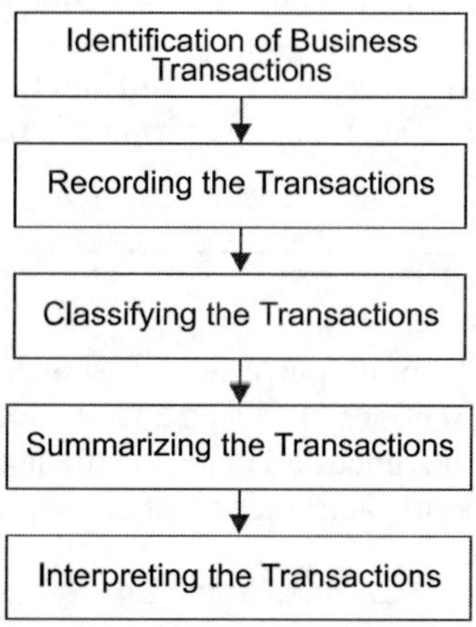

Thus, accountancy is both art and science in which accounts are maintained systematically under book-keeping. Accounting information should be prepared and presented in such a way that it is able to depict a clear and orderly view of the business enterprise.

As an art accounting is viewed as a language of business because it prepares reports and statements which communicate information regarding the business enterprise. It is viewed as chronological record of all financial transactions in the books of accounts according to specified rules.

It is also regarded as a means of determining the true profit or loss of a business enterprise.

Accounting is now regarded as an information system because it is capable of providing the kind of information which managers and other interested parties require for taking appropriate decisions.

Accounting is regarded as a service activity because it provides quantitative financial information which is helpful to the users in different ways.

Scope of Accountancy

Accountancy is often regarded as a language of business. Since the main aim of a language is to serve as a means of communication, accounting communicates the result of business activities to management, owners, investors, creditors, lenders, government etc. Accounting as an information system is a process of identifying, measuring, recording, summarising, and communicating the information about business to interested users of such information. Different groups of persons have vested interests in business organisation. Accounting provides useful information to all these interested parties.

Management now-a-days requires various types of information to perform its functions more efficiently. To meet the increasing requirements of management, various specialised branches of accounting come into existence such as Financial Accounting, Cost Accounting, Management Accounting, Tax Accounting, Social Responsibility Accounting, etc. These branches are explained as under:

1. *Financial Accounting.* The main purpose of this branch of accounting is to record the business transactions in a systematic manner, to ascertain the profit or loss of the accounting period by preparing a Profit and Loss Account and to present the financial position of the business by preparing a Balance Sheet. It includes:

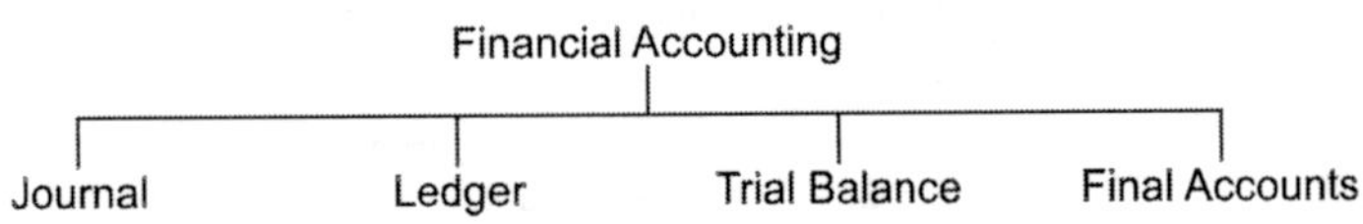

2. *Cost Accounting*: The main purpose of cost accounting is to ascertain the total cost and cost per unit of goods produced and services rendered by a business. It also estimates the cost in advance and helps the management in exercising strict control over cost. The following activities are included in it:

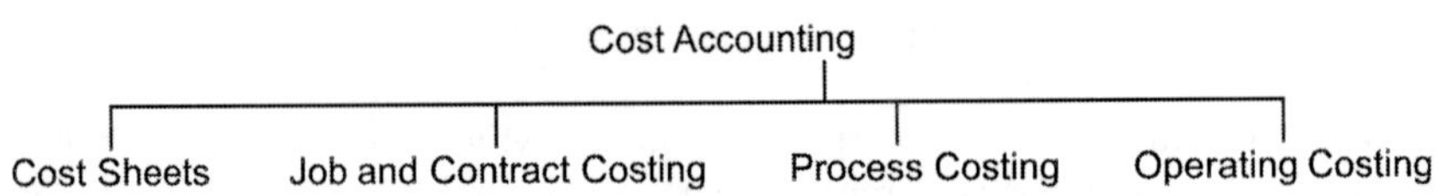

3. *Management Accounting*: The main purpose of management accounting is to present the accounting information in such a way as to assist the management in planning and controlling the operations of a business. The management accountant uses various techniques and concepts to make the accounting data more useful for managerial decision making. These techniques include:

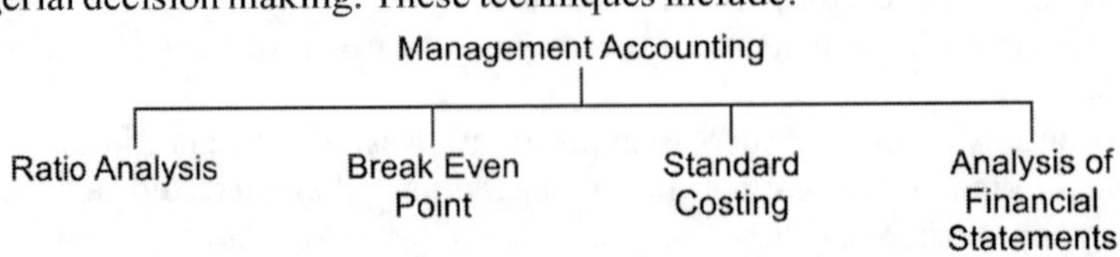

4. *Tax Accounting*: The branch of accounting which is used for tax purposes is called Tax Accounting. It includes:

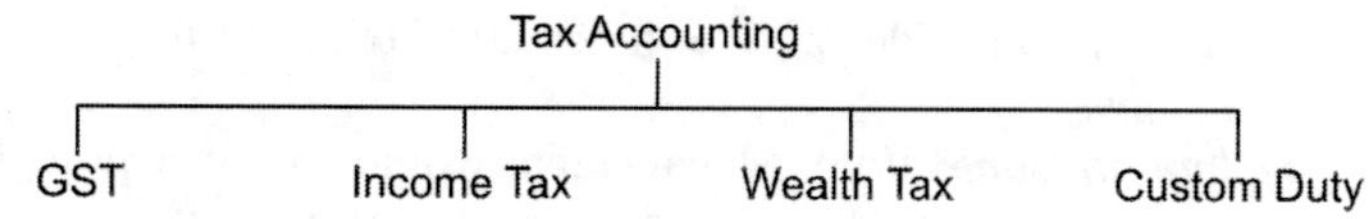

5. *Government Accounting*: Government accounting is done by Central Government, State Governments and local governments. It is the systematic process of collecting, recording, classifying, summarizing and interpreting the financial transactions relating to the revenues and expenditures of government offices. It reveals how public funds have been generated and utilized for the welfare of the general public.

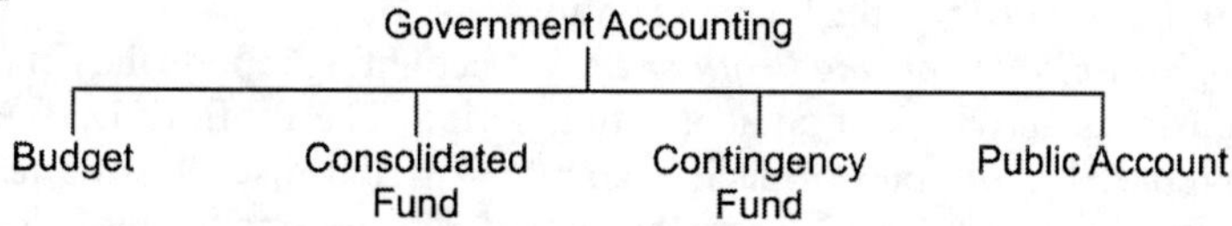

6. *Social Responsibility Accounting*: The society provides infrastructure and the facilities without which business cannot operate at all. Hence, the business also has a responsibility to the society. Social responsibility accounting is the process of identifying, measuring and communicating the contribution of a business to the society. It consists of providing employment to under-privileged, providing financial and manpower support for future programmes, environmental contribution, product safety, product durability, customer satisfaction, etc. In social responsibility accounting, techniques have been developed for measuring the cost of these contributions and the benefit to the society.

Thus, accountancy has a wide scope because its informations are used by various groups of people who have contact with business enterprise whether it can be a business firm or production house, professional organisation or bank, transport company or an insurance company.

Value of Accountancy/Accounting

Accountancy is an important subject in the field of commerce. Accounting or accountancy is no doubt the universal language of business and figure Its importance is increasing in the modern era as:

1. *Helpful in Management of Business*: Management needs a lot of information for the efficient running of the business. All such information is provided by the accounting which helps the management in the following:
   (A) *Helpful in Planning*: Management would like to know whether the sales are increasing or decreasing and also the speed of increase in the cost of production. All such information is provided by the accounting, which helps the manage-ment in estimating the future sales and expenses. It also helps them to estimate the cash receipts and cash disbursements during the next accounting period.
   (B) *Helpful in Decision Making*: At times, the Management has to take a number of decisions. For example, What should be the selling price of the product? How much discount should be offered to the customers?

Accounting provides all the information required for making such decisions.

(C) *Helpful in Controlling*: Management would like to see that the cost incurred is reasonable and that no department is overspending. Accounting provides information to the management in this regard.

2. *Provides Complete and Systematic Record*: Business transactions have growth in size and complexity and it is not possible to remember each and every transaction. Accounting keeps a prompt and systematic record of all the transactions and summarizes them in order to provide a true picture of the activities of the business entity.
3. *Information regarding Profit or Loss*: Accounting reports the net result of business activities of an accounting period. The Profit & Loss Account prepared at the end of each accounting period discloses the net profit earned or loss suffered during that period. The information regarding profit is of great use to the owners and various other interested parties.
4. *Information regarding Financial Position*: Accounting reports the financial position of the business by preparing a Balance Sheet at the end of each accounting period. Balance Sheet discloses the position of assets and their values on the one hand and liabilities and capital on the other hand.
5. *Enables Comparative Study*: By keeping a systematic record accounting helps the owners to compare one year's costs, expenses, sales and profit, etc. with those of other years. Such a comparison provides the useful informations on the basis of which important decisions can be taken more judiciously.
6. *Helpful in Assessment of Tax Liability*: Properly maintained records will be of great help when the firm is assessed to income tax or sales tax. Such records when audited are trusted by the taxation authorities.
7. *Evidence in Legal Matters*: Properly maintained accounts, supported by authenticated documents are accepted by the courts as a firm evidence,
8. *Facilitates Sale of Business*: If a business entity is being sold, the accounting information can be utilised to determine the proper purchase price.
9. *Helpful in Raising Loans*: Accounting information is of great help while raising loans from banks or other financial institutions. Such institutions before finalising the loans supervise the financial positions of the firms as final accounts, cash flow, etc.
10. *Knowledge of Accountancy Concepts*: In order to make the accounting a language convey the same meaning to all people and to make it more meaningful, most of the accountants have agreed on a number of concepts which are usually followed for preparing the financial statements. Following may be treated as basic concepts:
    - *Accounting period concept*: According to the amended income tax law, a business has to compulsorily adopt financial year beginning on 1st April and ending on 31st March in the next calendar year, as its accounting period. Apart from this, companies whose shares are listed in the Stock Exchange are required to publish quarterly results

to depict the profitability and financial position at the end of three-month period (Quarterly).

- *Business entity concept*: According to this, business concept is treated as a unit separate and distinct from its owners, creditors, managers and others. Because of the concept of separate entity, the proprietor's house, his personal investment in securities, his personal car and personal income and expenditure are kept separate from the accounts of business entity.
- *Money measurement concept*: Only those transactions and events are recorded in accounting which is capable of being expressed in terms of money. An event, even though it may be very important for the business, will not be recorded in the books of the business, unless its effect can be measured in terms of money with a fair degree of accuracy.
- *Going concern concept*: As per this concept it is assumed that business will continue to exist for a long period in the future. It is in this concept that we record fixed assets at their original cost and depreciation is charged on these assets without reference to their market value.
- *Cost concept*: According to this concept, assets be recorded as the cash amount (or the equivalent) at the time that an asset is acquired. This cost becomes the basis of all subsequent accounting for the asset since the acquisition cost relates to the past; it is referred to as historical cost.

11. *Provides Knowledge about Basic Accounting Principles*: In order to make the accounting information meaningful to its internal and external users, the process of accountancy is based on certain principles which are fixed, uniform and consistent. They are:
    - *Principle of Revenue Realisation*: It is an important principle of measuring the revenue of a business. Revenue means amount which is added to the capital as a result of business operations. Revenue is earned by sale of goods or by providing a service. It should be remembered that revenue realisation is not related with the receipt of cash.
    - *Principle of Expenses*: The cost incurred on the purchase of goods and services to get services is termed as expenses. It includes cost of raw material, salaries, bank interest, depreciation of the fixed assets, etc.
    - *Principle of Matching*: This principle is very important for correct determination of net profit. In determining the net profit from business operations, all costs which are applicable to revenue of the period should be charged against that revenue. Accordingly, for matching costs with revenue, first revenue should be recognised and then costs incurred for generating that revenue should be recognised.

- *Principle of Dual Aspect*: According to this concept, every business transaction is recorded as having a dual aspect. In other words, every transaction affects at least two accounts. If one account is debited, any other account must be credited. The system of recording transactions based on this concept is called as "Double Entry System".
- *Principle of Accrual*: In accounting, accrual basis is used for recording transactions. It provides more appropriate information about the performance of business enterprise as compared to cash basis The idea behind the accrual principle is that financial events are most properly recognized by matching revenues against expenses when transactions – such as a sale – occur, rather than when the actual payment for the transaction may be received.
- *Principle of Objectivity*: This principle requires that accounting transactions should be recorded in an objective manner, free from personal bias of either management or the accountant who prepares the accounts. It is possible only when each transaction is supported by verifiable documents and vouchers such as cash memos, invoices, sales bill, pay-in slip, correspondence, agreement, etc.

12. *Provides Knowledge about Accounting Conventions*: An accounting convention may be defined as a custom or generally accepted practice which is adopted either by general agreement or common consent among accountants. The students of accounts get knowledge about these conventions through the subject of Accountancy. The main accounting conventions are:
    - *Convention of full disclosure*: It means that there should be a sufficient disclosure of information which is of material interest to the users of the financial statements such as proprietors, present and potential creditors, investors and others.
    - *Convention of consistency*: This convention states that accounting principles and methods should remain consistent from one year to another. These should not be changed from year to year, in order to enable the management to compare the Profit and Loss Account and Balance Sheet of the different periods and draw important conclusions about the working of the enterprise.
    - *Convention of conservatism*: According to this convention, all anticipated losses should be recorded in the books of accounts, but all anticipated unrealised gains should be ignored. In other words, conservation is the policy of playing safe.
    - *Convention of materiality*: This convention is an exception to the convention of full disclosure. According to this convention, items having an insignificant effect or being irrelevant to the user need not be disclosed. These unimportant items are either left or merged with other items, otherwise accounting statements will be unnecessarily overburdened.

13. *Provides Knowledge of Accounting Terminology*: There are certain basic accounting terms which are daily used in the business world. The students of accountancy will not be able to understand the accounting procedure without the knowledge of these terms. The important terms used in it are:
   (i) *Assets*: Anything which is in the possession or is the property of a business enterprise including the amounts due to it from others is called an asset. It may be classified with the following categories:

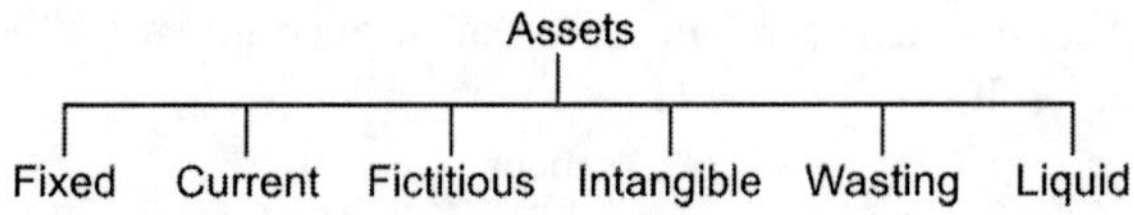

   (ii) *Liability*: It refers to the amount which the firm owes to outsiders (excepting the amount owed to proprietors).

   Liabilities = Assets – Capital

   It can be classified as:

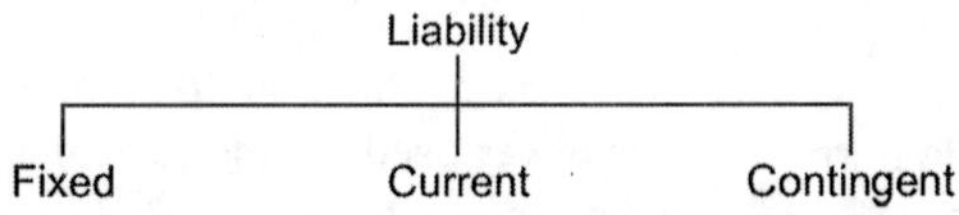

   (iii) *Capital*: It refers to the amount invested by the proprietor in a business enterprise. It is the amount with the help of which goods and assets are purchased in the business.

   Capital = Assets – Liabilities

   Capital is also known as owner's equity or net worth or net assets. It can be classified as:

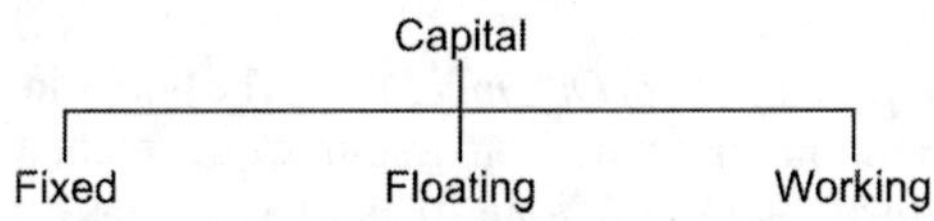

   (iv) *Expenses*: Expense is the cost incurred in producing and selling the goods and services.
   (v) *Income*: Surplus revenue over expenses is called income.

   Income = Revenue – Expense

   (vi) *Expenditure*: Any disbursement of cash or transfer of property or incurring a liability for the purpose of acquiring assets, goods or services is called expenditure. It may be classified as:

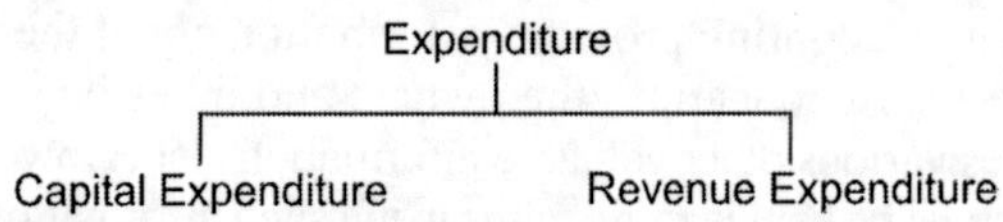

   (vii) *Revenue*: It consists of the amount received from sale of goods and from services provided to customer. It also includes receipt of rent, commission, dividend, interest, etc.
   (viii) *Debtors*: It represents those persons or firms to whom goods have been sold or services rendered on credit and payment has not been received from them.

(ix) *Creditors*: It represents those persons or firm from whose goods have been purchased or services procured on credit and payment has not been made to them.

(x) *Gain*: It is a monetary benefit.

(xi) *Stock*: It includes the value of those goods which are lying unsold at the end of accounting period. It may be of two types i.e. opening stock and closing stock.

(xii) *Discount*: It is a rebate on an allowance given by the seller to the buyer. It is of two types.

Discount

Trade Discount | Cash Discount

(xiii) *Drawing*: Any cash or value of goods withdrawn by the owner for personal use or any private payments made out of business funds are called drawings.

(xiv) *Sales*: It is used for sales of those goods which are purchased for resale purposes. It is never used for the sale of assets. It includes—

Sales

Cash Sales | Credit Sales

14. *Development of Skill to Prepare Accounting Equations*: With the help of accountancy the pupils learn to prepare accounting equation. It signifies that the assets of a business are always equal to the total of capital and liabilities.
15. *Learn to Prepare Books of Original Entry*: The books in which a transaction is recorded for the first time from a source document are called 'Books of Original Entry'. Journal is one of the basic books of original entry in which transactions are originally recorded in a chronological order according to the principles of double entry system.

Thus, the students of commerce learn about different terms related to accountancy, writing of accounting equations, preparation of balance sheets, journals, etc.

Limitations of Accountancy

It is a hard fact that accounting provides information about the profitability and financial soundness of a concern to the owners and other interested persons. In addition, it provides various other valuable information also. However, it has certain limitations which must be kept in mind while using such information. The limitations are as follows:

1. *Influenced by Personal Judgements*: Accounting is as yet an exact science and accountant has to exercise his personal judgement in respect of various items. For example, it is extremely difficult to predict with any degree of accuracy the actual useful life of an asset which is needed for calculating depreciation. The same is true about method of valuation of stock and making provision for doubtful debts.

Different persons are bound to have different opinions in respect of such things and hence it will result in ascertainment of different figure of profit or loss of a business by different persons. Hence, the figure of profit cannot be taken as an exact figure.

2. *Based on Accounting Concepts and Conventions*: Accounts are prepared on the basis of a number of accounting concepts and conventions. Hence, the profitability and the financial position disclosed by it may not be realistic. For example, fixed assets are shown in the balance sheet according to the 'going concern concept'. This means that the fixed assets are shown at their cost and not at their market value. The values realised on their sale may be more or less than the values stated in the balance sheet. Similarly, on account of convention of conservatism, the profit & loss account does not disclose the true profit of the business because future losses are provided whereas future incomes are ignored.

3. *Incomplete Information*: Accounting statements provide only the incomplete information because the actual profit or loss of a business can be known only when the business is closed down.

4. *Omission of Qualitative Information*: Accounts contain only the information which can be expressed in terms of money. Qualitative aspects of business units are completely omitted from the books as these cannot be expressed in monetary terms. Thus, changes in management, reputation of the business, core management-labour relations, firm's ability to develop new products, efficiency management, satisfaction of firm's customers etc. which have a vital bearing on the profitability of the firm are all ignored and omitted from being recorded because all of these are qualitative in nature.

5. *Based on Historical Costs*: Accounts are prepared on the basis of historical costs (i.e. the original costs) and as such the figures given in financial statements do not show the effect of changes in price level. The assets remain undervalued in many cases particularly land and building. The outcome of this practice is that balance sheet value of assets are not helpful in estimating the true financial position of the business.

6. *Affected by Window Dressing*: Window dressing refers to the practice in manipulating accounts, so that the financial statements may disclose a more favourable position than the actual position. For example, the purchases made at the end of the year may not be recorded or the closing stock may be over-valued. Hence, correct decisions cannot be taken on the basis of such financial statements.

7. *Unsuitable for Forecasting*: Financial accounts are only a record of past events. Continuous changes take place in the demand of the product, policies adopted by the firm, the position of competition etc. As such, the financial analysis based on past events may not be of much use for forecasting.

Thus a**ccountancy** is the occupation of maintaining and auditing records and preparing financial reports for a business. It includes cost accounting, book keeping, inventory accounting etc.

3

Aims and Objectives of Teaching Commerce

"An aim is a foreseen end that gives direction to an activity and motivates behaviour".
– John Dewey

Trade, Commerce and Industry constitute a vital part of our life's activities. These aspects of our life's experiences are extremely important and if we despise these, all our educational efforts will be fruitless toils.

The question of aims and objectives of teaching a particular subject should be the first to occur to a conscientious teacher because the objectives of teaching a particular subject strongly influence the organisation of the curriculum, and at the same time provide guidelines for the methods of its approach.

Objectives are usually governed by the needs of the young pupils. These are of two types:

(*i*) Firstly those which can be satisfied by acquisition of ideas and skills and are known as short term or subject matter objectives.

(*ii*) Second type of needs are those which are satisfied by matured thinking and acting. These are summed up under long term objectives because their function is an overall development of a person which may continue throughout his life.

These two types of objectives are interrelated and interdependent. The subject matter objectives control the framework of the syllabus, whereas the long term objectives determine how the course material of the syllabus has been tackled. The long term objectives in commerce will require a learner:

1. To acquaint a basic knowledge of the subject.
2. To develop his own observational skills.
3. To understand the inter relation of the subject and the economy.
4. To infuse thorough understanding of its concepts and theories.

These long terms objectives aim at providing young pupils such types of knowledge, skills and attitudes as would develop an acceptable behaviour in a democratic society in which they live. In other words, it means continuation and expansion of ideas initiated at the earlier stage till the end of schooling. The commerce teacher is as much responsible for the achievement of these goals as the teachers of art, science and mathematics. In fact, it is the joint responsibility of the entire staff engaged in teaching.

The subject matter objectives are transitory and may be for a specific purpose. It may be achieved in a particular lesson or in the course of the academic year or it may be prolonged to the whole period of schooling.

Aims of Teaching

Before teaching any subject it is necessary to determine its aims because without the knowledge of aims the educator is like a sailor who does not know his goal and the child is like a rudderless vessel which will be drifted along somewhere ashore. When a person is going to start an activity he fixes up certain aims to carry out that activity successfully. Aims are the means which bring desired changes in the behaviour of the students. Determination of aims is necessary due to following reasons:

- Aims are necessary to explain the desired nature of any subject.
- They help in determining the learning process.
- They help in curriculum construction.
- They fix limit to the teaching process.
- By evaluating the teaching on the right basis they help in fixing the effectiveness of the teaching and learning experiences.
- Aims give guidance for the working of teachers as well as students.

Objectives of Teaching

The objective is a statement which suggests a certain kind of change in the children and we try to bring about it in the child.

"Objective is desired change in behaviour of pupil as a result of experiences directed by school."

"An objective is a point or end in view of something towards which action is directed, a planned change sought through any activity what we set out to do."

– NCERT

Difference between Aims and Objectives

The difference between aims and objectives can be clarified with the help of the following table:

Aim	*Objective*
1. The scope of aim is wider.	1. The scope of objective is narrow.
2. Aim is a normal statement.	2. An objective is a determined statement.
3. The complete school environment, society and nation are responsible to attain the aim.	3. Objectives are the small steps to achieve the aim. So the responsibility lies with teacher and the teaching material.
4. Aims are ideal in nature. So it is difficult to achieve it completely. It may or may not be.	4. Objectives are not ideal in nature. They are behavioural. They can be achieved easily.

(*Contd.*)

Aim	Objective
5. Much time is needed to achieve aim.	5. Less time is needed to achieve objective.
6. It is vague.	6. It is specific.
7. It does not help in determining the teaching strategy in the class.	7. It helps us determining the teaching strategy in the class.
8. It does not provide clear educational instructions to the learners.	8. It provides clear and fixed instructions to the learners.
9. Aims are the ultimate goals, the destination, the target.	9. Objectives are immediate.

Aims of Teaching Commerce

Commerce teaching is very useful and practicable in the present day society. In the developing economy like India its utility increases more. This is the reason that it becomes necessary to provide the knowledge about commerce in schools. Thus, the general aims of teaching commerce may be listed as follows:

1. *To Provide Mental Discipline*: The aim of teaching commerce is that it provides mental discipline which means that the subject trains the pupil's whole mind of thought which in its turn influences his intellectual life and studies in the same field. This mental discipline comes through the application of scientific attitude in distinguishing facts, interpreting their effects, and drawing correct conclusions and inferences. Commerce encourages independence in thought and action. An independent person will come to his conclusions only after thoughtful deliberations.

2. *Development of Common Sense*: Commerce teaching develops simple cleverness among the pupils. The pupil does many activities in his daily life and if he does not have the knowledge of commerce then he can't get success in his day-to-day activities. Commerce teaching includes accounting of income-expenditure, getting maximum utilization with limited resources, markets and the trade in them, etc. The pupils can learn about trading process. They can learn to have control on their wants according to the law of demand and supply.

3. *Development of the Sense of Humility and Service*: The qualities of humility and service are developed among the pupils with the help of commerce. A successful trader is always polite and sweet tempered. With his politeness only he can attracts the customers towards him. Commerce makes the pupils tolerant. It develop the feeling of cooperation.

4. *Development of Logical Power and Critical Judgement*: The power of thinking and reasoning cannot be developed without the acquisition of facts. If the pupils have been taught about the function of banks, different financial markets, etc. they can think about the solution of financial problems easily. If purely mental process are involved, this is logic, judgement also must be based on facts. The commerce must be the chief media for training pupils to render business judgements and to draw generalizations after sufficient and proper data have been gathered. Such abilities must be trained so that pupils may be able to render constructive

judgements and decisions about business problems, like insurance, office management etc.

5. *To Promote Nationalism and International Understanding:* Commerce teaching aims at creating a desire in the pupils to perpetuate those principles of justice and humanity that controls the life of a nation as well as other nations for it they can be taught about the duties of a shopkeeper towards his customers, or duties of a factory owner towards his shareholders. Commerce may overplay the interdependence of the nations and underplay the diversity which will result in the development of every nation of the world. If there is something wrong in the business world in any country, it will not affect that country alone but the whole world may be affected by that.

6. *To Provide Solution of Contemporary Problems*: Every sphere of individual's life as well as of society is full of complex problems. Commerce should develop the abilities of the pupils to provide mature judgements on immediate trade issues, trends and prospects in the fields of industries, businesses, national and international affairs.

7. *To Prepare Efficient Traders*: The child of today is the citizen of tomorrow. They can became traders, producers and capitalists in the future. It is the function of the commerce to make them effective traders. The pupils can help in the development in different spheres of a nation. Commerce teaches the pupils what type of trade they should do? What type of goods should be imported and exported? Thus teaching of commerce helps in preparing efficient traders.

8. *To Provide Skilled Labourers*: Commerce education helps in making the pupils skilled. It teaches the pupil, that how they can get maximum wages? How they can become skilled labourers? How they can protect their rights in the future? Skilled labourers help in increasing the productivity of the nation. Thus, commerce education helps in increasing the productivity of the nation by providing skilled labourers.

9. *To Help Students become Accountant, Stenographers, Auditor etc.*: Pupils study book keeping and accountancy, business methods, banking, insurance and commercial economics in commerce. Book keeping and accountancy help in becoming accountants. Commerce develops the attitude among the students from its initial stage that they can become insurance agents, they can go for banking services etc. Curiosity arises among the commerce students for these services. They have attraction for these posts. Commerce education develops interest in them and the pupils acquires practical knowledge with the help of different subjects related to commerce.

10. *To Acquaint the Students with Economic Conditions and Problems of the Country*: Commerce education tells the students that the citizens of a country can remain happy if it develops economically. So, it is the duty of every citizen to provide help in economic development. Commerce education creates awareness towards economic problems and with the help of acquired knowledge they can be successful in solving these problems. Commerce education develops economic consciousness among the pupils.

11. *To Impart Practical Training of Commercial Principles*: The main aim of

commerce education is to impart practical training of commercial principles to the pupils. Commerce provides the knowledge of basic principles of business. For example, if there are two currencies in a country then the good currency will outward the bad currency. With the clarification of this principle, commerce education clears the practical aspect also. If the currency is in limited amount then this principle will not apply. Commerce provides another type of practical knowledge also. For example, the knowledge of letter writing, methods of getting the copies of letters, filing system, tools to save time and energy, etc. is provided. This knowledge helps the pupils in their real life. In book keeping and accounting the knowledge about the principles of book keeping and its related problems is provided. The practice is being made of those principles. The pupils get the knowledge about the functioning and practicability of companies, business organisations, cooperative societies, banks, government offices and factories. Pupils get the understanding of the organisation of factories. How to control the prices? Pupils understand that which persons and agencies are helpful in this process. Thus, the students of commerce get the knowledge by analysing the facts and understand the accounting of banks, companies and gov offices.

12. *To Train the Pupils to Become Spendthrift and Honest*: Commerce education makes the pupils spendthrift. They understand how to get maximum satisfaction with the limited money. How the wastage of money can be prevented? The pupils learn to become honest. Only the honest trader can get success in trading. Thus, the habit of becoming spendthrift and honest is developed among the pupils with the help of commerce education.

13. *To Equip with the Capacity of Accepting Responsibility*: The life of man is full of responsibilities. Our many responsibilities are related with society and nation. These can be of many types, as pupils can serve the nation by becoming efficient traders, they can cooperate in successive implementation of five-year plans etc. Thus, commerce education provides training in bearing the responsibilities.

14. *To Enable the Pupils to use their Leisure time properly*: A man is a whole personality. Commerce education not only provides knowledge but also tries to help the students in the proper utilization of leisure time. It helps the students in acquiring the knowledge of banks, post office, share market, business letters etc. in a play way manner.

15. *To Develop Desirable Qualities for an all round development of a Rich Personality*: In the modern society, the foremost aim of education is the all round development of personality. To fulfill this aim of education, commerce is to develop qualities like tolerance, clear thinking, flexibility of mind, initiation, courage to face the problems of life. Not any single phase of personality should be ignored.

16. *To Develop Human Values*: Commerce education aims at developing human values i.e., students can be told that each business has two things – one is profit and second one is loss. So, we should have patience for getting fair profit in the business.

17. *To Provide Knowledge of Vocational Skills*: Commerce education aims at providing knowledge about different vocational skills as how to do the typing, how to prepare trial balance sheet, how to write in short hand, etc.

18. *To Provide Practical Training in Cooperation*: Man is a social animal. His

life is developed in the society. Commerce education provides training in cooperation as a business can't be run solely. It is a cooperative affair of different persons as wholesaler, labourers, retailers, etc. Production is impossible without the cooperation of labour, risk, manager, etc. Today there is much need of cooperation for the development of individual society, nation and the world.

In this way, we can conclude that commerce education seeks to promote the trading activities. It should inculculate right type of attitude, right type of interests and various skills. NEP 2020 focuses on building skill sets that are useful in employment with vocational learning and internships from grade 6th.

Other Aims of Teaching Commerce

1. To provide knowledge about general laws of commerce so that pupils may utilize them in solving business problems.
2. To develop economic citizenship among the students, so that pupils may work with the feeling of responsibility.
3. To acquaint the students about the measures helpful in industrial and business progress.
4. To develop scientific attitude among the students so that they may be able to understand each concept clearly.
5. To develop the potentiality among the students to test the economic data and events provided by the government analytically on the criterion of their reliability.
6. To make the pupils cooperative citizens for the increase in national income and to make the standard of living high of the nation.
7. To provide knowledge about the natural resources of the nation to the students so that they may be able to utilize them fruitfully.

Objectives of Teaching Commerce

Teaching objectives are to be determined for the effectiveness of teaching activities. To the attainment of objectives of general education, the subject matter objectives are the necessary stepping stones. While the educator has his eyes focussed on the ultimate aim of education, the commerce teacher should give his contribution towards the realisation of the primary objectives of education by taking such measures as might ensure sound factual knowledge, a clear understanding of factual relationships and a keen discipline of intellectual powers.

A. Objectives related to Knowledge and Understanding

Through commerce students can acquire the knowledge and understanding of:

1. The language of commerce in terms of definition.
2. The various concepts such as trade, business, banking, insurance, organisation behaviour, etc.
3. Commercial ideas in terms of facts, figures, principles and relationships.
4. The nature, functions and responsibilities of commerce in society.
5. Better use of services of business.
6. Contribution of commerce in various fields.

7. Different subjects related to commerce as accounting business studies, taxation, etc.
8. The basic nature of the subject commerce.
9. Interrelationship among different areas of commerce.
10. Economic environment to adjust in a better way.

B. Objectives related to Skill

Through commerce, the following skills can be developed as:

1. Ability to think correctly, to draw inferences and generalise.
2. Ability to serve in different sectors of trade, commerce and business.
3. Ability to prepare notings and draftings of official activities.
4. Ability to apply commerce knowledge to practical situations.
5. Ability to develop skills of organising and managing different business machines so that the students get acquainted with the daily activities of an office.
6. Development of techniques of problems solving.
7. Development of essential skills to understand and use of business laws.
8. Development of skill of survey.
9. Ability to inculculate attitudes and values leading to the integration of business with the social system with a positive approach.
10. Ability to apply the principles and functions of management to specific aspects of business.

C. Objectives related to Application

The students will be able to apply the knowledge and skill:

1. To analyse a given data.
2. To predict new happenings.
3. To find relationships that exist between various facts, concepts, phenomenon learnt by the pupil.
4. To infer correctly the observed facts.
5. To develop originality and creativity.
6. To solve the problems of trading independently.
7. To develop the ability to make use of commerce learning in the learning of other subjects.
8. To develop the habit of systematic thinking and objective reasoning.
9. To enable the students to analyse financial statements and interpret the results for decision making.
10. To enable to think and express precisely and systematically by making proper use of commerce language.

The Central Board of Secondary Education (CBSE) has listed the following objectives of teaching commerce at the senior secondary stage as follows:

1. To acquaint pupils with the theoretical foundations and practices of organising, managing and handling routine operations of a business firm.
2. To enable students to apply the principles and functions of management to specific aspects of business.

3. To generate and promote awareness of students in modern techniques of maintaining accounting records with the help of computers.
4. To acquaint the pupils with practice and procedure of determination of cost from the point of its elements.

Objectives of Teaching Accountancy

In the modern age, the subject of accountancy has become a subject of practical utility for every firm, whether it is a business firm or production industry, professional organisation or bank, transport company or an insurance company. Accountancy fulfils business objectives of all these. The students learn this subject because it will not only help in present time but in future also. The objectives of accountancy are as follows:

1. *To keep systematic record of business transactions*: The main objective of accounting is to keep complete record of business transactions according to specific rules. Complete record of business transactions helps to avoid the possibility of omission and fraud. For this purpose, all the business transactions are first of all recorded in Journal or Subsidiary Books and then posted into Ledger.
2. *To calculate profit or loss*: The second main objective of accounting is to ascertain the net profit earned or loss suffered on account of business transactions during a particular period. For this purpose, Trading and Profit & Loss Account of the purchases, sales, expenses and revenues (incomes) of the business are recorded in Trading and Profit & Loss Account. If the amount of revenue exceeds the expenditure incurred in earning that revenue, there is said to be a profit. In case the expenditure exceeds the revenue, there is said to be a loss. In addition, a businessman is able to get the following information by preparing a Trading and Profit & Loss Account:
   I. How much goods have been purchased during a particular period?
   II. How much goods have been sold during a particular period?
   III. How much goods have remained unsold and what is its value?
   IV. How much amount has been spent on various heads of expenditure and how much amount has been earned by various heads of revenue?

   By attaining these information a businessman can keep effective control of expenditure.
3. To know the exact reasons leading to net profit or net loss.
4. *To ascertain the financial position of the business*: For a businessman merely ascertaining profit or loss of the business is not sufficient. The businessman must also know the financial health of the business. For this purpose, after preparing the Profit & Loss Account a statement called 'Balance Sheet' is prepared which shows the assets and their values on the one hand and the liabilities and capital on the other hand. A Balance Sheet is actually a screen picture of the financial position of the business. At one glance, one would know the following by looking at the Balance Sheet:
   I. How much the business has to recover from Debtors?
   II. How much the business has to pay to Creditors?

III. How much the business has in the form of (a) Cash in hand, (b) Cash at Bank, (c) Closing Stock, and (d) Fixed Assets?

5. To ascertain the progress of the business from year to year.
6. To prevent and detect errors and frauds.
7. *To provide information to various parties*: Another main objective of accounting is to communicate the accounting information to various interested parties like owners, investors, creditors, banks, employees and government authorities, etc. The information helps them in taking sound and judicious decisions about the business entity.
8. *To help to know and understand the basic terms of accountancy*: There are certain basic accounting terms which are used daily in business world. Before recording the transactions in the books, it is essential to understand these terms as these terms have their specific meaning in Accounting. These basic terms are:
   - Assets
   - Liability
   - Capital
   - Expenses and income
   - Expenditure and revenue
   - Debtors and creditors
   - Goods
   - Cost
   - Gain
   - Stock and its types
   - Voucher
   - Discount
   - Drawings
   - Loss and profit
   - Purchase and sales
   - Business transactions
9. *To help to know and understand the basic principles of accountancy*: Theory base of accounting consists of principles, concepts, conventions, rules and guidelines developed over a period of time to bring uniformity and consistency to the process of accounting in order to enhance its utility to various uses of accounting information. The objective of accountancy is to provide knowledge and to make the students able to understand these principles. Accounting principles are described in various terms such as assumptions, conventions, doctrines, postulates, etc.
10. To make the students able to understand accounting equations.
11. To provide knowledge about different taxes.
12. To prepare the students to keep their individual and family accounts in a systematic way.
13. To prepare the students to solve the problems regarding accountancy.
14. To make the students able to understand the application of computer in accounting.

15. To develop the skill of preparing financial design, records and drafts.
16. To develop the capability to analyse the records and drafts.
17. To familiarise the students with the finance function and acquaint them with working knowledge of various techniques of financial decision-making.
18. To provide knowledge and develop skills in the construction of accounts of companies and specialised business entities.
19. To provide knowledge to the students about application of accounting principles in different situations.
20. To acquaint the students with the basic concepts and tools used in cost accounting management control.

Objectives of Teaching Business Studies

Objectives are the end towards which the activities of the students are directed. These are the goals established to guide the efforts of the students. The Central Board of Secondary Education (CBSE) has listed the following objectives of teaching Business Studies at school level.

1. To develop in the students an interest in the theory and practice in business, trade and industry.
2. To acquaint students with the theoretical foundations and practices of organising, managing and handling routine operations of a business firm.
3. To inculcate attitudes and values leading to the integration of business with the social system with a positive approach.
4. To enable the students to apply the principles and functions of management to specific aspects of business.
5. To equip the students with essential fundamental knowledge for setting up, organising and handling routine operations of a small scale factory.
6. To make the students able to understand business problems, techniques and administration of personal management and human resource development.
7. To provide knowledge of various labour laws which are applicable to business units.
8. To impart knowledge about the handling of industrial disputes and maintaining industrial relations.
9. To provide knowledge about different forms of business.
10. To familiarize the students with the basic concepts and practices of marketing.
11. To provide knowledge about the characteristics, advantages and disadvantages of sole trade and united Hindu family business.
12. To learn the comparison of organization and financing of Internal and Foreign trade.
13. To understand the concept of business capital.
14. To impart knowledge of policies, procedures and techniques of sales management.
15. To impart knowledge about different financial institutions.

16. To provide understanding of the general theory of management.
17. To impart knowledge of the concepts, techniques and management of advertising.
18. To provide knowledge to the students of the organisation, management and functioning of cooperative banking institutions.
19. To acquaint students with the application of statistical tools in the area of business decision-making.
20. To provide understanding of the economic factors governing the operation of industry.

BLOOM'S TAXONOMY OF OBJECTIVES (1956)

One of the most important aspect of teaching learning process is the specification of instructional objectives. They are achieved in terms of change in behaviour of learners. They may be termed as behavioural objectives. The ever increasing aspect of various courses, services and activities in the secondary schools lay more emphasis on instructional objectives.

The Taxonomy of Educational Objective, often called Bloom's Taxonomy, is a classification of the different objectives and skills that educators set for students (learning objectives). The taxonomy was proposed in 1956 by Benjamin Bloom, an educational psychologist at the University of Chicago. Bloom's taxonomy divides educational objectives into three domains – Affective, Psychomotor and Cognitive. Like other taxonomies, Bloom's is hierarchical, meaning that learning at the higher level is dependent on having attained requisite knowledge and skills at lower levels. Domains can be thought of as categories. Trainers often refer to these three domains as KSA (Knowledge, Skill and Attitude). This taxonomy of learning objectives can be thought of as "the goals of the training process". That is, after the training session, the learner should have acquired new skills, knowledge and attitudes.

Most references to the Bloom's Taxonomy only notice the cognitive Domain. A goal of Bloom's Taxonomy is to motivate teachers to focus on all three domains, creating a more holistic form of education.

1. Cognitive Domain

The cognitive domain involves knowledge and the development of intellectual skills. It includes the recall or recognition of specific facts, procedural pattern, and concepts that serve in the development of intellectual abilities and skills. There are six major categories, which are listed in order, starting from the simplest behaviour to the most complex. The categories can be thought of as degrees of difficulties. That is, the first one must be mastered before the next one can take place. Skills in the cognitive domain revolve around knowledge, comprehension and 'thinking through' a particular topic. Traditional education tends to emphasize the skills in this domain, particularly the lower order objectives.

There are six levels in the taxonomy, moving through the lowest order processes to the highest.

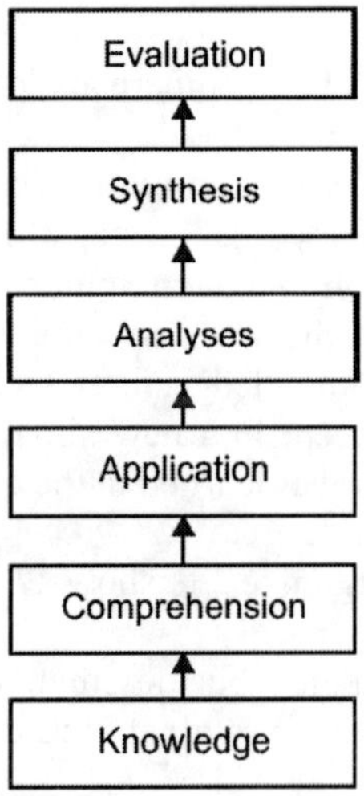

Fig. 3.1: Categories in the cognitive domain.

(*i*) *Knowledge:* This is the first and lowest level of cognitive domain. It exhibits memory of previously learned materials by recalling facts, terms, basic concepts and answers. This level gives more emphasis on memory. From content point of view, this category is further divided into the following ways:

(*a*) Knowledge of specifics.
- Knowledge of terminology.
- Knowledge of specific facts.

(*b*) Knowledge of ways and means of dealing with specifics.
- Knowledge of conventions.
- Knowledge of trends and sequences.
- Knowledge of classifications and categories.
- Knowledge of criteria.
- Knowledge of methodology.

(*c*) Knowledge of Universals and abstractions in a field.
- Knowledge of principles and generalizations.
- Knowledge of theories and structures.

Questions like: What is....?

Examples: Recite a policy. Quote prices from memory to a customer.

(*ii*) *Comprehension:* This category also indicates the lowest level of understanding. It exhibits demonstrative understanding of facts and ideas by organising, comparing, translating, interpreting, giving description and stating main ideas.

(*a*) Translation
- Translation from one level of abstraction to another level.
- Translation from one symbolic form to other.
- Translation from one verbal form to other.

(*b*) Interpretation

(*c*) Extrapolation

Questions like: How would you compare and contrast...?

Examples:

- Rewrite the principles of communication.
- Explain in one's own words the steps for performing a complex fare.
- Translate an equation in to a computer spreadsheet.

(*iii*) *Application:* It exhibits the use of new knowledge, solve problems to new situations by applying acquired knowledge, facts, techniques and rules in a different way. It deals with using a concept in a new situation or unprompted use of an abstraction, application of what was learned in the classroom into novel situations in the work place.

Questions like: Can you organize... to show...?

Examples:

- Use a manual to calculate a businessman's profit.
- Apply laws of statistics to evaluate the effect of advertisement on the sale of a product.

(*iv*) *Analysis:* This category indicate the medium level of under-standing. It exhibits separation of material or concepts into component parts so that its organisational structure may be understood. It includes examining and breaking of information into parts by identifying motives or causes. It deals with making inferences and finding evidences to support generalizations. It distinguishes between facts and inferences. It has three categories:

(*a*) Analysis of elements

(*b*) Analysis of relationships

(*c*) Analysis of organizational principles.

Question like: How would you classify....?

Examples:

- Gather information from different organisations and classify them.
- Recognise logical fallacies in reasoning.

(*v*) *Synthesis:* In this category all the elements are organised in such a way that they can form a unique whole, with emphasis on creating a new meaning or structure. It exhibits compiling all the information together in a different way by combining elements in a new pattern or proposing alternative solutions. It develops the creative ability of the students.

It includes the activities of three levels:

- Production of a unique communication.
- Production of a plan, or proposed set of operations.
- Derivation of a set of abstract relations.

Question like: Can you predict an outcome?

Examples:

- Write a company operations or process manual.
- Design an advertisement to promote the sale of computer.

(*vi*) *Evaluation:* It is the highest level of objectives of cognitive domain. It deals with presenting and defending opinions by making judgements about the information, validity of ideas or quality of work based on a set of criteria. It has two levels:

- Judgements in terms of internal evidence.
- Judgements in terms of external criteria.

Question like: Do you agree with....?

Examples:

l Select the most effective solution.
l Hire the most qualified candidate.
l Explain and justify a new budget.

Some critique on Bloom's Taxonomy (Cognitive Domain) admit the existence of these six categories, but question the existence of a sequential, hierarchical link. The revised edition of Bloom's Taxonomy has moved synthesis in higher order than evaluation. Some consider the three lowest levels as hierarchically order, but the three higher levels as parallel. Others say that it is sometimes better to move to Application before introducing concepts. This thinking would seem to relate to the method of Problems Based Learning.

Revised Bloom's Taxonomy (2001)

In 2001, a group of cognitive psychologists, curriculum theorists and instructional researches; and testing and assessment specialists published a revision of Bloom's Taxonomy with the title 'A Taxonomy for Teaching, learning and Assessment'. This title represents a more dynamic conception of classification. The revision to the cognitive taxonomy well spearheaded by one of Bloom's former student, Lonn Anderson and Bloom's original partner in defining and publishing the cognitive Domain, David Krathwohl. The newer version has a number of strong advances that make it a better choice for planning instruction today. One of the major changes that occurred between the old and the newer version is that the two highest forms of cognition have been reversed. In the older version the sequence from simple to complex functions was ordered as knowledge, comprehension, application, analysis, syntheses and evaluation, where as in the revised version the steps change to verbs and are arranged as remembering, understanding, applying, analyzing, evaluating and the highest function creativity.

Table : Bloom *vs.* Anderson & Krathwohl

Bloom's Taxonomy (1956)	*Anderson and Krathwohl's Taxonomy 2001*
1. *Knowledge:* Remembering or retrieving previously learned material. The verbs related to this function are: know, identify, relate, list, define, recall, recognize, acquire, name, memorise, repeat.	1. *Remembering:* Recognizing or recalling knowledge from memory. Remembering is when memory is used to produce or retrieve definition, facts, or lists, or to recite previously learned information.

(*Contd.*)

Bloom's Taxonomy (1956)	*Anderson and Krathwohl's Taxonomy 2001*
2. *Comprehension:* It is the ability to grasp or construct meaning from material. The verbs related to this are: differentiate, describe, discuss, identify, explain, interpret, illustrate, locate, review etc.	2. *Understanding:* Constructing meaning through written or graphic messages or activities like interpreting, comparing, explaining, classifying, summarizing, exemplifying etc.
3. *Application:* The ability to use learned material or to implement it in new and concrete situations. The verbs related to this are: apply, relate, demonstrate, dramatize, exhibit, calculate, practice, interpret, restructure, operate, organize etc.	3. *Applying:* Carrying out or using a procedure through executing, or implementing. It relates to where learned material is used through products like model, presentations, interviews or stimulation.
4. *Analysis:* The ability to break down or distinguish the parts of material in to its components to understand the organizational structures in a better way. The verbs related to it are: analyze, compare, examine, contrast, categorize, deduce, discriminate, separate, experiment, scrutinize dissect, detect etc.	4. *Analyzing:* Breaking materials or concepts into parts, determining the relationship between parts or how the parts relate to on overall structure or purpose. It relates to creating spreadsheets, surveys, charts, or diagram or graphic representation.
5. *Synthesis:* The ability to put parts together to form a unique new thing. The verbs related to it are: compose, design, assemble, modify, construct, originate, derive, propose etc.	5. *Evaluating:* Making judgement based on criteria and standards through checking and critiquing.
6. *Evaluation:* The ability to judge, check and even critique the value of material for a given purpose. The verbs related to it are judge, assess, compare, evaluate, rate, argue, decide, validate, criticize, infer, appraise etc.	6. *Creating:* Putting demerits together to form a functional whole; reorganizing elements into a new pattern or structure through generating, planning or producing. It is the most difficult mental function in the new taxonomy.Æ

Bloom's Digital Taxonomy (2008)

Andrew Churches developed Bloom's Digital Taxonomy in 2008 as an extension of the original Taxonomy. As now a days we are living in digital era, so he created a hierarchy of learning activities in a digital environment.

Churches' Taxonomy uses this approach with students using digital tools to complete a learning ability at different levels.

1. Remembering is the act of retrieving knowledge. Digitally a student can produce definition. It is the lowest level of learning. At this level, the student would need to be able to identify search engines as Google, Bing, yahoo and understand how it works. The most important part in this is that the student should be able to identify the correct keyword to use so that he may receive the required information. In the digital age he/she has access to a vast sources of information. Thus in the

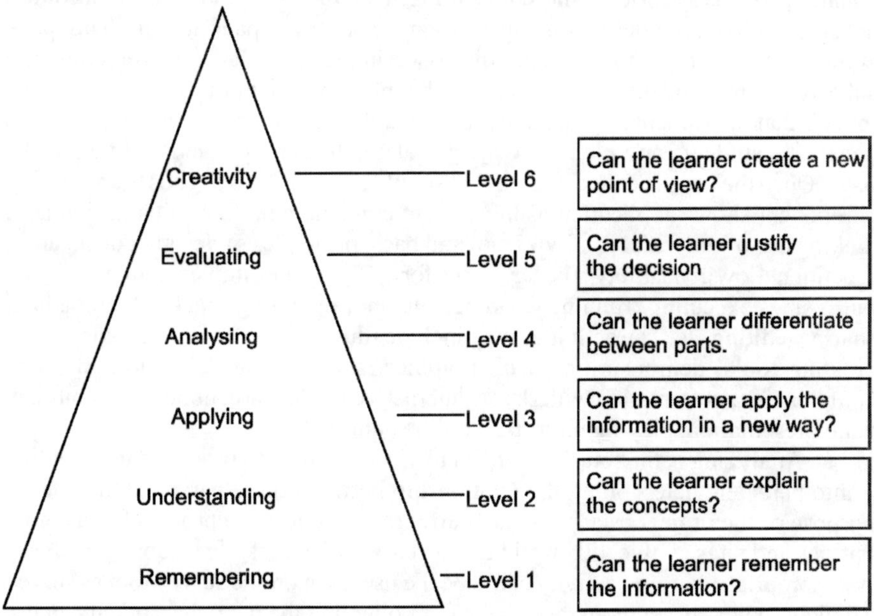

Fig.: Revised Bloom's Taxonomy

digital age, it is not important to remember the information, but the important is how the retrieve the information. The abilities to find and access necessary information from different resources should be developed among the students in the present era. The action verbs can be used as: copying, locating, quoting, googling, retrieving, networking, searching, highlighting, identifying, bullet, pointing, matching etc.

2. The next level of this taxonomy is understanding under which students are to learn the meaning of different concepts at their own and to find the relationship between the concepts. A learning activity at this level can involve the categorizing and tagging of bookmark through a social book marking application. For example, the student would register an account with a social networking site and then bookmark a number of relevant websites. Once the links have been created, the

student would spend sometime adding tags to the bookmarks. These tags will provide the information about the original date object. It is a progression from level one. Students require a greater depth of understanding to be able to create, modify and refine searches to suit their search needs. A variety of tools exist that allow the user to comment and annotate on web pages, pdf files and other documents. The user is developing understanding by simply commenting on the pages. The key terms are: Advanced searches, Boolean searches, blog journaling, twittering, categorizing and logging, Annotating, commenting, subscribing. This is a rubric for using advanced and Boolean searches. This search requires an understanding of the keywords, Boolean logic, advanced search features, structuring and refining searches and suitable search engines.

3. Applying is the level where the student applies learned knowledge to a situation. This is a rubric for the Wiki editing. The student would register an editing account with Wikipedia and navigate to an appropriate page to edit. This page could relate to a topic that is being discussed in the class. It can be regarding the subject that the student has researched. The most important thing required at this level is that the student should have relevant and original information to add to the page. The student can upload any image related to the topic and add that to the page. Once the page is edited, the student should then click save. Thus the authoring component shows application as the student edits the wiki to a suitable standard, making use of the features of wiki tool and basic principles of design–consistancy, repetition, flow, readability. The key terms for applying are : implementing, carrying out, using, executing, running, loading, playing, operating, hacking, uploading, sharing, editing etc. The activities may include illustration with online tools, comic creating tools; demonstration with graphics, screen capture, audio and video conferencing; presentation with skype, interactive whiteboard, google presentation, zoho presentation; playing mmorpg's online games etc.

4. Analyzing is the fourth level where student learns to process data, dividing it into parts and determining the relationship between these parts and the overall purpose of the project. Mashing data currently is a complete process but as more options and sites evolve, this well become easy and accessible means of analysis. An appropriate learning activity could be the use of an online survey tool as survey Monkey (www.surveymonkey.com). After collecting the data, the student can use the tool to analyse the data, comparing response, relationship between different groups etc. The important key words are as: comparing, organizing, marking, linking, reverse engineering, coaching, mind-mapping etc.

5. Evaluating is the fifth level and related to higher order thinking. It requires the student to make criteria based judgements through the process of critiquing and checking. In the present digital era, multiple opportunities are available for discussion and an ease of participation through comments and forum posting. The student can use a free blogging platform as word press (www.wordpress.com) and write a blog post on any topic or subject, encourage comment and interaction. The student should evaluate the comment in context and decide the value of the contribution. If it is valuable, they can make the comment publicly visible by using the tools supplied by word press. If the comment is not appropriate, they can delete

it by using the tools provided. Thus constructive criticism and effective practice are often facilitated by the use of blogs and video blogs. Students of today and tomorrow must be able to validate the veracity of their information sources. The key terms included in this are: monitoring, (Blog/vlog) commenting, reviewing, posting, moderating, networking, reflecting, collaborating etc.

6. Creating is the sixth and highest level of thinking and concerned with taking various elements and creating a new coherent product. The student could participate in publishing and distribution of an e-book. The student would write the text, then decide about the inclusion of illustrations, graphs, examples etc. Once all the chapters are complete, the student can create an account on Amazon Direct Publishing Website. He/she can put the e-book metadata (author's name, description etc.) and upload the Microsoft word version of the book. By using available tools on Amazon, he/she can create a cover page and decide on the price of a e-book. The Amazon website's software would then convert these elements in to e-book format that can be read on kindle e-reader. The staff members will review it and after their approval, the e-book will be available for sale. The students can also create their own application, programming macros or developing games or multi media applications with in structured environment. The students can frequently capture, create, mix and remix content to produce unique products. The student can create video blog; create, add and modify content in wikis also. The key terms for creating are: designing, programming, blogging, animating, video blogging, mixing, remixing, wiki-ing, publishing, videocasting, podcasting, etc.

Before finalising the digital document, the student should check that is it suitable for the purpose? Is it suitable for the audience? Does it convey information easily? Is it effective? A digital document is not limited to a word processed product, rather it could be a blog or wiki entry, a web page, slide show presentation, DTP product, etc.

Example:

Level	*Activity*
1. Remembering	Identify a legitimate search engine and understand its working process.
2. Understanding	Categorise and tag bookmark through a social book marking application.
3. Applying	Produce a presentation.
4. Analyzing	Conduct a survey online and analyse the result.
5. Evaluating	Moderate and respond to comments on a blog post.
6. Creating	Construct a video blog, wiki-page.

Thus in the digital era, the student could apply the digital tools available online to collect the information, to understand the concepts, produce an effective presentation, apply the knowledge to edit a wiki-page, analyse the data to find the results and compare between different categories, evaluate the effectiveness of the comments posted on the blogs as well as create new video blogs, publish e-books etc. The aim of the taxonomy is not to focus on the specific tools but ensure that the student progresses through the hierarchy of levels. The teacher should have the information about the availability of digital tools, so that they can prepare their students accordingly.

2. Affective Domain

It is clear that emotions, attitudes, interests, feelings, and values exist and affect all human behaviour. This domain includes the manner in which we deal with things emotionally such as values, feelings, appreciations, enthusiasms, motivations and attitudes. Skills in this domain describe the way people react emotionally and their ability to feel another living thing's pain or joy. It typically targets the awareness and growth in emotions, attitudes and feelings. There is a confusion among educators whether this aspect should be included in the curriculum or not. But in fact, it is the school where various values and feelings of the students are developed and shaped through engaging them in different activities in the rich social environment.

The five major categories are listed from the simplest behaviour to the most complex:

(*i*) *Receiving:* It is the lowest level. In it the student passively pays attention. On the other hand it is the important level because without it no learning can occur. The learners are sensitive to the existence of certain stimuli. It includes three types of activities:

- Awareness about the stimuli.
- Willingness to hear.
- Control the attention of the learner.

Examples:

- Listen to others with respect.
- Listen for and remember the name of newly introduced people.

(*ii*) *Responding:* It involves active participation on the part of the learners. The pupils are motivated to response. The pupil attends and reacts to a particular phenomenon. It includes three types of activities:

- Obedience to respond.
- Willingness to respond.
- Satisfaction in responding.

Examples:

- Participates in class discussion.
- Gives a presentation.
- Questions new ideals, concepts, models, etc. in order.
- Knows the safety rules and practises them.

(*iii*) *Valuing:* It includes the worth or value a person attaches to a particular object, phenomenon, or behaviour. This ranges from simple acceptance to the more complex state of commitment. Valuing is based on the internalization of a set of specified values, while clues to these values are expressed in the learner's overt behaviour and are often identifiable. It has three types of activities:

- Acceptance of value.

- Preference of value.
- Commitment of value.

Examples:

- Demonstrates belief in the democratic process.
- Is sensitive towards individual and cultural differences.
- Shows the ability to solve problems.
- Informs management on matters that one feels strongly about.
- Propose a plan to institutions' improvement and follows through with commitment.

(*iv*) *Organization:* In this category, a student organizes values into priorities by contrasting different values, resolving conflicts between them and creating a unique value system. It has three types of activities:

- Comparing values.
- Relating values.
- Synthesizing values.

Examples:

- Recognizes the need for balance between freedom and responsible behaviour.
- Accepts responsibility for one's behaviour.
- Explains the role of systematic planning in solving problems.
- Accepts professional ethical standards.
- Creates a life plan in harmony with abilities, interests and beliefs.
- Prioritizes time effectively to meet the needs of the organization, family and self.

(*v*) *Internalizing values (Characterization):* At this level the pupils have a value system that controls their behaviour. The behaviour is *pervasive*, consistent, predictable and most importantly characteristic of the learner. Instructional objectives are concerned with the student's general pattern of adjustment. (Personal, Social, Emotional)

Examples:

- Shows self reliance when working independently.
- Cooperates in group activities.
- Uses an objective approach in problem solving.
- Displays a professional commitment to ethical practice on daily basis.
- Revises judgements and changes behaviour in light of new evidences.
- Values people for what they are, not how they look

3. Psychomotor Domain

The psychomotor domain includes physical movement, coordination and use of motor skill areas. Development of these skills requires practice and is measured in terms of speed, precision, distance, procedure or techniques in execution. It is very important in taxonomy of educational objectives because motion is a necessary condition of survival and of independence. This domain is based on the concept of coordination among various organs of the body. In this domain learning depends on mastery of a physical skill. There are various taxonomies for this domain as follows:

Simpson's Taxonomy (1972)

(*i*) *Perception:* It is the ability to use sensory cues to guide motor activity. This ranges from sensory stimulation, through cue selection, to translation. The presence of interest and inspiration among the students is a prerequisite for perception.

Examples:

- Detects non-verbal communication cues.
- Estimates where a ball will land after it is thrown and then moving to the correct location to catch the ball.

(*ii*) *Set:* It relates with readiness to act. It includes mental, physical and emotional sets. These three sets are dispositions that predetermine a person's response to different situations (sometimes called mindsets). This is closely related with the 'Responding to Phenomena' – a subdivision of Affective Domain.

Examples:

- Knows and acts upon a sequence of steps in a manufacturing process.
- Recognises one's abilities and limitations.
- Shows desire to learn a new process.

(*iii*) *Guided Response:* It is the early stages in learning a complex skill that includes imitation and trial and error. Adequacy of performance is achieved by practising.

Examples:

- Follows instructions to build a model.
- Performs a mathematical equation as demonstrated.

(*iv*) *Mechanism:* This is the intermediate stage in learning a complex skill. Learned responses have become habitual and the movements can be performed with some confidence and perfection. It is the condition which helps the students in responding properly.

Examples:

- Use a personal computer.
- Drive a car.
- Prepare an advertisement.

(*v*) *Complex Overt Response:* The skillful performance of motor acts that involve complex movement patterns. It is the highest level of psychomotor domain. Proficiency is indicated by a quick, accurate and highly coordinated performance, requiring a minimum of energy. This category includes performing without hesitation and automatic performance. For example, players often utter sounds of satisfaction or expletive as soon as they hit a tennis ball or throw a football, because they can tell by the feel of the act what the result will produce.

Examples:

- Operates a computer quickly and accurately.
- Displays competence while making an advertisement.

(*vi*) *Adaptation:* Skills are well developed and the individual can modify movement pattern to fit special requirements.

Examples:

- Responds effectively to unexpected experience.

- Performs a task with a machine that it was not originally intended to do.
- Modifies learning style.

(*vii*) *Origination:* It includes creation of new movement patterns to fit a particular situation or specific problems. Learning outcomes emphasized creativity based upon highly developed skill.

Examples:

- Construct a new theory.
- Develops a new and comprehensive learning programme.

Dave's Taxonomy

He classified psychomotor domain in five categories as:

(*i*) *Imitation:* Observing and patterning behaviour after some one else. Performance may be of low quality.

Examples:

- Copying the work of art.

(*ii*) *Manipulation:* It involves being able to perform certain actions by following instructions and practising.

Examples:

- Creating work on one's own, after taking instructions, or reading about it.

(*iii*) *Precision:* It includes refining, becoming more exact. Few errors are apparent.

Examples:

- Working and reworking something, so it will be 'just right.'

(*iv*) *Articulation:* It includes coordinating a series of actions, achieving harmony and interval consistency.

Examples:

Producing an advertisement that involves music, drama, colour, sound etc.

(*v*) *Naturalization:* It is the highest level having high-level performance become natural, without thinking much about it.

Examples:

- Nancy Lopez hitting a golf ball.

Thus, every teaching learning process should include all the three domains for the all-round development of the students. Bloom and his colleagues never created subcategories for skills in the psychomotor domain, but since then other educators have created their own psychomotor taxonomies. The teacher of commerce should always give proper attention to these domains while formulating instructional objectives of his subject.

4

Writing Instructional Objectives in Behavioural Terms

"Behavioural objectives are the measuring rods to evaluate learning outcomes. They are the crux and keys of the entire process of teaching and learning."

Learning objectives have central place in teaching. The teacher is to use them in his teaching. He /she can make his lesson-plan balanced and well organised on the basis of these objectives. So, it is necessary for a teacher to make the objectives more clear and precise. While writing objective two things should be kept in mind:

Firstly, laws of teaching and learning should be defined. For this Bloom's taxonomy is to be utilized. Bloom has categorized all the changes that are to be needed in the pupils' behaviour. So in lesson planning or teaching instructional objectives and learning objectives are used precisely. They help in providing the definite environment in teaching process.

B.S. Bloom has shifted the emphasis from content to the objectives. According to him, specification of objectives in a task of teaching learning may prove more effective and purposeful if they are written in behavioural terms. The following points should be kept in mind while writing the objectives in behavioural terms:

(*i*) Relationship of objectives and expected behaviour or outcomes.
(*ii*) Mastery over subject matter.
(*iii*) Clarity of levels to be achieved in objectives.

Thus, instructional objectives can be stated by identifying the product of instruction in terms of observable performance. These outcomes have been referred to as behavioural objectives or terminal performances. Thus, when we formulate instructional objectives for students we have to ensure that they are observable or measurable.

An instructional objective certainly tells us about the change(s) proposed to bring about in the student but it will be still clearer if we isolate the critical aspects of a particular change. Statements of objectives in terms of the change in the behaviour of the students are called *behavioural objectives*. Instructional objectives can be transformed into behavioural objectives.

Example

- To develop in the student a sense of business responsibility.

  This objective acquires concreteness, clarity and meaning when we get answers to the following questions:

  (*i*) What does a person who has a sense of business responsibility usually do?

(*ii*) What does a person who has a sense of business responsibility usually not do?

(*iii*) What kinds of behaviour distinguish one who has a sense of business responsibility from one who lacks a sense of business responsibility?

An objective, when it is defined in terms of student's behaviour, becomes tangible and capable of attainment. It is clear from the above, illustration that a clearly formulated objective has two dimensions: one deals with the behaviour and the other deals with the content area in which the behaviour operates.

Need of Writing Objectives in Behavioural Terms

As a matter of fact, the objectives are meant to help us bring about changes in the individual in the desired direction. The achievement of objectives enables the individual to perform certain tasks, develop certain understanding, sustain thinking process, develop attitudes, add to the stock of knowledge etc. and this leads to a happy, productive and socially acceptable life. Now a days it is important to write the objective in behavioural terms because the teacher has to do different activities as:

1. For effective learning the teacher can select teaching strategies and tactics on the basis of the objectives modified in behavioural terms.
2. Testing and evaluation can be made objective centered in the form of behavioural terms of the objectives.
3. Specification and delimitation of teaching activities becomes possible and it does not include undesirable activities.
4. The integration of teaching and learning activities can result in expected learning achievements.

Scaffold has given the following needs to write the objectives in behavioural terms.

1. To specify objectives.
2. To select test items for test construction.
3. To integrate learning experiences and changes in behaviour.
4. To select appropriate teaching strategies, tactics and teaching aids.
5. To distinguish between various aspects of learning.
6. To make learning functional.

The above are some of the reasons why we need to write instructional objectives in behavioural terms. The instructional objectives in behavioural terms help in planning the instructions. They tell us where we are going i.e. what the students will be able to know to do at the end of instruction. Proper statement of objectives will help the teachers plan the steps or procedure to reach the terminal outcomes to behaviours. The instructional objectives in behavioural terms also help in designing performance assessment procedures and help in test construction. The assessment of students' performance reveals the gap between the expected outcomes and achieved outcomes. The students will also know in advance the areas of knowledge, attitudes or skills on which they will be tested.

We should remember that just writing objectives in behavioural terms does not serve the purpose unless you also know how to achieve them. Some experts or administrators may suggest you various short cuts (routes) to reach the undertaken objectives but you may end up nowhere. You therefore should know the systematic way for evaluation/ assessment of objectives.

Procedure for Writing Behavioural Objectives

The statement of objectives in behavioural or performance terms i.e. in term of expected terminal behaviour of the students has received attention. For example, Mager's (1962) and Miller's (1962) works are devoted entirely to writing good performance objectives. Mager's work is devoted to the cognitive and affective domain, while Miller worked on psychomotor domain.

Robert Mager's Approach for Writing Instructional Objectives

Robert Mager has suggested three steps for writing performance objectives. They are:

- Decide what the students will be able to do at the end of learning activities.
- Decide under what condition the behaviour will be expected to occur i.e. indicate the condition(s) under which the behaviour will be observed.
- Decide what will be the expected level of performance i.e. indicate how will the students be expected to perform.

These steps can be elaborated with the help of an example as '*At the end of the lesson, the students should be able to identify at least five constellations in the sky at the night, with the help of a star chart as a guide.*'

The above statement fulfills all the three characteristics of a good behavioural objective. Conditions one and three are fulfilled by the first half of the statement and the second condition is fulfilled by the later half of the statement.

(*i*) *Cognitive Objectives*

Mager approach has adopted the Bloom's Taxonomy of objectives as the basis for writing behavioural objectives. He laid much stress on action verbs for stating different objectives. Only those associated verbs should be used which are direct and unambiguous. The following list of verbs will help you understand and formulate acceptable behavioural objectives.

	Objectives	*Associated Action verbs*
1.	Knowledge	Define, describe, identify, know, label, list, match, name, outline, recall, recognize, reproduce, select.
2.	Comprehension	Comprehend, convert, defend, distinguish, estimate, explain, extend, generalize, give, rewrite, translate.
3.	Application	Apply, change, compute, construct, demonstrate, discover, manipulate, modify, predict, relate, participate, prepare, project, utilize.
4.	Analysis	Correlate, diagram, differentiate, discriminate, distinguish, focus, illustrate, infer, limit, point out, selects, separate, deconstruct, etc.

(*Contd.*)

	Objectives	*Associated Action verbs*
5.	Synthesis	Adapt, anticipate, categorize, collaborate, combine, communicate, compare, compose, compile, contrast, create, design, express, facilitate, formulate, initiate, integrate, rearrange, reconstruct, reinforce, reorganize.
6.	Evaluation	Appraise, compare and contrast, conclude, criticize, critique, decide, defend, interpret, judge, justify, reframe, support, etc.

Verbs open to many Interpretations (To be avoided)	*Verbs open to proper Interpretation (To be used)*
– to know	–to write
– to believe	– to compare
– to respect	– to list
– to appreciate	– to predict
– to understand	– to solve
	– to construct
– to grasp significance of	– to recite
. – to enjoy	– to identify

Examples:

1. The students are able to recall the meaning of double entry system– *knowledge - recall*
2. The students are able to explain the features of double entry system– *comprehension - explain*
3. The students are able to assess the books of accounts under double entry system– *Application - assess*
4. The students are able to analyse principles of double entry system–*Analysis - Analyse*
5. The students are able to generalize the principles of double entry system– *Synthesis - Generalize.*

Example of Revised Taxonomy by Anderson & Krathwohl

1. The students are able to retrieve the general meaning of internal trade.
2. The students are able to find a specific example of the goods used for internal trade in India.
3. The students are able to construct a model to demonstrate the process of internal trade.
4. The students can distinguish between internal and external trade.
5. The students are able to detect the appropriateness of the procedure for internal trade.
6. The student are able to devise a procedure for effective internal trade.

Example of Bloom's Digital Taxonomy

1. The students are able to access the resources regarding meaning and features of internal trade.
2. The students are able to create links between resources and construct meaning of internal trade.
3. The students are able to upload the images of various goods used for internal trade in India and add them to the trade.
4. The students are able to analyse the data regarding internal trade for the last 2 years collected from a survey.
5. The students are able to evaluate comments related to benefits of internal trade on a blog spot using a set of criteria.
6. The students are able to create their own content using various computer based and online tools.

Behavioural Objectives of Affective Domain

Robert Mager has also developed the associated action verbs for each category of an affective domain which indicates the behaviour which is required for a student to demonstrate. The list of action verbs is as follows:

	Objectives	*Associated Action verbs*
1.	Receiving	ask, choose, describe, follow, give, hold, identify, locate, name, point to, select, reply, use.
2.	Responding	answer, assist, aid, comply, confirm, discuss, help, label, perform, practise, present, read, recite, report, select, tells, write.
3.	Valuing	Complete, demonstrate, differentiate, explain, follow, form, initiate, invite, join, justify, propose, read, report, select, share, study, work.
4.	Organization	alter, arrange, combine, compare, complete, defends, explain, formulate, generalize, identify, integrate, order, organize, prepare, relate, synthesize.
5.	Internalizing values	act, discriminate, display, influence, listen, modify, perform, practise, propose, qualify, question, revise, solve, verify.

There is no doubt that a lot of confusion prevails with regard to the statement of objectives in affective domain, as compared to the cognitive domain. Terms like interest, appreciate, values, attitudes, etc., give varying shades of meaning. The objectives related to these characteristics are hard to define and hence to achieve. Affective learning is not completely separable from cognitive learning.

Examples:

1. The students are able to name the types of internal trade. *Receiving - Name*
2. The students are able to discuss the features of internal trade. *Responding - discuss.*

3. The students are able to share their views about internal trade in India. *Valuing - share.*
4. The students are able to compare different types of internal trade. *Organizing - compare.*
5. The students are able to verify different types of internal trade in India. *Characterization - verify.*

Limitations of Mager's Approach

1. There is overlapping of action verbs.
2. It explain only cognitive and affective domain objectives.
3. It is useful only in programmed learning.
4. It lays no emphasis on mental processes.
5. Only lower level objectives can be written, not the higher order objectives.

Robert Miller's Approach

Miller's method of task description is somewhat difficult to describe because it is a product of research on training process in the Air Force and has not been fully adopted to the school setting. It is related to development of skills and physical activities. According to him, there are three elements that are essential in any task description:

- Indication i.e. the task which calls for a response. In psychology we call this the stimulus or the stimulus condition.
- Activation i.e. the response to be made.
- Feedback i.e. information on the adequacy of the response.

Miller also provided the list of action verbs for writing objectives in behavioural terms as follows:

	Objectives	*Action Verbs*
1.	Perception	Choose, describe, detect, differentiate, distinguish, identify, isolate, relate, select.
2.	Set	Begin, display, explain, move, proceed, react, show, state, volunteer.
3.	Guided Response	Copy, trace, follow, recall, reproduce, respond.
4.	Mechanism	Assemble, display, construct, fix, heat, manipulate, measure, mend, mix, organize, sketch.
5.	Complex overt Response	Assemble, build, change, create, locate, connect, more accurate.
6.	Adaptation	Adapt, alter, change, rearrange, reorganize, revise, vary.
7.	Origination	Arrange, build, combine, compose, construct, create, design, initiate, make, originate.

Examples

1. The students are able to identify business activities. *Perception – Identify.*
2. The students are able to display different business activities. *Set – Display.*
3. The students are able to recall the activities related to production. *Guided Response – Recall.*

4. The students are able to sketch different business activities on the chart. *Mechanism – Sketch.*
5. The students are able to revise the difference between industry, commerce and trade. *Adaptation – Revise.*
6. The students are able to design the goods to be produced in industries. *Origination – Design.*

The RCEM Approach

The teachers of Regional College of Education Mysore realized the limitations of Mager's and Miller's approaches and worked out a very systematic approach called RCEM approach to write objectives. They converted Bloom's taxonomy of cognitive domain into four categories and these four categories were further divided into 17 mental processes or abilities. These are as follows:

Bloom's cognitive system	*RCEM system*	*Mental Processes or Abilities*
1. Knowledge	Knowledge	1. Recall 2. Recognition
2. Comprehension	Understanding	3. See relationship 4. Cite examples 5. Discriminate 6. Classify 7. Interpret 8. Verify 9. Generalize
3. Application	Application	10. Reason out 11. Formulate Hypotheses 12. Establish Hypotheses 13. Infer 14. Predict
4. Analysis synthesis Evaluation	Creativity	15. Analyse 16. Synthesise 17. Evaluate

This method also requires the structure of the content and the objectives are identified in taxonomic category considering entry behaviour of the students. Here we want to emphasize the mental process and the selection of the content so as to achieve the objectives i.e. the modification of the behaviour or learning taking place in the students.

Examples:

Topic: Outsourcing of services.

- Students are able to *recall* the meaning of outsourcing of services.
- Students are able to *classify* different types of outsourcing of services.
- Students can *predict* the effect of outsourcing of services.
- Students can *analyse* the needs of these services.

Thus, with the help of writing objectives in behavioural terms teaching activities/ learning experiences are determined and delimited. Teaching is organised for the development of the child. Teaching learning process may be integrated for effective learning outcomes with all the three domains. It leads to systematization of instructions. The interaction process in teaching learning can be represented as follows:

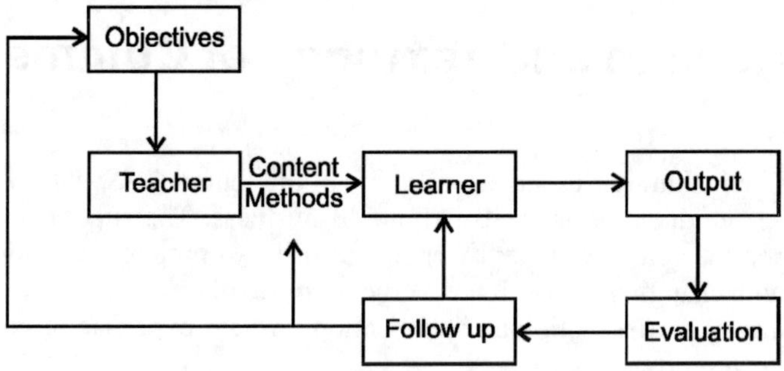

Fig. 4.1: Teaching learning process

In this way teaching learning process can be made effective if the objectives are stated properly in well defined terms and clear language. These should be in direct relation with the particular content of a topic. Objectives of instruction, learning experiences and evaluation techniques must be interrelated and interdependent.

5

Curriculum and Textbook of Commerce

"The Curriculum represents the total life of the school." – *Spears H.*

Commerce education is the backbone of business. The success in business depends upon the quality of manpower, etc. utilised. Commerce education should keep pace with changing trends. It has a crucial role to play in our society including various political parties, religious organisations, where expertise in commercial knowledge is required.

Our country is getting integrated in to the global economy, where the world has predominantly become interdependent in term of trade, culture and communication. The knowledge of state of commerce is expanding and diversifying. As social culture shifts from ideal to material, commerce education has shifted from abstract thinking to thoughtful actions, perceptions and practices. In response to the widely recognised need for broader and integrated content, emphasis in commerce curriculum, teachers, curriculum workers and professors are effecting, searching, analysing and extensively revising the existing programme of commerce education to achieve the following goals of education:

- Development of total integrated personality of the child.
- Commitment to society through involvement in development programmes and actions.
- Application of new methods of science and technology effectively in line with industry and agriculture.
- Improving productivity of human efforts towards improving quality of life and entrepreneurship of the society.

The present world is characterized by fast changing conditions of demand and technology. There will be much uncertainty than in the past. Our research and development organisation will have to acquire, and adapt latest technologies in improving the quality so as to stay in the competitive world. The speed of LPG (Liberalization, Privatization and Globalization) has tremendously influenced the various dimensions of commerce education. It demands that the schools of today equip future citizens with two essential ingredients for successful living: *Knowledge* and *skill in working effectively with each other.* This require systematically planned learning experiences in which the pupil has the opportunity to apply what he has learned about the commerce activities theoretically. These kinds of learning activities are the essence of what is commonly referred to as *commerce education.* Content alone, without practical work, is not enough for commerce education. Commerce curriculum should now be mostly practical oriented. Content alone cannot constitute the whole commerce education curriculum any more than practical activities alone

– both are essential and complementary, both must be in sensible proportion in a sound programme designed for society's needs.

Meaning of Curriculum

The curriculum is the important part of the education process. The subject of commerce forms that part of the school curriculum which schedules subject matter and activities that enable the pupil to acquire an understanding of different concepts related to business or trade as banking, insurance, management, book-keeping, advertisement, etc., a knowledge of business management, dedication to the principles and values of society and commitment to participate in different activities of the society.

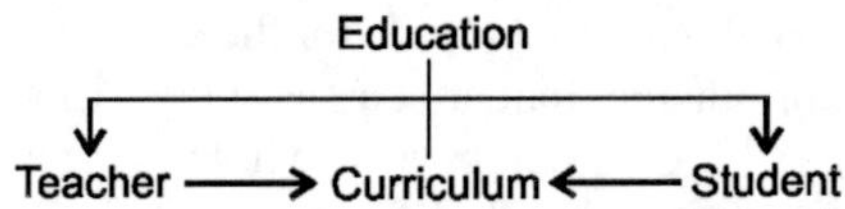

The three important elements of education are the teacher, curriculum and student. From these, curriculum is the most important because it works as the medium for the interaction between teacher and students.

Etymologically the world 'curriculum' is derived from the Latin word 'currere' which means–'A Race course.' In the field of education, curriculum is like a race course for children who run to win the race/educational achievements in the limited time duration. Thus, it means a runway, a course on which one runs to reach a goal.

Concepts Related to Curriculum

There are two concepts of curriculum prevailing in the society.

1. Old concept 2. New/Modern concept.

1. Old Concept

According to old concept, it was often interpreted as a syllabus or a course of study. Most of the part of the curriculum was regarded as a written course.

In the words of C.V. Good, "Curriculum is a general overall plan of the content or specific material of instructions that the school should offer to the student by way of qualifying them for certification for entrance into professional or vocational field."

According to R.N. Safaya, "Curriculum is a group of subjects or courses of study arranged in a particular sequence for instructional purposes in the school."

In the words of Elizabeth Maccie, "Curriculum is a prescribed instructional material for the students."

2. New/ Modern Concept

According to the modern view, curriculum consists of all the educative experience under the conscious guidance of the teacher in the school. Just as the assigned lesson was the basic unit in old concept, so an experience is the unit of the new. In the overall context, it means a rounded programme of learning, doing and living for every child as opposed to the curriculum as a series of lessons or a collection of courses.

Cunningham, "It (Curriculum) is a tool in the hands of an artist (teacher) to mould his material (students) according to his ideals (objectives) in his studio (school)."

Froebel, "Curriculum should be conceived as an epitome of the rounded whole of the knowledge and experiences of the human race."

Secondary Education commission, "Curriculum does not mean only the academic subjects traditionally taught in the school but it includes the totality of experiences that a pupil receives through the manifold activities that go in the school, in the library, in the classroom, laboratory, workshop playground and in the numerous informal contacts between teacher and pupils."

Education commission, "We conceive of the school curriculum as the totality of learning experience that the school provide for the pupils through all the manifold activities in the school or outside, that are carried under its supervision."

According to Kilpatrick, "Curriculum is the whole living of the pupils or students so far as the school aspects responsibility for its quality."

Curriculum = Content + Activities + Various parts of educational environment

Thus, curriculum is the sum total of the content and activities which the school employs for the purpose of training the pupils. Today the child is regarded as being far more important than school subjects. The best preparation of the child for future life is to give him as many experiences and activities as possible in the school, so that he may feel the necessity of learning different kinds of skills and acquiring various forms of learning. There is an urgent need to introduce a vast range of course including traditional academic areas of learning and research, as well as more practical course with a vocational orientation. It is necessary that the curriculum be designed in such a way that more importance is placed in developing the ability of students to think creatively and independently, read widely and critically participate in seminars, debates, workshops and function as a team. The end users need should be borne in mind and the above said attributes are those, which the present day employers look for.

In the words of Owen, "The new curriculum will be based not on traditions, but on analysis."

Characteristics of Curriculum

On the basis of above definition, the curriculum has the following characteristics:

1. It is more than teaching and learning.
2. It includes content, methods of teaching and purpose of education.
3. It is an ever-changing product.
4. It caters to the individual differences of the learners.
5. It includes social, physical and psychological environment.
6. It includes the totality of the experiences.
7. It is a medium to achieve the objectives of education.
8. It is framed and reframed according to the needs of the society.
9. It is the mirror of the prevailing educational system.

Thus, curriculum is a tool to fulfill the objectives of education.

Difference between Syllabus and Curriculum

The difference between syllabus and curriculum is the same as in the old concept and new concept. The difference can be described according to the following criteria:

	Criteria	*Syllabus*	*Curriculum*
1.	Scope	Syllabus is the part of the curriculum, its scope is limited.	Curriculum is a complete teaching process, its scope is wider.
2.	Knowledge Imparted	Syllabus provides theoretical knowledge.	Curriculum includes theoretical knowledge as well as practical based on interest, aptitude of the students
3.	Preparation	Educationists, NCERT, CBSE prepare syllabus.	Curriculum is prepared by the teachers.
4.	Aspect	Syllabus lays emphasis on theoretical aspect i.e., cognitive.	Curriculum lays emphasis on the aspect of all round development of the personality i.e., it includes cognitive, affective and psychomotor aspect.
5.	Importance	It gives importance to the subject matter	It provides importance to the students.

Importance of Curriculum

Curriculum plays an important role in education process because without it the teacher can't imagine what to teach and the students can't imagine what to learn. The knowledge is so vast that we can't teach /learn everything at once. So, we are to divide it in different parts according to the mental level of the students. Education is a tri-polar process which has important three elements:

– The Teacher – The Child – The Curriculum

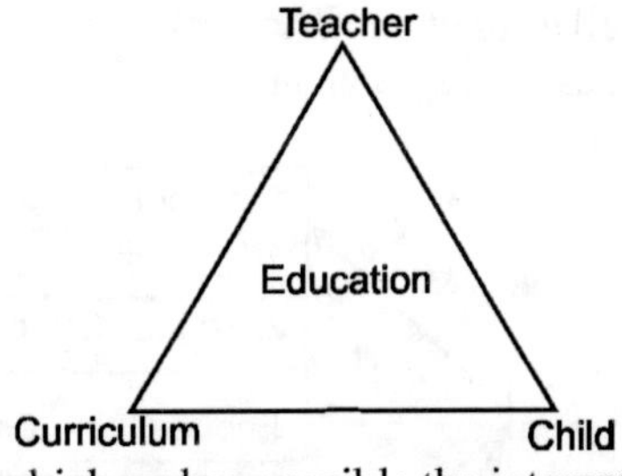

It is the curriculum which makes possible the interaction between teacher and student. The following points will demonstrate the importance of curriculum:

- It helps in all round development of a child.
- It helps in selecting the appropriate method of teaching.
- It can help in satisfying the educational, vocational and psychological needs of the students.
- It helps the child in providing various opportunities to prove himself.
- It helps in achieving the aims and objectives of education.
- It helps in providing the limits to teachers and students both for teaching and learning.

- It helps in developing self confidence in the child.
- It helps in developing the thinking, understanding, reasoning of the child to achieve his maximum mental growth.
- It helps in bringing uniformity in educational system throughout the whole country.
- It helps the students in solving real life problems.
- It helps in achieving the educational and instructional objectives in school.
- It helps to maintain the good relation between school and community.

Bases of Curriculum Construction

The curriculum construction depends upon the educational system and there are mainly four bases of education:

- Philosophical → Why we need curriculum?
- Sociological → What should be in curriculum?
- Psychological
- Scientific → How the curriculum should be used in schools.

So, our education system tries to follow the above bases in the construction of curriculum because with the help of these it can be in the position to fulfill its aims and objectives.

Development of Curriculum in Commerce

Generally, it is believed that the development and change in the curriculum is a continuous process and no nation can tolerate the slow speed in this process. The curriculum should fulfill the needs of the learners, expectations of the society and international comparison. In the era of globalisation there should be minimum differences in the curriculum of the commerce at the world level because it is the subject through which the economy of the nation can provide knowledge about the trade of that nations as well as of other nations also. The curriculum as a system is the sum total of all that goes on inside in an institution which leads the students to achieve the particular goals.

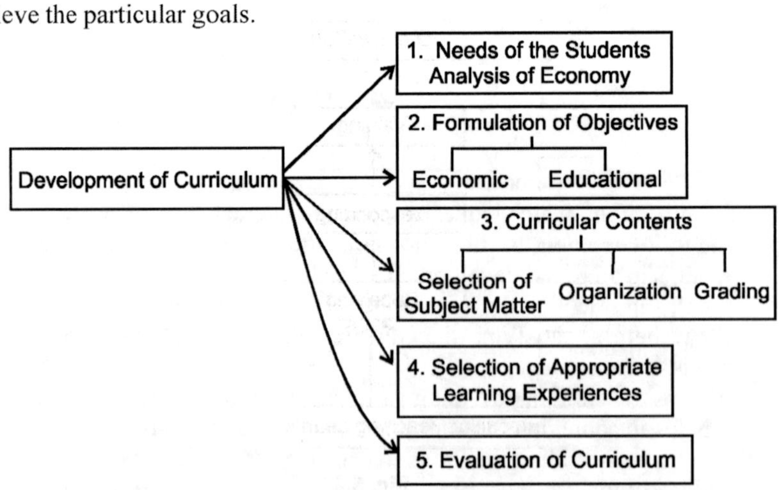

Fig. 5.1: Process of Curriculum Development in Commerce.

1. Analysis of Economy: Commerce is related with the trade and trade is related with economy; so the first step of developing the curriculum is analysis of economy. This analysis will provide the knowledge about the elements of trade about which the teacher and pupils of commerce should know. The analysis also indicates towards the changing trends in the business world. Whenever there will be change in the trading process, the curriculum will also change accordingly. The changing trends point out towards the aims of the economy. Besides this, the needs of the students should also be kept in view. While constructing the curriculum the educationists should also analyse the beliefs and important values of the society.

2. Formulation of Objectives: It is generally believed that a student should be provided knowledge and skills needed for activities to make the solution of the problems in business. The curriculum of commerce should indicate specific objectives according to the class and these should be classified as – knowledge, skills, application, attitude, appreciation, interest etc. Besides this, these objectives should be expressed in terms of desired change in the behaviour of the students as thought, feeling and action. The curriculum should not only provides the knowledge about the existing information and skill but should also enable the students to be continuous self learners. The educational institutions are those organised sources through which the society tries to fulfill its basic desires, expectations and goals.

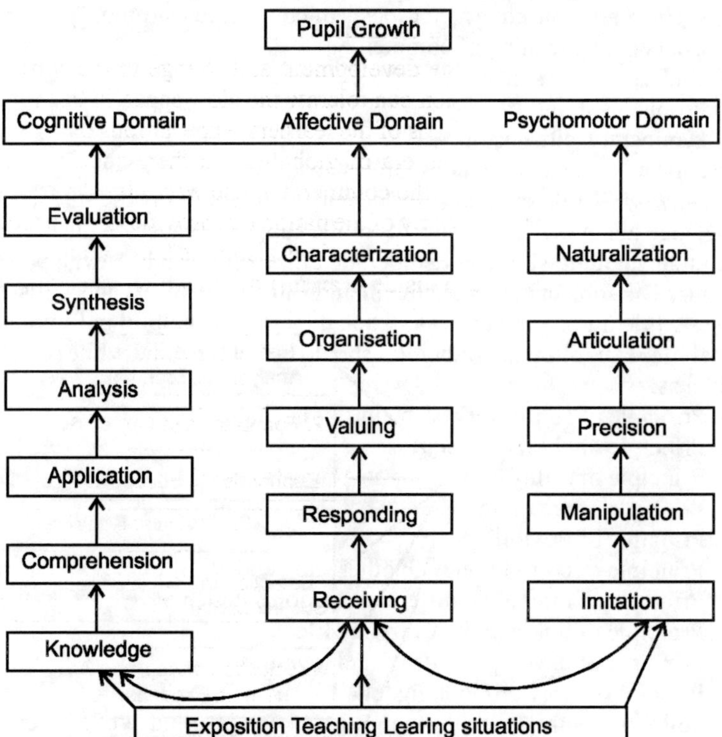

Fig. 5.2

These expectations of the society become its aim. The educational aims depend upon the aims of the society. It should be kept in mind that the aims should be in specific forms so that they may help in deciding the proper learning experiences.

The Fig. 5.2 shows that when a child is exposed to a certain teaching learning situation, the exposure is likely to generate growth in one or more aspects which could also be in varying degrees. This means that the growth will be cumulative and concomitant. It will be necessary for the instructional objectives when stated and defined, to satisfy some criteria to motivate purposeful instruction and evaluation. This implies that they should be:

- Stated specifically and in unambiguous terms.
- Stated in terms of pupil behaviour.
- Stated with both the content and the modification part.
- Achievable with the available resources.
- Testable.

3. Curricular Content: All the experiences of past as well as present can't be included in the curriculum. Only those elements should be included which can be effective in achieving the desired educational objectives. In this way the selection of the curricular content depends up to a certain extent on the objectives of education. There are four important aspects of commerce learning.

- Concept or Meaning of commerce
- Understanding skill
- Problem solving
- Democratic citizenship.

The curricular content includes three steps:

(i) Selection: While selecting the curricular content firstly the students should get knowledge about the basic concepts of the subject because on the basis of this only the understanding skill and democratic citizenship can be developed among the students. The subject matter should include all those aspects and skills which a trader uses while trading in business so that they may be helpful in future for their vocational life. The following principles should be kept in mind while selecting the curriculum as:

- Principle of conformity with aims of education
- Principle of child centredness
- Principle of utility
- Principle of creativity
- Principle of flexibility
- Principle of correlation with other subjects
- Principle of individual differences among students
- Principle of linking with everyday life
- Principle of developing ideals and loyalties
- Principle of forward looking, etc.

The following subject matter should be kept in mind while selecting the curriculum so that useful topics can be selected according to the level/ stage of the students:

- Stenographic sequence
- Clerical sequence
- Secretarial sequence
- Book-keeping sequence
- Business problems
- Economic problems
- Corporate Organisation
- Finance
- Management
- Administration
- Different Activities

(ii) Organisation: The selection of the subject matter is not sufficient to make the teaching of commerce effective and objective based but it should be well organised also. For this the following methods of organising the subject matter can be adopted:

- Unit Method.
- Topical Method.
- Concentric Method.
- Spiral Method.

(iii) Grading: After organising the curriculum the question arises that how the curriculum should be graded at different levels at senior secondary level, graduation level and post graduation level. In this process, the principles of curriculum construction play an important role.

Thus, while selecting the subject matter new thoughts, prevailing conditions and circumstances of the society should be kept in mind. The subject matter should be such that which is full of experiences, diversified and flexible, according to the needs of the business community and useful for leisure time. Its subject matter should be systematic, organised and graded according to the psychological needs of the students.

While preparing the curriculum content, it has to be kept in mind that curriculum is not one man's job and certainly not the monopoly of the subject specialists as has been the case in the past at several places.

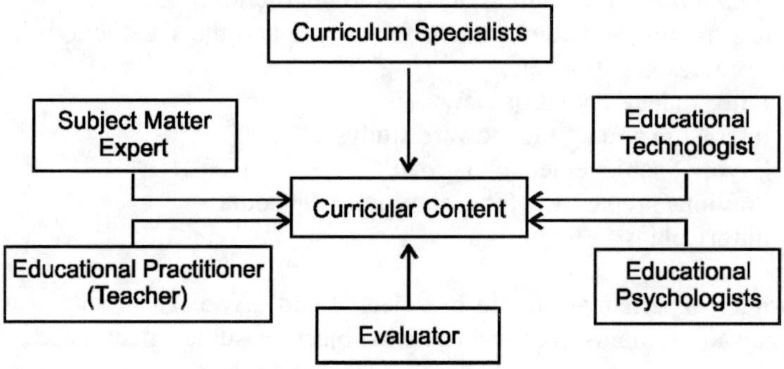

Fig. 5.3

Thus, curricular content development is a process requiring inputs from several areas of specialisation. At the present times, it has become more necessary than ever before, to collaborate with *business and industry. This may not just be limited to consultation but their active involvement in the development of courses and their transaction for incorporating elements relevant to the needs of the job market.* But the sole responsibility for constructing the curriculum and having curriculum and evaluation material prepared should rest with the core body. It will be only then a coordinated curriculum development will be possible.

4. Selection of suitable learning Experiences: This is a crucial step. It is here that the use of the vast inputs in curriculum construction is made. This is mainly the teacher's jurisdiction where he is the master of the situation in manipulating or providing learning experiences to the students as envisaged by the curriculum. This is the stage of interaction between the curriculum on the one hand, the teacher and the students on the other hand.

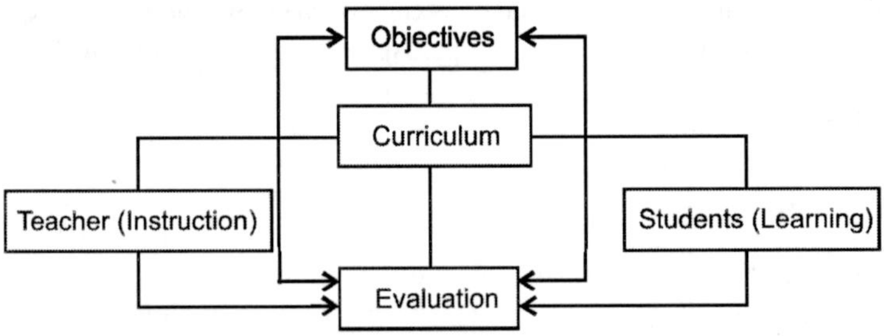

Fig. 5.4

Objectives are the anchor of the curriculum which in turn are the bases of the work of teachers and students. Both work for the achievement of the objectives through the curriculum transaction which are ultimately evaluated through a well defined procedure of evaluation.

It may be noted that several forces both internal and external influence the aforesaid process of providing teaching learning experiences. From the teacher's point of view, they are:

- Personal academic background and training.
- Availability of resources and aids to instruction.
- His interest and commitment for the job and the satisfaction he derives from its execution, etc.

From the student's point of view:

- Interest in and attitude toward study.
- Level of achievement and growth.
- Previous preparation for assimilating the course
- Future plans
- Motivation

Learning experiences should be selected and organised in such a way that student may adjust themselves according to objective, subject matter and activities. From the point of view of both the teacher and the student, it may be the ethos and the atmosphere of the school and the encouragement and motivation, it provides besides the availability of instructional material and their use, etc. Thus, selection of learning experiences should remain with the teacher. We should have faith in enabling even the weakest student to attain the level of achievement of a bright student through a well designed and implemented curriculum programme.

5. Curriculum Evaluation: This is the weakest link of the Indian curriculum development scene. It involves the tryout of the curriculum and curriculum material to find out their adequacy and appropriateness for achieving the objectives. This is seldom done and even where it is attempted, it is not done as it should be. The try out could be unit-wise and when one is developed or that of the complete curriculum. Questions like the following could be sought to be answered through the try out:

- Whether the objectives of instruction set are within the competence of the students to achieve?
- What instructional material helps the students to achieve the objectives better than others?
- Which one of the various methodology tried is more suitable to be adopted as compared to others?
- Whether one set of content matter or another is more adequate and appropriate for enabling the students to achieve the objectives?

This step is mainly contemplated to put the effectiveness of the curriculum to test before putting it into practice. This step may no doubt mean substantial investment in terms of time, effort and money but it could save educational disaster which may mean losses multiplied several times over.

It may be mentioned that in an ideal scheme there should be a built-in system of continuous review and revision of the curriculum.

Principles of Curriculum Construction

No hard and fast principles can be laid down for the construction of the curriculum but these should be kept in the mind while framing the curriculum and these are based on the needs, situation, and expectations of the society.

1. Child Centredness: As all of us know that education is for the child, not the child is for education. So, the curriculum should meet the requirements of the child, which means that it should be in accordance with the interest, age, aptitude, attitude, capabilities and capacities of the child.

2. Community Centredness: Commerce as the very name indicates is the study of business and trading i.e. why its curriculum will have to be localized and determined by the needs and purposes of the business community. Each child is an individual but according to pragmatism, there is need of social development for the development of an individual. It is therefore quite desirable that his needs and desires must harmonize with the needs and desires of those persons amongst whom the child has to live. The purpose of society determines the purpose of the school and the purpose of school determines the purpose of curriculum. Thus, curriculum of commerce must be community centered.

3. Flexibility: Society is not static. It is dynamic and continuously changing. Society determines the goals of education and educationists through suitably designed curriculum help in the realization of such goals. So curriculum should as far as possible, be flexible and in accordance with the changing needs of the society. It cannot remain static; it must be readjusted in view of the prevailing business community.

4. Keeping aims and objectives in view: Aims and objectives of education are determined by the society and the education system tries to achieve these aims and objectives with the help of curriculum of different subjects. According to Wesley, "If *there is no discernible connection between objective and materials, one or the other ought to be modified. There are four pillars of every subject i.e. aims and objectives, curriculum, methods of teaching and evaluation.*"

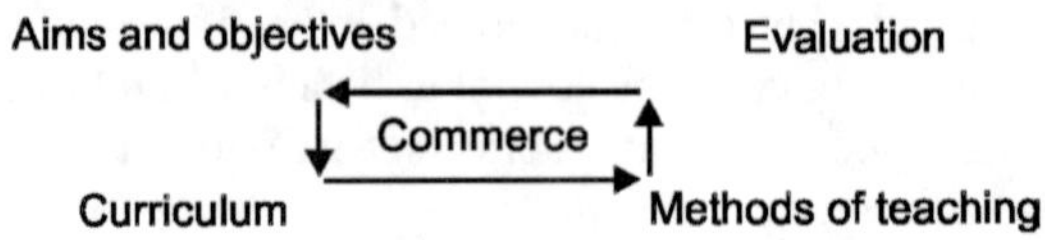

Fig. 5.5

There is interrelationship between these four pillars and the correlation goes on forever.

5. Utility: In the present age, many of the students do not want to get education because they think that it has no utility, because there is no combination between theory and practice. The curriculum should provides such type of knowledge, which will prepare them for the future life in such a way as to make them capable of facing the various challenges of the complex problems of the future.

6. Development of Democratic Values: India is a democratic country. Being the citizen of India society they should know about the past and present societies, their rights and duties to come up to the expectations of a democratic society. Relationship between knowledge and action is established and they turn out to be effective and enlightened citizens. The school itself should be organised on democratic values like liberty, equality, fraternity, justice, respect for dignity of the individual and group living.

7. Principle of Creativity: Children by nature are creative and the point should be kept in mind at the time of framing the curriculum. Raymount rightly remarked, "In a curriculum that is suited to the needs of today and of the future, there must be a definite basis towards definitely creative subjects."

8. Being Tentative Rather Than Final: Life is not static; it is changing day by day. There should be change in every year in the curriculum of the commerce because of the change in political, economic, social changes in the society.

9. Forward Looking: The curriculum should give important place to the future needs and requirements of the society. Child today is the future citizen of tomorrow. They should get such type of education, which will develop them as progressive minded persons. The curriculum should enable him to adjust according to the conditions of life in the world after he left the school. They must not stick with the past but preserve what is good.

10. Studying Current Affairs: In today's life for the development of an individual, study of current affairs can't be neglected. Students should be trained to appreciate critically and learn intelligently the current events so that they may be able to discriminate between what is authentic and what is not. The child is only to get the experiences of the past. What future will be it depends upon present activities, so child is concerned with present. The curriculum will provides the real life education when it includes topics of current affairs.

11. Developing Ideals and Loyalties: The curriculum should be planned in such a way that it helps in teaching the child a true sense of loyalty to family, the school, the community, the town, the province, the country and the world at large. It should help in fostering the desirable ideals among the pupils. The child must understand the maxim 'unity in diversity'.

12. Based on Actual Experience of the Student: The aim of every subject is not only to give information but the development of attitudes and skills. Maximum efforts should be made through the curriculum to exploit the actual experiences of the child. For this it is essential that some practical work should be prescribed.

13. Sensitivity to Changing Needs and Values: For the smooth running of life, change is necessary. Every human being in this world wants change because of his dynamic nature. What was considered good and useful yesterday has proved useless today. New inventions, discoveries, explorations are providing new explorations to past concepts. There is modification in old theories, principle, thinking and working. The curriculum should include the topics according to the changing needs and values of the business community.

14. Achievement of Wholesome Behaviour Pattern: The aim of the education is the all round development of personality. The curriculum of Commerce should be such which will result in the development of the child in the form of wholesome behaviour pattern *i.e.* economic behaviour, social behaviour, religious behaviour, moral behaviour, cultural behaviour, etc.

15. Principle of Readiness: The curriculum should follow the Principle of biological maturity *i.e.* according to the physical and mental level of the students, keeping in mind the different stages of development, the curriculum should be organised, otherwise, if they are not ready to attain the knowledge, we can't force them. It means requisite knowledge should be provided.

Principles of curriculum construction according to Secondary Education Commission (1952):

(1) Totality of experience
(2) Variety and elasticity
(3) Related to community
(4) Use of leisure time
(5) Correlated with life
(6) According to needs of society

Thus, commerce as core curriculum aims at enabling the student not only to adjust himself to the environment but also to improve his social, cultural, economic and physical environment as an active group member. The present day curriculum of commerce includes development of knowledge, skills, attitudes and values through the activities of reading, writing, observing, discussing, creating, processing, playing, problem solving, exhibiting, and developing relationships while living in one's own environment. Though interest in the revision and improvement in the commerce curriculum by experts is continuously increasing, much remains to be done in this regard.

Critical Appraisal of Curriculum of Commerce

A glance at the model national curriculum of commerce in India, recommended and developed by the National Council of Educational Research and Training (NCERT), the syllabus presented is in accordance with the latest demands of Indian education. It is good from the following points:

1. It fulfills the needs and interests of the students along the logical demand of the subject.
2. A lot of practical work has been recommended in the curriculum, while teaching the various components.
3. Students learn the technique of accounting and business.

On the other hand, the curriculum is full of many deficiencies. No deliberate efforts have been made in the curriculum to realize all the objectives of teaching commerce. It is really unfortunate that the curriculum is neither comprehensive nor provides any flexibility for the teachers and students to innovate.

There are some defects in the system of selection of courses and curriculum in commerce stream.

1. Experienced teachers are not represented. The business circle, for which learners are prepared, are also not represented. The result is that the courses of study suffer in quality and utility.

2. At present, of the two sequences i.e. book-keeping sequence and stenography sequence, only one sequence predominates (i.e. book-keeping) and the other sequence remains almost neglected. Even if it has been introduced in a very few schools the programme suffers considerably on vocational grounds.

3. The commerce curriculum lays more stress on the bookish knowledge rather than to practical approach. As a result it lays more emphasis on memorization and leads to cramming and very little initiative is provided for creative working. It has been viewed as body of information.

4. The present day curriculum of commerce does not lead the students to get employment because it is not related to the real life of the students as well as economy. The student feels difficulty in achieving the desired target.

In this way, it can be said the curriculum presented is not fulfilling aims and objectives i.e. preparing the students for future life or understanding the problems of the business community or becoming responsible citizen of a democratic nation or upholding the banner of business values. What to learn? What not to learn? How to learn? These choices are made by whom? All these will differ from one state to another whoever makes the decision or influences the decision should follow the process of rational planning.

Suggestions for the Improvement of Curriculum

A technique for the framing and selection of curriculum material is definite plan, criterion, standard or procedure, the application of which results in the inclusion of some material and reflection of others. The technique is applied within the frame of references provided by the conditioning factors and in accordance to the principles that have been accepted. Being an important and useful area, the curriculum of commerce should be improved to be an effective one. With the rapid growth in the field of trade, commerce and industry, the need for the right type of education of commerce was felt and to meet the needs an effective curriculum should be prepared with a great discussion among teachers, educators, planners and administrators so that every state may adopt it, maintaining uniformity in the curriculum and standard of achievement in different sequences. The following suggestions are recommended by different commissions, committees, educationists, teachers as well as students for its improvement:

1. The commerce curriculum should be need based.
2. It should be vocation oriented.
3. Contemporary events and problems of the business should be included.
4. The objectives should be clear-cut and the material should be so selected that it appears to offer a direct connection between objectives and material.
5. It must change according to the change in trade and business.
6. Representation of business and trade should be associated in the development of the curriculum.
7. The curriculum should be based on the principles of its constructions. Those most frequently mention are utility, accuracy, learnability, student needs, student interest, civic values and social needs. Whatever principles are accepted must be adapted to local needs and worked out through some practical techniques.
8. Some case studies should also be incorporated.

Thus, it can be said that the present commerce curriculum fails to achieve the expected and predetermined aims and objectives of preparing the students for future life or becoming responsible citizens. No doubt there will remain a gap between ideals and actual achievements, but efforts should be made to make it more and more objective oriented, flexible, industry centred by suggesting related activities and effective evaluation techniques. It should have horizontal as well as vertical correlations i.e. there should be correlation within the curriculum of commerce of different classes as well as in the industry and future life. It should have the totality of experiences in and outside the school to motivate and inspire the students to give practical shape to some new and creative ideas.

NEP 2020 envisages that education must develop higher order cognitive skills as critical thinking, problems solving and soft skills. For this, following suggestions are given:

- Curriculum needs to focus on academic flexibility and also on practicability through internship thereby improving employability.
- Commerce Education may need continuous revision and revamp of the curriculum which will develop the creative potential of each individual and create new career growth opportunities based on changing industrial and societal needs.
- The curriculum needs to be periodically revisited through curriculum conclaves involving various stakeholders to capture their changing expectations and also to meet the requirements of the education policy.
- Commerce curriculum needs to focus on developing a well-designed academic structure with continuous revamping at periodic intervals and deployment by a dedicated faculty team which lay emphasis not only making the students academically strong but also facilitates transforming them into true leaders.

- Curriculum content will be reduced in each subject to its core essentials, to make space for critical thinking and more holistic, inquiry based, discovery based, discussion based, and analysis-based learning.

COMMERCE TEXTBOOK

A textbook is a prescribed book for the students of a particular age group. It is a manual of instructions, a book containing a presentation of the principles of the subject used as a basis of instruction. It is equipped with the usual teaching devices. Textbooks are the most important tools in the hands of a teacher. It is highly desirable and essential for efficient teaching to see that this tool works well.

A textbook has been defined as an instrument of instruction that facilitates teaching learning process. It is organised logically according to the mental make-up and psychological requirements of the students. Most pupils and many teachers regard the textbook as a very humble and simple device. They too frequently assume that all its aspects and features are self-explanatory and that they can secure all its advantage without experience, application or special training. In reality, the textbook is a very compact and somewhat complicated product, the use of which requires considerable understanding and skill. If we are to get maximum benefit from it, the teacher should take care of its utilization for the maximum learning outcomes of the students.

Definitions

A textbook is "a book prepared specially to assist learners in mastering a subject or a part of a subject." – J.A. Lauwerys & Barnard.

"Text books are books that are designed to present the basic principles or aspects of a given subject for use as the basis of instruction, they can, in fact, be considered as an entire course of instruction, they are highly organised." – International Encyclopedia of Educational Technology.

"Textbook is any manual of instruction, a book dealing with a definite subject of study, systematically arranged, intended for use at a specified level of instruction and used as a principle of source of study material for a given course."

– *Dictionary of Education*

Characteristics of Textbook

1. It is a tool for achieving the instructional objectives of the subject.
2. It is a manual for instructions.
3. It fulfills the needs of students at different levels of intelligence.
4. It is used for formal as well as informal education.
5. It contains selected material according to the course of the study.
6. It is a learning instrument used by the students.
7. It is a teaching instrument used by the teachers.
8. It provides essential knowledge at one place.
9. It provides material in logical, systematic and comprehensive manner.
10. It is a source of stimulation.

Need and Importance

Good textbooks occupy an important place in the field of education. They are helpful for both teachers as well as students. Education Commission Report remarked, "A good textbook written by a qualified and competent specialist, in the subject, and produced with due regard to quality of printing, able illustrations and general get up, stimulates the pupil's interests and helps the teacher considerably in his work." It is an important aid to teaching as well as to learning. It is important due to following reasons:

1. Source of Knowledge: A textbook provides knowledge about the subject matter related to the subject. It represents the synthesis of material borrowed from many sources. It embodies knowledge worked over by masterminds.

2. Serve as the Basis of Almost All Other Methods: Almost all other methods can be used with the text book as a basis of study. The assignment procedure, discussion method, unit method can be effectively used only with the help of textbooks.

3. Presents Content Relating to Human Relationship: A textbook gives an accurate account of our environment the values and principles which guide our actions and processes through which we hope to improve ourselves. In this way, it helps in improving the physical and mental well-being of our pupils.

4. Helps in Developing Study Habits: A textbook provides a common basis on which the process of reading, analysing, outlining and summarizing can be mastered. It helps in developing the study habits of the students independently at home and understanding its content.

5. Uniformity of Good Standards: It provides a highway for carrying better practices to all schools. The textbook ensures some sort of uniformity of good standards. It furnishes a common basis to teachers for teaching.

6. Saves Time and Energy: In a textbook the relevant material concerning the syllabus of that class is readily available. Therefore, it guides the teacher about the boundaries and limits of his teaching in a particular class. The time and energy is saved of the teacher. On the other hand, it also helps in saving time and energy of the student. They are not to note down the lecture of the teacher in their notebooks. They can understand and complement it with self-study at home.

7. Suggests Application of the Material: A textbook also suggests application of the subject matter through assignments, drills, questions, projects and the activities.

8. Helps in Inculcation of Desired Interest and Aptitude: Textbooks written on the progressive lines have sufficient material for the inculcation of desired interest and aptitude. It provides opportunities for understanding and using the learned facts and this helps the students to achieve the objectives of commerce.

9. Reflects and Establishes Standards: A textbook indicates what the teacher is required to teach and what the pupils are supposed to learn. In this way, by its teaching and learning aid, it greatly affects methods and reflects and establishes the standards of scholarship. It furnishes a definite basis for specific assignments, problems and projects.

10. Helps the Teacher to Attain Instructional Objectives: In the absence of instructional objectives the teacher cannot make his teaching learning process effective. He has to make certain instructional objectives before entering in the class and it is the textbook that helps the teacher to organize learning material properly to attain his instructional objectives of teaching.

11. Helpful in Planning Day-to-day Teaching: A teacher can plan his day-to-day teaching with the help of textbook. It also helps in finding out new ideas. The teacher can give different assignments to the students and organize different activities in the classroom and outside.

12. Presents Different and Opposing Points of View: A textbook presents current affairs related to trading in such a way as to help pupils to develop an appreciation of different points of view.

13. Makes the Description Clear: It provides ample opportunities to make the description of the various terms of trading, banking, insurance, etc. and this description helps the teacher to understand the material clearly.

14. Meets the Needs of the Students: In classroom it becomes difficult for the teacher to cater to the needs of all types of students. Textbook helps in this direction by meeting the requirements of slow, average and fast learners. It meets their requirements by the use of simple language, heading, sub-headings, questions, assignments, maps, pictures and other illustrative material.

15. Expands and Limits its Scope: A textbook can expand and delimit its scope, size and content according to the changing needs of the education. Thus, it may sometimes lead and sometimes follow the educational process.

16. Helps to Make Generalization: Textbook helps the students how to make generalizations of different basic concepts, important ideas and certain important points given in the whole unit. They can make the generalization on the basis of summary given at the end of the unit.

17. Overcome Classroom Limitations: A good commerce textbook removes the worries of the students and the teachers to complete the syllabus in the prescribed time. It also overcomes the limitation of non-availability of various other teaching aids and devices and contains pictures, diagrams, etc, which are indispensable for effective instructions.

18. Essential for Some Teachers: While all teachers are not in a position to dig up facts. Some mature, well trained, experienced teachers may find it possible to dispense with a basel text book. However, most of the teachers, especially new teachers can not, as they need a definite base which can be from the text book.

Thus, the textbook is only one of many media through which teachers and pupil communicate with each other in an effort to carry forward to learning process. As C.P. Hill writes, "A text book is a structure of basic information which the pupils can use in a variety of ways."

Qualities of a Good Textbook

There is always a dire need of good textbooks on commerce, so, we now proceed to see what should be the qualities of a good text book ought to be. In the words to Kothari Education Commission, "A good text book written by a qualified and competent specialist in the subject and produced with due regards of printing, illustrations, and general get up, stimulates the pupil's interest, and helps the teacher considerably in his work."

A textbook is called good textbook if it contains certain qualities. The qualities of the text book can be divided into two parts:

(*a*) General Qualities (*b*) Specific Qualities

General qualities deal with the format, size, binding, printing, get up, etc., whereas specific qualities relate with language, illustrations, style, etc., which differentiate from subject to subject. Pupils are of varied interests and capacities, so the textbook should fulfill the needs of all types of students. A good textbook of Commerce should fulfill the following requirements:

1. Size of the Book: The size of the book depends upon one's attitude as to its proper function. Those who want logical outline syllabus or guides require only small books. Generally, the size of the book should neither be too small nor too big. It should be convenient in handling and carrying.

2. Table of Contents: The table of contents is supposed to indicate the scope and organisation of whole book. It should therefore, be a logical outline, one that shows the space developed to the major divisions and to the important minor divisions.

3. Title Page: The title page of textbook is supposed to convey some idea of its specific quality, view point or merit. It furnishes the full name of the book. It should give the author's name, publisher's name, and name of city in which the publisher is located and the year of publication.

4. Printing of the Book: The outlook of the book should be good and it depends upon its printing. It should be neat and clean, free from all type of errors. The spacing between the words, lines, paragraphs should be proper.

5. Paper Used in the Textbook: The paper used in the textbook should be of good quality *i.e.* adequately thick, durable and smooth.

6. Style in the Textbook: Everyone agrees that textbook should be written in excellent style. Sentence length is probably an index of clarity but short-sentences are in themselves a questionable cure. Extremely short sentences in textbook for the secondary schools should probably be regarded more as a liability than as an asset. The headings should be attractive and interpretative. The main headings should be accompanied by brief, logical and condensed headings.

7. Vocabulary in the Textbook: It is clear that a student can learn frequently a new concept by means of new words as early as he can expand the meaning of a familiar word. The introduction of new words may actually simplify a paragraph, provided, of course, that they are used in such a way as to reveal their meaning. A textbook should increase the vocabulary of the students.

8. Illustrations: The number and variety of pictures, graphs, tables and diagrams have increased markedly in recent years. Pictures can be the integral part of teaching. It, therefore, seems desirable for commerce textbook to include as many pictures as space allows. If they are judiciously selected, properly placed with respect to accompanying material and skillfully utilized, they furnish an effective teaching and learning aid.

9. Subject Matter in the Textbook: As commerce deals with the business and trading activities, so, the subject matter should be up-to-date and complete in itself.

10. Free from Indoctrination: A good textbook should not contain superficial and misleading generalizations. It should not contain extreme nationalism, which leads to be dogmatic, conclusive and official. The views presented in the book should be based on truth.

11. Suggest Good Methods of Learning: In a quality book subject matter is not only to be presented but its application should also be suggested. It should give practical suggestion for applying the knowledge gained through the construction of models, organisation of visits and field trips; preparation of charts, posters, illustrations, etc.

12. Proper and Adequate Exercises: It should provide different exercises, which will be helpful for the students in recapitulating and revising the important information. The activities like discussion, debates, etc. should be incorporated in it which will help the teacher in evaluating the outcomes of the students in terms of their acquisition of desired understanding, attitude and skill development.

13. Child-Centred: A good textbook should be child-centred *i.e.* according to the age, ability and interest of the pupils for whom it is written. It should be related to the daily life, i.e. real life of the students.

14. Developing International Understanding: It should contain the subject matter related to social, economic, political relations between the different nations and their contribution in the globalisation. It should create the feeling among the pupils that they are not only the citizens of their nation but the citizens of the whole world and one nation can't develop without the help of other nations.

15. Constant Modification and Revision: Commerce relates with business activities, so, the textbook should be kept quite up-to-date as regards its subject matter. It can't be possible unless it is revised and modified frequently in the latest development in business environment. In the world, life is changing very rapidly because of the changes in different fields as technology, industries, agriculture, education, science, etc. A good textbook should contain latest information.

16. Appendices: A good textbook should contain appendices also. It contains a great variety of materials. The materials presented in appendices are so varied and extensive that many of them, if used at all, are destined to be helpful. The examples are as:

(*a*) The population of India and other countries.
(*b*) List of states with pertinent data.
(*c*) List of things and trade.

Thus, the commerce textbook can be evaluated on the basis of above mentioned qualities. But even if a textbook is judged good, it should not be taken as an end in itself but only one of the means. It should only serve as a book of reference for both the teacher and the pupil. A teacher who depends too much on a text book, leaves a bad impression upon the mind of the student. He should present different views from different books to classify the concept and give a wider range of knowledge.

Defects of Existing Textbook of Commerce

There are some defects or shortcomings in the existing textbooks of commerce. They are as follows:

1. Present textbooks are written in such a manner, which always develop the

habit of cramming among students.

2. The subject of commerce is related with daily economic life of the people, but the knowledge related to new researches being 'carried on', generally do not find a place in the existing text books.
3. The authors do not care for the maxims of learning while writing the subject matter for the book. There is too much of abstraction, which always confounds a normal student when he tries to learn something with the help of the book.
4. Most of the textbooks are examination oriented and do not provide depth of the subject.
5. The authors do not keep in mind the standard, mental levels and age of the students while writing the textbooks.
6. The standard textbooks are very costly, not in the reach of the students, so they are to depend on non-standard books.
7. Some times publishers want those writers who can write for them at low cost. So, the authors write the book with the intention of money only not caring for the subject matter according to students.
8. The existing textbooks also suffer from unattractive get up and defective printing.
9. The textbooks also suffer from dead material. In some subjects, e.g. income tax, old textbooks may be out of date.
10. Sometimes authors have no conversant with the methods of teaching of commerce subject nor do they have any authority on the subject.

Thus, we should try to remove the defects in the existing text books as well as modify them as per the recommendations of NEP 2020. It envisages that

- The mandated content should focus on key concepts, ideas, applications and problem-solving.
- All textbooks should aim to contain the essential core material (together with discussion, analysis, examples and applications) deemed important at national level, but at the same time contain any desired nuances and supplementary material as per local context and needs.
- Quality textbooks will be produced at the lowest possible cost to mitigate the burden of textbook prices on the students.
- Additional textbook materials could be funded by public-philanthropic partnership and crowd sourcing that incentivize experts to write such high quality-textbooks at cost price.
- The textbooks will also be available in all regional languages.
- Access to downloadable and printable versions of all textbooks will be provided by all states/UTs and NCERT to help conserve the environment and reduce the logistical burden.

Criteria for the Evaluation of Textbook

A teacher can evaluate the textbook on the basis of different points discussed under the development. The fundamental questions that a teacher should ask concerning the textbook are:

1. it is it challenging?
2. Is it according to the mental level of the students?
3. Is it contents suitable to achieve the objectives of the subject?
4. it is it clear and simple in organising the subject matter?
5. it is it create interest in the pupils?

Usually we use 'Rating scale' for the evaluation of the textbook. Through the scale we can get the true knowledge of the present text book and can judge about its worth..

The points on the scale indicate:

Poorest	1
Poor	2
Average	3
Good	4
V. Good	5

S.No.	Criteria	V. Good	Good	Average	Poor	V. Poor
		5	4	3	2	1

1. **Physical Aspects**
   (*a*) Size
   (*b*) Original or Revision
   (*c*) Format
   (*d*) Printing Layout
   (*e*) Durability
   (*f*) Price
2. **Nature of the content**
   (*a*) Relevant content
   (*b*) Coverage of the course
   (*c*) Up-to-date content
   (*d*) Integrated content
   (*e*) Vocabulary
   (*f*) Clarity of the content
   (*g*) discussion
   (*h*) Analysis
   (*i*) Application
   (*j*) According to students and communities' needs
   (*k*) Critical issues facing local communities, states, the country and the world.
3. **Organization**
   (*a*) division
   (*b*) Proportions
   (*c*) Psychological Approach
4. **Presentation of the content**
   (*a*) Appropriate titles
   (*b*) Creative Approach
   (*c*) Adequate terminology
5. **Style**
   (*a*) Vocabulary
   (*b*) Vividness
   (*c*) Fullness

S.No.	Criteria	V. Good	Good	Average	Poor	V. Poor
		5	4	3	2	1
	(*d*) Concreteness					
	(*e*) Grammatically correct					
	(*f*) Appropriate use of technical terms					
6.	**Illustrations**					
	(*a*) Purposeful and clear					
	(*b*) Adequate					
	(*c*) Variety					
7.	**Exercise and Projects, etc.**					
	(*a*) Adequate					
	(*b*) Wide coverage					
	(*c*) Graded exercise					
8.	**General Nature**					
	(*a*) Title					
	(*b*) Nature of preface					
	(*c*) Fullness of table of contents					
	(*d*) Listing of diagrams and pictures					
	(*e*) Appendix					
	(*f*) Extent of Index					
9.	**References and Bibliography**					
	(*a*) Practical					
	(*b*) New					
	(*c*) Completeness					
	(*d*) Useful for teachers as well as pupils					
10.	**Access to downloadable and printable version**					

On the basis of rating scores, we can rate the textbook of commerce as –V. Good, Good, Average, Poor, Poorest. The textbooks can also be evaluated on the basis of assignments, exercises, glossary and summary also. Thus, the teacher must read the book carefully and evaluate the textbook before using it in the classroom.

Role of Library and Reference Books in Teaching of Commerce

The library has become an indispensable part of the structure of every school. Modern methods of teaching, which emphasize the need for training pupils to think independently, require the provision of a variety of materials. The library undertakes the administration of these materials, their acquisition and organisation, and guidance in their use.

Library means, "any collection of books organised for use." "Library preserves the knowledge so that none is lost, organise knowledge so that none is wasted and make the knowledge available so that no one need be deprived."

Good's Dictionary of Education defines library as:

1. A building or room equipped for housing books and other materials communication and for reading, listening or viewing purposes;
2. A collection of books of various kinds;
3. A collection of films, recording, etc.

Therefore, library is an instrument of education and it has much importance for teaching of commerce.

1. Encourage reading habits in pupils. Commerce is a vast subject and the pupils can't get detailed knowledge without self study.
2. Develop the ability to learn from books, when left to themselves.
3. It provides opportunity for training in trading.
4. It supplements the knowledge of the classroom.
5. It develops the habit of supplementary reading.
6. It helps the students to use their leisure time properly.
7. It influences the culture of the students.
8. It provides opportunities for intellectual development.
9. It gives aesthetic satisfaction.
10. Supervised study can be organised in a library.

Therefore a library is now regarded as a live workshop humming with activity. It is now a place where pupil go not only for study but for enjoyment also. In the words of K.G. Saiydain, "No school or university without a library, adequate for its needs and size, should be recognised as a worthy centre of education." NEP 2020 recommends that all the books will be developed including high quality translation (technology assisted as needed) in all local and Indian languages, and will be made available extensively in both school and public libraries. Public and school libraries will be significantly expanded to build a culture of reading across this country. Digital libraries will also be established. A National Book Promotion Policy will be formulated and extensive initiatives will be undertaken to ensure the availability, accessibility, quality and readership of books across geographies, languages, levels and genres. It shows the importance of library to enhance the learning of all.

Changing Role of Libraries

Libraries in our country as well as abroad were considered originally as '*Pustakalya*' or '*Granthalaya*' *i.e.* a store-house of books and literature meant for dissemination of knowledge to its users. In today's context when we look at the role of libraries, we are confronted with the new challenges, a new reality which has arisen because of the advent of the rapid changes in the knowledge base. In today's context of Information Technology driven education, it is important for us to realize that the books of 21st century have to be written from the point of view of facilitating interactive learning *i.e.* they should be user friendly enabling the cultivation of knowledge through, by and large self learning.

The libraries of 21st century have to be conceived not merely the store-house of knowledge but an effective mechanism to facilitate disseminations of knowledge, promoting information and knowledge sharing, while, at the same time, supporting the growth of knowledge and the growth of intellectual property. The libraries should facilitate the transition of today's literate society to a knowledge based society of tomorrow. We have to create local area network, national networks and link our local and national networks to the global network of libraries and information systems so as to facilitate global access of knowledge regarding the subject of commerce.

The library markedly influences the success or failure of the work in commerce where as some school subjects can be taught with relative success without any great use of books. The very essence of the commerce is found in an expanded realisation of the various forms and instances of business cooperation. Much of this knowledge can be derived only from books and other printed materials. The commerce teacher, therefore, should give constant thought to the acquisition of utilization of pertinent materials. The library is perhaps the best single index of the quality of instruction that is given in the commerce.

Contents of a Commerce Library

Commerce is a vast subject so the commerce teacher is interested in the whole library, but his major attention should necessarily be focussed upon the books that are most useful in his own field. The library should contain at least a few well chosen books in each of the following groups:

1. Supplementary Material: Following are the different types of supplementary material, which should be in the library

(*i*) Survey reports
(*ii*) Yearbooks
(*iii*) Encyclopaedias
(*iv*) Book Reviews
(*v*) Reports by Chairmen of public and private companies
(*vi*) Budget discussions in Parliament and state assemblies
(*vii*) Government documents and reports
(*viii*) Journals and Periodicals
(*ix*) Technical documents as bank documents, business documents, company documents, Income tax laws and documents, Post office documents, Telegraphs guides, etc.

2. Magazines and Journals: Commerce is a subject in which current knowledge is valuable. Many magazines contain interesting and latest material on different matters relating to commerce which can supplement classroom instructions. The knowledge about price trends, share markets and budget discussions are given in journals which can help in enhancing the knowledge of commerce.

3. Newspapers: Newspapers help in bridging the gap between information contained in the books and changing developments in trading, international relations, business activities, trends in advertisement and economic life.

4. Reference Books: Reference books provide a wider exposure to the teachers as well as students. In general they are state manuals, dictionaries and biographies. The commerce teacher finds these reference books very useful to enhance his knowledge as well as to communicate it to his students. Government Notifications, Government Gazettes fall under this category. Ready reckoners related to income tax calculations are also needed for reference purposes.

5. Pamphlets and Periodicals: Textbooks and reference books cannot include the latest trends and developments. Newspapers and magazines provide report on the current developments, but they cannot provide the background nor present in a systematic treatment. The gap between these two types of materials can best be filled up by current pamphlets. Apart from the pamphlets the library should consist certain periodicals which attempt to present mostly objective and factual information.

6. Parallel Texts: Students generally depend upon the class textbook but in addition to it, they should have access to at least two or three other texts of a parallel nature. If several copies of each additional text are available, the teacher can make occasional assignments. These texts will occasionally present a different view point. An awareness of such differences is one of the most valuable outcomes of critical teaching.

7. Books related to Local Aspects: The teacher should undertake to secure practically all that is available on local business and government, and on the economic conditions and activities of the neighbourhood. Local publications are useful as motivating material. They inspire a sense of concrete reality.

Thus, we can say that library is of great use in teaching commerce. The books should be according to the mental level of the students. The books should have a large variety and should be good in number. The teacher should have the thorough knowledge about the library. The teacher should visit the library frequently as evidence of his interest and in order to observe the way in which his students study. To achieve maximum benefits commerce teacher shall have to take pains by putting in more efforts. Thus, a good commerce library helps to keep the lamp of commerce knowledge burning so as to kindle light in the minds of the students as also the teacher.

6

Self Instructional Modules and Materials in Teaching Commerce

Self instructional modules require careful monitoring of students working on their own or in small groups on practice a new style. Before assigning students to work independently, a teacher has to provide necessary guidance to ensure that they are prepared to work on their own. Thus, self instructional modules demand teacher's active participation in the teaching learning process. The students may need periodic review with corrective feedback in their work.

All of us know that any instructional system comprises the teacher and the learner, besides the curriculum. It is not appropriate to say that the teacher alone controls the instruction system. Of course, there are certain instructional procedures in which the participation of the teacher is more in comparison to that of the learner. But, there also exist other instructional procedures in which the learner plays a pivotal role in the instructional process as compared to the teacher and these are known as *self instructional modules*. It does not mean that in such modules teacher has no role to play. It is a matter of shifting relatively more of the responsibility of learning to the students. The emphasis here is on learning rather than teaching. The teacher's role becomes of a manager, facilitator or a guide.

Self instructional modules include a number of techniques which range from the simple assignment to the most sophisticated computer-aided instruction. These can be divided into two broad categories:

I. Individualized instruction or self learning modules.
II. Group instruction or group learning modules.

INDIVIDUALIZED SELF INSTRUCTIONAL MODULES

Individualized instruction or self learning modules developed when teaching methods meant for all members of a group failed to meet the varying needs of individual students. An underlying assumption in this method of instruction is that human beings learn many things with the help of their own efforts. Each individual has a manual desire to learn on his/her own. Another assumption is that every individual is unique. He or she learns according to his or her abilities, interests, potentialities, capacities, etc. Hence, any system based on presentation of information to a group cannot take in to account the wide variations in the rates in which individual student learn.

Individualized self instruction is the only panacea to fulfill the needs of individual differences. The most common description of self-learning method is that teaching is directed towards the individual student rather than the group of students. However, self learning is not synonymous with independent learning or learning in isolation from other students. Self learning may encourage independence from the teacher, this, however is not usually the main aim. The important characteristics of self instructional module are:

1. Emphasis on learning rather than teaching.
2. Active student participation.
3. Recognition of individual differences.
4. Working at one's own pace.
5. Provision of feedback and evaluation.

Individualized self instruction modules help in self learning in the following ways:

1. They help the teacher to meet the varying needs of the students.
2. They prepare the students to face the problems in his/her real life.
3. They help the students in achieving desired goals.
4. They make learning more enjoyable, exciting and rewarding because the student learns at his/her own.
5. They promote self-discipline in the class.
6. They help in developing critical thinking in handling of study material on one's own and enhancing communicative skills and self reliance.
7. Students become self motivated.
8. Special skills (reading, comprehension, project, etc.) can be learned through individual efforts.
9. Learning becomes more effective.
10. They help in developing the habits of selection of study methods and work methods independently.

Forms of Individualized Self Instruction Module

Self instructional modules can be of various forms. There are two main categories: more structured or less structured. Under more structured methods, the most important are *programmed instruction, personalised system of instruction (PSI), and computer assisted instruction.* Less structured methods are *assignments* and *project work* .

A. Programmed Instruction

In the field of education, programmed instruction or learning represent the important innovation. It is completely individualized. It emerged out of the research conducted by B.F. Skinner in operant conditioning. The Law of effect propounded by E.L. Thorndike has direct relevance to programming. According to this law, learning which is associated with satisfaction is likely to be more permanent. Satisfaction in the form of reward reinforces the behaviour of the student to take interest in learning. In 1926, Pressey devised a teaching machine which required students to press keys to answer multiple-choice questions and the next question was presented only after the correct key had been pressed by the student. The idea behind such a teaching machine was that after being exposed to instruction the student would go through a test presented by a machine and achieve mastery on all the questions (content) till she/he ceased making mistakes.

The real landmark in the development of programmed learning was the work of B.F. Skinner. According to this theory of operant conditioning, behaviour is learned only when it is immediately reinforced. By applying the principles of operant conditioning in teaching, Skinner developed an instructional model which is popularly known as *programmed instruction.* The term 'Programmed' is used for arranging learning experiences or events in the most logical and psychological sequence so that the student gets minimum benefit from instruction.

Styles of Programmed Instruction

There are mainly three styles of programmed instruction:

1. Linear Programming
2. Branching
3. Mathetics

1. *Linear Programming*: The linear style of programming developed by B.F. Skinner is otherwise known as Skinnerian style. According to this style, the subject matter is broken into small pieces of information (steps) and is presented in a logical reference of small steps. These small steps are called frames. The student is required to go through these frames containing a bit or bits of information and respond to the question given at the end of each frame. The feedback in the form of correct answer is provided in the next frame. The frames are so designed and arranged that student's errors are kept to a minimum. In other words, programmed instruction ensures that the student commits minimum errors. In this type of programming, two types of responses are emitted by the learner:

(*a*) *Construct Response:* In every frame, blank is provided to construct a response by the learner. The response for the blank is related to new behaviour or desired response.

(*b*) *Discriminant Response:* In some situations, two alternatives are given for the response. The learner has to select the right response for the situation. The correct response is an integral part of the desired behaviour.

In this programming, the first frame leads to the second, the second to the third and so ($f1 \rightarrow f2 \rightarrow f3 \rightarrow f4 \rightarrow f5 \rightarrow f6 \rightarrow$) this leads to a sequence that resembles a straight line until the whole information is acquired by the student.

2. *Branching Programming*: The branching programming was developed by Norman, A. Crowder. His intention was to use the errors to direct the students to an appropriate explanation or remedial sequence. Therefore, he gave students some information followed by a multiple-choice question and provided a different response for each apparently correct answer choice. Students proceed through such a programme, following different routes or branches and care is taken to ensure that they understand each point before they proceed to the next.

The figure indicates that there are four main paths and others are remedial paths. If a learner does not make wrong response he will proceed to main path otherwise he will go to remedial path then to the main path. Thus, every student chooses his path of learning.

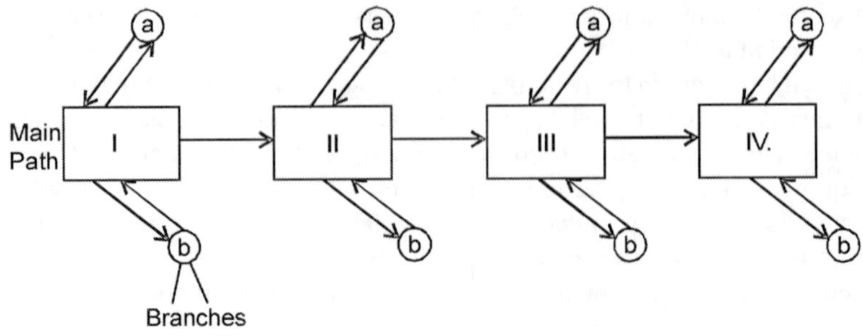

Fig. 6.1. Structure of Branching Programme

Types of Branching: The branching programming is of two types:

(*i*) *Backward Branching*:

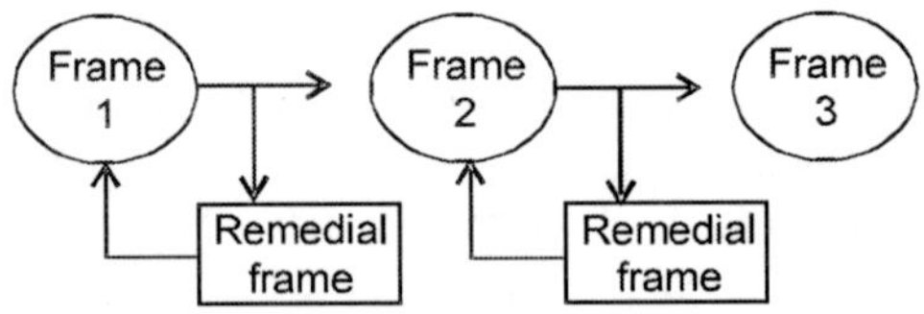

Fig. 6.2. Structure of Backward Branching

In this programme the student proceeds from frame 1 to frame 2 if he response rightly. If his response is wrong then he will proceed to remedial frame and then again to frame 1 and try to give right response. Thus, the student reads the same frame twice if he responds wrong.

(*ii*) *Forward Branching*:

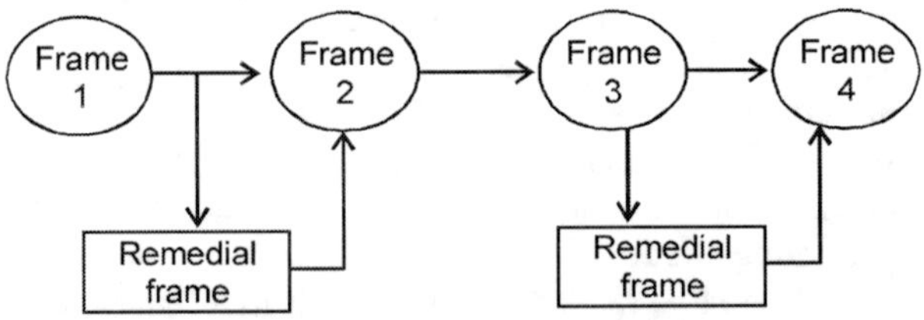

Fig. 6.3. Structure of Forward Branching

In this style the student always proceed to next frame even he responds wrong. If his response is incorrect then he will proceed to the remedial frame and then to the next frame.

Thus, branching programming provides remedial instructions to the learner simultaneously. The research findings have revealed that it is effective for realizing higher cognitive objectives of learning. It is used as an adjustive device to facilitate the individual variations. The branching is mainly concerned with teaching and instructions rather than learning. It works as a tutorial strategy. It gives emphasis to difficulties and needs of each and every learner. Branching programming is presented in the form of books. These books are known as *scrambled books* because the pages in these books are not in a sequence. The students are directed to different pages according to their response.

3. *Mathetics Programming*: This programming was developed by Thomas E. Gilbert. It is concerned with transfer of learning. In this, motivation is an important factor. In teaching, the teacher supplies the student with all the steps leading up to mastery step and prompts him to perform the mastery step. It proves very useful in learning difficult skills.

Development of Programmed Instruction Material

There are three major steps involved in the development of programmed instruction material. These are:

(*i*) Planning and preparation of the programme.
(*ii*) Writing of the programme.
(*iii*) Evaluation of the programme.

With the help of these steps you can acquire the skill of preparing programmed instruction material for your students.

(*i*) *Planning and Preparation of the Programme*: This step involves a few specific activities. These are:

- First, you have to select the topic which is to be programmed. This selection depends on the style of programming to be adopted, the scope of the use of the programme, the field of specialization and so on.
- Second, you have to find out the characteristics of the target population namely, their age, gender, interests, experiences, intellectual level, cultural back ground, etc.
- Third, you have to undertake task analysis of the topic selected for programming.
- Fourth, you have to specify the instructional objectives in observable and measurable terms.
- Fifth, you have to write criterion questions for all the objectives which form part of the pre-test and post-test to be administered when the programme is gone through by the student. It provides a basis for evaluating the effectiveness of the programme.
- Last, you have to arrange each frame/step in a sequence logically. Similarly, the elements of each frame are arranged logically in some sequence. For this, all the objectives are kept in mind. Expert opinions should also be sought. In preparing the list of contents, the relationship of teaching and learning should also be considered.

(*ii*) *Writing of the Programme*: In preparing the programmed instructions, the writing of the frames is the most difficult task. The first decision you have to take is whether you want to follow linear style or branching style or a combination of the both. The second task is to take a decision on frame development. There are mainly four types of frames:

(*a*) *Introductory frames* — The function of these frames is to link the new knowledge with the testing of previous knowledge. Its limit should not exceed 10 to 15 per cent.
(*b*) *Teaching frames* — In these frames, the content is presented in such a

form that the objectives can be achieved. In this, various prompt frames are constructed. The number of such frames should be 60 to 70 per cent.

(*c*) *Practice frames* — In these, the learnt frames are practised. The number of such frames should be 20-25 per cent.

(*d*) *Testing frames* — These frames are related with the evaluation of the learnt knowledge. These are without prompts.

While developing frames you should keep in mind the following points:

- The language used should be simple.
- The frames should be presented in the form of statements.
- Adjectives should not be used in the frames.
- The size of the frame should be according to the level of the students.
- The response of a good frame is stimulus for the next frame.
- Prompts or cues, wherever necessary, should be used to help the learners in selection of right answers.
- Irrelevant material must be avoided.
- Every frame has three parts — (*i*) Stimulus, in which content is presented, (*ii*) Response for each stimulus, and (*iii*) Reinforcement.

These instructional frames are arranged in logical and psychological sequence. Good frames are in clear terms. The responses of good frames are related to terminal behaviour. These are challenging and motivational. Before making it final, it should be thoroughly edited by the experts. It will help in eliminating the ambiguous and inadequate terms in the programme.

(*iii*) Evaluation of the Programme: When the writing of the programme is over, the next task for you is evaluation of the programme. This is done at three stages as:

(*a*) *Individual testing* — Individual testing means that you, as the programme designer, and one representative of the target group for whom the programme is meant are involved in the testing activity. The purpose of the testing should be clear to the student and as a teacher you should establish good rapport with him. While reading the frame, you should ask the difficulties faced by the student and those difficulties should be discussed with the student so that the inadequacies can be located and eliminated.

(*b*) *Small Group Testing* — After making necessary modifications in the draft programme on the basis of individual testing, the programme is ready to try out on a small group of students say 5-6 students. The data on the basis of pre-test and post-test are analysed to assess the effectiveness of the programme.

(*c*) *Field Testing* — This is the last stage for testing the programme. Entering behaviours are considered as the basis for selection of sample. To know the previous knowledge, criterion test is administered. After this programmed instruction material is given to the students. Post-test is administered to the students. The data thus collected are analysed and programme is modified and finalised.

The last phase is the preparation of manual. In this manual the information about the programmed instruction are described. Without manual, the use of programmed instruction is not possible. In this manual specification of objectives, detail of criterion test, detail of frames, detail of evaluation and important instructions about programmed material are described.

B. Personalised System of Instruction

The personalised system of instruction is another self instructional module which emphasizes individualisation of instruction. It is also known as *killer plans* and is widely used all over the world. This technique is called PSI because instruction is designed according to the need and ability of the student. It has following characteristics:

- It is a mastery oriented learning technique.
- It uses a few lecturers to stimulate and motivate the students.
- It is individually paced technique of teaching and learning.
- It uses tutors to evaluate attainment of the objectives by the students.

In PSI, the student is given carefully prepared assignments which generally include programmed learning material, handouts and other available material related to the subject matter. The student is instructed how and what to read. The teacher is available for necessary help whenever the student faces any difficulty. When a student thinks that he has completed the material, he can come to the teacher and you can conduct a short quiz or test in order to evaluate student's learning. It you are satisfied, then you can direct the student to proceed on to the next unit and vice versa. The student should not be given punishment if he commits errors. Thus, PSI helps in increasing retention power.

C. Computer Assisted Instruction

Teacher's position is in danger in the periphery of learning because the concept of learning is developing or changing day by day. The meaningfulness of learning depends on the teacher who is responsible for adequate classroom interaction. To fulfil this function the teacher should use modern techniques of teaching in the classroom. The computer technology has brought a great change in the classroom teaching and learning process.

CAI is referred to as an individualised method of self-study using information communication technology of which the computer is an essential part to deliver an educational activity.

Computer Assisted Instruction means instructions provided with the help of computer using multimedia approach for self-learning.

According to *Encyclopaedia of Britannica*, CAI means, "A programme of instructional material presented by means of a computer or computer system". Historically computer aided instruction, which is also called computer assisted instruction(CAI) has roots in Pressey's 1925 multiple choice machine and the punchboard device, which fore-shadowed the network supported tutorials of today. Pressey's multiple choice machine presented instruction tested the user, waited for an answer, provided immediate feedback and recorded each attempt as data. Later CAI researchers observed that algorithms for teaching with CAI had to incorporate both the physical programming or authoring to run computer programme and the instructional programming required to learn from the programme.

With the advent of personal computers during 1980s, which were cheap and powerful, use of CAI increased considerably. In 1980, only 5% of elementary schools and 20% of secondary schools in the United States had computer for assisted instruction. By 1990, nearly all schools in the United States, and in most industrialised countries, were equipped with teaching computers. Internet development, particularly since the 1990's has far-reaching implications for CAI. By connecting millions of computers worldwide, it enabled students to access huge stores of information, which greatly enhances their research capabilities. In the modern CAI systems and especially with visualisation systems and simulated environments, control over the progress of the instruction often rests with the student or with the teacher.

CAI encompasses a wide and rapidly expanding range of computer technologies that assist the teaching and learning process.

Types of CAI

Presently different types of CAI are available:

1. *Tutorial Mode:* In tutorial mode, information is provided in small units, followed by a question. The students' response is analysed by the computer and an appropriate feedback is provided. This is similar to programmed instruction. As in programmed instruction the information may be given in a linear fashion or in branched pathways.

2. *Drill and Practice Mode:* In this mode, the learner is provided a number of graded examples on the concepts and principles learnt earlier. The guided drill is a computer programme that poses questions to students, returns feedback and selects additional questions based on the students' responses. Some of the recent guided drill systems incorporate the principles of education in addition to the subject matter knowledge into the computer programme. The idea is to develop proficiency and fluency through doing. All the correct responses are reinforced and the incorrect responses are diagnosed and corrected. The computer continues the drill and practice until mastery is achieved by the learner. This remains very useful for practicing accountancy.

3. *Simulation Mode:* In simulation mode, the learner is presented with scaled down simulated situating bearing correspondence with the real situations. In Commerce, for examples many simulations may be given as consumer, as businessman, as manager, as accountant etc. These are made to avoid risk, save money and conserve time.

4. *Discovery Mode:* In the discovery mode, the inductive approach to teaching and learning is followed. The learner is encouraged to proceed through trial and error approach i.e. by solving a given problem, realising where and how he/she went wrong, trying again and finally solving the complex problem. The best example is preparing the balance sheet in accountancy.

5. *Gaming Mode:* In the gaming mode, the learner is engaged in playing opposite to the computer or opposite another learner. The extent of learning depends upon the type of game. Games on name of places, types of management, modes of advertisement, places of getting raw material and general knowledge are some examples of it.

Development in the Field of ICT and CAI

The computers facilitate communication between the tutor and the taught, either instantaneously through chatting or through e-mails. CAI tools such as word processors, spreadsheets and databases collect, organise, analyse and transmit information facilitate communication among students. The education system is developing on the basis of ICT and CAI in the following way:

ICT	*Education*
– Electronic tube	– Text based computer-based learning
– Standalone computer	– Multimedia computer based learning
– Multimedia computers	– Learning experienced in a networked computer laboratory
– Computer Network	– Local Area Network
– ICT based communication	– Internet & www
– E-mail	– Utilising the Internet
– Bulletin Board	– Information access
– Chatting	– Self-directed learning
– Video-conferencing	– Interdependent, collaborative learning
– Social network	– Virtual classroom & online learning

On the basis of above description we can say that CAI is the result of development in technology.

Characteristics/Importance of CAI

1. *Promoting interactive learning:* CAI helps in presenting interactive learning material in test or/and multimedia format which creates interest among the students towards the subject matter. CAI facilitates interactive learning activities by utilising video-conferencing facilities. It facilitates interaction with peers and experts in virtual reality. While interacting students can learn effectively and efficiently because they can express their views and discuss their view point.

2. *Promoting educational management:* While managing any class in different subjects, the teacher should know about the problems and needs of the students. CAI helps in establishing electronic databases for diagnosing learning needs and problems. On the basis of their needs, CAI also provides automated learning assessment and remedial activities so that the students may progress at their own. In this way the learning problems of the students can be solved.

3. *Providing additional learning opportunities:* The students of commerce may not get all the material related to their subject in the text book so they are to depend on the computers for getting the latest trends in the economy. CAI provides supplementary electronic learning material in addition to the traditional text books. The students can easily search the information by using internet.

4. *Based on behaviour approach:* Behaviour is defined as a muscle movement. It is a result of a series of conditioned reflexes, emotions and thought processes. Learning of every student is demonstrated through observable behavioural changed. It is based in stimulus response process and behavioural theorists propose that stimulus-response bonds are strengthened by reinforcement. The educators who

adhere to the behaviouristic approach could apply CAI that is based on the principles of programmed learning, mastery learning and drill and practice.

5. *Based on constructivism:* Constructivism is based on the premise that knowledge cannot be transferred from one person to another but is rather constructed by the learner. Knowledge is an understanding which is generated from past and present learning experiences. CAI supports student-centered learning and inquiry based learning. The educator mediates between information-communication technologies, learning experiences, the learning content and the students.

Cognitive constructivism focuses on how an individual student gains understanding of things, and social constructivism emphasis that meanings and understandings grow out of social encounters. Multimedia technologies and learning packages which support discovery learning, problem based learning and simulations are in accordance with constructivism. Social constructivism can be applied in CAI by utilising the principle of collaborative learning.

6. *Helpful for distant students:* CAI transmits information, facilitate communication among students, between students and instructors and beyond the classroom to distant learner, educator and experts.

7. *Presentation of information:* Through CAI the information can be presented on computer in the form of text or in multimedia format, which includes photographs, videos, animation, speech and music to stimulate interaction between the students.

8. *Development of sense of responsibility:* The process of CAI motivates the students to feel a sense of personal responsibility for their own learning because they learn at their own with own pace.

9. *Mastery learning:* Mastery learning is based on behaviourism. Its main goal is the attainment of excellence of performance. It is premised on the assumption that all tasks can be learned by students provided they are exposed to the appropriate stimuli and are given sufficient time to master the content. With the help of CAI students proceed through a pre-test, learning outcomes, content, activities and post-test. Successful completion of one level of learning is required to proceed to a higher level. The computer automatically keeps record of the students' progress. Thus CAI helps in mastery the learning in commerce.

10. *Discovery learning:* Discovery learning is an educational approach during which educators create opportunities for students to embark in a process of self-directed inquiry, which would result in learning. CAI challenges the students to obtain information or seek answers to difficult questions by using the information and communication properties of the internet. For example, gaming require the discovery or certain information or solutions in order to proceed through the game.

11. *Problem solving learning:* Problem solving learning involves confronting students with real life problems that provide a stimulus for critical thinking and self-directed learning. Under CAI, various printed and electronic resources are utilised to solve given problems or make appropriate decisions.

Recent development in ICT and educational software, paved the way for the development of computer-based multimedia learning packages that use complex scenario which are aimed at helping the students in developing critical judgements and problem solving skills.

12. *Gaming:* Multimedia computer technology supports the gaming teaching strategy. Electronic educational games focus on either the content or the process of learning. Content games focus on teaching or reinforcing factual information. Process games are those that emphasise problems solving, decision making or application of information.

13. Networks and internet enable groups of students to participate without the players having to use the same computer or having to share a geographical space. Thus it develops socialisation skills among the students.

14. *Simulation:* Simulation is an imitation of some facts of life usually in a simplified form. It aims to put students in a position where they can experience some aspects of real life by involving in activities that are closely related to it. For example, when a student simulates the role of a manager through CAI, he learned the experiences of it which will be fruitful for him in real life later. A simulated situation can be created in virtual reality in which students interacts with a virtual world. They obtain automatic feedback on their decisions and actions and have the opportunity to rectify poor decisions and actions.

15. *Collaborative learning:* CAI provides opportunities for teams of students to complete their learning assignments or engage in problem based learning cooperatively. The students can form face-to-face or virtual groups. Collaborative learning can be promoted in virtual reality by establishing an interdependent, interactive learning environment and by creating a virtual classroom.

16. The communication abilities can be developed effectively because under CAI, communication can be verbal, or electronic through e-mail, blogs, chatting and video conferencing.

17. It provides freedom to experiment with different options.

18. The teachers can devote more time to individual students.

19. Privacy helps the shy and slow learners to learn.

20. It provides the opportunities for self-directed learning. The students can decide when, where and what to learn.

21. Multimedia helps to understand difficulty concepts through multi- sensory approach.

22. Individual attention can be provided.

Thus we can say that CAI is successful in raising the examination scores of students in commerce, improving student attitudes and lowering the amounts of time required to master certain material.

Demerits and Limitations of CAI

There are some disadvantages in using CAI. These can be as follows:

1. Learner may feel overwhelmed the information and resources available.
2. In the topics involving abstract reasoning and problem solving process, CAI is not very effective.
3. If the instructional software is poorly designed, it can reduce students' interest and motivation to learn.
4. Learning becomes too mechanical.
5. All the subject matter of commerce is difficult to be programmed.

6. Long working hours using computers poses health hazards like tiring of eyes, neck pain, back pain etc.
7. Inadequate training of the teachers with the operation of computers could hamper the usage of CAI.
8. Children may become addicted to computers and ignore other activities of life.
9. Overuse of multimedia may divert the attention of the students from the content.
10. Acquiring and maintenance of computer systems and authorised software is a costly affair.
11. Students also require training in the use of computers, which may cause distraction from the main instructional process.
12. It is a hard fact that in face-to-face mode student-teacher interaction takes place and there is a scope to deal with emotions and feelings. Computers cannot handle this aspect of learning.
13. The availability of reliable and stable supply of electricity is essential which is lacking in India.
14. Lack of infrastructure.
15. Speech and writing analysis through computers is still in its nascent stage.

In spite of the above disadvantages and limitations considerable efforts has, over the years, been directed at developing CAI systems that are easy to use and incorporate expert knowledge of teaching and learning. However, such systems are still far from achieving their full potential. In the coming years, when the sufficient packages and good infrastructure will be available, these can be very fruitful for the teaching and learning process to be more effective than the present scenario.

D. The Assignment

Assignment is one of the most important self instructional modules of teaching commerce at senior secondary level. Some significant topics or sub-topics can be assigned to the pupils for preparation, for study, for revision or for some remedial work. The written assignments help in organisation of knowledge, assimilation of facts and better preparation for examination.

Types of Assignment

The teacher of commerce can use following types of assignments:

1. *Preparatory assignments* — These are means to prepare the pupils for the work which is to follow the next day.
2. *Study assignments* — These are given after the lesson has been taught, in the form of problem, or listing the main points, or making chart, graph, etc.
3. *Revisional assignments* — These are given for providing drill to the work done by the students, for checking the understanding of the topic, for checking the retention of facts of the topic, etc.
4. *Evaluative assignments* — These are given to check the knowledge about the topic. These can be in the written as well as in oral form.

5. *Remedial assignments* — The purpose of these assignments is to remove weak points and clear understanding.
6. *Project assignments* — These can be in the form of project.
7. *Experimental assignments* — These could take the form of performing experiments in the laboratory and answering questions put forth by the teacher.

Development Process of Assignment

The first step is to analyse the prescribed course. The next step is to list the assignments and lay down the objectives for each assignment, with the cooperation of the pupils and guide them through the following steps:

1. Reference to previous experiences
2. Discussion
3. Explaining and clearing difficulties
4. Distribution of tasks.
5. Starting the activity
6. Evaluation

Thus, assignments rouse children's interest, stimulate their thinking, elicit their cooperation, encourage initiative, clear up misunderstandings, develop insight and boost morale. It is a technique of teaching yet to be recognised by education. The importance of it is based on the premise that the desire for self learning is more important than of learning through teaching. If good assignments are prescribed, pupils can and will study independently with success.

E. Project Work

Project work, as a self instructional module, is less structured as compared to PLM, PSI and CAI. In schools, you may be giving assignments of various kinds to your students, sometimes, certain assignments demand that students work on them for a longer period, say one week or two weeks, and produce something concrete or describe the process of certain experiences in the form of a report. Such assignments are called project work. Through this, the students get experiential learning. This provides the students an opportunity to learn at their own pace and time, while they do certain activities more or less independent of the teacher.

Types of Project Work

It may be of the following kinds:

(*i*) *Laboratory Work* — It aims at developing certain skills in the students through activities conducted in controlled conditions.

(*ii*) *Field Work* — It is conducted in real life situations. It provides first hand knowledge of the subject.

(*iii*) *Library Work* — Such project has potential to promote individualised learning.

Development of Project Work

It is an effective self instructional module which require participation of the students as well as of teacher.

(*i*) Preparation stage.
(*ii*) Implementation stage.
(*iii*) Reporting stage.
(*iv*) Evaluation stage.

Thus, individualised self instructional modules help in the development of the students at their own pace according to their interest, potentiality and abilities.

GROUP DIRECTED SELF INSTRUCTIONAL MODULES

In Indian classrooms there is a lot of emphasis these days on cognitive development due to the instructional procedures adopted in the schools. This is mainly because we depend heavily on teacher-controlled instructions. Due to this development of certain skills in students, remain ignored. Therefore, it is essential, that group directed self instructions should be organised in schools.

In group-directed self instruction the students carry out the instructional activities together in a group. These are based on the fact that every member of group activity participates in the instructional activity. Learning takes place due to interaction among the group members and learning by doing work in the group with the support of each other. Thus, learning in this mode of instruction is controlled by the interactive climate generated by the group working as a team with mutual support.

Group directed self instructions provide deeper understanding of knowledge through participation in group work including discussion. It develops the power of expression, critical thinking, tolerance, belongingness, trust, team spirit, habit of helping each other etc. Thus, this type of instructions can help in preparing knowledgeable and skilled human beings who could support a society with democratic values leading to harmonious life, prosperity and happiness. Some of the group directed self instructional modules are as follows:

— Discussion
— Debate
— Symposium
— Brain Storming
— Group Projects

In all the above instructional modules group interactive sessions take place. In these sessions, the group members interact with each other by asking questions, seeking classifications, giving their own views, examining other views, arguing the decisions etc. You, as a teacher can initiate these instructional modules in the class and then allow the members of the group to participate and manage it.

Elements of Group Directed Instructions

There are four main elements as:

- Chairperson
- Speaker
- Participants, and
- Recorder.

In such group interactions, the students play the role as chairperson, speaker, participants and recorders.

Procedure/Steps of Group Directed Self Instructions

1. Preparation

For the organisation of group directed self instruction firstly the teacher is to prepare the students as well as pre arrangements. For preparation the following activities are to be performed:

(*i*) *Allocation of topics* — The topic should be allocated to the students in advance so that they can prepare for presentation. It is better to give students only a small portion. As a teacher, you should keep a record of the portions allotted to various students.

(*ii*) *Decide the date of presentation* — The dates of presentation should be fixed for each student is the beginning itself. This may be notified also.

(*iii*) *Guiding and Motivating students for preparation of write-ups* — The teacher should guide the students regarding reference books and also in the preparation of write-ups. In order to ensure that every student prepares a write-up, you should encourage students to start work immediately.

(*iv*) *Making seating arrangements* — A proper seating arrangement is needed to enable all participants to see and listen to each other. For this circular seating arrangement is the most effective.

(*v*) *Orientation of the students* — The students should also tell them that they will be evaluated on the basis of the write-up, presentation they make and their participation in the interaction. The student should know their role and the process of evaluation.

2. Conducting

For conducting the group interaction, the teacher should initiate, encourage and guide the students. He can function as an elaborator, moderator and controller. In order to ensure that every student participates in discussion, the teacher should make some efforts to motivate the students. He should appreciate the views expressed by the students. The teacher is required to moderate the overall environment of interaction with a view to maintain the warmth of the interpersonal feelings and providing all participants a chance to take part in the interaction.

3. Closing the Session

Before closing the session, the teacher should highlight and summarise the views and agreements expressed during the discussion. This may be done without personal references and without hurting the feelings of the participants. He should commend desirable behaviour and caution against undesirable one.

Thus, self instructional modules are very useful and effective for self learning. In these the instructional activity is controlled more by the students than the teacher. In other words, the students depend more on themselves for learning rather than on the teacher. Learning in group directed instructions takes place with the mutual support of group members.

SELF INSTRUCTIONAL MATERIAL IN COMMERCE

It is now well-organised fact that to keep teaching interesting and to make it effective there is need of utilizing certain instructional aids. A teacher must explore a wide variety of materials to find suitable aids for instruction to provide additional information and to broaden the concept. The instructional material needed for different branches of commerce are almost limitless. The subject of commerce is so vast that a teacher, to help the students in understanding the content, must use different types of instructional materials. But, the material for use should be selected carefully and special care to be taken to eliminate that type of material which distorts facts.

The process of education is dynamic and has been changing with the advancement to scientific inventions and discoveries. The present day society is proceeding towards materialism in which everyone desires to do a lot in a very short span of time. Educational field is also being affected with this feeling that a teacher want to achieve the set objectives in limited period of time. This can be done only with the help of using instructional material. They have brought about a revolutionary change in the education system. Even more sophisticated instructional material will be available in the near future.

> "Instructional material is all material used in the classroom or in other teaching situations to facilitate the understanding of the written or spoken words."
>
> — *E.C. Dent.*

Meaning of Instructional Material

The word 'Instructional material' is the summation of two words:

(*i*) Instruction
(*ii*) Material
(*i*) *Instruction*: To give the knowledge, to provide information, to instruct, to teach or to train.
(*ii*) *Material*: That provides help or support.

Thus, instructional materials are those materials which help the teacher to make clear all the concepts, ideas or thoughts, develop understanding and create coordination in them by interrelationship.

Need and Importance of Instructional Material

Kothari commission while emphasizing on the importance of these material said, "The supply of these material to every school is essential for the improvement of quality of teaching." National education policy has also stressed on the use of this type of material, specifically, self made material to make the teaching-learning more effective, permanent and real. The need and importance of instructional material is due to the following points:

1. Clarity of the Subject Matter: There are various concepts in commerce e.g., banking, insurance, management etc. which are difficult to understand theoretically. If the teacher takes the help of some material, he can make the concepts clear, understandable and meaningful to the students.

2. Attention and Interest: The instructional material helps in creating the attention and interest of the students in the learning of commerce with the help of graph, diagrams, chart, model, etc. The teacher can attract the attention of the students.

3. Development of Scientific Attitude: The use of instructional material helps in developing the scientific attitude of the students instead of agreeing by listening the subject matter, they observe or use practically with the help of these materials. This will help in developing the habit of generalizations through actual observation and experiments.

4. Provide Direct, Representative and Meaningful Experiences: Instructional materials provide direct, representative and meaningful experiences which make learning permanent when a child sees, hears, touches, tastes and smells, his experiences become concrete.

5. Spontaneity: Self instructional material provide occasions for the pupils to move about, talk, laugh and comment upon. They work because they feel like working and not because the teacher wants them to work.

6. Best Motivators: While utilizing self instructional material, the pupils work with more zeal and interest. These materials possess vividness, clarity and dramatic appeal. They remain more attentive. These material can motivate them to learn faster, remember longer and gain more accurate information and to understand meaningfully.

7. Antidote to the Disease of Verbal Instruction: Sometimes students feel boredom in the class while listening the verbal explanation of the teacher. These materials help to reduce verbalism. They help in giving clear concepts and this help to bring accuracy in learning.

8. Maximum Use of Senses: As senses are the gateways of knowledge, therefore, lessons should have a multiple sense appeal. It has been observed that stimuli which appear to more than one sense organ, are perceived and remembered easier and better. As research done by Cobun (1968) indicated that 83 per cent of what is learned is from the sense of sight, 11 per cent from hearing, 3.5 per cent from smell, 1.5 per cent from touch and 1 per cent from the sense of taste.

9. Based on Maxims of Teaching: While utilizing instructional material it becomes easier for the teacher to follow the maxims of teaching as from 'simple to complex', 'known to unknown', etc.

10. Encourage Class Room Interaction: The teacher while utilizing the instructional material has to be friend and guide in the class. He can make the students active. The success of teaching learning process depends upon this type of interaction.

11. Effective for Slow Learners: Psychologically it has been proved that there are individual differences in the intelligence and personality of the students. Not every student is able to understand through verbal explanation only. Such students can understand and remember the facts more easily with the help of these materials.

12. Saving of Time and Energy: The subject matter of commerce is much wider and it is not easy for the teacher to explain all the subject matter thoroughly.

These materials help in clarifying the concept with less explanation in a short span of time.

13. Discouragement of Cramming: The use of instructional material develops interest of the students in the subject matter and are motivated to learn themselves. As a result they are not to cram the subject matter.

14. Helpful in supplying New Experiences and New Energies: The verbal explanation given by the teacher in the class clarifies only the concept which is given in books whereas a picture, a model or a specimen actually extends the limits of experiences. On the basis of these experiences they can generalize, analyse, synthesize the subject matter and correlate it with the other subjects also.

15. Vividness: Instructional material gives vividness to the learning situation. A film on the banking process, advertising techniques, management of an organisation provide a vivid picture.

16. Development of Higher Faculties: Verbalism promotes memorization. Use of instructional material stirs the imagination, thinking process and reasoning power of the students, and calls for creativity and inventiveness and other higher mental activities on the part of the students and thus helps in the development of higher faculties among the students. These higher faculties help in development of understanding level of the students.

17. Helpful in Getting Desired Behaviour Outcomes: Instructional material help the teacher to clarify, establish, correlate and coordinate accurate concepts, interpretations and appreciation and enables them to make learning more concrete, effective, interesting, inspirational, meaningful and vivid.

18. Positive Environment for Creative Discipline: A balanced, rational and scientific use of instructional material develops motivation, attracts the attention and interests of the students and provides a variety of creative outlets for the utilization of their tremendous energy. This type of environment keeps the students busy in the classroom work. In this way use of instructional material help in providing positive environment for creative discipline.

Thus use of instructional material provides significant gains in informational learning, retention and recalling, thinking and reasoning, activity, interest, imagination, better assimilation, personal growth and development. The materials are the stimuli for learning 'why', 'how', 'When' and 'Where'. The 'hard to understand principles' are usually made clear by the intelligent use of skillfully desired instructional material. These materials are very helpful for teacher to make teaching learning process more effective and for students to learn in an interesting, effective and inspirational environment.

Criterion for the selection of Effective Instructional Material

1. They should be meaningful and purposeful.
2. They should be economical.
3. They should be durable.
4. They should be easily handled, manipulated and used.
5. They should be according to the mental level of the students.
6. Their repair should be easily possible.

7. Their appearance should be attractive.
8. They should be free from any undesirable propaganda and advertising.
9. They should be interesting, comprehensible, concrete, clear and concise.
10. They must represent correct and real examples.
11. They should be simple.
12. Their size should be such that they must be perceptible by the students for whom they are meant.
13. They must supplement the textbook information.
14. They should help in the realization of desired learning objectives.
15. They should have specific educational value besides being interesting and motivating.

Difficulties and Problems in the use of Instructional Material

Inspite of the increasing effectiveness on teaching learning process by the use of instructional material in the present educational system, there are following problems which are faced in using them:

1. Non-availability of material in schools.
2. Apathy of the teacher.
3. Ineffectiveness of the material.
4. Lack of suitable storage facilities.
5. Lack of finance.
6. Lack of facilities for the use of material — proper space, electricity, etc.
7. Lack of training on the part of the teachers in the use of material.
8. Lack of availability of suitable instructional material in the languages of different states.
9. Improper selection.
10. Not catering to the local needs.
11. Lack of coordination between centre and states.
12. Indifference of students.

In spite of all these problems, the future of utilization of these instructional materials can be bright if there is proper planning on the part of the government and proper coordination between producers, teachers and students.

Classification of Instructional Material

The instruction materials are classified in different ways but the main purpose behind it is that the teacher can quickly examine a range of possibilities in any one of the several classifications. They can easily select the most suitable one for use in specific classroom situation.

I. Classification on the Basis of Projected and Non-projected Material

1. Projected Material

Still	*Motion*
• Slides	• Film
• Filmstrips	• Television

- Transparencies.
- Micro image system: microfilm, micro-card.
- Close-circuit television
- Video cassettes

2. Non-projected Material

(*a*) *Graphic Aids*

- Charts
- Posters
- Graphs
- Cartoons
- Pictures
- Comics
- Diagrams
- Maps
- Flash cards
- Strips

(*b*) *Display Boards*

- Chalk board
- Magnet Board
- Flannel Board
- Bulletin Board
- Peg Board

(*c*) *Three-Dimensional Material*

- Globe
- Specimen
- Puppets
- Model
- Real objects
- Mock-ups

(*d*) *Equipment Material*

(*i*) Audio Material
- Radio
- Tape Recorder
- Disc Recorder
- Language Laboratory
- Sound distribution system

(*ii*) Audio-visual material
- Television

(*iii*) Activity Material
- Computer Assisted Instruction
- Demonstration
- Dramatisation
- Experimentation
- Field Trips
- Programmed Instruction
- Teaching machines

II. Classification on the Basis of Traditional Approach

Audio Material	*Visual Material*	*Audio-Visual Material*
• Radio	• Bulletin Board	• Demonstration
• Gramophone	• Flannel Board	• Films
• Linguaphone	• Chalk Board	• Printed Material with recorded sound.
• Tape-Recorder	• Charts	• Sound film strips
• Disc Recorder	• Graphs	• Television
	• Tables	• Videotapes
	• Exhibits	
	• Illustrated Books	
	• Maps	
	• Magnetic Board	
	• Posters	
	• Photographs	
	• Silent films	
	• Slides	
	• Pictures	
	• Models	
	• Self-Instructional material	

III. Classification on the Basis of Technological Approach

Simple Hardware	*Hardware*	*Software*
• Magic lantern or slide projector	• Radio	• Pictures
• Epidiascope	• Tape Recorder	• Chart
• Films strip Projector	• Television	• Maps
• Slide cum film strip projector	• Audio cassette Recorder	• Diagram
• OHP	• Educational films	• Graph
	• Computers	• Cartoon
	• Teaching Machines	• Posters
		• Three Dimensional material
		• Programmed Learning Learning
		• Newspapers
		• Slides
		• Film strips.

IV. Edgar Dale's Classification

Edger dale classified the instructional material by using cone of experience

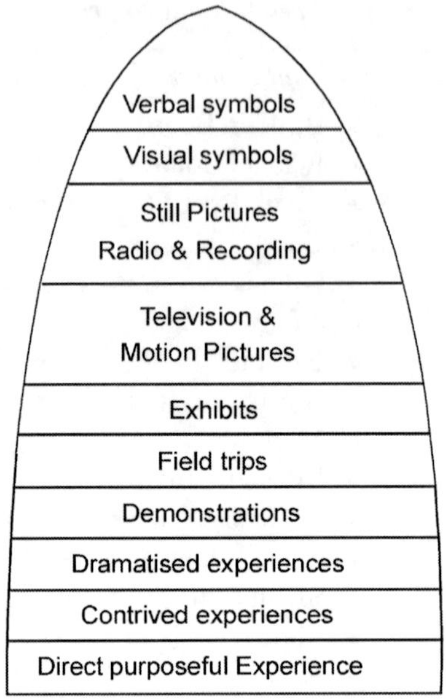

Edgar Dale's Cone of Experience

Use of Various Instructional Materials in Teaching and Learning of Commerce

There are various instructional materials which can be used in teaching and learning of commerce to make it effective as:

1. Films

In the field of education there is too much development of films. It is a good audio-visual aid in teaching learning process. It is complementary or substitute of physical teaching. It affects the whole environment of class with the mixture of sound and light. It coordinates pictures, words, colours, objects and diagrams according to the objectives. It is gaining much popularity as a self instructional material.

An educational film is one which contributes to the achievement of desirable educational goal by making effective use of motion pictures as a medium of communication.

Types of films

(a) Instructional Films: They are concerned with instructions. They can be very useful for certain topics. They are of 15 to 20 minutes duration and provides direct instruction for an unit. They can provide effective instruction in commerce like how to organise business, what type of advertisements can be effective etc.

(b) Documentary Films: The documentary films are the constructive presentation of the reality. They presents the artistic view of the actual material. They help in developing the attitudes. They not only present the reality but analyse, synthesise and explain the facts in an interesting way also.

(c) News Reels: They are the best source of providing the information regarding current affairs in the world.

(d) Dramatic Films: They provide the information with the help of dramas.

(e) Narrative Films: They provide the information regarding any event or events in a systematic way.

(f) Discursive Films: They present the subject matter related to a topic or different topics in a discursive, systematic and organised way.

(g) Factual Films: They provide the information regarding the occupations or facts of the economy.

(h) Problematic Films: They present some problems before the students and some fundamental facts for thinking also.

(i) Drill Films: They provide the opportunities for drill.

(j) Emulative films: They present some ideals related to any behaviour or activity and the pupils can simulate them.

Advantages

1. It helps is modifying the interests and attitudes of the students by providing information regarding different business activities.
2. They can bring past and present in the classroom.
3. They may prove as effective sources for recreation and entertainment.
4. They provide variety to the methods of instruction due to the presentation with movements, change in visuals and life related. They attract the attention and create interest.
5. They are true to life experiences. We can get the experiences from every corner of the world.
6. They can provide the students the latest changes and developments in various areas of the subjects like preparation of balance sheets, recent income tax rates, new advertising process, etc.
7. The knowledge gained through the films becomes permanent.
8. They help in inculcating right values among the students as well as the development of national and international outlook.
9. They work as controlling time factor also.
10. They help in developing thoughts and actions.

Limitations

1. Too much costly.
2. Lack of trained teachers.
3. It is not possible to revise the visual at a time.
4. It is difficult to think on the important facts while depicting the films.

How to use

1. The teacher should have up-to-date list of films related to his subject.
2. He should present the film step by step.
3. Before depicting the films, he should present explanation talk.
4. He should ask the students to note down the important points side by

side.
5. He should delete superfluous portions.
6. There should be no interruption in the presentation.
7. He should ask questions, encourage discussions to make the students attentive.
8. He should use follow up programmes as to write a short note, to complete the project presented through film, etc.

2. Television

Television is a commonly used teaching material in U.S.A., but in India, a beginning has been made. It presents a projected representation of reality and can be used to present past, present and the future perspectives. Television lesson coordinates both visual and auditory senses which makes the subject matter easy to understand and interesting. The students can be made conscious about the various events and progress being made in business economy in India as well as outside the country. It provides clear knowledge about the progress made by the different industries and actual process of different industries. Now a days many educational programmes are telecasted by UGC, NCERT, SCERT etc. to make the subject matter more interesting and understandable.

Advantages

1. It helps the students to understand the subject of commerce deeply and clearly.
2. It helps in bringing the most talented teachers to educational institutions throughout the country.
3. It helps in making difficult lessons intelligible through acting and dramatization.
4. It can present the reality of the economy.
5. It helps in professional growth of the teacher.
6. The students can get current knowledge about the commercial activities prevailing in the economy.
7. It is a motivational device and creates interest among the students to gain knowledge about the business activities.
8. It provides knowledge about the new researches made in economy.
9. It provides knowledge about processes of different industries as well as share market.
10. It helps in realising educational objectives.
11. Educational programmes help in upgrading the curriculum.

Precautions

The following precautions should be taken while utilizing television for teaching-learning process:

1. The teacher should acquaint himself with the broad casting programmes or schedule before hand.
2. While selecting the programme, the age, interest and mental level of the

students must be kept in mind *i.e.,* the programme should be student-centred.

3. The teacher himself should be fully prepared before showing the television programme to the students.
4. The students should be fully prepared mentally and psychologically before the start of the television lesson. The teacher should instruct the students to focus their attention on the important points of the lesson.
5. The teacher should be careful to place the T.V. set at such appropriate place from where it is clearly visible and audible to all the students.
6. He should take care of providing proper environment in the classroom.
7. It is essential to maintain proper learning environment and discipline while observing the T.V. programme.
8. Teacher should ask the students to take brief notes while observing the programme.
9. After the programme the teacher should remove the individual difficulties of the students regarding the lesson. The students should be allowed to clear their doubts, if any.
10. The students should be guided and provided opportunities for seeking practical application of the subject matter seen by them in the broadcast.
11. The students should be assessed properly by suitable tests. This test can be written and oral.
12. Remedial measures should be taken to correct the weaknesses or errors of the students as diagnosed by testing.

Thus, television can be used as an instructional material for commerce to bring about qualitative improvement at all levels. It will help in bringing clarity and stability in the knowledge of the students about commerce. Taking into account the usefulness of television, Government of India has been making efforts to provide free television sets to all the institutions. Group discussions among specialists can be telecast on the T.V. directly. It can enhance the knowledge of students about economic development, working system of share market, insurance companies, transportation and communication, etc.

3. Computers

Computer as an instructional material is the latest arrival in the field of education. In its technological advancement and educational utility, it has surpassed all the audio-visual equipments including teaching machine. Its demand is increasing day by day in serving the various purposes in the field of education. The day is not far off when every educational institute and each classroom will be equipped with computer sets.

Advantages

A computer is essentially a device for storing large amount of information and handling the information in specified ways in extremely short period of time. The information supplied through the computer can be very useful for the students of commerce in the following ways:

1. The students can get answers to their questions without feeling any hesitation and fear.
2. The curiosity of the students can be easily satisfied and they can get valuable information regarding the different areas related to commerce as accounts, share market, business activities, etc.
3. Computers can help a lot for practice and drill work to be done by the students for the fixation of knowledge and skills already learnt in the classroom.
4. It can play an effective role in providing appropriate tutorial services to a number of students at a time on individual or collective basis.
5. Through problem solving programmes available on the computer the students can have enough practice for solving different types of problems thinking new strategies, originating new ideas and constructing and developing something new.
6. Through the provision of some artificial situations and made ups computers can help in a big way to arrange for simulation and gaming techniques.
7. Teachers can make the students more productive and creative in terms of their outcomes.
8. Computer can work according to the pace of the student.
9. It helps in providing current knowledge related to business activities to teachers as well as students.

Commercial Software or Software used in Business

However, many softwares are available in the market but generally the following softwares are used in business:

a. Electronic Spreadsheet/Ms-Excel
b. Word Processor/Ms-Word
c. Data Base Management

a. *Electronic Spreadsheets/MS-Excel*

Spreadsheet is a type of a large page which is a type of a programme, e.g. MS-Excel. There are number of software packages available in the market used for preparing spreadsheets. These packages are the application programmes having vast capabilities of creating, editing and formatting the spreadsheets. There are many columns in a spreadsheet made with the help of horizontal and vertical lines. We write data in these columns. The length and breadth of every column can be increased or decreased according to the need. Electronic spreadsheet is very useful when some numbers are related with each other and some numbers are based on other numbers. Spreadsheet gives answer to such type of questions as 'What will be the outcome after this?' For example, while preparing wage sheet, if there is an increase of 10 per cent in the wage, then we can find out immediately what will be the extra cost. It allows you to analyse the information in the variety of ways. You can establish the financial analysis, estimated cost, graphs and charts of numerical data. This programme is useful for arithmetical calculations and maintaining data. This programme is useful for maintaining the accounts as:

(i) Payroll Accounts: It is useful in calculating the pay of an employee. In a spreadsheet a row is used for each employee in which there are separate columns for basic salary, dearness allowance, house rent allowance, other allowances, total salary, taxes and balance salary. If the name and basic salaries are filled in the columns then on the basis of given formula, other amounts fill automatically in the columns of spreadsheet.

(ii) Recalculation if Some Values are Changed: With the help of spreadsheet we can get the answer immediately if there is any change in the formula. For example, if we change the formula of dearness allowance then we can know the new amount of dearness allowance permissible to each employee and his total salary.

(iii) Graphic Representation: In the MS-Excel data can be displayed graphically in a chart. Worksheet data is linked with the charts. You can also create charts from cells or ranges. Ms-Excel can also create a chart from a pivot table. We can use twelve types of charts to present the data:

- Columns
- Bar
- Line
- Pie
- XY (Scatter)
- Area
- Doughnut
- Radar
- Surface
- Bubble
- Stock
- Cone, Cylinder and Pyramid

Thus, the data of sales, expenses, profits, costs, etc. can be represent with the help of graph, diagram or chart.

(iv) Depreciation Accounting: Spreadsheets can also be used to select the depreciation method on fixed assets and to determine the rate of depreciation.

(v) Budgeting and Financial Forecasting: Spreadsheets can also be used to prepare the budget of the business as well as to forecast the trend of sale profit.

b. *Word Processor/MS-Word*

Word processors are the applications programmes having vast capabilities of creating, editing, correcting and formatting the text with number of additional components. A word processor can also be known as typewriter of jet era. We can write letters, reports and other documents with the help of word processor and we can do changes in it if we need to change on the screen. Most of the business organizations are using word processor in place of typewriter because it has following advantages:

(i) You can save the word document you are working on; it may be new or existing one. You can also save all open documents at the same time. A copy of the active document can be saved with a different name and also in a different location. You can save a document in another file format for use in another programme. Word sets automatically to save a backup copy of a document you saved.

(ii) Word saves multiple versions of a document within the same document so that you can go back and review, open, print and delete earlier versions.

(iii) A powerful word processor is one, which has number of advanced features of editing and formatting the text or document. Editing and formatting tools are useful to improve the presentation of the text in the manner in which you want.

(iv) As you know, we do number of mistakes while typing and retyping of text. Word processor provides auto features to reduce or eliminate the same. It has different types of auto features as auto complete, auto text, auto correct, auto format and auto summarize.

(v) Sometimes it is the requirement of the document or text to improve the presentation by inserting objects like pictures, graphs, typical shapes, etc. Generally, we use page breaks, page numbering, date and time, footnotes during the creation of the document. Word processor provides such type of components.

(vi) It provides facilities of correct spelling and grammar of the text.

There are different examples of uses of word processor as:

(i) Letters of Common Reply: Many letters received in the office for which we have to give same reply. So, the reply of these letter can be stored in word processor and only by changing address we can send the reply.

(ii) Reminder to Debtors: With the help of word processor, we can prepare the reminders for the debtors by changing only the debited amount.

(iii) In Case of Contracts: Every big company has same contract details with different companies/shareholders. So, these contract details can be stored as MS-word and these can be used while making new contract.

c. Data Base Management

In this, all useful data related to the business can be stored at one place. This type of data are stored in storage devices. Data Base Management is useful information. The stored data can be related to different activities of the business like daily purchases, day-to-day sales, income-expenditure under different heads etc. The data stored in the computer can be reorganized and different calculations can be made based on these as we can find out real accounts any time, we can get the number of debtors in every city. Thus, data base management is useful in stock control, production planning and control, budgeting, billing, making payroll sheet etc.

Limitations

The use of computers for commerce has some limitations also as:

1. Repairing of the computer is difficult.
2. It is an expensive material.
3. Good Softwares related to the subject of commerce may not be easily available.

4. Students may get bored and fatigued on account of mechanical instructions with the computer machine.
5. Computer assisted instructions are basically the learner's controlled instructions. The learner has to proceed at his own will. Such unrestricted freedom may lead to carelessness, indiscipline and mere wastage of time on the part of the learner.
6. Every computer, how good it may be, is a machine. It can never match a teacher in providing living instructions to the students in terms of heart to heart links, sympathy, affection and emotional warmth.
7. For making an effective use of computer every student should be computer literate but it is lacking uptil now in India because many students belong to rural areas.

In spite of these limitations, computer is a very helpful and effective device for making teaching learning process effective.

4. Chart

The charts are very useful instructional material because they help the teacher to explain difficult points. In teaching of commerce charts are inevitable material aids. A chart is a visual instructional material through which a sequential relationship can be established between lines, figures and words as well as with the facts and ideas of the content. It possesses a unique speciality to express the extensive content. The charts help in creating a suitable subject atmosphere in the classroom and in elucidating various points. Charts help in saving time and energy because instead of drawing them on the chalk-board, the teacher can depend upon the pre-drawn diagram. Moreover, it is not always possible to draw a diagram on chalk-board with accuracy. They also help to raise issues, which will help in the process of systematic thinking and intelligent understanding.

Types of Chart

The charts may be classified in terms of arrangements and kinds of ideas which they may express as:

I. The Narrative Charts: Such a chart is an extended left to right an arrangement of facts and ideas for expressing.

(*a*) Contrasting views of individuals or organizations on important topics or issues.

(*b*) Technological development over a period of years such as improvement in transportation, communication, manufacturing, advertisement, etc.

(*c*) The events in a process such as trading, banking etc.

(*d*) The flow of different business organizations, different business laws, development procedure and classification in a systematic way.

II. The Tabulation Chart: These charts are used to express facts and ideas with the help of different tables as.

(*a*) The time sequences of a series of events to arrange chronologically all the happenings important to the development of process, organisation or nation, etc.

(*b*) Numerical data for making comparisons.
(*c*) List of products or the like in selected area.
(*d*) List of things for internal or international trade.

III. The Cause and Effect Chart: These charts depict the subject matter from left to right as:

(*a*) Relationship between rights and responsibilities.
(*b*) Relationship between advertisement and sale of the product.
(*c*) Relationship between community workers and the community that supports them.
(*d*) Relationship between trading and different factors as economic system, availability of product, etc.
(*e*) Relationship between standard of living and different factors as availability of material resources, level of technological advancement, etc.
(*f*) Relationship between economic environment pollution and different factors as problem of food, problem of unemployment, anti social development, etc.

IV. The Chain Chart: This can be used to represent the facts and ideas as:

(*a*) Distribution of population in a circular form.
(*b*) Different transition in the business activities.
(*c*) Different economic activities.
(*d*) Establishment of a business.

V. The Evolution Chart: These can be used to depict the facts and ideas as:

(*a*) Change in the standards in food consumption, length of work, purchasing power of a rupee, etc.
(*b*) Change in the type of advertisement, trading, etc.
(*c*) Change in the specific items from beginning to date, perhaps with projects into the future.
(*d*) Change in banking system.
(*e*) Change in the process of trading.

Uses/Functions/Advantages of Chart

Chart is useful at every step of teaching learning process whether it may be introductory phase or presentation phase or evaluation phase. It is useful for the following reasons:

1. It is an effective means for the classification of the important information.
2. Whenever the students feel any difficulty, it helps in making easy the difficult ideas and present the complex data in an easy and summarised form.
3. It is helpful in creating the interest of the students in the subject matter.
4. It provides motivation for instructions.
5. It helps in the process of intellectual understanding and systematic thinking.
6. It saves time and energy of the teacher.
7. It is easy to prepare.
8. It is easy to store.
9. It helps in presenting abstract ideas in the visual form.

10. It encourages utilization of other media of communication.
11. It helps in presenting materials symbolically.
12. It helps in showing relationship by means of facts, figures and statistics.

Suggestions/Precautions for the Proper Use of Chart

Chart is a useful and important visual aid. While utilizing it the teacher should keep in mind the following points to make its utility effective for teaching learning process:

1. A chart should not contain too much subject matter.
2. It should be according to interest and mental level of the students.
3. It should be related to the subject matter.
4. The presentation on the chart should be easy, attractive, clear and according to the understanding of the students.
5. The subject matter displayed on the chart should be perceptible to all the students.
6. It should be used at proper time.
7. Definite objectives should be fulfilled by the chart.
8. A chart should not be used too much for only one point.
9. The chart should be used at that time, when it is needed.
10. If the chart is depicting more than one fact then they should be displayed one by one.

Thus, charts can be used to convey both verbal and graphic message. Students should be involved in preparation of charts. Self-made charts should be used by the teacher. The pictorial charts are available in the market but they should be used according to the needs of the instruction. In modern times, these can be prepared with the help of computers also.

5. Graphs

Graphs are defined as such visual graphic aids that help in the representation of numerical data in form of dots, lines or pictures so that the students may be able to understand the subject matter clearly. The purpose of graph is to make the subject matter easy, interesting and understandable. It fulfills the psychological law of learning, i.e. 'learning by doing'.

Preparation/kinds of Graphs

The teacher can prepare a graph on the chart or on transparency with the help of the students to present the subject matter related to commerce as:

1. Bar Graph: In bar graphs facts are presented through bars. The different facts can be shown with the help of bars of different lengths, breadths and/or colours. The bars can be presented horizontally or vertically. These graphs are more useful for comparative study if the number of facts is small. For example, export credits of India in different years can be depicted through bar graphs.

2. Picture Graph: In picture graph, the numerical data can be depicted through pictures. It can be easy, attractive, interesting and effective way of presenting the data because the children like pictures the most. The facts can be easily understood with the help of pictures. These graphs are self-explanatory. They also possess the capacity to explain even the abstract ideas clearly. For example, in order to compare the growing Indian population with the world population picture graph can be used.

3. Pie Graph: Pie graph can be known as circle graph also. In it, a circle can be divided into parts to present numerical data. This kind of graph is more useful to compare the parts of a circle with the whole circle. Pie graphs attract attention and instantly reveal their message.

4. Line Graph: In line graph figures or numbers are depicted through lines when the number of facts is large and the number goes on increasing, in that case line graph is more useful for presenting the data. For example if we have to show the expenditure of a business on advertisement in different years for sales promotion, we can use line graph. This is perhaps the most frequently used graph.

The teacher can make use of any kind of graph according to the needs and mental level of the students. But the graph must serve the desired purpose clearly and correctly. The facts being compared numerically must be stated clearly.

Precautions while Preparing the Graph

The following points should be kept in mind while preparing graphs:

1. Graph should be of proper size.
2. It should have proper and clear heading.
3. It should be according to the topic.
4. It should be easy and clear.
5. The students should be familiar with the symbols used in it.
6. At a time single fact, thought or concept should be depicted by it.
7. The scale of graph should be clear.
8. Horizontal graphs should be given preference over vertical graphs.
9. Sufficient space should be left between two bars.
10. If different colours are used in bars then the instructions should be kept on the right corner.

Uses/Advantages/Functions of Graphs

1. Graphs help in elucidating the subject matter comprehensively.
2. They help in making the subject matter interesting and understandable.
3. Graphs especially pictorial graphs provide a lot of help to the students with lower intelligence quotient.
4. They are useful for comparative studies.
5. They make the data clear.
6. They are useful for students at every level.
7. Generalisation can be done with the help of data related to any concept on the basis of graph.

Thus, the teacher of commerce can use the graph in the class by preparing them according to the mental and intellectual level of the students and make his teaching interesting and effective.

6. Model

Models are three-dimensional visual aids. If, while teaching about an industry, bank etc., we take the students out to show these places, they will understand them better. But it is difficult to take the students out to far off places. To overcome this difficulty models are used in place of real objects or places. A model is a replica of a thing or a place or a person or an event, which is easy to be kept in school. Models represent the real objects. Models may be simple, sectional or working. They can be solid, hollow or may just show the outlines for demonstrating the external features of the real things.

Uses/Functions/Advantages of Model

1. It can be used as an effective aid when it is difficult to bring real object in the class.
2. It makes teaching effective and interesting.
3. Learning becomes permanent.
4. It helps in increasing motivation to learn.
5. Students also become active.
6. It helps in creating a background situation for verbal activity.
7. It brings great variability in course of instructions.
8. It monitors the attainment of instructional objectives.
9. It intensifies the learning process.
10. It reinforces the processes of comprehension.
11. It develops the creative power of the students.

Thus, a variety of models can be prepared with the help of students for illustrating various contents of commerce.

Precautions while using models

1. Model should be simple and comprehensible.
2. The model must help in the process of illustrating some definite facts.
3. It should be light and handy.
4. A model must be accurate.
5. It should be made of proper material, colour and form.
6. It should be according to the needs and interests of the pupils.
7. A model must have the quality of solidity i.e., it has its inherent strength.
8. Every student should be given an opportunity to observe the model minutely.
9. The students should be encouraged to ask questions about the model.
10. Students should be motivated to prepare the model themselves.
11. Models should be used properly at proper time.
12. Only those aspects or parts should be shown in the model which are in accordance with the content matter.
13. While using the model the teacher should explain each and every aspect related to the content to make the model understandable.
14. Model should correctly represent the thing, the place or the event.

The use of models in class teaching creates an informal atmosphere and motivates learning. Teaching is no longer confined to any one instructional device but it is a help to explain the subject matter in an easy, interesting and correct way.

7. Tables

Generally the teacher finds it convenient to depict the data in the tabular form. Tables are useful to depict certain data, results etc., particularly when we have to make clear inter-relationship. In commerce we are concerned with the data related to various business activities which are to be analysed. Commerce is a scientific subject and it must be taught in a way that the students may make a practical use of their knowledge of commerce. While teaching accounts it is not possible without framing tables. If we are to draw a graph to present something, it is not possible without table.

Table for layout is a special case, since table based layout has some specific properties, which cannot be achieved through simple lecturing. When tables are used to represent logical relationships among data-text, preformatted text, images, links, forms, form-fields, other tables, etc., that information is called **'tabular information'** and the tables are called **'data tables'**. The relationship expressed by a table may be rendered visually (usually on a two-dimensional grid), aurally (often preceding cells with header information), or in other formats.

The tables should be simple and with caption so that it may be easily understandable to the students. The data presented in the table should be neat and clean. It should not be too lengthy. It should impart maximum knowledge in the short period. The teacher should speak while showing the table.

8. Original Material

In commerce, the teacher is to use some original material to make his teaching and learning process effective. They are as follows:

1. Journal
2. Ledger
3. Cash Book
4. Time and energy saving material
   (*i*) Punching machine
   (*ii*) Time Recorder
   (*iii*) Book-Keeping Machine
   (*iv*) Cheque Protector
   (*v*) Calculating Machine
   (*vi*) Type-writer
   (*vii*) Photostat Machine
   (*viii*) Stapling Machine
   (*ix*) Folding Machine
   (*x*) Addressing Machine
   (*xi*) Sealing Machine
   (*xii*) Balancing Machine
5. Post office forms, telegraph forms, money-order forms, etc.
6. Cheque, *Hundi*, exchange bill, etc.
7. Different currency notes, etc.

The original material will help in providing the knowledge of commerce effectively. It makes the subject matter more clear. In the lecture of Book-keeping, the use of journal, ledger, etc. can be taught by showing them originally.

9. Internet

Internet is a set of computers connecting over telephone lines, fibre optics, satellite links and other media including probably, the one on your desktop. In technical words Internet is "the network formed by the cooperative interconnection of computing networks". These connected networks usually use the TCP/IP (Transmission control protocol/Internet protocol). Since its creation in the 1960s, it has grown exponentially and is now used by millions of people from those in commercial and educational institution to individual consumers.

No one owns the Internet. Every person who makes a connection owns the slice of the Internet. It was the best outcome of the world war, when a network of computers was set up by the military. It was established to communicate effectively at the tune of war. Later on the military allowed some universities to join the network. It was especially for the research and development.

Internet itself is responsible for development. Newer technologies are coming up in this field. Today, the new hot-words are WAP, WML, XML, .Net etc. In future mobile phones will be no longer "just telephones" but will be wireless Internet terminals. Microsoft's. Net technology aims to provide a single platform for web and personal computing. Remain updated at all times.

Millions of Internet users are taking the benefit of the information explosion by getting on line connectivity. Many Personal Information Browsers are available in the market to meet the requirements of the various categorised users. In these days of competition, various connectivity options are also playing roles of different kind. As a part of emerging advanced technology for information source, every one should know the basic and fundamental terms of the Internet.

Every one is now aware of the Information Technology. On line banking, Online shopping, Online payments are the outcome trends from E-commerce scenario. It is possible because of the Internet. Communication by E-mail, Chat and Instant Messaging is fast and reliable.

History of the Internet

Around 1959, United States' Department of Defence has started a network called, "ARPA Net". It is the acronym for Advanced Research Projects Agency of United States' Department of Defence. "ARPA Net" began in a modest way with one computer in California. It was an experiment carried out to see whether networking would be reliable. The Department of Defence has also started the involvement of agencies for sharing of the software and hardware resources. "ARPA Net" quickly gets the success to encompass the entire American continent and became a huge success.

Number of universities in that country wanted to become a part of "ARPA Net" and hence the network was broken into two parts "MILNET" for managing the military sites and the new "ARPA NET" for managing the non-military sites. "BIT NET" and the "CS NET" were parallel and complementary efforts to the "ARPA NET'. In the "BIT NET" large number of computers were used for academic and administrative computing. "CS NET" stands for Computer plus Science Network. In 1980 network called the "NSF NET" was created. The National Science Foundation Network (NSF NET) allowed universities and research institutions to link up with their super-computers. It was the first step towards the path of increased demand. Using modern technology, it permitted any computer in the system to link up with any other computer connected to the system. The "NSF NET" backbone was retired in April 1995. It's network connections were replaced by Network Access Points (NAPs).

Use of the Internet

Today you have a choice to make the use of Internet in the field selected by you. The explosive growth of the Internet has led number of its applications; few of them are listed below.

1. *Internet Newsgroup*: Internet Newsgroups are discussion groups on the different topics from recreational activities to scientific research. Any Internet surfer can access many of the newsgroups. Some of them are commercial so that you have to subscribe to them for accessing and agree not to forward the information to others. You can also post the follow up articles and write any articles in that newsgroup. You can use the E-mail facility of such Newsgroups to communicate with users and the hosts.

2. *E-mail (Electronic Mail)*: It is a popular communication and fast working feature on the Internet. This e-mail service is available by means of two ways:

1. Email account provided by the ISP (Internet Service Provider) Examples: dut@scpl.net.in, skk@bom6.vsnl.net.in
2. Web based E-mail accounts:

Some of the popular web based free e-mail providers are:
www.rediffmail.com, www.hotmail.com, www.yahoo.com, www. netscape.com
Examples: dut@rediffmail.com, skk@hotmail.com, asg@netscape.com

E-mail is becoming very popular because, unlike in regular mail there is no delay in the delivery. Postage is not required. Printing e-mail addresses on the letterheads and business cards is becoming as common as printing the telephone numbers. A variety of e-mail management software makes it a useful tool in the many areas like ECRM (Electronic Customs Relations Management), e-marketing, e-banking, etc., Replying, deleting, replying all, file attachments, forwarding messages and address book is possibly done in the e-mail management more effectively than traditional one.

3. *Information Downloads through FTP (File Transfer Protocol)*: This application is used to transfer files between host servers. It means it is an Internet tool that copies a file from one Internet site to another. It is the specific programme that implements this transfer. FTP also downloads file to your server from any remote server that is connected to the Internet. Several FTP sites permit you to access their files without establishing an account with them. These sites are called anonymous sites. You generally login to such machines as Anonymous. Many times special kind of security is provided to make sure that no one could access this information without permission. This concept provides password requirement to access.

4. *Information Access through WWW (World Wide Web)*: The WWW is a series of servers that are interconnected. The information in the www is in the hypertext Form. It can be accessed from any location connected to the Internet. The highlighted contents are linked which help you to move from one document to another that may be present in same or different servers. Generally, website is having number of documents linked with each other. Such documents are called homepages. In addition the Web offers another service, called URL (Uniform Resource Locator) it defines a universal locator mechanism for a group of logical data placed anywhere on the Internet.

Examples: Some of the popular sites are:

www.yahoo.com, www.netscape.com, www.indiatimes.com, www.microsoft.com, www.mitconindia.com, etc.

5. *Online Banking*: You can make transactions by using on line account of the banks. You can access bank account through an Internet PIN. Under any circumstances, never disclose your bank PIN or credit card PIN to anyone. Credit Card, e-cash are the other ways of making transactions on the Internet. You can supply your bank account number and other details i.e. amount debited to the PKN enabled web sites during the transaction with PKN (Personal Key Number).

6. *Online Shopping*: It is also called e-shopping. It is quite enjoyable and far from the risk if you take proper precautions. E-shopping offers more choice, comfort, better convenience, required information and best prices. In this type, there is no need to suffer the crowd, pickpockets and even other scares. Most of the shopping sites have a return policy. You can return the unwanted material within the certain days and request for refund. It increases the utility value of the e-shopping.

7. *Online Communication*: Internet is widely used and accepted communication media. e-mail, Chat through typing the text, e-fax, Internet telephony, instant messaging, voice mail, video mail are the various methods of Internet communication. This type of communication is very fast and having compatibility feature with the other communication devices. In the era of Internet communication, e-mail has played a distinct role. E-mail communication is fast, reliable and cheap. As you know e-mails is a natural way of communication with your friends and business associates those who are at distant locations, and this is the essence of networking.

10. E-learning

The present age is the age of science. Technology is developing day by day. The era of digital age has brought its amazing change in almost all fields, the education field being the most leisurely one. But now many research studies points out the need for the effective teaching-learning opportunities and time to develop new ones which incorporate e-learning into classroom lessons. This century demands the teacher to be skilled enough to incorporate e-learning procedures.

The origin of e-learning is not certain, although it is suggested that the term more likely originated during 1980's within the similar time frame of another delivery mode online learning.

Nicholas defines e-learning as strictly being accessible, using technological tools that are either web-based, web-distributed, a web-capable.

E-learning not only covers content and instructional method delivered via CD-ROM, the internet or an intranet but also includes audio-video tapes, satellite broadcast and interactive TV.

Tavangarian et al included the constructivist model as a framework for their definition by studying that e-learning is not procedural but also shows some transformation of an individual's experience into the individual's knowledge through the knowledge construction process.

There is a perceived need for students to become digitally literate and this has led to an ever increasing focus on the use of a number of technologies within and beyond the classroom. Various pedagogical perspectives or learning theories may be considered in designing and interacting with e-learning programmes.

E-learning or electronic learning field creates a dynamic environment that stimulates learning through self-directed training. This field applies theories of constructivist learning action-orientation and activity theory. Learners are affected positively because it motivates that accelerate learning, enables knowledge transfer through retention and provides manipulative experiences unavailable in a normal training environment negative implications include problem resulting from self-guidance, diminished media richness and issue regarding technology compatibility.

In the words of Bassoppo and Moyo, "The e-learning industry refers to the integration of a range of technologies across all areas of learning. E-learning technologies are designed to support learning by encompassing a range of media, tools and environment. It allows for both synchronous and asynchronous learning environments. E-learning acts as a catalyst for authentic and meaningful learning experiences.

An important characteristics of e-learning is its interactivity. It captures and holds learner's interest. It is individualised, allowing user to navigate through information to build their own unique mental structure based on exploration.

The learning theory that is best applied to e-learning is the constructivist theory, which is a theory of learning where humans construct meaning from current knowledge structures. Thus e-learning is learner-controlled, because they can decide how much training is needed by what they already know. In this way, e-learning is designed to be 'adjustable' by the learner.

Another applicable theory to e-learning is action-orientation, which is a learner-centered pedagogy that emphasises the importance of learners' activation. Through activities based on the interaction with their environment, learner construct knowledge.

Motivation is critical for e-learning of motivation to learn is low, very little learning will occur. If motivation for learning is high, it will occur even when materials are poor. E-learning promotes disinhibition because those normally shy can become more extrovert. This is because there is no identity or physical visibility in e-learning. Nobody knows who they are, so learners can express themselves more openly. There is no culture, age, or gender present in e-learning. This result in an equal opportunity for learners to voice themselves.

Economical – The accessibility of e-learning is also a positive effect because there is no waiting or travelling. It also supports just-in-time learning, which means learners can access the learning at their own convenience. The learners can pace the learning at their own needs, those that work faster are not held up by slower participants. Another benefit is that they do not need to travel anywhere. Minimal travel and shorter learning time results in less time away from productive work and lower cost.

No Boundaries, No Restrictions – E-learning facilitates learning, without having to organise when and where everyone who is interested in the course of commerce can be present.

More Fun – E-learning makes the course interactive and fun through the use of multimedia or the more recently developed methods of gamification.

With e-learning the teacher has the ability to host a guest lecture without having to spend much money. It can be done virtually, with cameras and with the use of microphones to facilitate the same level of interaction that would be possible of the teacher was physically present in the classroom. The recording can be watched again to further understanding.

Demerits of E-learning

E-learning needs self-directed learners and this becomes problematic for those who are uncomfortable by the lack of an instructor. These variations on learner's preferences may result in a hesitancy and reluctance to learn. Thosewhose learning style requires more structure and guidance may become frustrated. Some less-experienced or less well-disciplined learners may also make poor decisions about how much information they need, resulting in information overload.

E-learning may be time consuming for first time learners because the instructional systems are more complex than conventional learning requiring more time to master.

Social implications of a classroom environment keep learners from walking out, whereas the online environments causes attention problems. Learners can get confused, or lost in cyberspace if instruction is on the web, or even get distracted by the environment.

Learners need to be able to access computers with exact software capabilities to view and play. Computer capabilities including bandwidth that affect online speeds may prevent many learners from accessing multimedia efficiently or reliably. Assuring accurate computer facilities, as well as the initial purchase of e-learning training centre very costly. Also, there is a high cost and difficulty of converting current traditional training and instructional material into e-learning for the institutions who opt to use their own material.

The practical skills regarding accounting are harder to pick up from online resources.

Isolation: Though e-learning offers ease, flexibility and ability to remotely access a classroom in the student's own time, learners may feel a sense of isolation.

Health: E-learning requires the use of a computer and such other devices; this means that eye strain, bad posture and other physical problems may affect the learner.

Commerce is a vast subject and the related knowledge can't be limited to books only. E-learning is very much required to have detected knowledge. In essence, e-learning is a computer based educational tool a system that enables you to learn anywhere and at all time. Technology has advanced so much that the geographical gap is bridged with the use of tools that make you feel as if you are inside the classroom. E-learning offers the ability to share material in all kinds of formats such as videos, slide shows, word documents & PDFs.

In the fast paced world of e-learning the available technologies to make a course exciting are always charging, and course content can and should be updated quickly to give students the very latest information. Thus e-learning is faster, cheaper and potentially better.

E-learning in commerce can be done with different methods as Blogs, World Wide Web, Social Networking, Video, Conferencing, Podcast etc.

Blogs

A blog (sometimes referred to as a weblog) is a web publishing tool that allows authors to quickly and easily self-publish facts, artwork, links to other blogs or websites and a whole array of other content. Blog is short for web log. It is a big like an online diary or journal, except blogs aren't necessary private, instead they're created for an audience. And just like a diary or journal a blog is relaxed, making it an easy and comfortable way for students to get writing.

Blogs are written on all kinds of topics. Readers can usually leave comments, which lead to discussions about the blog's content.

Using Blogs to Integrate Technology in the Classroom

We all know that in the present era, internet becomes an increasingly pervasive and persistent influence in people's live, the phenomenon of the blog stands out as a fine example of the way in which the web enables individual participation in the market place of ideas. Teachers can use blogs to publish assignments, resources, and keep students and even parents up-to-date on class event, due dates, and content being covered. The education blog can be a powerful and effective technology tool for students and teachers alike.

Educational Benefits of Blogs

In addition to providing teachers with an excellent tool for communicating with students, there are numerous educational benefits of blogs are:

1. Students can use blogs to publish their writing and educate others on a particular topic.
2. Highly motivating to students, especially those who otherwise might not become participants as classrooms.
3. Teachers can use blogs to help students' master content and improve their writing skills.
4. Effective forums for collaboration and discussion.
5. Powerful tool to enable scaffold learning or mentoring to occur.
6. Publish assignments, resources to keep students and even parents up-to-date.
7. Helps students become subject matter experts.

Using the Blog in the Classroom

The first step in blog creation is choosing a platform. A platform is where you build and publish your blog. Edublog.com is the number one site for education blogs. It lets you create and manage teacher and student websites. You can customise your design and even add photos, videos & podcasts. Kidblog.com is a safe, secure publishing platform designed for grades K-12. It is free for up to 50 students per class. Thus as an educational tool blogs may be integrated in a multi-faceted manner to accommodate all learners. It can serve the following functions in the classroom.

1. *Collaboration:* Blogs provide a space where teachers and students can work to further develop writing or other skills with the advantage of an instant audience. Teacher can offer instructional tips, and students can practice and benefit from peer review. Online mentoring is also possible. The older students can help the younger student in developing more confidence in their writing skills. The students can also participate in cooperative learning activities that require them to relay ideas or suggestions.

2. *Integrate Curriculum:* Blogs can be used across the curriculum. From Maths and Economics to Commerce and Science. It is a great way to take literary across the curriculum and it is a fact also that knowledge is not divided in different compartments. It is a complete whole.

3. *Classroom Management:* As blogs are easy to create and update efficiently, these can be used to inform students of class requirements, notices, post handouts and homework assignments or act as a question and answer board. These blogs can serve as a portal to foster a community of learners.

4. *Guidelines and Expectations:* On blogs you can develop clear goals, guidelines and expectations for you and your students. Guidelines can be published and updated right on your class blog for easy access by students and parents.

5. *Development of Writing Skills:* Blogs not only require subject knowledge, these also help in developing good writing skills. Even if you are using blogs in commerce, you should sit some issue aside to teach a bit of writing and grammar.

6. *Discussions:* A blog opens the opportunity for students to discuss topics outside of the classroom. With a blog, every person has an opportunity to share their thoughts and opinions. Students have time to be reaching to one another and reflective. Teachers can also bring together a group of knowledgeable individuals for a given unit of study for students to network and conference within a blog.

7. *Commenting:* Initially, it is a good idea to teach students the dos and don'ts of commenting on the blogs. The teacher should encourage students to contribute quality comments while discouraging put down and inappropriate language. Monitor comments and provide feedback.

8. *Warning about Plagiarism:* The teacher should explain the students that plagiarism will not be tolerated. Students must contribute their own work. They should not post copyrighted images. If you want to post, then include a site there.

9. *Consistency:* Blogging takes commitments. If posts are haphazardly published, student interest will most likely decline. The idea is to keep building and expanding.

10. *Student Portfolios:* Blogs present, organised and present student work as digital portfolio. As older entries are achieved, developing skills and progress may be analysed more conveniently. Additionally as students realise their efforts will be published they are typically more motivated to produce better writings.

11. Increases student interest and ownership of learning.
12. Gives students legitimate chances to participate.
13. Provides opportunities for diverse perspectives, both within and outside the classroom.

As with most new ventures, there is also a learning curve with blogging. Manoeuvring platforms to create one or more blogs while also mentoring students and class blogs can be time-consuming. But there is a good chance most of our students will be excited about blogging and will want to take more responsibility, perhaps for some extra credit.

The traditional classroom system is changing nationwide, current and future careers are dependent on strong computer skills, blogging helps the students develop necessary skills for their continuing education and gainful employment. Consider the world of blogging as a creative, fun way to bridge literacy and across the curriculum and cover other learning standards at the same time. Thus we can think of a blog as a web based multi-media publishing system, which is very low cost (often face), easy to use, customisable in terms of appearance, content, target audience and hyperlinked to other content over the internet #. All these features highlight the great potential of blogs as a teaching- learning tool facilitating the integration of traditional education system.

It promotes learning styles, i.e. autonomous, reflective and active learning. It has high versatility, both in face and distance teaching. Blogs should not be seen merely as a technological tool for teaching and learning but as a situated practice that must be brought into appropriate alignment with particular pedagogical and disciplinary practise. A model of blogging as a networked approach to learning suggests that blogging might achieve best results across the curriculum not through isolated use in individual units.

Elde and Eide, experts in brain structure and function, work with children with learning difficulties. They discuss the following functions of blogs:

- Blogs can promote critical and analytical thinking.
- Blogging can be a powerful promoter of creative, intuitive and associational thinking.
- Blogs promote analogical thinking.
- Blogging is a useful medium for increasing access and exposure to quality information.
- Blogging constitutes the best of solitary perfection & social interaction.

Social Networking

Social networking is a software that allows people to come together around an idea or topic of interest. In a quite short period of time, social networking have been a marked effect on colleges and schools, on teaching and learning. Schools should reflect the world we live in today. And we live in a social world. We need to teach students how to be effective collaborator in that world, how to interact with people around them, how to be engaged, informed 21st century citizens. At the institutional level, tertiary sectors and secondary sector vibrating needs innovative social networking sites for knowledge mapping, managing knowledge, collaboration, self-directed learning and multiple reflective learning. ICT tools are also playing vital role in the institution for such tasks as accounting, inventing content, communicating document preparation and printing.

Sometimes question is raised that faculty and students in routine use Facebook, Twitter and other social media in their personal lives, so how might those same tools be put to academic use? We need to teach kids the powerful ways networking can change the way they look at education, not just their social lives. We don't talk enough about the incredible power of social networking technology to be used for academic benefit. Let's change the terms. Let's not call it social networking but we can call it academic networking.

11. Power Point Presentation

Power point is a presentation programme known as MS Power Point. It has become the world's most widely used presentation graphic programme. It runs on Microsoft Windows and the Mac OS computer operating system.

It was initially developed in 1984 by Forethought, Inc., Sunnyvale, California, for the Macintosh computer. In 1987, Forethought was bought by Microsoft and seesaw Microsoft's Graphics Business Unit, which continued to further develop the software.

In present scenario it has become the most popular presentation software. It is regarded by many as the most useful and accessible way to create and present visual aids to the audience. Supporters and critics generally agree that the use of presentation software can save a lot of time for people who otherwise could have used other types of visual aids—hand-drawn or mechanically type set slides, white boards, charts, models, OHP etc. Ease of use also encourages those who otherwise would not have used visual aids. These help in use of various presentation material like text, graphic, pictures, charts, tables, diagrams, movies, animation, sound and Internet to share information. Users can easily and quickly create presentation for lectures, research reports, meeting handouts, speaker's note and outline etc.

Power Point can be an effective tool to present the subject matter in the classroom and encourage students' learning. For example, in Accounts class, a single Power Point Presentation would project the process of maintaining debit-credit record, questions which students ask about the Balance Sheet, a chart of related terms, and a mini-quiz about what was just discussed that provides students with information that is visually challenging and engaging.

It has become an integral part of many instructional settings, particularly in large classes. It has many advantages and disadvantages as:

Advantages

1. *Useful in large classes:* If we see in Indian situation, many times the size of the class is big and it becomes difficult for a teacher to handle the class by using some visual aids as chart, model etc. Power Point slides are generally easier to see by a large audience when projected.

2. *Quick and Easy:* The teacher can quickly and easily master the subject matter with the help of slides. He can present the subject matter in an organised way.

3. *Easy to create an attractive design:* Sometimes the teacher does not have much knowledge about the basic graphic design principles as well as he is not good in art, then with the help of power point by using standard templates and themes he can create colourful and attractive design to make the slides more appealing and students will take interest in the subject matter.

4. *Easy to modify:* When a teacher uses handouts in the class then it becomes very difficult to do some changes in that, if needed, but when the teacher uses power point presentation, he can make changes several times according to the requirements.

5. *Easy to re-order:* The sequence in many visual aids as graph, chart, pictures cannot be changed as per the requirement but with a simple drag and drop or using key strokes, he can move slides to re-order the presentation.

6. *Easy to present:* The teacher can easily advance the slides in the presentation one after the other with a simple key stroke or by using remote. While doing it, he can maintain eye contact with the students. On the other hand, if the teacher is using the whiteboard in the class, every time he has to turn towards it to write something on it and the students can create indiscipline in the class.

7. *Easy to carry:* Power Point presentation is portable. You can download it in pendrive, or CD etc. Wherever you want you can carry it with you. Thus, it can be easily shared with students and colleagues.

8. *Support Multimedia:* Power point presentations not only contain the text material but also multimedia as video, audio, images and animations.

Disadvantage or Limitations

Some people are not the supporters of using power point presentations believing that it has its own mind set which forces presenters to spend countless hours of thinking in developing slides. The following limitations may be there as:

1. *Need of equipment:* The basic equipment required to present are laptop/ Desktop/Smart board, LCD projector for projection equipment, electricity to run all these equipments. Sometimes these equipments are not available in every school and in each classroom.

2. *Power Point excess:* Sometimes teachers use the presentation only as a compulsion by the authorities. Such teachers create presentations, so they have the slides to present rather than outlining, organizing and focusing on the message.

3. *Design:* The teacher should have the basic knowledge of designing the presentations. Sometimes the slides made by the teachers give the illusion of content and coherence, when in fact there is not much substance or connection between the different points on the slides in reality.

4. *Over simplification of subject matter:* There is a set procedure of framing and presenting the Power Point slides. Sometimes the linear nature of Power Point forces the teacher to reduce complete subject matter to a set of bullet items that are too weak to support decision-making or show the complexity of the subject matter.

5. *Focus on medium, not message:* Many teachers forget that they are making a presentation first and that Power Point is just a tool, so they frame the unnecessary slides which are not meaningful and fruitful to give the message regarding the

subject matter. They try to use all the features of Power Point in one presentation. Too many flying letters, animations and sound effects without seeing much original thought or analysis can be a real issue. In such type of presentations the medium shoves the message aside.

6. *Less classroom interaction:* Power Point presentations can reduce the opportunity for classroom interaction. It will be possible when the teacher is using only the PPTs to disseminate the information to the students.

7. *Less scope for creative teaching:* Sometimes the teacher feel easy to utilise the PPTs in the classroom to present the subject matter. These can drive the instruction and minimize the opportunity for spontaneity and creative teaching. Besides using PPT, the teacher can use different methods to make the teaching learning process effective.

Points to remember while creating an effective Power Point Presentation

- Plan carefully
- Knowledge about your students
- Available time for the presentation
- Practice your presentation
- Speak comfortably and clearly
- Essential points to be covered in the presentation
- Availability of required equipment in classroom.

Effective Power Point Slides

- Avoid text dense slides—better to have more slides than trying to place too much text on one slide.
- Use brief points instead of long sentence or paragraph.
- Use Italics, bold and colour for emphasizing content.
- Use of a light background with dark type face or a dark background with light type face.
- Avoid using underlines for emphasis which typically signifies hypertext to digital media.
- Include only necessary information.
- Use design template.
- Content should be self evident.
- Be consistent with effects, transitions and animations.
- Too many slides should be avoided.
- Font size should be large enough. Titles and headings should not be less than 36-40 points and subtext not to be less than 32 points.
- Use clip art and graphics sparingly. Use graphics only when they support the content.
- Use 2-dimensional pie and bar graph rather than 3-D styles which can interfere with the intended message.
- Size and place of graph should be appropriate.
- Photographs can be effectively used to add realism.
- Add motion, sound and music only where necessary.
- Excessive movement within or between slides should be avoided.

Thus, Power Point presentations should be done carefully. Now we will discuss that how a teacher can enhance teaching and learning with Power Point.

Ways to Enhance Teaching and Learning

The main purpose behind using Power Point presentation is to make the subject matter more interesting and to enhance the learning of the learners. The teacher should use the following ways.

1. *Class Preparation:* The teacher can prepare the Power Point presentation depicting the salient points and content of the subject matter to be taught in the class. Lecture notes can be prepared as notes pages. The slides should not be over loaded.

2. *Students' Learning Preferences:* The presentation can be prepared by using colour, images, clip art, video and shapes for visual learners; sound and music for auditory learners means keeping the students' learning preferences in mind. Some slides should be based on intera sessions also.

3. *Type on Live Slides:* Power Point allows user to type side by side during slide show which will provides the chance to the learners for interaction. For this, students' comments and ideas can be used. It will help to remain active in the class.

4. *Just-on Time Course Material:* The teacher can make their slides and notes pages online. The students can take their print out before class and can understand meaningfully in the class while listening to the teacher. They will come prepared in advance for discussion in the class.

The teacher should keep the students engaged while doing the presentation by asking questions, brain storming, think pair share, two minutes proper note check, students' questions, asking muddiest points, most useful points etc. Thus, Power Point presentation is an effective way to enhance the learning of the learners and to make the subject matter of commerce interesting and understandable.

Thus, commerce is not a new subject, but it should be taught with the help of different audio visual aids. Today e-commerce, e-marketing are introduced in the curriculum and these can't be taught theoretically. The commerce subject is fully based on practical and directly related with business and market. The community itself has the capacity to provide a large number of teaching aids. The local newspapers, the national dailies, the economic and business magazines are all full of enrichment material for teaching of commerce. If the instructional materials are prepared neatly and used intelligently, then they can have a great impact on the minds of the students.

7

Effective Skills and Methods of Teaching Commerce

The National Education Policy 2020 envisages inclusive education while aiming to address the growing developmental imperatives of our country. With the fast-changing landscape and globally diverse ecosystem in education, it is becoming critical that one should not only learn but also know how to learn. Skills and methodology help in knowing this.

SKILLS

"Teachings skills are specific instructional activities and procedures that a teacher may use in his classrooms. These are related to various stages of teaching or in the continuous flow of the teacher performance." – *Gage*

The possession of skills is an essential feature of any profession. Skills provide means for professionals to put theoretical knowledge into practice. Effective teacher should possess skills and competencies that set him apart not only from non-professionals i.e. non-teachers but also from ineffective and inefficient teachers.

A method is a procedure, a personalised combination of basic facts. A skill is a mean of achieving a particular purpose. It is immediate means and incidental to a large purpose. In order to achieve certain objective of the subject, the teacher has to use different skills. It is a procedure that makes the learning and teaching more interesting and more effective. It initiates, stimulates and reinforces the process of learning.

These days an aim is to provide mass education. The teacher we need can be made available through appropriate education and training. Effective teachers cannot only do things in the classroom that others cannot but they can also understand the relationship between their action and the effects of those action on the students. The skills required by them can be taught, practised, evaluated, predicted and controlled. These skills can be acquired through education and training.

In the words of Macintyr and Whine, "Teaching skill is a set of related teaching behaviours which are specific types of classroom interaction situations tends to facilitate the achievement of specific educational objectives."

We assume that the effective teachers need three essential kinds of knowledge before they can teach the class confidently. These are knowledge of content; knowledge about the students they are going to teach and the learning process; and knowledge of teaching strategies. We know that learning is neither easy nor difficult. Teaching too is difficult as well as complex. The teaching skill is a set of strictly overt behaviour of the teacher (verbal and non-verbal) that can be observed, measured and modified.

Singh and Joshi has described that teaching skills have essentially following three components.

1. Perception: Teaching skills have a perceptual component for observing and receiving feedback. The teacher observers and selects appropriate skill to be acquired by him.

2. Cognition: It refers to the behaviour or experience of knowing in which there is some degree of awareness as in thinking and problem solving. Skills are thus cognitive strategies that allow the teachers to complete their assigned tasks *i.e.* teaching learning activities which they learn through education and training.

3. Action: Teaching skills demand every teacher to actually practise his perceived and acquired knowledge in an effective way in the classroom.

While using difficult methodology, the teacher can use different skills as explaining, illustrations, narration, etc. to make his teaching learning process more effective. The effective teacher must not only possess a good repertoire of skills, but also understand when and why to use certain skills. A skillful teacher understands that educational objectives require different teaching skills and behaviours.

Classification of Skills

There is no demarcation in different types of skills because all teaching skills are inter-related and have bearing on one another. The classification of skills according to the teacher tasks is as follows (Lalitha 1975).

Pre-Instructional Skills: This category includes the tasks performed by the teacher before he starts teaching. The teacher has to plan teaching activities and prepare and motivate the students to learn. The skills for deciding appropriate content and its organisation, pacing of delivery, grouping the students, identifying appropriate activities etc. belong to this category.

Instructional Skills: This category includes the tasks performed by the teacher during teaching in the classroom. The tasks related to setting the climate of classroom can be as presenting content, organising discussion, explanation, maintaining the motivation of the students, using audio-visual material, using blackboard, managing the classroom, etc.

Post-instructional Skills: These skills are used only after the delivery of the content i.e. actual teaching is over. The tasks involved are summarizing what is taught, giving assignments, providing feedback, testing and grading, etc.

Some of the teaching skills, which can be used by the teacher while teaching Commerce are:

Fig. 7.1: Teaching Skills

It should always be kept in mind that skills are means to end. While the development of skills is a vital part of the Commerce programme in terms of objectives, skills themselves do not constitute any part of the substance of Commerce content. The substances of the content are cognitive in nature. Skills are partly ways of dealing with this content and partly a way of life within the framework of the classroom and school. Now we will discuss these skills in detail.

Attempts have been made to list teaching skills. Alter and Ryan listed the following teaching skills at Stanford University in the U.S.A.

1. Stimulus variation
2. Set Induction
3. Closure
4. Teacher silence and non-verbal clues
5. Reinforcing pupil participation
6. Fluency in questioning
7. Probing questioning
8. Use of higher questions
9. Divergent question
10. Recognizing and attending behaviour
11. Illustrating and use of examples
12. Learning
13. Planned repetition
14. Completeness of communication

B.K. Passi has given the following list of Teaching skills in his book 'Becoming Better Teacher, Micro Teaching Approach'.

- Writing instructional objectives
- Introducing a Lesson.
- Fluency in questioning
- Probing questioning
- Explaining
- Illustrating with examples
- Stimulus variation
- Silence and non-verbal clues
- Reinforcement
- Increasing pupil participation
- Using blackboard
- Achieving closure
- Recognizing attending behaviour

NCERT (National Council of Educational Research and Training) in its publication Core Teaching Skills (1982) has laid stress on the following teaching skills:

1. Writing Instructional objectives
2. Organizing the content
3. Creating set for introducing the lesson
4. Introducing a lesson
5. Structuring classroom questions

6. Question delivery and its distribution
7. Response management
8. Explaining
9. Illustrating with examples
10. Using teaching aids
11. Stimulus variation
12. Use of blackboard
13. Promoting pupil participation
14. Pacing of the lesson
15. Giving assignments
16. Management of the class
17. Diagnosing pupil's learning difficulties and taking remedial measures.
18. Evaluating the pupil's progress.
19. Achieving closure of the lesson

Core Teaching Skills

It is not possible to train all the pupil teachers in all these skills in any training programme because of the constraint of time. Therefore, a set of teaching skills which cut across the subject has been identified. They can be very useful for every teacher. The set of these skills are known as Core Teaching Skills.

1. Skill of Introduction

Skill of introduction is also known as set-induction skill. This skill is concerned with the lesson's initiation. The success of every lesson depends on its introduction. If the starting (Introduction) of the lesson is good, it means the whole lesson will go on properly and the teacher will be known as effective and successful teacher. The skill of introducing the lesson may be defined as proficiency in the use of verbal and non-verbal behaviour, teaching aids and appropriate devices for making the pupil realize the need of studying the lesson. In introducing the lesson the creativity and imagination of the teacher plays an important role. The following components should be kept in mind while preparing the micro-lesson related to the skill of introducing the lesson.

Components of Introducing Skills

1. Previous Knowledge: The effective teaching should be based on principles and maxims of teaching. According to 'known to Unknown' maxim of teaching, pupil's new knowledge should be based on previous knowledge. If the new knowledge is presented before the students at once, it becomes very difficult to acquire it. If it is linked with the pupil's previous knowledge than the student will take interest in that new knowledge. With the help of testing the previous knowledge, teacher will be able to know about the student's level of knowledge. He/She can estimate that whether the level of knowledge is very high or very low or mediocre. On the basis of this level, he can bring changes in the lesson-plan.

2. Relationship between Subject-matter, Objectives and Statements: While introducing the lesson, the statements used should be related with the subject matter to be taught and that subject matter should be in relation to pre-determined objectives. If the teacher is not able to establish this relationship, his introduction of the lesson will not be effective. In this duration if the teacher becomes able to attract the students towards the concepts, ideas and objectives related to the subject matter, it means the effectiveness of teaching starts from it.

3. Proper Sequence: There should be coordination between the ideas, statements and questions used during introduction. This is possible only if there is a proper sequence. The use of uncoordinated statements will result in the disturbance in the process of understanding of the students.

4. Objectives and Aids: Appropriate aids are selected keeping in mind the objectives of the lesson. Use of one kind of aids brings monotony. It will not help in creating the interest of the students in the lesson. The various devices used for introducing the lesson are questioning, narration, examples, story-telling, drama, experiment and demonstration, and audio-visual aids, etc. But one thing should be kept in mind that the selection of all the devices and audio-visual aids should be according to the mental level of the students.

5. Duration of Introduction: While introducing the lesson, it should also be kept in mind that it should be neither too lengthy not too short. It should be confined to creation of interest and motivating the pupils.

6. Capability of Creating Interest and Motivation: The teacher should have the capability of creating interest and motivation in the pupils because if it is not so he can't be able to become an effective teacher and his teaching will become boring. The students will not take interest in learning the new lesson.

Thus, the teaching starts from introducing the lesson. If it is not proper and effective, the students will not take interest in the new knowledge due to lack of motivation.

2. Skill of Reinforcement

Reinforcement is psychological in nature. It is condition or situation which increases the probability of desirable responses and also decreases the probability of undesirable responses. It helps in influencing the responses or behaviour of the learner. It is not only used to promote learning but also to secure attention and provide greater motivation to the students. For this, the academic activities should be meaningful and worthwhile so that the students can get the intended benefits from them. For example, if the teacher approved the behaviour of the student in the class, it reveals that he feels initiative in instructional activities.

There are two types of reinforcement:

(i) Positive Reinforcement and

(ii) Negative Reinforcement

In this way, the reinforcement, in the teaching process, means use of such stimulus or their presentation or their removal so that the possibility of recurrence of some responses may increase.

Components of the Reinforcement Skills

There are four broad components of the skill of reinforcement, as under (*i*) *Positive Verbal Reinforcement:* It involves the use of verbal or linguistic expressions which reinforce learning just saying 'Good', 'Yes', 'Fine', 'Right', 'Excellent', 'Well done' after the student has answered can reinforce him. Teacher's utterances like 'aha', 'humm', etc. can encourage the student to continue with his answer. The statements accepting pupil feelings, repeating and rephrasing pupil responses, summarising pupil ideas, etc. fall in this component.

(*ii*) *Positive Non-verbal Reinforcement:* It involves the use of teacher's gestures in order to reinforce the pupil's behaviour. Nodding, smiling, moving towards the students, giving him an encouraging look, etc. are examples of positive non-verbal reinforces.

(*iii*) *Negative Verbal Reinforcement:* The use of certain undesirable reinforces can strengthen occurrence of a particular behaviour. Expressions like wrong, no, incorrect, not true, etc. are the examples of negative verbal reinforces.

(*iv*) *Negative Non-verbal Reinforcement:* The teacher uses this type of reinforces in order to make the students aware of certain undesirable behaviour. Frowning, nodding the head disapprovingly, moving away from the students, etc. are examples of negative non-verbal reinforces.

With the help of these components practised in the behaviour, the pupil teacher can get efficiency in this skill.

Precautions while Using the Reinforcement Skill

There is need to follow the following precautions while using this skill:

1. Different new statements should be used for reinforcement. A few statements should not be repeated again and again.
2. Too much use of reinforces should be avoided. Each and every response should not be reinforced.
3. Reinforcement should be for all children not only for those who respond or for brilliant children. In every class, there are shy students, they should also be reinforced. The students who do not participate in the class discussion or other activities should also be reinforced.
4. Proper words and statements should be used for reinforcement. The teacher should be impartial in providing reinforcement.

3. Skill of Probing Questions

The art of asking questions plays an important role in teaching learning process. Its success depends upon the desired answer (or Response) of the students. When the questions are asked, the students — according to their ability, type of questions, knowledge of the subject, behaviour of the teacher towards the students —, may respond in many ways as no response, partially incorrect response, wrong response, partially correct response or correct response, etc. How the students' responses should receive and how the teaching should take place on these bases is skill of probing questions. When a student does not give response or gives incorrect and wrong response then he is to be motivated to give correct response. For getting correct response, the teacher takes help of such questions which help the students to reach at the correct response on the basis of their previous knowledge. These questions help in searching the right response.

The skill that deals with student response, going deep into the students' knowledge by asking a series of questions, is called 'probing'. The main thing in this skill is that the teacher proceeds his teaching on the basis of the responses given by the students. Such probing questions are asked from the students that help in getting detailed knowledge of the subject matter. In this skill the stress is given to handling of the responses given by the students i.e. why Jangira and his associates named this skill as response management.

Components of the Probing Questions Skills

The components of this are:

1. Prompting: Sometimes students are unable to give the response of different questions, in that situation the teacher doesn't give response but gives clues or hints and helps the students by prompting them. These prompts can be in the form of questions which have answer in itself or by reframing the question or by asking question step by step or give suggestions or give hints, etc. Which type of technique is to be used in a situation depends on the previous experiences, maturity level, understanding of clues and the nature of responses given by students.

Example–

T What is business?

P No response.

T What it is called if some people are busy in producing things?

P Business.

2. Seeking Further Information: This component is used by the teacher when the student gives incomplete or partially correct response. The teacher expects from the student that he will complete his incomplete response. For this teachers should ask well prepared questions so that the student may give desired response for seeking further information, probing question can be asked in different ways as to give examples to clarify it, give reasons to prove it, explain it in detail, etc.

Example–

T What are the characteristics of business?

P Profit motive.

T What are the other characteristics?

3. Refocusing: Refocusing is used to initiate the student to make his response more correct, meaningful, clear and more effective. The main aim behind this is to make the student aware of the implications of a given response in more complex and novel situations. It helps in strengthening of the responses. The teacher relates the answer with the topic already taught. For example, the students are already familiar with the word advertisement.

T What do you mean by advertisement?

P A public announcement.

T How it can be useful in promoting business?

4. Redirection: Redirection is used when a student does not respond or gives incomplete answer. The teacher can change the form of question or ask the same question from the other student. The help taken from other students to reach at desired answer helps that student to learn correct answer. The main purpose behind it is to probe and increase student participation.

Example–

T What is human activity?

Ram No response.

Sohan An activity that a person performs.

5. Increasing Critical Awareness: When a student gives correct answer then this technique is used to increase the critical awareness of the student. The teacher asks questions to justify the students' response rationally. Therefore, the teacher can ask the reason behind the response, how can you prove it? How it can happen? Thus, it helps in understanding the subject matter and property utilising it.

Teacher pupil interaction is an integral part of most classroom instruction. The teacher can maintain and direct the interaction by the type of questions he/she asks and the kind of encouragement he/she gives. Two teaching skills, involving the ability to ask probing questions and offer accepting reactions, are especially helpful in eliciting and encouraging responses from pupils. In addition, these skills can be used by the teacher to test the level or degree of students' comprehension through:

(*a*) Discussion of classroom interchange techniques,
(*b*) Examples of probing questions and accepting responses,
(*c*) Examination of appropriate film transcript, and
(*d*) Communication exercises.

Read this schedule before planning and teaching your micro lesson on probing question:

1. Your questions were usually clearly understood by the pupils.
2. Your questions were usually coherently expressed.
3. You used pause after asking most of the questions.
4. You varied the pace at which you asked questions.
5. You directed some of your questions at individual pupil.
6. You distributed your questions amongst the whole group of pupils.
7. You used prompting techniques to help pupils formulate their answers.
8. You used probing techniques to help pupils think more deeply about their answers.

Thus, there are skills involved in asking questions. I suggest you use the term 'fact' and 'thought' questions when you are teaching the pupils about questions. A useful approach is to write on the chalkboard or OHP two lists of questions. One list should contain only simple 'fact' questions and other should consist of only 'thought' questions. Ask the pupils to look at the list and to work and find out what the difference is between them. Then ask them which type of questions they prefer and why. You will probably need to use directing and redirecting, prompts and probes to obtain answers to this question. The pupils should be asked to decide which are 'fact' and 'thought' questions by setting a simple exercise consisting of a list of ten simple questions. You should end the lesson by explaining that knowing what kinds of questions are being asked will help them to give better answers in class.

4. Skill of Explaining

What does a teacher do most frequently during a lecture? Obviously, he/she spends most of the time 'explaining something to students'. But exactly what is explaining? According to Brown and Hatton (1982), explaining is "giving understanding to another person".

The act of explaining usually involves a teacher, one or more students and the subject matter. Thus there are three corresponding elements to take note of:

(*i*) The teacher's skill in explaining,

(*ii*) The students' background, interest and thinking skill, and

(*iii*) The nature of the subject matter.

An effective explanation is pivotal on its delivery. Therefore, the teacher should choose the words carefully and present the information in an appropriate order. Because students usually have to sit through many periods in a day, it is important that the teacher's explanation stimulates students' interest in the subject matter. This could be achieved by using metaphors and/or examples, humour and creating opportunities to apply what is being taught.

The nature of most classrooms explanations can be divided into these categories namely, 'what', 'how', and 'why'. When teachers explain the 'what' to students, the main aim is often to deliver basic knowledge to the group in the most economical way. This type of explanation often stresses on the 'definition'.

For example, to answer the question "what is double entry system?" the teacher may start by explaining:

"This system seeks to record every transaction in money or money's worth in its double aspect. The receipt of a benefit by one account and the surrender of a like benefit by another A/C." Essentially, the teacher's attempt to explain what double entry system is now become a definition. Students may mistakenly think that they have learnt something about double entry system but in fact they only have a minimal understanding of the concept.

Explanation based on 'how' questions are concerned with structures, processes or procedures. Specially most 'How' questions in the classroom address the mechanism by which things work. With respect to the above example, the question could be "how it works?" This lead to the explanation of it follows set rules, personal and impersonal A/C, preparation of trial balance, preparation of final accounts.

Explanation to 'why' questions are especially important to help students to understand the subject matter. Such explanations identify reasons, causes, motivation and justification for ideas or behaviour. In relation to double entry system, a good 'why' question is: Why should double entry system be adopted? The explanation here requires an understanding of advantages as — scientific system, complete record of transactions, less possibility of fraud and mistakes, possibility of comparative study and facility of adjustments.

So what makes an explanation effective? An effective explanation should address all these types of questions: 'what', 'why' and 'how'. In addition, the information must be appropriately required to transit smoothly from the type of explanation to another.

Components

A good explanation is one which is understood by the pupils. It has some components and can be divided into desirable and undesirable categories. It the teacher wants to make his explanation more effective, he has to increase the occurrence of desirable behaviours and avoid the use of undesirable behaviours.

I. Desirable Behaviours: The teacher should practise the following desirable behaviours in order to master the skill of explaining. These are:

1. Use of Introductory Statements: With the help of introductory statements, the teacher is to announce the topic or concept of which he is going to explain in the class. It helps in creating mental alertness and readiness in the class to listen to what is going to be explained. These statements provide background to the explanation.

Example: As all of us know that there is need of ethics for the betterment of the society, so, in the same way business ethics are needed to run the business effectively. Ethics means the ideals which motivate an individual to work honestly.

2. Use of Explaining Links: There are certain link words which increase the effectiveness of explanation. Such links make explanation clear by bringing continuity in statements. The teacher should use appropriate explaining links to make his explanation effective and understandable. A few examples of explaining links are 'if', 'then', 'but', 'hence', 'due to', etc.

Example: Business ethics means discharging of responsibilities *in respect of* all the parties related to business.

3. Use of Visual Techniques: The teacher can make his explanation effective with the use of some visual techniques as, charts, diagrams, pictures, etc. The students can better understand the concepts with the help of these visual techniques by using their different sense organs.

4. Covering Essential Points: The explanation will be complete in itself if the teacher covers all the essential points as specified in instructional objectives in her explanation.

5. Interesting: The students will be able to learn effectively if the explanation is interesting. The teacher can make the explanation interesting by providing different examples from the daily life of the economy or society. He can use different media of communication also.

6. Defining Technical Words: Sometimes a topic consists of difficult technical and ambiguous terms then it is the responsibility of the teacher to explain these technical words in a simple, easy and understandable language otherwise students may not be able to understand the subject matter. In commerce some technical words are — Insurance, cargo insurance, liability insurance, freight insurance, etc.

7. Testing Pupil's Understanding: If the teacher wants to test whether the students have understood the subject matter or not then he is to ask some questions. But the teacher should take the precaution that only a few questions should be asked.

8. Use of Concluding Statement: When the teacher is to finish his lesson, then he is to conclude it with some statements. These statements give a consolidated picture of what has been explained to the students.

II. Undesirable Behaviours: There are some behaviours that the teacher should avoid while explaining any concept:

1. Use of Irrelevant Statements: Those statements which are not related to the concept being explained and which do not help in understanding the concept by the students should be avoided. It is because such statements create confusion and distract the attention of the students.

2. Lack of Continuity: Lack of continuity in explanation makes it difficult for the pupils to understand the concept. A continuity is generally broken in the following situations:

* When the statements are irrelevant.
* When there is no sequence either of place or of space or of time.
* When new information is introduced without relating it to the previous knowledge of the students.
* When the statement is not logically related to the previous statement.

3. Lack of Fluency: It is related to the flow of interrupted statements for explaining a concept. If the teacher speaks half of sentence and reformulate in the midst of the sentence, it disturbs fluency of the explanation. When a teacher uses fumbling ideas or inappropriate words or statements, it distracts students' attention from the subject matter they are learning.

4. Use of Vague Words or Phrases: Some expressions which may not clear the concept or the idea are called vague. The use of such words and phrases hinders the clarity of explanation. Examples of some vague words or phrases are: *theek hai*, understood, as you know, I mean, etc.

5. Use of Inappropriate Vocabulary: Sometimes in explanation, teacher uses inappropriate vocabulary not according to the mental age and chronological age of the students. It makes the explanation ineffective and difficult.

Thus, if the teacher wants to make his/her explanation effective, understandable, interesting and according to the mental age of the students, then, these components should be kept in mind. Simple and comprehensive language should be used. The speed of the explanation should confirm to the linguistic abilities of the pupils. It these components are take care of, then only the teacher can be able to fulfill the aims of the lesson.

5. Skill of Illustration with Examples

To illustrate means to make a point or idea clear and intelligible. It means to explain or to elucidate or exemplify ideas with the help of verbal or non-verbal aids as examples, figures, comparisons or some concept material like chart, diagram, etc. Sometimes when the teacher teaches some abstract concept, thought or any concept of accounts, then, mere explanation does not help the students to understand the concept. They need more than explanation. Such demand of students fulfills when the teacher uses some illustrations to make clear that concept, thought or theory. Illustrations mean the employment of those aids which will make ideas clear to the children and help them acquire correct knowledge. They make the subject matter clear, simple and understandable. They help in securing attention of the students towards the subject matter and result in better learning. The value of illustrations depends upon the skill with which easy and familiar things can be used to explain new and difficult ideas in the subject.

Types of Illustrations

Mainly there are two types of illustrations:

1. Non-verbal Illustrations: These illustrations act directly through senses. They may be called as non-verbal, concrete, material or objective illustrations.

2. Verbal Illustrations: These are illustrations which influence the mind through the medium of related ideas expressed in words. Their chief function is to make clear the meaning of a general statement or an abstract idea by the aid of verbal examples, analogies, etc. These can be divided into three categories:

(*i*) Similes and words.
(*ii*) Analogies and comparisons.
(*iii*) Stories, anecdotes and descriptions.

Components

Some questions arise in our mind that whether all examples help in understanding the abstract concept? If not, then what are the chief characteristics of these examples? The knowledge of these characteristics will help the teacher to make meaningful examples for the students.

Examples provide important contribution in the process of teaching learning because they help in taking the students from unknown to known. Examples make the subject matter interesting and provide motivation to the students to learn. It has following components:

1. Formulating Simple Examples: Simple is a relative term. One example can be simple for 12th class but it can be difficult for 6th class. In the same way an example can be simple for the urban students but difficult for rural students. One example may be simple for one country's students but difficult for the students of other country. So while formulating simple examples for the students, then age level, grade level, previous experiences, family background should be kept in mind. The students' participation in asking questions will be an authenticity of the examples being simple.

2. Formulating Relevant Examples: Sometimes teacher presents such type of examples which have no concern with the topic discussed or the examples are again to be explained to understand them. Such examples are not fruitful for the learning of the students.

3. Formulating Interesting Examples: Interesting examples are those which attract the attention of the students and create curiosity among the student. Interesting is a relative term. An examples which is interesting for the students of 11th class may not be meaningful for 6th class. So, the teacher should keep in mind the age level, grade level and maturity level of the students while formulating examples. The encouragement, curiosity, behaviour of the students are the criterion of the example to be interesting.

4. Using Different Medium for Presenting Examples: The examples can be categorised on the basis of their presentation–

- *Visual Examples:* In this the illustrations in the form of such types of objects are given which can be seen with the help of eyes. Chart, model, diagrams come in this category.

- *Auditory Examples:* This category includes examples in the form of story-telling, explanation of events, etc.
- *Actual Examples:* This category includes the presentation of an actual object in the form of examples.

There is no proper media to give examples in the class. Mainly two types of medium can be used as:

(*i*) *Non-verbal Medium*: Sometimes to clear the concept, thought, or an idea there is need of showing original objects or somewhat similar objects which help in developing the interest of the students in the subject matter. They can be as:

(*a*) *Use of objects:* In general, the use of actual objects in the class to clarify the subject matter provides effective learning. Means of communication, Ledger Books, Journals, etc. can be used while teaching commerce which will help in providing first hand experiences to the students.

(*b*) *Use of Models:* Very often it is not possible to bring actual object in the class and still more difficult to take the children out to show actual place or thing, like to give an idea of Bank, an industry, etc. Here model can be used to provide learning experiences to the students. These will help in making the subject matter interesting. These will help in teaching of any principle, theory, law or concept.

(*c*) *Diagrams, Maps and Charts:* A commerce teacher should be able to make his own devices of teaching. While planning to teach a difficult term in business studies, he can easily illustrate it by drawing a diagram on the chalk-board. One of the essential qualities of a commerce teacher is the ability to draw diagrams, showing of maps and charts whenever they are needed.

(*d*) *Picture, Photographs and Posters:* Sometimes it is difficult to bring actual object or model in the class, then the teacher can use pictures, photographs or posters. This type of material is economic and easily available. The internal trade and international trade commodities can be explained with the help of pictures and photographs. Business ethics can be illustrated with the help of posters.

(*ii*) *Verbal Medium:* Verbal medium means that the teacher uses words to classify thoughts, concepts, principles, laws related to business activities in the class. Some important verbal mediums are as follows:

(*a*) *Examples:* In illustration skills examples play an important role. The accounts can be made understandable with the help of examples only.

(*b*) *Verbal Pictures:* When a picture is captioned with words then it is known as verbal picture and the teacher can explain it easily because sometimes without caption the students are not able to understand that picture.

(*c*) *Comparisons:* Sometimes the teacher compares two concepts, principles or ideas to make them more clear as e-commerce and e-business.

(*d*) *Story:* Business activities or accounts can be classified with the help of story-telling.

5. *Use of Different Approaches:* Different approaches are needed to use verbal

and non-verbal mediums for presentation of examples as:

(*i*) *Inductive Approach*: Teacher gives different examples to clarify any theory in the class and the students are motivated to make generalizations or to give other related information. This approach is known as inductive approach. In this approach principles of known to unknown, specific to general, etc. are followed. The teacher should use simple, interesting and related examples to make the subject matter understandable.

(*ii*) *Deductive Approach*: In this approach, the teacher states the idea, concept, principle or law and then gives examples to illustrate it. In this teacher goes from general to specific, abstract to concrete.

Both the approaches can be used simultaneously also. For example, with the inductive approach firstly the concept is explained with illustrations and then on the basis of deductive approach by telling the concept and analysing the illustrations and examples given by students, the learning level of the concepts is to be developed. Thus, the use of both approaches in illustration with examples will be more effective.

Importance of Illustrations

1. With the illustrations, concrete description to the abstract ideas and thoughts is possible.
2. They are useful for the young children, as they do not indulge in abstract thinking.
3. It develops the retention power of the students.
4. Teacher can stimulate the imagination of the students by using illustrations.
5. Illustrations help in the cultivation of the power of observation and judgement and provide training to the sense to greater acuteness of perception.
6. Illustrations help the teacher in emphasising any particular point in the lesson.
7. They help in breaking the dullness of the lecture and make students attentive.
8. Illustrations make the instructions complete.
9. They help in simplifying and giving explanation.
10. Illustrations in the form of comparisons, examples or analogies make the subject matter interesting.

Precautions while Using Illustrations

1. Illustrations should be exact and accurate.
2. Use of many illustrations should be avoided.
3. These should be prepared in advance.
4. They should be interesting, stimulating and according to the mental level of the students.
5. Technical vocabulary and hyperbola should not be used.
6. Students should be motivated to observe illustrations well.
7. They should be used properly at proper time.
8. They should be self-explanatory, obvious and meaningful.
9. Use of metaphors and conceits should also be avoided.

10. There should be variety and novelty in the illustrations.

Thus, illustrations should be wisely selected, effectively prepared, timely presented and interestingly used. They should be understandable.

6. Skill of Stimulus Variation

Stimulus means something that helps to develop better or more quickly, in other words, something that produces a reaction in human beings. Student's learning advances with the increase in the relevant sources of information. The child directly perceives every situation and tries to receive relevant information. Psychologically it has been proved that the learner should be attentive to the information if he wants to learn something. Teaching depends upon the stimulus provided by the teacher during teaching because it is his responsibility to think that what, when and how much change in behaviour is required for sustaining and securing attention of the students in the class and it is known as skill of stimulus variations.

Stimulus variation means that we are deviating from the standard habitual teacher behaviour. It involves both verbal and non-verbal stimuli. Examples of stimuli would be things like movement, gesture, focussing, interaction with students, pausing and shifting sensing. For example, many teachers use their hands when they are talking and explaining things.

A good teacher goes on varying the stimulus in order to bring in variety in his/her teaching. It generates interest among students towards their learning and helps in their academic achievement i.e. why the teachers are trained in movements, gestures, focusing, etc.

The skill of stimulus variation is based on the principle that changes in the stimulus in one's perception capture the attention. It has been observed that it is difficult for one to attend the same stimulus for more than a few minutes and in some cases a few seconds and even less. The teacher should imbibe in himself the capabilities of attracting and holding the attention of the students. He should deliberately change his attention drawing behaviour in the class.

The teacher can attract the attention of the students with the help of different activities and behaviour.

Components of Skill of Stimulus Variation

One of the areas of effective teaching that is very important but quite difficult to prepare is knowing how to approach subject delivery. The other thing which is certain is that an organized and pre-planned lesson will have an edge over many aspects. Stimulus variation enhance the teaching learning process manifold. It is normally a variation and application of systematic techniques in three main areas:

1. Personal Teaching Styles (Teacher's Mannerism)
2. Media and Materials of Instructions (Resources) and
3. Teacher students Interaction (Inter-personal communication)

The idea of variation is closely linked with variety since changes introduced in teaching inevitably lead to instructions characterized by variety. Variation is more inclined towards actual process. The main objectives of stimulus variations are to make teaching skill more professional and demanding. The impact of this skill is concerned basically with:

- Arousing Student's attraction and further sustain it.
- Motivating learning through new exploration and investigation.
- Promoting edu-tainment (Education + entertainment)
- Promoting learning by involving students.
- Catering to individual sensory preferences and facilitating learning.
- Building positive feelings towards teachers and school.

I. *Variations in Personal Teaching Styles:* Variation in teacher's manner can be infinite. The change could be instant or otherwise. If carefully executed, these changes can be very effective and productive. The impact and efficiency also depends on the teacher's showmanship. Teacher's behaviour includes the following elements:

1. Modulation: Modulated voice with loud and slow pitch according to the situation brings greater impact in attracting attention of the students. A pleasant conversational talking style is best for the teacher to adopt and this will naturally include moderate vocal variation. Students often like a kind of voice that is friendly, free, smooth and agreeable to hear. However, the teacher should dramatize an event, emphasize points and relate quietly to individual in the classroom.

2. Focusing: Focusing is narrowing student's attention to a particular point or an object. This is often accompanied by gestural focusing where the teacher points to an object or taps the table for emphasis. This will help to focus attention on a point.

3. Pausing: As required, insertion of space for silence in the teacher's talk and teaching activity is yet another focusing device. Before starting a lesson, a teacher should pause for a few seconds which will focus the attention of students. This will doubly increase the lesson objective it captures attention by changing the stimulus from one of noise to silence.

4. Eye Contact: The teachers should shift his/her gaze around the classroom, possibly meeting every student's eye with his/her's, establishing positive relationship and avoiding impersonality. The teacher can gain cues on student's interest and understanding. It can also be used to help convey information, reinforcement and agreement.

5. Gesturing: Variation on facial expressions, bodily movement and hand gesturing are very important aspects of communication. The impact of gesture synchronized with variation in voice and words will yield tremendous positive results in teaching; not only conveying information but helping convey the meaning of oral message.

6. Movement: The movement of the teacher in the teaching space helps sustain students' attention and also personalize his/her teaching. As the occasion demands, the teacher needs to move back and forth, left and right, behind and beside the pupils.

The most important point which should be kept in mind is that these stylistic variations must be purposefully employed and executed, and not overdone. It is a fact that teachers can overplay or otherwise under play their roles; in either of these cases, the teaching will not be effective.

II. *Variation in the Media and Materials:* The media and material of instructions may be listed into these broad components on the basis of the predominantly secondary mode of communication and the type of effect they yield.

1. Aural – Concerned with hearing / audio.
2. Visual – Concerned with sight / vision, and
3. Tactile – Concerned with touch.

Alternating between these components necessitates a large number of sensory adjustments for high level of attention. The novelty or materials and the technical delivery encourage the curiosity and motivation of the students.

1. Aural Variation: The teacher's voice is the most common mode of communication in every classroom anywhere. This general aural mode needs sufficient voice modulation and abundant switching with visual and tactile media. Anything recorded could be gainfully introduced into a relevant situation. Student(s) own voice can be taped and played.

2. Visual Variation: Visual variation can be used as an added advantage. Simple objects like chalk board, sketches, pictures, bulletin board, film, T.V. items, library, resources, field trip etc. can enrich and enhance teaching.

3. Tactile Variation: The final element of variability related to media and material is the teacher's provision of opportunity for the pupils to touch and manipulate real objects and materials of the instructions. They could involve children in construction or modelling activities.

III. *Interaction Variation: Change in teacher-students communication:* Change in general pattern of interaction with students will definitely produce a very effective situation in teaching-learning process. Some of the teachers are very conventional and traditional ones. They are the sort of pedagogical terrors. Of course, the pattern of interaction may range from a situations dominated by teacher talk to a situation where students work independently of teacher. The teacher might provide opportunities for students, possibly working in pairs and small groups to exchange ideas, ideals, thoughts, opinions and problem through exposition, discussion or demonstration without teacher's intervention.

The teacher should create a friendly atmosphere in the classroom for a healthy teaching learning process. Students should feel that their opinions are also taken account of. They also should feel that their right of sitting in the class, right to learn, and right of individuality is duly taken care of and protected.

Therefore, the teacher should take utmost care of the students' individuality through genuinety:

- accepting their feelings.
- accepting the ideas of the students.
- solving problems.
- counselling.
- praising and encouraging them.
- asking questions.
- giving direction.
- taking their opinion into account.

The teacher may vary the cognitive activities of the students by moving from levels of their intellect and understanding. Besides listening to the teacher, pupils may contribute is small buzz-groups, discussion, projects, seminars, and mock sessions or in various learning activities. Therefore, the degree of dominance by the either side – teacher or student – is perfectly balanced, invigorating the teaching learning process.

Thus, the skill of stimulus variation can be in the following ways:

1. Kinetic variation
   - Teacher movements
   - Volume variation
   - Get into space
   - Move behind
2. Focusing
   - Verbal as this is important, write it down
   - Gestural as point out, bang on the desk.
   - Verbal-Gestural-point out and look at it.
3. Shifting Interaction
   - Teacher to student
   - Student to teacher
   - Student to student
   - Teacher to student to teacher to student
4. Pausing
5. Shifting sense
   - Hearing
   - Seeing
   - Feeling
   - Tasting
   - Smelling

Thus, all the individuals have different movement styles, actions, gestures and expression as they are different and they use different speech styles and tones. Unless this skill is well understood by the teacher, the students will miss the essence of teaching and teaching remains incomplete. It is essential that all possible stimulus variations in accordance to the situations be purposefully employed with smoothness and continuity.

7. Skill of Classroom Management

You must be aware that learning is effective if the children actively participate in the learning activities of the class. The main purpose of the skill is to achieve the maximum participation of pupils in the development of the lesson.

Components of the Skill

1. Calling pupils by their names: Pupils are attentive when they are called by their names by the teacher. Though this seems to be simple but has great significance in obtaining pupil participation. Good pupil participation controls the learning activities.

2. Making Norms of Class Room Behaviour: It includes the pinpointed instructions by the teacher to the pupils.

(*i*) Stand up and answer when you are asked a question.
(*ii*) Raise hands if you know the answer to the question.
(*iii*) Never give group response.
(*iv*) Listen to the teacher attentively when he / she is teaching.

3. Giving Clear Directions: Here the teacher gives clear directions to the pupils to follow the norms of the classroom behaviour. They should not be engaged in any other activity when the teaching is going on in the class.

4. Ensuring Sufficient work for each child: The teacher should allot work to each child keeping in view the individual differences. This act of teacher will prepare each child for active pupil participation.

5. Keeping pupils in eye span: After teaching the concept the teacher should check the effects of his / her teaching. He / she can assign some activity like drawing the diagram and labelling its parts or should ask some short questions. The teacher should go to each student to check his work. If needed, he should give instructions for further improvement.

6. Shifting from one teaching activity to another smoothly: While teaching any concept, the teacher is engaged in many academic activities as explaining, illustrating, questioning, etc., so, he should smoothly change from the activity to another. Before shifting the activity, the teacher must ensure himself that the concept under study has been followed by the pupils.

7. Recognising and Reinforcing Attending Behaviour: The teacher should use verbal and non-verbal (nodding head) for the correct response of the pupil. This type of the behaviour of the teacher is very effective to stimulate classroom learning environment.

8. Checking Inappropriate Behaviour Immediately: It means that if the student is not behaving properly in the learning situation or may not be attentive to the teacher, then he / she should be immediately checked. He should be directed to behave properly to the needs of the situations. This will increase the attending behaviour of the pupil leading the teacher to better management of the class.

The practice of the skill does not need any sort of lesson planning. It may be practised simply by keeping the above components in view.

Integration of Teaching Skills

For effective teaching there is need of integration of teaching skills. It involve the following steps:

1. Perceive and analyse the teaching situation.
2. Select and organise appropriate skills in effective response to produce best results.
3. The teacher should be innovative in his / her approach of teaching.

The teaching should be such as to enable students to identify themselves with the subject matter. The teaching should encourage learning habits. It should raise the standard of students work. It should encourage students to bring their critical and reflective skills to bear on the topic they are studying.

INSTRUCTIONAL STRATEGIES AND METHODS

Teaching methods are best articulated by answering the question, "What is the purpose of education?" and "What are the best ways of achieving these purposes?" For much of pre-history, educational methods were largely informal, and consisted of children imitating or modelling their behaviour in that of their elders — learning through observation and play. In this sense the children are the students, and the elder is the teacher. A teacher creates the course material to be taught and then enforces it. Pedagogy is usually the different ways a teacher can teach. It is the art or science of being a teacher, generally referring to strategies of instruction or style of instruction resources that help teachers to teach better are typically a lesson plan, or practical skill involving learning and thinking skills.

For effective teaching to take place, a good method must be adopted by a teacher. A teacher has many options when choosing a *style* to teach by. The teacher may write lesson plans of his own, or borrows plans from other teachers. When decided what teaching method to use, teacher will need to consider students' background, knowledge, environment, and learning goals. Teachers know that students learn in different ways but almost all students will respond well to praise. Students have different ways of absorbing information and of demonstrating their knowledge. Teachers often use techniques which cater to multiple learning styles to help students to retain information and strengthen the understanding. A variety of strategies and methods are used to ensure that all students have equal opportunities to learn.

After 3000 B.C., with the advent of writing, education became more conscious or self-reflective, with specialized occupation referring particular skills and knowledge on how to be a describer, an astronomer etc. In his dialogues Plato describes the Socratic Method. It has been the intent of many educators, since then, such as the Roman Educator Quintilian, to find specific, interesting ways to encourage students to use their intelligence and help them to learn.

Some critical ideas in today's education environment include:

- Instructional Scaffolding
- Graphic Organizers
- Standardized Testing

"While only a small portion of faculty can be outstanding teachers, nearly all are capable of being responsible ones" —*Renner, Greenwood and Schott.*

In the words of William Lyon, "In my mind, teaching is not merely a life work, a profession, an occupation or a struggle but a passion. I love to teach as a painter loves to paint, as a musician loves to play and as a strong man rejoices to run a race."

In the words of Epestin, "What all the great teachers appear to have in common is love of their subject, an obvious satisfaction in arousing this love in their students, and an ability to convince them that what they are being taught is deadly serious."

The instructional strategies are concerned with the ways and means of transmitting the content of the subject or the skills to the learner. The strategies are dependent on the input variables. Whatever are the capabilities of the learner in accordance with them the structure of knowledge of his subject matter is planned and the content transmitted.

The instructional strategy may extend from simple narration to an elaborate set up of teaching approach. In the elaborate approach the instructional strategies are based on input variable. This was referred to earlier as the preparation of the learner for receiving new knowledge. This step is followed by actual process of instruction. Here by techniques of questioning, exposition, narration, explanation, etc. are employed for the transmission of the content or knowledge of the subject matter. The use of various strategies can also be made at this stage.

Teaching entails learning. It is an activity which leads to learning. When we talk of method, model and strategies of teaching we are considering the functioning of the teaching process which leads to learning. Teaching is a process of building a person's mind and character through its methodology.

According to Scheffler, "Teaching is intended behaviour for which the aim is to induce learning."

Every learner at the entry point of his learning has certain capabilities, potentialities and skills. These are input variables. Besides these on the part of the teacher also there are input variables in the form of his knowledge, communication skills, dynamism etc. with which he starts teaching. The material facilities available in the instructional environment are also included in input variables.

There is a need for using a variety of instructional inputs in Commerce. Based on research evidence Woolever and Scott (1998) say that Commerce teachers, left to themselves, use only a limited number of teaching strategies which students find boring. The boredom could be relieved if teachers use a variety of instructional strategies not just large group lectures and discussion. Variety in instructional strategies promotes and maintains students' interest, accommodates individual learning styles, adjusts for different stages of development and helps in achieving diverse types of instructional objectives.

The output or product variables is the terminal behaviour resulting after teaching. It can be spread to three dimensions—cognitive, affective and psychomotor. The process variables comprises of content, instructional process and the media through which learning is imparted.

The instructional strategies, methods, models or designs are all the various ways of achieving the goals of teaching that is they provide a structure to instructional process which leads to the desirable terminal behaviour. All of these take into consideration the input aspect as well.

Instructional Strategy

The simple meaning of the word strategy is a plan/method for obtaining a specific goal or result. If we use a *strategy* in our teaching learning/instructional situations, it is known as *instructional strategy. Thus the instructional strategy is that process which is designed explicitly, and systematically to ensure that the learners acquire the terminal behaviours and achieve the expected instructional objectives.*

One cannot learn swimming by only reading books on it or watching a film on swimming. To learn swimming, one has to enter the water (deep enough, but not so deep as to drown) and try to swim. Similarly, to learn how to design a strategy, you must design one yourself. Designing an instructional strategy requires a number of steps. The steps are presented diagrammatically in Fig. 7.2 as:

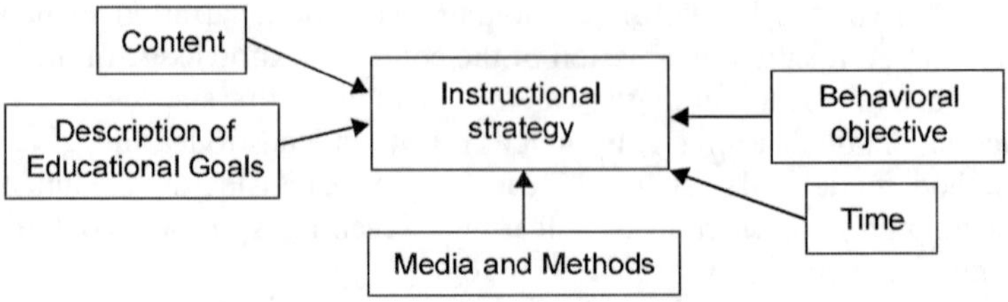

Fig. 7.2: Steps of Instructional Strategy

The contents are provided in the syllabus. Generally a textbook gives some details — the sub-topics, the procedures regarding that topic. The general goals of education like thinking, analytical reasoning, open-mindedness, scientific outlook, etc. also indicate the levels at which one should treat that subject. The goal of teaching is to produce learning, that is, some change in the behaviour of the learner. For this purpose some specific instructional objectives shall have to be in the behavioural terms but not vague or ambiguous in terms of learner's behaviour which is observable and hence, measurable.

After this, there will be a problem about the time duration. Some objectives take long time — may be years to attain, while some others can be learnt in a few minutes. Fortunately, however in many of these objectives, the ability dimension goals are cumulative, *i.e.,* students learn them through different apparently dissimilar topics and over a long period of time. So a teacher's job will be to select methods and media which will give opportunities to student to exercise his thinking modes, learn new ones if he does not already have that mode, etc.

The teacher can choose any one or combination of different methods that can be used to help learners to achieve the instructional objectives. No teaching method is singularly good or bad. It can be effective or ineffective with respect to a particular goal. Media is vehicle for message. One may present a message (or messages) through his voice (what we call lecture) or through a tape recorder, or through a visual chart, a film, a map, etc. Thus, a strategy for helping students to achieve a specific educational goal may include more than one method and media. As the goals become more and more complex and comprehensive, the necessity of integrating of more than one method and media increases.

Thus, a teacher as a manager of learning experience has to be flexible, innovative and open-minded while planning an instructional strategy to suit the requirements of the learners.

Importance of Instructional Strategies

What to teach is followed by how to teach to make learning effective and meaningful. Thus after selecting and organizing the content matter of commerce, it needs to be placed before the students in such a way that the teaching becomes most effective. Educationists now agree that the strategy adopted is more important than the matter learnt. The instructional strategies are useful because:

1. To Achieve Pre-determined Objectives: The instructional strategies help the teacher and pupils to achieve predetermined objectives that are psychologically and educationally sound. If psychological soundness relates to learner factors in the teaching learning process, then educational soundness may be thought of as relating to the knowledge, skill or value component to be learned.

2. Assist the Learner to Achieve his Goal: The type of learning task confronted by the pupils will also determine the instructional strategy employed by the teacher. It makes some difference if a teacher is developing a concept, teaching a skill or helping pupils clarify a value question. Not all learning goals are achieved in the same way, and the process of instruction will assist the learner to achieve his goal.

3. Helping in the Development of Certain Intellectual Skills: Instructional strategies are selected and used because they help in the development of certain intellectual skills. Today investigation-oriented approaches to instruction are getting much attention under the labels of discovery, inquiry, induction and problem solving. Some strategies force the learner to apply the skills of reflective thinking, problem solving etc.

4. Essential to Good Teaching: It is evident that the teacher must be thoroughly trained in the instructional strategies in their field and must also possess a broad understanding of all phases of method-including psychology—as a part of that philosophy of education which is essential to good teaching.

5. Teaching becomes Interesting and Effective: With the help of using different instructional strategies the teacher can stimulate the interest by presenting the outstanding aspect of the events and the achievement of significant persons in an interesting way. The use of different instructional strategies will help in making teaching effective and interesting.

Thus, there is great need of knowledge about different instructional strategies. According to Secondary Education Commission, "Even the best curriculum and the most perfect syllabus remains dead unless quickened into life by the right method of teaching and the right kind of teachers."

Instructional Method

Method is nothing but a scientific way of presenting the subject, keeping in mind the psychological and physical requirements of the children. Method may be regarded as a process or procedure whose successful completion results in learning, or as the means through which teaching becomes effective.

The term 'method' can be thought of as the most effective and economic way of learning to take place among students. Communication of ideas and development of concepts in a precise manner based on a logical development of subject is the most important pre-requisite in teaching the subject of Commerce.

In the words of Bining and Bining, "Methodology should be conceived as dynamic function of education and not as static aspect or the process of teaching."

A method is not merely a device adopted for communicating certain items of information to students and exclusively the concern of the teacher who is supposed to be at the 'giving end'. Any method good or bad links up the teacher and his pupils into an organic relationship with constant mutual interaction. It reacts not only on the minds of the pupils but on their intellectual and emotional equipments, their attitudes and values. Good methods which are psychologically and socially sound, may raise the quality of pupil's life.

The content of the subject is becoming even more closely related to method. In recent years many methods of teaching Commerce have been developed. Attempts have been made to discover the best method of teaching. From a study of the theory and practice of various methods of teaching Commerce, together with much experimentation, it is evident that there is not one best method. The successful teacher will avail himself/herself of many methods or phases of different methods, varying them to suit the conditions that surround him/her, the materials of instruction, and the mental status of the pupils.

Difference between Instructional Strategy and Method

Instructional strategies and methods are used for the same meaning but they are quite different from one another. We all are familiar with the term method as we make use of different methods as lecture method, project method, problem solving method etc. in the class for teaching. In this way method reflects a particular mode of presentation of the subject matter where as strategy is selected and employed not only for the presentation of the subject matter but also for the realisation of pre-determined teaching objectives. Some points of differences are as follows:

Instructional Strategy	*Instructional Method*
1. It is used to create appropriate teaching learning environment which helps the students in attaining the teaching learning objectives.	1. It is used for the effective presentation of the specific content of the subject which helps the students to understand it.
2. It is a new term belonging to educational technology.	2. It is an old term related with pedagogy.
3. Its assumption is that teaching is science and quite technical in nature.	3. Its assumption is that teaching is an art.
4. It is quite flexible in its application.	4. The steps taken in instructional method are quite rigid and fixed.
5. In it the emphasis is laid over teaching activities for the proper organisation of teaching learning environment.	5. In it the emphasis is laid over the instructional steps taken for the proper presentation of the subject matter.

(Contd.)

Instructional Strategy	*Instructional Method*
6. The effectiveness of an instructional strategy is evaluated in terms of the realization of the set objectives by using criterion references test.	6. The effectiveness of an instructional method is evaluated in terms of mastery over the subject matter by using achievement test.
7. Instructional strategy comprises use of different methods, audio-visual aids, techniques, etc.	7. Instructional method comprises the use of teaching techniques and audio-visual aids.

Owing to the development of instructional strategies and their importance at the present time in educational theory and practice, it is essential that the teacher who is to achieve success should make a careful study of this phase of educational thought. The method or methods including classroom procedures that a teacher uses from day-to-day determined to a great extent *his success or failure.* Teaching is not an easy task and everybody is not fit to be a teacher. Some persons may have a *flair* for teaching and such persons have the ability to awaken interest and arrest the attention of the students. Some others who are not so fortunate can improve their teaching through practice if they are fully acquainted with various instructional strategies. In order to make teaching effective the teacher has to adopt the right kind of method at proper time. It is well to keep in mind, however, that the best methods are those which:

- Arouse interest and effort.
- Develop self activity and initiative.
- Stimulate independent thinking.
- Stimulate judgement on the part of the pupil.
- Make for cooperation and socialization.
- Initiates to learn.
- Must be artistic.
- Related to the experiences of students.

***Teaching Should*:**

(*i*) Focus on desired learning outcomes for students, in the form of knowledge, understanding, skill and attitudes,

(*ii*) Assist students to form broad conceptual understanding while gaining depth of knowledge,

(*iii*) Develop an awareness of the limited and provisional nature of much of current knowledge in the field,

(*iv*) Encourage the informed and critical questioning of accepted theories and views,

(*v*) See how understanding evolves and is subject to challenge and revision,

(*vi*) Engage students as active participants in the learning process, while acknowledging that all learning must involve a complex interplay of active and receptive processes,

(*vii*) Respect students' right to express views and opinions,

(*viii*) Incorporate a concern for the welfare and progress of individual students,

(*ix*) Engage students in discussion of ways in which study tasks can be undertaken,

(*x*) Proceed from an understanding of students' knowledge, capabilities and backgrounds,

(*xi*) Utilize instructional strategies and tools to enable many different styles of learning, and

(*xii*) Adopt assessments methods and tasks appropriate to the desired learning outcomes of the course and topic and to the capabilities of the students.

The variety of teaching and learning methods which is used within a course is an important ingredient in creating a course with interest to students.

With in recent years, many methods of teaching Commerce have been developed. Attempts have been made to discover the best method. It seems that the good teacher must have a method and the best teacher is bound to be aware of his method. He must know not only the materials but also the problem of the learner. He must facilitate the learning process.

Many methods have been devised for teaching Commerce. The teacher must familiarize himself with all of these in order to determine which will be most effective in attaining the aims and objectives.

Classification of Methods

1. Methods based upon equipment
   (*a*) Textbook Method
   (*b*) Library Method
   (*c*) Laboratory Method
   (*d*) Construction Project Method
2. Methods based upon economic realities.
   (*a*) Verbal books
   (*b*) Graphic representation
   (*c*) Specimens
   (*d*) Excursions
   (*e*) Participating for purpose of training
3. Methods based upon organization of material.
   (*a*) Chronological (*b*) Psychological
   (*c*) Logical (*d*) Topical
   (*e*) Integration (*f*) Correlation
   (*g*) Fusion (*h*) Units
   (*i*) Problems
4. Methods based upon teacher purpose.
   (*a*) Explanatory (*b*) Reasoning
   (*c*) Diagnostic (*d*) Development
5. Methods based upon pupil purpose.
   (*a*) Problem (*b*) Project
   (*c*) Socialized

6. Methods based upon physical activity
   (*a*) Visual (*b*) Auditory
   (*c*) Motor
7. Methods based upon theories of learning
   (*a*) Drill (*b*) Problem solving
   (*c*) Activity
8. Methods based upon goals of education.
   (*a*) Democratic (*b*) Authoritarian
   (*c*) Cooperative group work
   (*d*) Creative self realization

The above classification of methods may have logical and suggestive values. It certainly has the practical value of demonstrating the complex, over-lapping of the methods that are in daily use. Now we will discuss some important and effective methods of teaching which can be used to make learning effective.

I. Discussion Method

There are issues where there is a likelihood of differences of opinion or problems admitting different solutions or some conceptual confusions needing clarifications where some consensus is required to be obtained. These are to be put up for discussion. Commerce deals with the problems of business, trading, etc. Discussion may be said to be an important means of discovering the problem and to suggest the suitable steps for proper solution.

In the words of Johnson, "Discussion is a special action in its purest form."

In the words of James Lee, "The discussion is an educational group activity in which the teacher and the student talk over some problem or topic."

Discussion can be profitably used to plan a new activity, or take certain decisions, or to provide some important information to the students, or to analyse certain aspects and ideas or to develop the interest of the students in the subject of commerce.

In the words of Sattler and Miller, "Discussion is a reflective thinking by two or more persons who cooperatively exchange information and ideas in effort to solve a problems or to gain understanding of a problem."

Analysis of the above mentioned definition shows the following characteristics of the discussion method:

1. It is based on the exchange of ideas and concepts among the teacher and the students.
2. It permits students to freely express their points.
3. It develops the clarity of the ideas while presenting the ideas and facts in the group.
4. It stimulates group thinking.
5. It is an active oral method.
6. It enables students to agree or differ from other co-students.
7. It is a systematic process of collective decision making among the teacher and the students through competitive cooperation.
8. It promotes public speaking.

Types of Discussion

1. Formal Discussion: When objectives and principles are pre-determined, each student will have to follow the pre-determined objectives and principles. This type of formal discussion are — panel discussion, symposium, forum, debate, etc.

2. Informal Discussion: When objectives and principles are not pre-determined, no one is bound to follow the principles to participate in the discussion. It is clear that the classroom discussion is a kind of informal discussion.

Constituents of Discussion

According to Johnson, the essential parts of a discussion are:

1. A Leader
2. A Group
3. A Problem, and
4. The content

1. A Leader: In the discussion method, the teacher works as leader. The planning of the discussion, selection and organization of the subject matter, etc. is all done by the teacher in the capacity of the leader. But the teacher should keep in mind that he must not dominate the entire scene. The role of teacher as a leader in holding the discussion is quite a responsible one. The teacher as a leader by way of his personal contact with the pupils enters into their life experiences. He helps his students to participate in the discussion seriously because, 'the function of a discussion is to educate young people in the process of group thinking, a process in which they are continually engaged in more or less amateur fashion.'

2. A Group: The class of the students is clearly the group in the discussion. Generally, the group is composed of all types of temperament and all varieties of mind.

It is the teacher's duty to encourage and motivate each and every student to take part in the discussion. Not even a single student should be ignored.

3. A Problem: A topic or problem on which the discussion is to be done should be the problem of the group and of the leader. It should be as precise and exact as possible. The problem should be selected by the teacher with the cooperation of the students. The teacher should not impose the problem on his pupils. It must be real and functional and within the reach of the pupils.

4. The Content: The content of the discussion as envisaged by Johnson is, "the body of knowledge-facts and generalization which must be drawn upon if any problem is to be discussed and resolved." Facts, of course, cannot be discussed because facts remain facts. But sometimes these may be proved true or false. Such statements are to be discussed and interpreted as to their validity and importance with regard to human relationships.

Process/Steps of Discussion

In order to secure the valuable results of the discussion the teacher and the pupils representative should do considerable planning. The whole process may be divided in to three steps.

1. Preparation for the Discussion.
2. Conducting the Discussion.
3. Evaluating the Discussion.

1. Preparation for the Discussion

First of all the teacher with the help of student representatives is to plan for the preparation for the discussion. The following suggestions can be helpful for the preparation:

(*i*) They should have already in mind the problem, topic or unit on which the discussion is to be proposed.
(*ii*) Find and utilize the sources to collect the material for discussion such as encyclopaedias, year books, reference books, magazines, journals, pamphlets and other specialized studies.
(*iii*) To get the latest development, read the newspapers.
(*iv*) Read purposively. They choose the relevant material and concentrate on them.
(*v*) Read critically, note contradiction and in consistencies.
(*vi*) Read objectively. Discard prejudices.
(*vii*) Read discriminately. Distinguish between facts and opinions. Do not ignore opinions, because world policies are based upon them, but recognize them as interpretation rather than facts.
(*viii*) Read appreciatively. Try to understand the viewpoint of the writer even though you do not accept it.
(*ix*) Expand your information and be prepared to be convinced, even though it involves a change in your attitude. So read receptively.
(*x*) Read constructively, deduce conclusions and generalizations.
(*xi*) Utilize the material to prepare an outline, a speech or a written report.
(*xii*) Arrange the point in a logical sequence.
(*xiii*) Prepare conscientiously.

In this process, the students prepare their subject matter for the presentation as well as for the discussion. They study each and every aspect of the topic from different sources.

2. Conducting the Discussion

A good discussion is one which the participants are able to communicate easily, freely and purposively. Firstly the teacher or the moderator or the organizer should announce the details of the procedure thus enabling everyone to adjust his participation to fit the plan. A prearranged procedure may inhibit the free exchange of opinions. He is to make sure that each participant will assume his share of the discussion. He is to set some boundaries for possible, determine what question need to answered, make sure that the meaning of special terms or phrases is known to all. After this the main part of the discussion comes *i.e.* conduction. It involves the skillful use of factual information and informed opinions that are relevant to the problem under discussion. Each participant should observe.

1. Do you share?
2. Hear the other person's views.
3. Speak clearly and concisely.
4. Speak with modesty.
5. Admit that you have not enchanted the topic Admit your limitation of knowledge and insight.
6. Respect other people's contributions.
7. Be sincere.
8. Try to inform rather than convince others because it should not be narrowed.
9. A good discussion is a planned and well mannered conversation, so be courteous.
10. If possible present a map, picture, chart, diagram.
11. Words used should be simple because sometimes strong language is likely to stir the emotions.
12. Allow every one to participate.
13. Avoid being forcedly humorous.
14. Be good natured because an annoyed person is neither a good speaker nor a good listener.
15. Ask sincere questions.
16. Encourage sincere question and comments, but do not coax or wheedle the members.

After conducting the discussion, the teacher/moderator/recorder is to prepare the summary of the discussion. While preparing it the following points should be kept in mind:

1. Point out opposing or divergent point of view.
2. Restate the problem and briefly indicate the scope and limitation that the participant placed upon the discussion.
3. Simple language should be used.
4. Major generalizations should be stated.
5. The major conclusions should be pointed out.
6. Indicate general trend and major emphasis that developed during the discussion.

The discussion remains incomplete if it is not evaluated on proper lines.

3. Evaluating the Discussion

The evaluation of the discussion should be objective means free from biases. The ultimate purpose of discussion, as with all learning experiences, is to bring about desirable change in the pupils. There are several areas as knowledge and information, intellectual abilities (using generalization to predict consequences, etc.), intellectual skills (communication reading, organizing, etc.) interests, attitudes, personal social adjustment, qualities of good citizenship, group cooperation, appreciation, etc. in which the change may take place as a result of discussion. On these criteria the discussion may be evaluated.

Advantages/Merits of Discussion Method

The following are the advantages of discussion method:

1. Group Decision: The pupils learn to take decision in a group with the help of discussion. It is a process to take decision cooperatively.

2. Development of Communication Ability: The pupils use the available time to communicate with each other. They communicate to others in a group by verbal and non-verbal signs as facial expressions, hand gestures, bodily movements etc. The other students as participants receive communication by listening and by visually attending to the verbal and non-verbal signs.

3. Achievement of Broad Instructional Objective: It is a flexible method. It helps in achieving the broad instructional objectives as subject matter mastery, change in attitude, moral development, development of problem solving ability, acquisition of communication skill, etc.

4. Development and Testing of Understanding: It develops an understanding that there is not one but several approaches to solve a business problem and that in democratic country solution to the problem are arrived at through consensus. During discussion, pupils are also able to test their own understanding of concepts and principles. This helps them to take corrective actions at an early age.

5. Activity Centered: This method is based on the principle of activity. The pupil remains active throughout the discussion. He becomes active participator in the process of learning. The knowledge become permanent because it gained through activity. On the basis of this it becomes psychologically sound.

6. Provides Feedback: It provides feedback both to teacher as well as students. The teacher gets the feedback on students progress and students gets the feedback as the supportiveness or discardness of their views.

7. Related to Life: Discussion method affords the opportunity to the pupils to apply knowledge in the real life. Decision making power is also developed which helps in later life.

8. Discourage Cramming: Through discussion method students find themselves the facts, analyse them and seek removal of doubts. The newly and actively acquired knowledge is deeply rooted in their minds, so, there is no need of cramming, but they only understand the concept.

9. Development of Self Expressing Ability: Naturalism believes that every human being should get an opportunity to express his ideas, without any fear. This method provides this opportunity which helps in development of personality of the students.

10. Clarify the Issues: Commerce is a very wide subject that needs clarification of many concepts, facts and events. The textbook is not sufficient to clarify them properly. During the discussion these issues can be clarified effectively.

Thus, discussion method is very useful to provide the knowledge related to real life. It takes into account not only the favourable majority of opinions but also the dissenting minority opinions.

Demerits and Limitation of Discussion Method

1. Wastage of Time: While using this method much time of students being wasted in the un-meaningful discussion. There is always a fear of irrelevant discussion. On the other hand when all the students are provided opportunities to express their views, a single problem/topic/issue takes much time.

2. Not Applicable for All Classes: This method can be applied only in higher classes where students have much knowledge about the subject matter and have the habit of self-study. It is not useful for junior classes because they don't have so much understanding about the problem and are not mentally mature.

3. Not Useful for All Types of Students: Psychologically it has seen proved that there are individual differences among the students. It is useful for the bright students not for the shy and slow learners. These type of students depend upon the lecture or the other methods of teaching.

4. Lack of Skilled Teachers: An able, skilled and efficient teacher is needed to plan, conduct and evaluate the discussion. Every teacher cannot make use of this method. There is lack of efficient-teachers needed for discussion.

5. Monopoly of Few Students: Sometime the discussion may be dominated by few clever and gifted children. Other students remain inactive in the process. As a result the dull student become more dull and the bright more bright. In this process all the students can't get equal opportunities for learning.

6. Not Applicable for All the Topics: Every topic in the curriculum is neither of same difficulty level nor of same importance. All the topics of Commerce are not amenable to discussion.

Inspite of these limitations this method can't be discarded due to its usefulness. If used with some suggestion, it can be the best method for achieving the educational objectives.

Suggestions for the Improvement of Discussion Method

1. Some one should be ready to lead.
2. Important aspects of the topic/problem/issue should be included.
3. The participant should be free to express their views and ideas without any pressure.
4. The interest of the student should be maintained.
5. Important facts and point of views should be evaluated critically.
6. The students should be encouraged to make interpretations.
7. More than one period of time should be given to enable more and more students to participate.
8. Conclusions should be made in such a way that all aspects are covered.

Usually the most important person determining the success or failure of discussion is the organizer/moderator. His role should be that of facilitating discussion rather than that of dominating the procedure.

Role of the Organizer/Moderator

The organizer/moderator can be a successful leader if he:

1. accepts all contributions,
2. is tactful and friendly,
3. have a good knowledge of the topic/problem/issue to be discussed,
4. takes no particular view point in the discussion,
5. keep the group to recognize the main issues in the discussion,
6. have no preconceived notions about where the discussion should lead,

7. prevent bad feelings from developing among participators,
8. sees that every member of the group gets an opportunity to express his views,
9. periodically summarizes discussion to let the group realize what has been achieved so far, and
10. at the end of the discussion, make certain that all participator know, what conclusions have been arrived at by the group.

The above discussion leads us to believe that this method is learner-centered method and it should be used at least once in a month. With proper planning, preparation and efficient conduct this method can result in vicarious advantages mentioned above.

II. Project Method

Project method is a self learning method. The dictionary meaning of the *project* is *scheme* or *design*. Projects have been defined as that form of coordinated activity that is directed towards the learning of a significant skill or process. It is based on the philosophy of pragmatism. Through this method students get experiential learning. This provides the students an opportunity to learn at their own pace and time, while they do certain activities more or less independent of the teacher. John Dewey wanted that education should be for life and through life. He put the child in real life situations of learning. He assigned spontaneous, purposeful and socialized activities to the child. The credit of developing the ideas of John Dewey into a method goes to William Kilpatrick *i.e.,* why this method is named after him as 'Kilpatrick Method'. In 1918, he defined it as, "Whole hearted purposeful activity proceeding in a social environment."

In the words of S.C. Parker, "A project is a unit of activity in which pupils are made responsible for planning and purposing."

In the words of Thomas and Lang, "Project is voluntary undertaking which involves constructive effort or thought and eventuates into objective results."

In the words of Stevenson, "A project is a problematic act carried to completion in its natural setting."

On the analysis of above mentioned definition, we come to know the following characteristics of this method as:

1. A project is a whole hearted activity.
2. It is cooperative work of the students.
3. It is based on information through experiences.
4. It develops the logical and analytical power of the students.
5. It is a purposeful activity.
6. It provides natural environment.
7. It is related with life.
8. It is child-centred method.
9. It follows psychological approach to individual differences among the students.
10. It involves mental and physical powers of the students.

Types of Projects

According to Kilpatrick, projects can basically assume four forms:

1. Constructive Project: These can also be known as producers' type projects. Those projects which involve mental activities are called constructive projects as development of material or object or article.

2. Aesthetic Project: These can also be known as consumers' type projects which involves artistic feeling of the students as listening, presenting a musical programme, beautifying the classroom, reading the stories, etc.

3. Problematic Project: These type of projects involve problem solving requiring the exercise of mental processes as why does demand of a commodity increases as a result of advertisements?

4. Drill Project: These type of projects involve learning mainly by repetition of the processes like drawing the sketch, learning the terms used in banks, etc.

Principles Involved in the Project Method

The principles governing the project method are:

1. Purposefulness: A project must be meaningful and purposeful to the pupils. This offers incentives and motivation to the pupils to learn and yields them the satisfaction and gratification at having been successful in accomplishing the task. A psychologist says that purposeful activities arouse the curiosity in the students to take part in the project willingly.

2. Activity Centredness: A project is woven around some activity and offers opportunities to children to learn by doing by getting involved in the activities. They are also required to plan, think, evolve strategies of functioning and in accomplishing tasks independently, with a sense of achievement and fulfillment.

3. Life Centredness: A project is planned around an actual life situation which is specially created simulated in the school environment. The situation so created enable children to demonstrate their special abilities, competencies, capacities and talents.

4. Freedom: The project method offers full freedom to the children to express their initiative and ingenuity in planning and executing the steps of the process on their own. Incidently this also helps them develop a sense of accountability for their activities.

5. Utility: Utility of the knowledge and experiences gained, through personally initiated and executed tasks, yields children the satisfaction of having realised something, which is of utility in life. This imparts meaningfulness to the educational ventures undertaken.

6. Based on Experience: In project method, learning is based on experiences, which will be long lasting. The child also learns the value of team work and participatory learning and the resulting social and democratic values.

Stages/Steps in the Project Method

Quite like some other approaches, in project method too children learn by doing. The steps for using project method in teaching commerce can be as follows:

1. Providing Situation: In project method, the first step is teacher's job to provide a situation which may give pupils a spontaneous urge, to carry out the project according to their interests, attitudes, competencies etc. This step refers such problematic situations in which the students themselves feel several problems but try to choose one out of them according to their attitude, needs and interest. The teacher can provide project situations both inside and outside the classroom through:

- Conversation.
- Discussion on different themes.
- Educational Trips.
- Story telling.
- Excursions.
- Video films.
- Pictures.
- Using audio-visual aids.

2. Proposing and Purposing a Project: The next step is that each student starts thinking over the selection of the project according to his interest, need and attitude. The teacher should help the students in choosing a project of the several projects chosen by a student through evaluating the merits and demerit of all the chosen projects. Thus, the teacher enunciates the purpose. While selecting a problem/topic/situation, following questions should be raised:

- Is it adapted to the needs and abilities of the student?
- Is it challenging?
- Is it worthwhile?
- Is it economical?
- Is it feasible and practical?
- Is it selected by the student?
- Is it purposeful?

The enunciation given by the teacher serves as a motivating device as the children discover its usefulness and its compatibility.

3. Planning the Project: Planning could be ideally done by the students themselves but in regard to the younger folk, some hints could be offered by the teacher, who may keep on watching them doing things on their own. In fact the students may be encouraged to think of alternative approaches for realising the goal and then to select the one that they consider most appropriate. This paves the way for the internalisation of the idea, which serves well in later life situations where an individual has to learn to be flexible in weighing situations for taking own decisions. The students also come to learn that whatever they may have planned, need not always be rightly followed even if the plans do not work. It requires time and much consideration before a really good plan can be made. The concept of 'mid-way correction' for realising success is a valuable mental attitude of accepting the need for making changes in plans and finally making them.

4. Executing the Project: It is the most important and longer step in the process and therefore needs a great deal of patience on the part of the students as well as of the teacher. While the project execution goes on, the teacher mainly remains an observer. Pupils distribute the various responsibilities among themselves according to their interest and capabilities. The teacher has also to establish a balance between the over-enthusiastic and comparatively inert pupils. Encouraging and guiding the latter can yield them confidence and enthusiasm to work and effectively contribute to team effort.

5. Evaluation: While evaluation is considered to be a teacher's activity the pupils can also be motivated to assess their own efforts and the resulting outcomes themselves. The teacher should evaluate the project from the academic angle, diagnosing and identifying the outcomes of the project in real terms by way of the development of competencies by the pupils, cooperation in the team work, voluntary willingness to make a contribution to the project while in process, identification of gainful outcomes in terms of the development of interests and abilities.

The pupils also can undertake, "self-evaluation of the gains, the new things learnt, the capacities improved, the insight into various operations gained, the confidence in oneself, motivation for further improving one's competencies and achievement of predetermined objectives."

6. Recording: At this step, all the activities concerned with the project work must be maintained with full details. It should contain:

(*i*) Procedure of providing a situation.
(*ii*) Procedure of choosing the project.
(*iii*) Discussion.
(*iv*) Proposals advanced and accepted.
(*v*) Allotment of work.
(*vi*) Books, newspapers and journals consulted.
(*vii*) Places visited.
(*viii*) People contacted.
(*ix*) Difficulties felt and experiences gained.
(*x*) The task remained incomplete.
(*xi*) Guidance for future.

Merits of the Project Method

1. It is based on 'learning by doing' and the principles of individual differences. This is the reason that it is very helpful in developing self-discipline and self-confidence among the students.
2. No place for rote and monotonous learning in the classroom.
3. It helps in encouraging pupils to cooperate, to think, and act together for a common project. This method prepares the pupil to live in democratic community like India.
4. It provides the opportunities to children for getting the incidental knowledge through practical and experimental work.
5. It establishes the correlation between the subject of commerce and the real life and also establishes coordination in the knowledge of different subjects.
6. It helps in developing the reasoning power and scientific thinking among the students through mutual exchange of ideas.
7. It provides child centred and activity centred education.
8. It develops the feeling of dignity of labour.

9. Students learn much in short span of time.
10. The pupils learn to direct their own activities, their power of judgement and training in independence are fastened.
11. It develops the habit of proper interaction among the pupils.
12. The students learn according to their own interests, aptitudes, attitudes and capabilities.

Demerits/Limitation of Project Method

Project method, though a great educational innovation, does suffer from some limitations. The main of which are stated below:

1. It is a time consuming method of teaching and learning.
2. It is not applicable to all the students and all the themes therein.
3. The teacher cannot always think of completely original themes for projects and therefore quite often they become repetitive.
4. It provides scattered and disorganised knowledge.
5. It does not fit a class with large number of students.
6. An inexperienced teacher can't use this method effectively and efficiently.
7. As commerce education needs planned teaching process, so, this can't be applied fruitfully for commerce teaching.
8. Sometimes suitable text-material is not available for the project work.
9. It ignores practices and development of various skills.
10. Collective project neglects the individual difference of the children.
11. In rigid time table of the school, this method is not applicable.
12. Teaching through this method fails to complete the whole syllabus in time.

Examples of Project in Commerce

— Collection of data of Internal and External Trade.
— Study of functions of Bank and Post Office.
— Study of usefulness of Insurance.
— Study of usefulness of Advertisement.
— Arranging commercial fairs.
— Study of school budget.
— Study of export-import procedure.

Student's Role in the Project

The students have to play important roles in the project method though the teacher is always there to help them throughout but the main responsibility of carrying out the project lies with the student. There are three major steps where the student role is important.

1. Planning Stage: At the planning step, the students have to consider the following tasks:

(*i*) They should have a clear cut idea about the objectives of the project.
(*ii*) They should understand the scope and limitation of the project.
(*iii*) If there is any ambiguity, the help should be sought from the teacher.
(*iv*) They should design a suitable plan for dealing with the project.

(*v*) They should discuss with teacher the various aspects of planning the project.

(*vi*) They should arrange the work in a sequence and fix a target to complete the project.

2. *Implementation Stage:* At this stage, the students should carry out the following tasks:

(*i*) Collect all necessary information.

(*ii*) Decide about suitable method of enquiry.

(*iii*) Use available resources as equipment, material, teachers, experts, etc. effectively.

(*iv*) Work cooperatively.

(*v*) Carry out the processes involved in the project as analysis, synthesis, application, decision making, etc.

(*vi*) Stick to the schedule for the project time

(*vii*) Secure guidance and help from the teacher throughout this stage.

3. *Reporting/Presentation Stage*: The students are expected to carry out the following tasks at the reporting stage:

(*i*) Interpret information and use material properly.

(*ii*) Secure help from the teacher.

(*iii*) Draw appropriate conclusion.

(*iv*) Compile an effective project work.

(*v*) Present the report in a systematic order effectively.

The students can learn themselves with the help of various activities which provide them experiential learning.

Teacher's Role in the Project

The workability of the project is not possible without the help and guidance of the teacher. The teacher helps the students at every step. He is expected to help the students in the following ways:

(*a*) While presenting the projects in the class, he should use different aids to clear them.

(*b*) The teacher should remain just behind the curtain while choosing the projects.

(*c*) As a keen observer and a true sympathizer, the teacher should win the goodwill of the pupils so that they may feel encouraged.

(*d*) The teacher should be able to anticipate the difficulties and suggest remedies as and when necessary.

(*e*) The teacher should supervise the students in manipulative skills closely enough to prevent waste of materials, time and energy.

In this way, project-method is very much valuable for teaching and learning. What the students learn from the experiences gained through the project work cannot be learnt through by any other method. No doubt, there are some wrong conceptions about this method but these can be removed wisely. All the problems in conducting project work can be removed when it is combined with direct learning, with systematic study, with experiments and with discussional development of subject matter. Thus it will help the teacher to attain understanding of each pupil's abilities, and potentialities, and for students to get valuable experiences from business point of new which will be helpful in later life.

III. Problem Solving Method

Any method of solving a problem scientifically involves thinking, reasoning, planning and execution by following logical steps in a scientific method. The process of problem solving method results in the development of cognitive abilities, affective abilities, attitudes and psychomotor skills. It is in this context that the '*Problem solving method*' is called a *scientific method.*

Meaning and Definition

Problem solving method is a teaching method in which the teaching work is planned and organized related to a problem. It is an activity centred approach in which a problem is presented before the students and they are trained to discover the solution of that problem. 'Problem' means a thing that needs attention and needs to be solved.

Risk explains problem solving as "a planned attack on a difficulty, perplexity or problem to find a satisfactory solutions." Ross interprets problem solving as "an educational device whereby the teacher and the pupils attempt in a conscious, planned and purposeful manner, to arrive at an explanation or solution to some educationally significant difficulty."

Gates and others define problem solving as, "a form of teaching in which the appropriate solutions must be discovered."

Skinner defines it as, "Problem solving is the framework or pattern within which creative thinking and reasoning takes place."

Thus, a problem occurs in a situation in which a felt difficulty to act is realised. It may be a mental difficulty or physical one, slowing or blocking the path of progress for reaching the goal. It may be therefore impress upon the pupils (who may meet it) as needing a solution and is recognized and realised by them as a challenge to be picked up and squarely met.

Characteristics of a 'Problem'

A problem in commerce ought to possess and actually possesses some distinct characteristics as follows:

1. The problem is normally related to life and is, therefore, normally within the ambit of common experiences of pupils.
2. The problem should have a practical value and the outcomes ought to be taken as of practical utility by the pupils.
3. The problem must be a part of the curriculum to realise the goals of which, is the prime concern of the students.
4. The problem should pose a challenge before the students.
5. The problem identified on the subject of instruction/learning ought to be clear, definite, understandable, interesting, aligned to the age group of the pupils, within the capability of the learners, and based on the knowledge they already possess. Above all, it should be thought provoking.

6. The problem should be such which can be solved in congenial and co-operative atmosphere.
7. The process of problem solving as a method of teaching/learning should not put unnecessary burden of finances on the instruction as well as on the students. At the same time, it should also be possible to accomplish the total task, within the available time.
8. The problem should be correlated with the environment of the pupils.

Approaches to Problem Solving

Basically there are two main approaches which can be used to solve the problem:

1. The Inductive Method: The inductive method carries the thinking process from particular to general situation. Conclusions by way of generalizations are arrived at from particular principles and concrete examples.

2. The Deductive Method: The deductive method carries reflective thinking from general to particular/specific.

Two other important methods also help to reinforce the problem solving method as:

— Heuristic Method
— Discovery Method.

Stages/Steps of Problem Solving Method

Many educationists have used problem solving method successfully. John Dewey suggested certain steps that should be followed by the teacher while using problem solving method for teaching/learning. Afterwards many scholars refined them. In commerce, the following steps can be used as:

1. Selection of the Problem: The teacher should help the students in selection of the problem to be solved by analysing the hurdles and handicaps posed by it. Necessary motivation for solving it should also thus be generated among the students. Students should also be enabled to be alert in spotting and recognising the problems in and when they crop up in different situations.

2. Defining (Interpreting and delimiting) the Problem: The teacher should present the problem before students in an easy and understandable language. The nature of the problem should help in charting the path for overcoming it. Hulfish and Smith suggest the following questions to be raised in defining a problem:

— What exactly is the problem? Can it be broken into sub-problems?
— Does the problem bear any similarity to any of those encountered in the past?
— In which way does the particular problem differ from the others?
— What do differences imply — new approaches?
— Is it necessary to redefine the problem in view of the above?

3. Collection and Evaluation of Relevant Information/data: After the problem has been defined and interpreted in collaboration with the pupils, they should be stimulated to collect information/data needed for solving it and to commence the process of its collection with a view to initiate this, the teacher may identify:

- The sources from which the data can be collected — books, documents, reports, etc.

- The personnel — experts and functionaries to be consulted.

The collected information should then be checked for its:

- Appropriateness and relevance,
- Adequacy, and
- Applicability in the given situations of the problem.

Thus, after the collection of information/data from different sources, the students should be asked to select the relevant material and to discard the superficial one and arrange the selected data a systematic way. This is possible only if students' attention is all the time focussed on the main problem.

4. Formulating Alternative Solution and Selecting one: Different possible approaches for solving the problem could be listed and their pros and cons discussed by pupils and the teacher. This process of churning would enable the identification of the one most suitable. Tentative solutions could also thus be arrived at. Care should be taken that solution is made only when sufficient data is collected. The teacher's role in this step is very important.

5. Arriving at the Final Solution: The next natural step is to pool together the possible solution. These may then be discussed from different angles, for reaching an appropriate solution. At this point of time, teacher's in-depth knowledge and ingenuity will be called for, for guiding students to reach apt and appropriate judgemental inferences.

6. Testing the validity of the Solution arrived at: No conclusion should be accepted without being properly verified. The correctness of solution must be proved. The students must be taught to be critical. The validity of the solution finally arrived at, could be arrived at through:

- The applicability of the hypothesis to new situations.
- Further exploration, experimentation and investigations.
- Additional investigations for gathering new information.

One thing should be kept in mind that students should be open minded and free of every bias in the process of problem solving.

7. Recording: The students should keep a record of the whole proceedings. The note book should give a comprehensive picture of the problem solving as a whole. It should give the procedure of selection of problem, duties assigned, difficulties felt and experiences gained etc. It will help in further guidance.

Problem Solving and Project Method

In spite a host of similarities, the problem solving and project methods do stand out prominently in respect of marked differences. Problem solving requires a solution in thought or action or both, whereas project method aims at the successful completion of a task or unit of work. Problem solving could be taken as a project work but a project need not always be a problem solving exercise.

Current Problem Solving Model

Cognitive research done in the last 20 years has led to a different model of problem solving approach. Today we know problem solving includes a complex set of cognitive, behavioural and attitudinal components. In 1983, Mayer defined problem solving as a multiple step process where the problem solver must find relationships between past experiences and the problems at hand and then act upon a solution. He suggested three characteristics of problem solving:

1. Problem solving is cognitive but is inferred from behaviour.
2. Problem solving results in behaviour that leads to a solution.
3. Problem solving is a process that involves manipulation of or operations on previous knowledge.

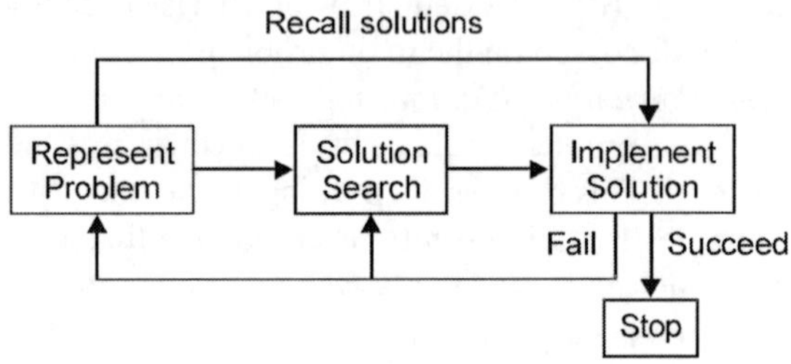

Fig. 7.3

This model identifies a basic sequence of three cognitive activities in problem solving technique:

- Representing the problem includes calling up the appropriate context knowledge, and identifying the goal and the relevant starting conditions for the problem.
- Solution search includes refining the goal and developing a plan of action to reach the goal.
- Implementing the solution includes executing the plan of action and evaluating the results.

There is an important 'shortcut', however, if the learner recognizes that he or she has solved a similar problem before, then all that is needed is to recall how it was solved last time and do it again.

Merits of Problem Solving Method

1. It helps students to learn more meaningfully.
2. It enables students to think and reason.
3. The students also acquire valuably desirable work habits and self-reliance.
4. As problem solving requires a higher order of mental abilities, it also helps students develop mental self-discipline.
5. It affords opportunities for participation in economic activities.
6. Discussion helps to develop the power of expression of the students.
7. Knowledge is easily assimilated as it is the result of a purposeful activity.
8. It helps to verify an opinion.
9. It is a goal-oriented method.
10. It helps in solving the problem of life.
11. It helps in developing the habit of self-study.
12. It helps is developing the close contact between teacher and student.
13. Students learn to struggle for solutions to selected problems.

14. It arouses a natural interest by creating a condition of strong mental perplexity or by setting up a challenge.

Demerits and Limitations of Problem Solving Method

The limitations of this method, however, mainly relate to logistic and the perpetual paucity of resources. The demerits and limitations are as follows:

1. It is time consuming both for the teachers and the students and hence cannot be used extensively and frequently.
2. Paucity of resources too often become hurdles in using it.
3. Quite often when problem solving is used as a method of teaching the elaborate and intensive focus it requires, turn out to be the only mental activity with others relegated into the background and in fact they get grossly neglected.
4. Sometimes due unavailability of relevant data and lack of experiences of the students result in unsatisfactory result and pupils may become discouraged.
5. The use of this method does not lend itself to a broad understanding of the subject.
6. A large number of students do not possess sufficient background information and therefore, they do not take interest in the discussion.
7. It is not applicable for all types of students because dull students do not have much abstract thinking power.
8. There is always a possibility of drawing out a wrong conclusion.
9. The whole commerce subject can't be taught through this method.
10. It does not help in acquiring important factual information and understanding of the commerce subject.

The pursuit of problem solving method imparts valuable personality attributes to the students. The limitations and demerits of the method can be removed because they are the result of ineffective use of this method. The teacher has, therefore, to use his discretion in establishing the needed balance among different methodologies of instruction. He has particularly to guard against the situations when he may assign problems without the problems coming from the students as that kills their interest.

Examples of Problems in Commerce

- Ware housing helps in price stabilisation.
- Coordination is the essence of management.
- Requirement of public sector enterprises in India.
- Finance is the lifeblood of a business.

IV. Socialized Recitation Method

The socialized recitation is often designed as a method. In reality it is an ideal rather than a procedure, but as an ideal it has had great influence in promoting better understanding among students and between teacher and students. It was designed to eliminate the formal and stilted air that seems to pervade many classrooms and to substitute a sense of freedom and naturalness.

In the words of Wesley, "Socialized recitation is the natural dialogue between student and teacher that takes place in an educational setting."

In the words of Bining and Bining, "Any class session that exhibits group consciousness and the feeling of individual responsibility toward the group is socialized recitation."

Socialized recitation may be called socialized discussion. The form of organization of a class for a socialized recitation varies from a simple, informal organization to a complex, parliamentary one. The socialized procedure has brought about more significant assignments, more student activity, and in some instances, a liberalization of school control.

Teaching is not a mechanical process. The use of the socialized recitation will depend much on the class, on the teacher, and on the aim that the teacher has for the lesson. Some teachers are well adapted to teach by this method, other might create an atmosphere of artificiality by using it too liberally. Classes vary, then again, the mental ability and the social background of the individual propels if different classes vary greatly. What one can do with one class cannot be done with other class.

Prof. Harol Benjamin has described the following aims of socialized recitation:

1. To develop useful technique for cooperative works.
2. To arouse intelligent thinking.
3. To proceed previous knowledge.
4. To encourage creative expression.
5. To develop desirable social attitude by providing different socialized situations.
6. To develop, the skill of cooperative thinking.

The socialized procedure can make use of all the devices, projects, problems and activities that are available under other methods. For example, the students may hear reports, an assignment, make a survey, hold contest, have a debate or carry on one of a hundred activities.

Plans of Socialized Recitation

Many plans can be made for utilizing socialized recitation method. One plan may be that a class has a president, a secretary and four or five committees. Each committee is responsible for a work. The work can be divided in various ways. The other plan may be that the class can be divided into four committees. They work as one for national affairs, one for foreign affairs, one for state affairs and one for local affairs. Each committee will be responsible for a knowledge of the important happenings in its respective fields. Another plan can be made by inviting some individuals to prepare discussion on certain topics.

The other plan may be the lesson or topic is divided into four or five parts and a leader is chosen for each part. It is the duty of each leader to plan and prepare his work carefully. To do this, he will be required to make an outline of his part of the topic and to work out a procedure that he will follow in conducting the work in the classroom. All his planning must be approved by the teacher. During the class, every leader will assume responsibility for his part of the topic. He will ask question, call for discussion and seek comments. He can call upon anyone in the group. The members of the group are free to ask questions to any point that has not been made clear. After the completion of the discussion, the leader offers any additional information that he thinks essential. If the work has been thoroughly done, the teacher will offer no remarks. If certain points have remained left *i.e.* not been touched upon or if definite conclusions have not been reached, the teacher by a selected procedure – questioning, discussing or commenting will bring out those essentials.

Role of the Teacher in Socialized Recitation Method

The part that a teacher plans in the planning of the socialized recitation is most important. The teacher who wishes to introduce this procedure/method should prepare the ground work by allowing more freedom and self direction. If one entered a classroom in which the method was being used, he would probably think that the teacher was having an easy time of it. The use of this method requires greater leadership and better planning than most forms of teaching. The burden of responsibility for the success of the method rests upon the teacher. He must make better preparation and must plan more cautiously to insure that the lesson will be of permanent value to the class.

He must not expect the student to initiate worth while procedure without direction. He should know when and how to stop the useless debate. He will have to see that the class is not dominated by a few individuals. This method demands well trained and efficient teachers. He must have a broad background of the subject because each pupil has a point of view, his ideas on the subject and the questions to ask. He must possess a thorough knowledge of the subject matter and source otherwise his defects will be painfully evident to the class. In the assignment, he must know where each pupil can find the material without loss of time. He must work a little harder to bring about group consciousness which is necessary for the recitation.

Merits of Socialized Recitation Method

The advantages/merits of this method are:

1. Help to Accomplish the Ideals of Education: The demand of the education, especially of the Commerce is to develop the subject matter that will aid in the socialization of the child. The socialised recitation method helps in achieving this ideal. The pupil regards himself as a member of a group and has a social motive in doing his work. It will help in creating group consciousness which will result in the development of spirit of cooperativeness and brotherhood with its by-products of courtesy and good will. It will also help in developing the individuals as well as social virtues of initiativeness, truthfulness.

2. Development of Right Attitudes: Bining and Bining has rightly remarked that "Attitudes of scientific mindedness, of loyalty, of truthfulness, of tolerance, of cooperation, of civic gratitude and above all intelligent optimism are among the right attitudes that the teacher must seek at every opportunity to develop in his pupils," Socialized recitation method helps in developing these attitudes of the students. Today, we are beginning to stress attitude and ideals even more than knowledge.

3. Develop Friendly Relations Between Pupils and Teacher: In socialized recitation method teacher has to be a true friend and guide. The attitude of the teacher remains very friendly throughout the process. The pleasant atmosphere thus created greatly helps in proper learning.

4. Provides Training in Leadership: Socialized recitation method provides training in leadership and initiative. The pupils remain active, with ample opportunities to develop the latest powers with in him. He plans the procedure himself under the guidance of the teacher. Each one has a chance to express what he feels and thinks.

5. Development of Democratic Outlook: Socialized recitation method provides ample opportunities to develop the much needed spirit of cooperation, brotherhood, open-mindedness, tolerance to develop democratic outlook. This is very timely in the generation in which we are living. Many evils of the past generation have seen due to the spirit. "Every man for himself and the devil takes the hindmost," and this still exists. The need of feeling one's dependence on others and the willingness to sacrifice self for the group, to tolerate views of others are much needed in our present complex society.

6. Development of Self-expressing Ability: One of the greatest advantages of the method is to provide ample opportunities to pupils to express themselves freely. This is of great educational value, not alone because it develops the self expressing ability, but also because of its importance in the learning process. It is a hard fact that if the child remains passive, the learning will be slow and temporary, but if he is given opportunities to express himself or he remains active, his thinking will become clarified and a better understanding will be reached and the gained knowledge will become permanent.

7. Provides Motivation to Learn: In socialized recitation method pupil is not reciting to a teacher but is engaged in a cooperative work with the rest of the group. Interest is aroused and each feels his responsibility. Every one wants to do his best as well as the desire to stand well with the group motivates him. Each pupil tries to put forth his efforts to accomplish the task at hand. But in this process the teacher should remain useful in the development of social relationship that none of the individuals will strive to advance his own prestige at the expense of the group.

8. Develops the Skill to Think Clearly: The aim of the education is to provide opportunities to the student to think clearly. Under many of the methods, the pupil is not expected to think at all. All he must do is to give back what is in the textbook. But Socialized recitation method provides the opportunities to discuss, to criticize, and to evaluate the public questions that are ever before us. Clear thinking is our great need today.

9. Pupils Become Self-reliant: With this method the students become self dependent to complete their work. They learn to direct their activities, their power of judgement. Their choice and training in independence are fastened. They learn to take their own decisions.

10. Helps in Developing the Qualities of Good Citizenship: Socialized recitation method helps in developing certain qualities as independence, initiation, sense of responsibility, cooperation, habit of discussion, of sharing responsibilities, of resourcefulness, self respect, tolerance of other's opinions, open-mindedness, etc. It helps in providing the training in real citizenship.

Demerits/Limitations of Socialized Recitation Method

Despite the advantages that can be found in this method, it has some disadvantages and limitations also. Most of the disadvantages has been aimed as the abuse of the method rather than at its use. Some of the demerits and limitations are as follows:

1. Lack of Specially Trained Teachers: For the effective use of this method, there is need of specially trained teachers because they are to do much work and they are supposed to have detailed knowledge of the subject matter to guide the students. There is always lack of efficient and trained teacher to utilize different methodology.

2. The Process may become Mechanical: One great lacuna lies in the use of the method that the lesson will be socialized in name only. The process may become mechanical, and the pupils respond not through any social urge but through habit or desire to please the teacher. Under such procedure, the method will have less value. When and how to use this method are of utmost importance to the teacher.

3. Inadequate Mastery of Subject Matter: This method does not provide mastery in the subject matter because the pupil is to prepare only one part of the topic efficiently, so the other parts will be ignored or have little knowledge. Many other methods are much more efficient in this respect. The socialized recitation is the wastage of time. The pupils may not be fit to take their examination at the end of the year.

4. Time Consuming: The method is a very time consuming process. If there is an urgent need for saving time during a class period other method should be used. The curriculum can't be completed with the help of this method.

5. Danger of Wander Away from Topic: One of the important disadvantages in the use of this method is the tendency of the class to wander away from the topic or subject matter. Careful guidance is required on the part of the teacher. Sometimes when the students are busy in discussing the matter they may go beyond the topic which will result in wastage of time and energy.

6. Danger of Futile Discussion: The socialized recitation method also is in danger of degenerating in to futile discussion. Sometimes some pupils may argue simply to prove their point, whether it has a direct bearing on the lesson or not.

7. Danger of Domination by a Few Pupils: In socialized recitation, there is always the danger that a few pupils may dominate the lesson. As a result dull becomes more dull and brilliant becomes more brilliant. The students of different mental abilities are present in the class. The slow pupil feels at disadvantage among the superior mentalities. He feels that his contribution might be ridiculed. More and more the desire to recede into the background becomes evident.

8. Not Applicable for Every Topic: This method cannot be utilized exclusively in Commerce. So far as socialization is concerned in itself, however, every lesson should be more or less socialized in the sense that pupils are given a chance to participate, and especially not in a stereotyped manner. It can be applicable for some topics or to review work or to solve some problems.

Thus, socialized recitation method has many desirable outcomes. It is basic that socialized class procedures will help to break down the bars of artificiality in the classroom. It will promote better pupil-teacher relationships and conform to the latest ideas in regard to the nature of learning. But it has some disadvantages and limitations also. If the teacher wants to use it effectively, some suggestions can be helpful.

Suggestions for the Improvement

1. The teacher should interfere in the discussion carefully. He should not be merely a passive spectator of the lesson.
2. The teacher must be alert to prevent useless debate.
3. The teacher must plan the recitation period in such a way that the lesson should not be monopolized by a few. Various means should be used where all are led to participate. How to make slow learner pupils feel that their contribution are of worth and how to make the bright pupils appreciate such contributions require ingenuity, tact and patience.
4. A friendly and controlled atmosphere should prevail during socialized recitation period.
5. The topics for socialized recitation should be carefully selected keeping in view the student's needs.
6. This method should not be used exclusively.
7. Seating arrangement should be proper.

To conclude, there is no doubt that this method provides motivation to the pupils to learn Commerce in an effective manner, but it all depends upon the skill efficiency of the teacher to use this method successfully, for which he requires training and experience in organizing, conducting and guiding the pupils. The teacher should make better preparation and must plan more carefully to ensure that the lesson will be of permanent value to the class and will not only help in the knowledge acquisition but also development of understanding, skill, attitudes and interest. All recitation should be socialized in the sense that the work is carried on in an atmosphere of freedom which encourage pupils to look upon their teachers as guides rather than an autocratic ruler. This method can be associated with other methods as debates, supervised study, discussion etc.

V. Supervised Study Method

It is important and useful method for teaching Commerce because, it is a very vast subject and the students are to depend upon their self-study. Although the term in itself is self-explanatory, but, it may be wise to define the word.

In the word of Bining and Bining, "By supervised study, we mean the supervision by the teacher of a group or a class of pupils as they work at their desks or around their tables."

In this process, we find pupils busy at work that has been assigned them by the teacher. When they find any difficulty that they can't overcome, they ask the teacher for direction and assistance. The teacher, when not called upon, walks quietly up and down the classroom or remains at his desk, watching the pupils doing their work, continually on the alert for any wrong procedures that the pupils may follow. The teacher is always ready to direct and help the pupils whenever they needed.

Some may call it as the narrow meaning and they think that it has some broader meaning i.e., it is made to include all the activities that may be taken up in the class under the name of this method. The term would then include supervised study, the teacher's assignments, socialized procedures and forms of recitation that may be used in conjunction with this method.

It can also be called as 'directed study'. It is not, of course, a very inclusive method. It arose from the unsatisfactory conditions and results of home study and so places emphasis upon the development of study skills.

In the words of Wesley, "Supervised study makes for study periods under the guidance of the teacher."

In the words of Clark and Star, "The supervised study is the study under the guidance for students and the observation and guidance of the study for the teachers."

Thus, it is a directed study procedure, which has to be implemented under the direction of the teacher. It is an effective technique to understand the subject matter of Commerce. It is an aid in helping to solve the problem of individual differences, because teacher provides individual attention to every student. Individuals have different abilities and capacities and the teacher through this method can be able to recognize the individual progress, study skills, study habits of the individuals. The students get direction while studying, which is very useful because the mistakes have been omitted at the same time, which helps in avoiding the wastage of time. Each pupil proceeds on his own responsibility, but in order that he should not be discouraged, the teacher guides and directs him until he becomes independent and efficient in his study.

With the help of supervised study procedure, under careful and efficient supervision, a pupil can do much more and better work in less time, especially if at the same time he is being trained in the technique of study.

Role of the Teacher

In supervised study, its effectiveness depends upon the efficiency of the teacher. He must demonstrate analytical reading, outlining, summarizing, making of graphs, and all other activities which he expects the students to perform. The instructions given by the teacher should grow directly out of student's need and should have a specific application to the lesson. The instruction can be given to the whole class, to small groups or to an individual.

The teacher should have some scientific insight in to the principles of learning and a keen realization of how to apply them. He should know how to help the students as well as when to help and when not to help. He may modify assignments and guidance in such a manner as to fit them to the needs of all kinds of students. He may sometimes decide to use the whole period for guided study or some time to the recitation and guidance with supervised study. In this way the effectiveness of this method depends upon the insight of the teacher that how and when to use this procedure.

Plans of Supervised Study Method

Many plans have been evolved for the supervision of the study. In general, Bining and Bining explained it in two ways:

1. These plans which have to do with the expression of pupils who are having difficulty with their work and are in danger of failing in their course, and
2. Those which have to do with supervised study as a class procedure.

The plans which can be used for the first category are as follows:

(*i*) *The Conference Plan*: In the plan, the teacher provides individual guidance to those pupils who cannot keep up their work and are in danger of failing, so that they can be brought to the normal standard of the class. The teacher remains in school each day for a period after the class work is over to provide individual attention to the weak students. In some cases the plan is voluntary on the part of the teacher; in other cases, the principal requires it as a part of teacher's work. In some plans, the conferences are optional on the part of the pupil; in other, they are compulsory. This plan can be of much use in aiding weak pupils and thereby preventing failures.

(*ii*) *The Special Teacher Plan:* Under this plan, one teacher devotes his entire time to coaching or supervising pupils individually or in small groups. Pupils needed assistance or those who are doing unsatisfactory work are required to meet the special teacher at stated hours. It is evident that this type of teaching calls for a teacher who have a special training and qualification and also a wide knowledge of different subjects, but not so deep as the subject teacher have. A sound knowledge of the learning process and of the psychology of students is also essential to the special teacher because the difficulties of pupils generally arise through the lack of training in how to study, although they may be due to mental, physical or other causes.

Other Plans: The above two plans are for the first type of category i.e., for the weak pupils or those who are failing in their work. Various other plans have been evolved for all pupils as:

(*i*) *Supervised Study and the Study Hall:* The term 'supervised study' is sometimes applied to the activities carried on in the study hall. There is differentiation between the work done during the study hall period and supervised study in the classroom. Study hall is a big room where the students who do not have a scheduled class come to study whatever they choose. The teacher is the incharge of the room. The teacher is to take care in maintaining the discipline in the study hall. For this, it is important that every one in the hall be busy and have work to do. The method can be useful for backward, normal or gifted students.

(*ii*) *The Divided Period Plan of Supervised Study:* This plan was the result of the work of superintendent of schools. John Kennedy conceived the idea of having large classes and two teachers in each of the large classroom. While one teacher conducted a recitation with one group, the other supervised the study of the rest. The results of the experiment were far beyond the expectations. Backward children made considerable progress and failures were few. The result was not due to having two teachers in the classroom, but to having class instruction supplemented by supervised study.

(*iii*) *The Double Period Plan of Supervised Study:* The double period plan is similar to the divided period plan, except that two whole periods are given to the class, instead of one. During the first period, the class engages in the recitation work and the second in supervised study. In some cases it may be reversed, this depends upon the aim of the recitation. Use of this plan makes the school day lengthy as well as increases the cost of instruction.

(*iv*) *Periodical Plan:* Some teachers and educationists are not in favour of double period plan or divided period plan. They have devised other plans. In one of them, every other day is given to supervised study by the classes. In another plan, an extra period has been added to the school day for this method. A third plan sets aside an hour a week for supervised study in each subject.

(*v*) *Study Guidance Sheet:* It is a sad fact that many pupils in school do not know how to study, simply because they have never been taught. The teacher assumes too much on the part of the pupil and have been guilty of leading him to establish wrong study habits. Many teachers have seen the need for teaching pupils the facts relating to methods of study and have therefore devised guidance sheet for the benefit of the pupils. The terms in the sheet deal with the technique of study and with the physical conditions necessary for effective study. The emphasis has been given on the following points:

1. Be sure that the assignment is definitely understood.
2. Review the main points of the previous lesson.
3. Read over the assignment rapidly, to get the main points.
4. Consult dictionary for new words and their pronunciation.
5. Read the assignment carefully.
6. Keep the main topic clearly in the mind and relate the substance of each paragraph and division to the same topic.
7. With the textbook closed, go over in your mind the main points of the lesson in detail and order.

The sheet contains valuable suggestion as the art of study, but it will be helpful only when the pupils will follow them in action. We see a wide discrepancy between knowledge and action. The teacher must develop in his pupils the habits necessary for independent study and this can be achieved best through the use of supervised study method.

Merits/Advantages of Supervised Study

Supervised study method is of immense value due to the following reasons:

1. It aids in preventing failures.
2. It promotes the progress of slow learners.
3. The additional work that can be given to the bright pupil affords him a better chance to make the most of his abilities.
4. It fulfills the needs of different pupils. The pupil work along his own mental level and at his own capacity. Assignment can be given to meet all levels of ability.
5. It promotes better pupil-teacher relationship. The usual class teaching procedure often produces a class vs. teacher attitude, because the teacher

is frequently considered a hard task master and little more. Under this method, he works as the helper and guide. Many more opportunities are there for displaying sympathy and understanding. The teacher is able to understand the difficulties of the pupils and is in a position to solve them.

6. Supervised study helps in the development of certain skills. Teachers often assume that pupils possess such skills whereas a thorough use of supervised study method would reveal weakness in the learners. The different skills as how to read Commerce material, how to use dictionary, how to use encyclopaedias, maps, index as and how to read graphs and maps can be developed in the pupils. The teacher should be aware that the mastery of skills is most important for the skill that pupil has learned will remain long after much of the material has been forgotten.
7. Through this method, the teacher finds an opportunity to supervise his class.
8. It develops the habit of self study among pupils.
9. It is related with psychological laws of learning i.e. learning by doing.
10. Pupils learn to evaluate the subject matter critically. It not only develops the ability to compare the facts but they learn to evaluate the sources of facts.
11. When the pupils work under the supervision of the teacher, they know about their weaknesses and the teacher can provide feedback immediately and bring improvement in them.
12. The teacher continuously supervises the textbook, reference book and thus their use can be more effective.
13. The students remain active throughout the process.
14. It offers an unusual opportunity to care for all the students in group as well as individually.

The efficacy of any method depends largely on the teacher-in-charge. If he is not efficient in utilizing the plan, the chances of success will be small. Teaching is a very humane affair and cannot be put in a mould to ensure good results.

Demerits and Limitations of Supervised Study Method

The demerits and limitations of this method are as follows:

1. In some investigations, it has been found that the bright pupil is not helped and in some cases, is even hindered by the method.
2. The double period plan increases the cost and the school day becomes lengthy.
3. It destroys the self-reliance of the pupil because of the availability of the teacher to get guidance. The student while facing small difficulties, do not use his mind, and always ready to take guidance from the teacher. For this the teacher must watch him at work, note his weakness, and aid him in achieving the most economical and effective habit of study.
4. It is a time consuming process.
5. It depends upon the encouragement and curiosity of the student, which they do not prefer to exhibit.

6. It may encourage the process of discussion only.
7. There is always lack of efficient teachers because training is not provided in utilizing this method.
8. The students are not free to do the work at their own.
9. Some argue that this process finishes the importance of the teacher because he works as the second part in teaching learning process.

The demerits and limitation described above may be the result of a faulty use of the method. The proponents of the method, however, maintain that the cost would not be greater in the long run or, at best the increase would be negligible. It must always be borne in mind that methods are means and not ends. After all, the end in view is the training and education of the pupil. An overuse of any procedure would result in a neglect of many aims of education. It can be valuable if utilized in limit by an efficient and skilled teacher.

VI. Lecture Method

The lecture method is the procedure of teaching most widely used in colleges and universities. The term lecture has been derived from the Medieval Latin word 'Lectare' means 'to read aloud'. It consists of an oral reading of a text followed by a commentary. The method has been criticised in schools. In criticising the lecture, many have gone to the extreme of condemning any telling procedure on the part of the teacher. In Commerce, the acquiring and understanding of knowledge is important. It is true that teachers often talk too large a part of the class period. This is not the fault of lecture method: the fault lies in the teacher. The poor teacher, who does not know how to fill in the class period, resorts to talk that has little educational significance. The better teacher may come to class with a well-prepared talk that proves useful for the class. In a lecture, notes are usually taken by the recipients and it may be supplemented by handouts provided by the teacher. The purpose of the lecture are usually considered to be to convey information from the teacher to the learners. It will help in generating understanding and stimulate interest. The processes of lecturing include structuring and conveying ideas, procedures and facts to a group which receives, interprets and responds to messages received. In this, students are spoon fed and their power of observation and reasoning, the exercise of which is so essential in the learning process, are not stimulated. This is purely a teacher centred method. According to Thomas Station, "A lecture has been defined a process by which facts are transmitted from the note books of the instructor to the note book of the students without passing through the either."

When to Use the Lecture Method

The teacher of Commerce has many opportunities to use the lecture or 'telling method'. The following are some of the uses to which it may be put:

1. *To give an overview of a large unit or topic*: This is of great educational value to the pupils in Commerce. The syllabus of Commerce is very wide. A carefully planned overview delivered in a vital and interesting manner will be helpful in making the reading of the pupils meaningful.

2. *To aid and supplement the pupils reading*: The teacher must take time and care to make the aims of outside reading intelligible and to relate it to the work of the course. There is much material that the teacher can give that will lead to better understanding of the subject.
3. *To give a background*: The events of business become more meaningful when they are seen in relation to an adequate background. The teacher can provide such a background that the work will take on meaning. Before starting any new topic, the teacher can create interest of the students by giving its background.
4. *To save time for the pupil*: Pupil's time is limited and with the help of lecture, the teacher can provide the important information relating to the topic within a short span of time and the students can utilise his study time in the best advantages.
5. *To arouse interest*: We are not interested in what we know little or nothing about. It is the teacher's duty to stimulate interest. He can do it by presenting the outstanding aspects of the events and the achievements of significant business personnel in an in interesting way. A teacher can talk about a book for those pupils who will desire to read it.
6. *To give an assignment*: The assignment is the teacher's opportunity to show how the new work is related to the just completed work. It is also used to tell the pupils what is expected of them and how they are to do it and by giving such explanations, it will enable them to work efficiently and intelligently.
7. *To clarify concepts*: The lecture can be utilised to clarify the meaning of difficult terms and concepts so that they may become understandable to the students. It is especially necessary in the Social Science.
8. *To make summaries and give reviews*: In Social Science, material is complex that is why frequent reviews are necessary in order to give emphasis to that what is important. It will help in preparing the pupils for examinations. The aim of a summary should be to emphasise the important points of the lesson and to show the relation of the lesson to previous lesson and to the subject as a whole.

The process of lecture method can be shown with the help of the following diagram:

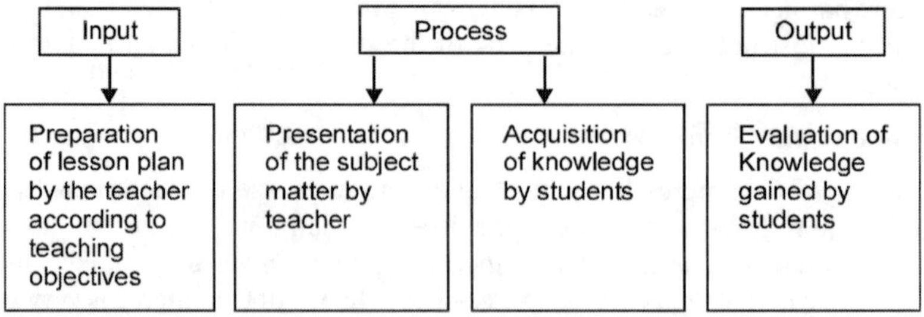

Fig. 7.4

These are the process of programmed instructions. Through these four steps, it becomes clear that the teacher is centre of information and the communication of knowledge through lecture is not possible without teacher. It is clear from the communication net.

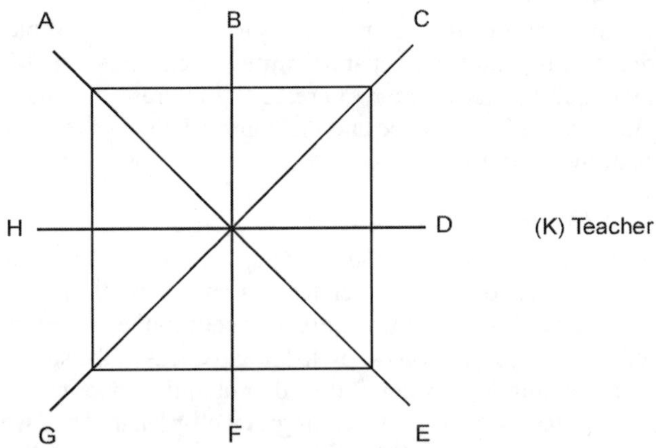

Fig. 7.5

It is clear from the net without the help of the teacher, there is no communication between A, B, C, D, E, F, G and H.

The following steps are to be followed while preparing the lecture:

1. *Lecture preparation and lesson planning hold much in common*: The lecture is essentially an experience in anticipatory teaching and as such must reflect the characteristics of anticipation required in the preparation of any good lesson. The laws of learning that govern lesson planning must be recognised in the preparation of the lecture.
2. *Preparation must keep objectives clearly in mind*: The objectives of education and the particular objectives of the lecture should be clear to the teacher.
3. *The lecture must be clearly outlined*: When exposition in the method employed to clarify an issue or develop the stages in the solution of problem, then it is important that the outline steps should stand out clearly.
4. *All pertinent illustrative devices should be carefully prepared*: When concrete devices are employed, every detail should be carefully prepared so that maximum class attention may be focused upon the idea illustrated and not upon the device employed.
5. *The lecture should capitalise the appreciative experience of the class*: This should be done in the selection of the illustrations, in adapting the lecture as far as possible to the known interests of the class and to the level of experience the students represent.

6. *When the lecture is expository in nature, the general principals of induction-deduction should be used*: The wise teacher will make every possible adaptation of these development procedures to the principles. Preparation for exposition may well follow some adaptation of the general outline of induction made famous by the Herbartian 'Five Formal Steps' namely—
   (a) Preparation
   (b) Presentation
   (c) Comparison association
   (d) Generalisation
   (e) Application
7. Where the lecture involves narration or description, simple clarity and interest are the features preparation must seek to assure. Many devices are available to the narrator to create the interest, and these should be carefully studied in advance and the appropriate ones chosen to meet the needs of the occasion.

Merits of Lecture Method

1. *Direct contact between teacher and pupils*: For effective learning, there is need of direct contact between teacher and students at the school level. Teacher can adjust his procedure in accordance with their interests, aptitudes, abilities, previous knowledge and needs of the students. Students can ask anything in between if they do not understand it.
2. *Help in making Commerce interesting*: A well-prepared and well-delivered lecture can make Commerce interesting. Through this method, event and subject matter can be correlated to make teaching learning process interesting.
3. *Less time consuming*: It covers syllabus in limited time provided by the timetable in the schools. Sometime students may spend a lot of their valuable time in going through other sources for the clarification of some complicated concepts. The teacher can clear those concepts in a short time.
4. *Provides training and experience in learning by hearing*: It helps the teacher to make a good example of oral expression. In democratic countries, children in schools must be trained for adult life so that they may be able to participate in national affairs. Lectures play an important part in adult life whether one is a leader or follower.
5. *Useful for factual information*: Factual information and a historical anecdotes can be easily imparted by this method. The interesting life histories of the great businessmen can be imparted effectively through this procedure.
6. *Inspiration value*: Good lectures have high inspirational value. Sometime students pick up motivation, inspiration, instigation, zeal and ambitious ideas and do something creative in life.
7. *Economical*: It is very economical because it can be applied easily at higher grade classes where sizes of the classes are very large in number. In this way, it is applicable in Indian situations where the size of the class is big.
8. *Based on personal teaching*: Through this method, the teacher can bring life, blood and colour to the various situations by his firm voice, tone, emphasis, stress, gesture, expression, and also by using various devices like dramatisation.

9. *Susceptible of immediate repetition and modification*: If a teacher feels that his pupils are not following his lecture, he may repeat the ideas with modified statements in an easy way.
10. *Help in stimulating brighter pupils*: As a lecture demands a lot of preparation on the part of the teacher, its advantages are transferred to the students. Teacher's own preparation, his enthusiasms and his interests stimulate brighter pupils. They like to pursue projects and consult more and more books and journals to gain more and more knowledge.

Demerits and Limitations

1. *Little scope for student activity*: In this method, students become passive listeners. Now-a-days effective method is that which involves the student's participation aspect in respect to Business Studies and Accountancy.
2. *More work load on teacher*: A teacher who is required to teach in the school from the first period up to the last, will not have the capacity to prepare so many lectures in a day. It is physically impossible for him to speak continuously for four/five hours a day.
3. *Spoon-feeding*: It does not encourage independent thinking, discovering, exploring and taking initiative. It is a type of spoon-feeding and all the traits of the child's personality are not allowed to develop.
4. *Unpsychological*: Students do not take opportunity to acquire learning by activity. The interests, attitudes, and capabilities of the students are ignored, which is opposed to the principles of psychology.
5. *Authoritarian*: This method is undemocratic, rather it is authoritarian. The pupils are encouraged to depend upon an authority i.e. teacher. They are not capable to challenge the verdict of the teacher.
6. *No development of critical thinking*: It fails to develop the creative, critical thinking and reasoning power. For the success of the democracy as well as for life this development is necessary otherwise the habit of evaluating the plans and procedures given by the government cannot be evaluated.
7. *Monotonous and dull*: The effective teacher to avoid dullness of the lesson uses a variety of methods. Only trained and exceptional teachers can stimulate interests through their lectures at all grade levels. The lesson most of the time becomes dull, when only the lecture method is used.
8. *Memory based*: It lays too much stress on memory work. Experimental work is ignored and the power of observation of a child is seldom exercised.
9. *Teacher-centered*: When the teacher provides lecture, talks and talks, there is no guarantee whether the pupils are concentrating and understanding all what the teacher is teaching.
10. *Less applicability*: It is not applicable for every student because of difference in their mental capability and it is also not applicable to teach every topic because some topics are easy and some are difficult.

It is a hard fact that lectures are still the most common method of teaching throughout the world.

According to James Lee, "The lecture is a pedagogical method whereby the teacher formally delivers a carefully planned address on some particular topic or a problem."

The teacher should not use it extensively but with some suggestive measures as use of maps, diagrams, in the lecture. Use of examples, stories and experiences can make lecture effective and interesting.

Teacher in Effective Lecture Technique

Suggestion on Lecturing

1. The teacher should choose the occasion for his lectures with great care.
2. Where lecture is to consume more time, it should be outlined and clearly thought through.
3. Illustrations should be provided, in the form of charts and diagrams.
4. Begin if possible, by arousing in the minds of the pupils a problem, a question upon which you propose to throw light.
5. As much as possible, keep the students in a problematic and expectant attitude.
6. Be careful as to pace. Adjust pace to difficulties of the material presented and to the ability of the pupils to take notes, if notes should be taken.
7. Be careful not to fall into the fallacy of assuming that what you say is as clear to your students as it is to you.
8. Use interested earnest conversational tones and in a personal conversational manner.
9. Pause occasionally for reactions.
10. Sometimes it is wise to furnish the class with an outline of the lecture in advance.
11. Phrase your remarks where possible in an attractive way.
12. Cultivate a good time sense.
13. Hold the pupils definitely responsible for the content of talks and lectures.
14. Check what the pupils have learned from your lecture, as a means of diagnoses and as remedial teaching. A short lecture may be used for this purpose.

VII. Lecture cum Discussion Method

It is generally believed that lecture method is teacher-centered method and the learners remain passive. It is a dull method because students remain inattentive in the class, therefore, to make the lecture methods interesting and effective, it is essential that it must be supported by other techniques as question answer, discussion, etc. If the discussion is also intended in lecture then it becomes lecture cum discussion method. Today there is need of such methods, in which learner remains active i.e. learners centered methods. This is an improvement over lecture method which is conducive for learning. It is based on the psychological laws of learning i.e. learning by doing. It involves the very useful social art of exchanging ideas with others. In it, teacher and pupils both remain active. Commerce deals with the problems of business and lecture with discussion can be helpful in finding the solution of the problems.

Procedure of the Method

The teacher introduces the topic with the help of lecture method. He puts some questions before the students to create interest in the topic. In this way, students become active in the teaching learning process. The subject matter is developed through the discussion i.e. active participation of the learners. The learning situations created by this method become effective and meaningful. It involves more senses of students which facilitate true knowledge of the subject matter. During discussion the teacher has to explain the concept with the help of lecture. The difficult and complicated aspects are explained by the teacher so that they may be understandable to the students. Thus, this process will go on with question-answer, discussion and lecture side by side. This method require systematic planning. Planning entails a number of activities. The teacher must prepare a plan for this. This contains the instructional objectives to be achieved, the amount of content to be covered, the kinds of instructional modes to be used, the discussion to be held, the feedback mechanism to be used, the kind of audio-visual aids to be used. Thus planning the lecture-cum-discussion boosts the confidence of the teacher. He knows in advance what to do, when to do, how to do and what not to do. Thus, method may be planned in three phases as follows.

(i) Introduction of the topic

Sometimes this introduction phase is also called the warm up phase. The main task of the teacher here is to establish rapport with the pupils, create interest and motivation among them and gradually lead the learner to the next phase. At this stage teacher uses question-answer technique to arouse interest and to make the students feel free to express their views. The teacher also uses different audio-visual aids to highlight the theme.

(ii) Development phase

This is the most important phase of the lecture-cum-discussion method. The transaction of ideas and information between the teacher and the learner takes place in this phase. The teacher explains the concepts and principle, provides facts, quotes, figures, etc. and asks examples from the students to make them active. The teacher also adopts different non-verbal communication techniques as gestures, posters, etc. to facilitate teaching and learning.

(iii) Consolidation phase

This is the concluding phase of the method. Here the teacher summarises the subject matter with the help of students. He also asks a few questions on the content matter covered in order to evaluate the students' understanding of the subject matter. The teacher gets the feedback about his methodology. The teacher also gives some assignments to the pupils.

Merits of Lecture-cum-Discussion Method

The lecture-cum-discussion method is more advantageous than lecture method as:

1. It can be used to impart knowledge pertaining to all branches of Social Science.
2. It can be adapted to suit a wide range of personality characteristics.
3. Students and teacher both remain active.
4. It is helpful in using more senses in learning processes.
5. The knowledge gained becomes permanent.
6. This method creates very conducive learning situations for the students.
7. It is based on psychological laws of learning.
8. The students get reinforcement in discussion.
9. The students are free to express their views.
10. The students get much exposure.
11. It is helpful for realising high order of cognitive objectives.
12. It develops the habit of discussion among students.

Demerits/Limitation of Lecture-Cum-Discussion Method

In spite of the above advantages, this method has following demerits/limitations as:

1. Lack of efficient teacher to use this method.
2. Few students may dominate the discussion.
3. The required weightage to lecture and discussion on a topic is the logical activity depends on the students.
4. Sometimes discussion may result in loss of time and energy.
5. Sometimes teacher may avoid discussion and depends upon lecture only.
6. It requires proper planning.
7. It requires proper training and practice.
8. It cannot be used at lower level.
9. Every topic can't be taught through this method.
10. Every type of student may not be able to understand the topic clearly.
11. It is a time consuming process.

To conclude, we can say that this method is an improvement over the lecture method and it can be used to make lecture more interesting and effective. It will help in removing the monotony of the method. If the teacher uses it properly, then it can be an effective teaching-learning process.

VIII. Role Playing Method

Commerce teacher can use various activities to make the teaching interesting and effective. Role playing provides useful learning experiences. Role playing proves useful to provide liveliness to commercial events, activities and prevailing thoughts in different ages. The students can establish contact with commercial and geographical places and goods by tours and travels. They can reach near the goods related to business with the help of charts and models. But business is not limited to place and goods only but it includes different events, geographical circumstances, economic problems, political thoughts and feelings etc. and commerce teaching can't be completed without the studies of these. Visual symbols can't make them lively. So, the educationists suggest the use of role playing method. But in this method one thing should be kept in mind that role playing is not the end like other sources but it is a means, through which we can achieve the specific objectives of commerce.

It can become a useful method if it is used carefully. The students are used to do different types of activities. As they observe their elders, they want to simulate them through role playing. They get recreation in such type of activities. They have the ability to simulation and dramatisation. It is the responsibility of the teacher to provide environment as well as opportunities to develop these abilities of the students. In present scenario teaching learning process tries to use different methodologies to make the students active and enthusiastic, so, role playing method can make the pupils hard working, reliable and resourceful and they can learn to remain cooperative to their peers. Role playing can also be useful in the development of creative powers. Froebel, stressed on the development of children's innate powers and abilities. According to him, 'play' is important in the child's development and through play his innate powers can be developed. Dewey also laid stress on the development of innate power through activity method. Thus, we can say that role-play can be helpful in the all-round development of the personality of the child. If role playing is used carefully then it can create enthusiasm, development of powers, provides opportunities for self-expression and develop the democratic qualities among the students.

Role play method is based on activity. It is just a transformation and extension of the activity urge of the child. It is governed by the principle of pleasure. It aims at the accompaniment of happiness and satisfaction which the role playing is undertaken. It is the experiencing of the pleasure of performing a role for its own sake.

Role play method is just the application of Thorndike's 'Law of Effect' to the learning process. In role play, a person experiences pleasure and happiness. Thus, an activity is said to be done and learnt in the role play when that activity is in accordance with a person's ability and inclination fulfilling his need and entails happiness and pleasure. Learning through role play becomes meaningful and significant. Effectiveness of learning lies not in reading and listening but in action, performance and experience.

Child's love of role play is proverbial. It is a natural means to provide opportunities to the child for free play of interest and spontaneous efforts. School education can be made a joyous activity, something tangible and practical if imparted on dramatisation lines.

Underlying Principles

The role play method is based on the activity principle, freedom and spontaneity of children's efforts. Learning process is not to be boring, taxing and abstract affair, but practical, joyous and autonomous. The accountancy, management and Business Studies can be taught effectively with role play method.

(i) Let learning take place through doing, in a natural atmosphere. There must be an active way of acquiring knowledge and also utilising it.

(ii) Methods should not be too rigid and too formal. There must be something of naturalness around them. These methods should be suited to the interests and needs of the students.

(iii) The information imparted, subject taught and knowledge gained should be related to life.

(iv) Ample and varied opportunities should be provided to the pupils for self-expression.

(v) The pupils should enjoy the learning process. Knowledge should not be trusted upon but desired after.

(vi) Teacher's attitude should not be authoritative to curb the natural expression of the pupils.

Role play is to be the basis of all progressive methods of education. Earnest and serious efforts should be made by all pioneers in education to explore the potentialities of the pupils. The role play method has a bright future to be applied as a potent medium for:

- Self-education
- Self-advancement
- Self-discipline
- Self-expression

Merits/Advantages of Role Play Method

The role playing carries with it great advantages. The principles underlying are now considered as the mainstay of good learning procedures. The major advantages may be as follows:

1. *Provides Motivation*: Role playing serves as a great motivating force for pupils. As it is based on their natural urge they gladly undertake to learn. It kills drudgery and boredom.
2. *Development of Proper Understanding*: Role playing helps in the development of proper understanding of the subject matter among the students. For instance, to prepare a skit on the business ethics, requires considerable reading and close identification with the ethics involved in the business. All this means a better understanding of the situation.
3. *Development of Democratic Behaviour Pattern and Social Skills*: It takes cooperation, discussion, intelligent decision-making and much self-discipline to play a situation. Role playing is especially useful as an instrument in developing attitudes and values important to democratic behaviour.
4. *Satisfies Individual Differences*: It satisfies the interests of the individuals. Role playing is valuable in providing variation in instructional procedure according to the individual differences in the classroom.
5. *Development of Memory*: Role playing is much useful from psychological point of view. It provides opportunities to the pupils for mental exercise and as a result helps in development of memory. The pupils are to memorise various dialogues.
6. *Development of Imagination Power*: Role playing helps in the development of imaginative power of the pupils. The students can imagine the business environment of different industries as well as the behaviour pattern of the employers, employees, customers, etc.
7. *Provides Opportunities for Learning by Doing*: Role playing provides opportunities to do different type of activities. The learning thus becomes lively and interesting.
8. *Sensory Training*: In lecture method students use most of the time the sense organ ears but it is not sufficient. In role playing the students get the

opportunity to use different sense organs. Besides it, the role playing helps in attracting the emotions etc.

9. *Helpful in Providing Recreation*: Everybody likes to see and act the plays and it provides education with recreation. In role playing pupils not only get the knowledge but it also helps in creating interests in them. The pupils get opportunities to act or indirectly play the role of an industrialist, customer, manager, cashier, etc. which may help them in real life also later on.
10. *Helpful in Initiation*: It is useful to initiate the study of a particular topic. Think of a situation in which the teacher wants to initiate the development of some basic understanding of business risks. He again seeks the description business risks with the help of dramatic situations.

Limitations of Role Play

1. *Lack of knowledge about art of role play*: Role playing is not an easy task. It is not used at a large scale in the schools of India, because on the one hand teachers are not much efficient and, on the other hand, students have no knowledge about it. It is necessary that teacher should help the students in role playing to a greater extent.
2. *Creates indiscipline in the class*: While using role play method there is need of free activity in the class, as a result it creates indiscipline in the class. But if the teacher remains alert then this problem can be solved.
3. *Lack of finances*: In India schools have lack of funds. Role play method needs finance to set a stage, to collect material etc. Without these, proper environment can't be created while role playing. The schools don't provide finances for such type of activities.
4. *Problem of dialogues*. The teachers have no time to write the dialogues for role play and many of them don't have aptitude. If the teacher has interest then this problem can be solved.
5. *Time consuming*: Generally it has been viewed that role playing takes so much time that it becomes difficult to complete the curriculum in time. But this also works as a means, not an end. If it is utilised in a limited way then this problem can be solved.

Precautions in Role Play

Undoubtedly, role playing is a useful method for teaching of commerce. It not only helps in making the teaching interesting, effective and understandable but it also helps in development of individual and civic values among the students. It will help in providing life skill education which is the need of the hour. But while using it, some precautions should be kept in mind as:

1. Such type of roles should be selected which can be easily played.
2. The roles should be according to the mental and intellectual abilities of the students.
3. The students should be involved while selecting the roles.
4. The roles should be given to the students according to their interests and abilities.

5. It should be well-practised before presentation.
6. The roles should be according to the lesson.
7. The role play should be used when it is needed.
8. After role playing it should be evaluated to test the fulfilment of objectives.

Thus, role play is not to be misconceived as frivolity or fun. Griffin has well pointed out, "It is the child's characteristic mode of behaviour and any system of education which hampers this natural direction for the expanding of energy endangers the health — mental and physical of the child."

It is not to be taken as an alternative to serious work or a relief from that, nor a mode of relaxation or a means of recreation. It is, in the words of Smith and Harrison, "an all-absorbing method, in which initiative, fore-thought control and skill can be exercised in full measure." The teacher is required to plan carefully and execute thoughtfully. The success of the role playing method depends on the wisely made labour of the teacher. He is to think out ways and means to make his lessons a success on role play method. It is not following the least line of resistance but a whole-hearted application to an arduous task of facilitating the learning process in a natural way and in an interesting manner. Role playing aims at making things interesting and to do that is a tough job and not soft-pedagogy.

Selection of a Good Method/Strategy

The main job of the teacher is to teach. There is not a single method or the method of teaching any subject which could suit in all the situations. As two children are not alike, in the same way all teachers are different. Thus, a teaching method is largely governed by the following three factors.

(*a*) The teacher
(*b*) The pupil
(*c*) The environment

A teaching method may prove to be suitable for one situation but completely inappropriate for another. If our objective is to provide factual knowledge of the subject matter, understanding of the basic concepts then lecture method will be more appropriate but by this method the laboratory skills, interests can't be developed and for this perhaps the laboratory method would be more suitable. So every method the teacher use should lead the pupil to a sense of achievement through interest and purpose. It should stimulate the pupils to think and cooperate actively. The instincts of play, imitation, curiosity, competition, etc. are concerned with the educational development of the child and which the teacher must consider while choosing and planning any method of teaching.

8

Specific Approaches of Teaching Book-keeping

"First write and then give, if forget then take from the paper."

Commerce is an integrated subject comprises of book-keeping, commercial practice, shorthand and typing etc. All these subject are separate from teaching point of use, so, the teaching methods are different for these subjects.

Book-keeping is the sum of two words — **book** + **keeping** means to keep the accounts in the book. Thus, it can be said that book-keeping is a science in which income-expenditure, credit-debit of money, sale-purchase, etc. are organised in a systematic way.

Principles of Teaching Book-keeping

1. Thoroughness in Teaching: A student must understand the concepts thoroughly. Learning in bits develops misunderstanding about the concepts.

2. Organisation: Each student must be very clear about what he is going to learn in the class. The subject matter should be organised in a systematic way so that students may be able to understand it fruitfully.

3. Effective Demonstration: The student should not only know what transactions to do but should also know how to do. For this the teacher is to demonstrate with the help of different instructional aids.

4. Determination of Teaching Method: By keeping in mind the subject matter, level of pupils and available resources the teacher is to determine that for the presentation of subject matter which method he should opt. There are several methods as — Text Book method, lecture method, Discussion method, project method, etc. — which can be utilised for teaching.

5. Determination of Approach: For teaching Book-keeping several approaches as journal approach, ledger approach, Balance sheet approach etc. can be used. After determining the approach, the teacher can decide how he will present the subject matter before the pupils in the class.

Instructional Objectives of Book-keeping

NCERT lists the following instructional objectives:

1. To acquire the knowledge of facts, concepts, principles and procedures, forms and statements related to book-keeping.
2. To develop an understanding of facts, concepts, principles and procedures, form and statements related to book-keeping.

3. To apply the acquired information and knowledge of the concepts and principles of book-keeping in new students.
4. To acquire the skills of maintaining account books.
5. To develop desirable interest in book-keeping.
6. To develop possible attitude towards book-keeping.

Approaches of Teaching Book-keeping

The important approaches for teaching book-keeping are:

1. Journal Approach

In this approach steps in a book-keeping are taught in the order they are used in different offices. After giving the preliminary knowledge of making journal entries and recording of business transactions in a book of original entry, three golden rules of journalizing and making entries into journal book, the ledger or the account is introduced. In journal approach there is certain system of presenting the subject matter of commerce. The teacher of commerce while teaching through this approach utilizes the following steps:

- Clarifying the meaning of double entry system.
- Defining debit and credit.
- Analysing transitions in terms of debit and credit.
- Writing of debit and credit in journal.
- Posting.
- Trial Balance — Arithmetical accuracy.
- Profit and loss account.
- Balance sheet.
- Closing entries.
- Learning of opening entries.

Characteristics of Journal Approach

Journal approach is a simple and practicable approach of presenting the subject matter in a systematic way. This approach is mostly applicable in Indian schools. It has following characteristics:

1. It is simple method of presenting the subject matter.
2. The knowledge of book-keeping cycle through journal approach is provided in the same way as a business office does in the book. From this point of view this approach is more practical.
3. Its steps are fixed.
4. While using journal approach firstly the principles of double entry system are made clear which makes the subject matter more easy.

Limitations

1. This approach is not psychologically sound because it is not based on the psychological laws of learning.
2. Pupils have to labour hard for weeks together in learning how to journalize and how to post into the ledger and due to such a long period, they don't understand where they are going and what is their final goal.
3. Pupils have to rely on teacher's words.

2. Ledger Approach

In this approach the basic and fundamental concepts of book-keeping are stated. The central idea behind the account is to prove the equality of debits and credits. The trial balances are taken to test it. The teacher starts teaching on the basis of ledger. He provides introduction of double entry system and then does exercise directly on ledger and then provides knowledge about journal. The steps of this approach are:

- Providing knowledge of elements and meaning of double entry system.
- Learning of opening entries.
- Knowledge of types of ledger.
- Analysing of transactions.
- Writing of debits and credits in ledger accounts.
- Balancing Ledger Account.
- Trial Balance.
- Journal writing of debit's and credit's.
- Posting.
- Final accounts and Balance sheets.
- Closing entries.

Merits/Characteristics of Ledger Approach

1. This approach is based on logic.
2. It provides meaningful and useful knowledge from the very beginning, so, the students understand 'why' and 'how' of every entry.
3. Students learn meaningfully the debit and the credit aspects.
4. Students learn easily to frame balance sheets of every type of accounts.
5. In comparison to journal approach, this approach provides meaningful and practical learning.

Limitations and Demerits of Ledger Approach

1. In this approach students have to start from the middle of book-keeping cycle i.e. preparation of final accounts.
2. In this approach the cycle is ledger → journal → final account but in practice the cycle is journal → ledger → final account. The students feel difficulty in this unsystematic order.
3. It puts confusion by going back to journal and again to preliminary knowledge.
4. This approach does not present the subject matter before the students psychologically.

3. Cash Book Approach

Some teachers start their teaching of book-keeping with cash book approach. They think that students take more interest in cash book, so, they learn this effectively. But if we see in actual practice, there is not much of a difference in cash book approach and ledger approach because the steps are almost same in both the approaches. They are of the view that cash book is same as ledger.

4. Balance Sheet Approach

In this approach students are shown the end product of book-keeping process. It lays emphasis on the need of records and how they are used. One starts with balance sheet and then learns profit and loss statements. It is based on the psychological principles of teaching, i.e. from simple to complex, from whole to part, etc. Firstly, one has a look at the complete book-keeping cycle and then parts are taken up. In this approach, ideas, principles and concepts are developed in a logical and systematic way. The teacher presents the subject matter before the students in the following way:

- Introduction of Balance sheet.
- A summary account of closing the income and expense account is presented.
- Some adjustment of inventory account is added.
- Liabilities accounts are introduced.
- Knowledge of Assets accounts.
- The inclusion of some more adjustment work may be undertaken.
- More formal statements are introduced about accounts.
- Introduction of security of accounts and then journalising.

In the end, practice set is provided to the students.

5. Equation Approach

At present, this approach is understood to be most important for teaching book-keeping. In this approach, the teacher provides the knowledge about these concepts i.e. *assets, liability* and *capital. Asset* refers to anything owned by the owner. *Liability* refers to anything owed or outsiders' interest *Capital* refers to owners interest in business. It includes all temporary accounts i.e. account of all expenses, losses, income and gains, etc.

Assets = Liability + Capital
Capital = Assets - Liability
Liability = Assets - Capital

The steps followed in this approach are as follows:

- Introduction of capital.
- Meaning of Balance sheet.
- Knowledge of opening 'T' accounts.
- Assets will always be equal to the sum of liabilities and capital.
- Learning of ledger entries.
- Closing entries.
- Preparation of Balance sheet.
- Balancing of ledger accounts.
- Clarity of meaning of debit and credit.
- Knowledge of preliminary entries.
- Entries in journal and their description.
- Final accounts.

Merits of Equation Approach

1. This approach is psychological because students can understand easily about assets and liabilities.

2. This approach seems logical because students know about the end point in advance.
3. Students are motivated to learn and to reach to the end point.

Limitations of Equation Approach

1. Book-keeping cycle moves from downward to upward and students find it difficult to understand.
2. It starts learning from the end point i.e. mastery point.
3. It is not very practical.
4. Students find it difficult to use this knowledge practically.

Inspite of these limitations, this approach is more useful and scientific to teach commerce and the teachers use this approach in India.

6. The Complete Cycle Approach

It is a good review device and could be adopted for remedial teaching. The requirement of this approach is that entire exercise on complete cycle be done on one side on one sheet. Many practices are to be given for learning. It gives a thorough knowledge of accounting procedure.

While teaching through this approach following points are to be kept in mind:

- Students make journal entries without giving explanation for debit and credit.
- Posting references are omitted and simple check marks are used.
- Students make use of cyclostyled forms.
- Account headings of assets, liabilities and capital are supplied to students on which they work.
- Books are allowed on the first day.
- Transactions with simple figures and whole numbers are used.
- Discussion on 'why' aspects are kept in abeyance.
- A new concept is introduced only after the basic cycle is mastered.
- Instead of mentioning debit and credit, it is better to start with left side and right side.

Merits of the Complete Cycle Approach

1. All entries are done on a single sheet, so are easily understandable.
2. Use of journal and ledger account gives students a realistic picture.
3. The students get a glimpse of the complete cycle on a single look.

7. Single Entry Approach

In this approach records of assets, liabilities and capital are to be maintained but no account of the sources of P&L a/c is maintained. An incoming asset is debited and outgoing asset is credited. Every entry is made for credit or debit. Cash payment for any purchase or expenses is always credited to cash only. This approach provides data and everything is entered in a single book. It provides only the position of debtor's and creditor's. This approach does not depict the picture of financial position of the business, as and when, the businessman wants to know it. This approach is mostly used in small shops only not in big business houses.

Thus, there are different approaches which can be used to teach book-keeping in an effective way.

9

Active Learning Strategies

Active learning strategies focus on learning rather than teaching. These strategies puts the student as an active learner not as a passive listener. These provide opportunities for students to meaningfully talk, listen, write, read and reflect on the content, ideas and issues in commerce. These strategies help to initiate learners and instructors into effective ways to help everyone engage in activities based on ideas how people learn. These put focus on the learner: What the learner does, what the learner thinks, and how the learner behaves.

Active learning does not simply happen with a few simple instructions. It occurs in the classroom where the teacher is committed to a learning environment that makes active learning possible. When students learn actively the knowledge gained retain for a longer time and they are able to apply that in a broader range of contacts. Many teachers assume they that are knowledgeable persons and their role is to teach. But they should think that their role is to help the students to learn more and more. Present day researches show that teachers who are facilitators, collaborators, and organizers are having great success in helping students prepare for life long learning and making them more capable to work in real life.

As a teacher, one of your biggest challenges is to plan lessons that inspire your students to remain actively involved in the learning process. You can use active learning strategies to empower, engage and stimulate a classroom by keeping students at centre of the learning process.

These strategies can be used individually or in pairs or in small groups. These can create the opportunity for deeper learning. However, these strategies conflict with the traditional view of teaching and learning, because the teacher may think that using these strategic won't permit him/her to cover the entire syllabus. Consider the statistics reported by Meyers and Jones as:

- Pupils retain 70% of the information in his first 10 minutes of a lecture but only 20% in the last 10 minutes.
- Pupils are not attentive to what is being said in a lecture 40% of the time.
- Four months after taking an introductory psychology course, pupil know only 8% more than those who had never taken the course.

Student attention often begins to declines after 10 to 15 minutes of lecture (Stuart, John & Rutherford), retention also drops considerably after the first 10 minutes (Hartley & Davies).

Neal defines active learning as educational methods in which students are involved in higher order thinking (analysis, synthesis, evaluation). The term therefore primarily reflects what is going on in a student's mind, whether or not the body (or the mouth) is physically active.

Thus, simply presenting course material may promote short term value, but physical practising, experiencing and learning through active engagements helps to hold the roots of that material. Educators who use active learning strategies are able to teach to a variety of learners: Visual learners, auditory learners, tactile learners, and apart from these, even those learners who have difficulty remaining seated. What is more, students of commerce are able to learn in a way that most closely simulates real, on the-job jobs business situations, making for more seamless transition into the workforce.

There are different strategies for active learning. These strategies range from short, simple activities like journal writing, problem solving and paired discussion, to longer, involved activities or pedagogical framework like case studies, role plays and structured team-based learning.

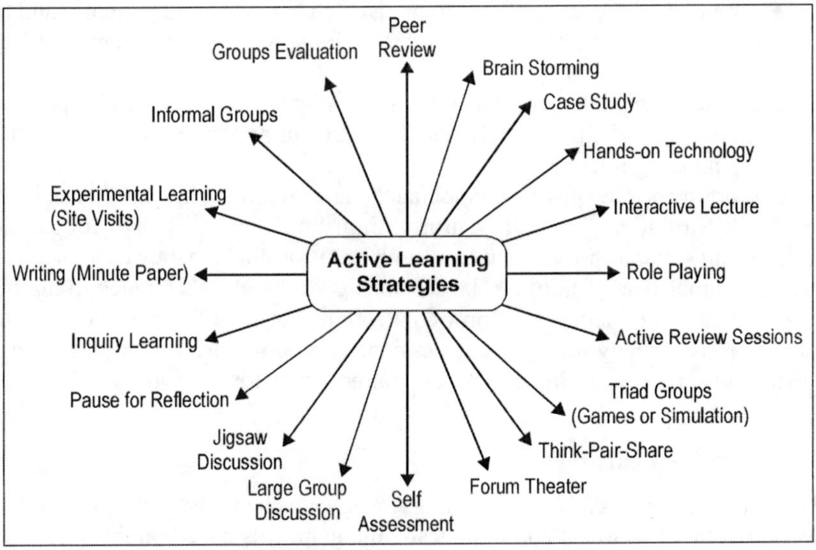

Now we will discuss some active learning strategic in detail.

1. Brainstorming

Brainstorming is an excellent strategy to generate ideas in the classroom on a given topic. It helps in promoting thinking skills. It promotes success for students with special needs as there is no one right answer. It can be used in different learning contacts as solving a problem, generating questions to ask about a visual presentation, or summarizing the key points of a lecture.

It is an excellent strategy to:

- Tap into individuality and creativity
- Tap into prior knowledge
- Eliminate fear of failure
- Show respect for each other
- Give all students to express their ideas

- Engage with the topic
- Make connections
- Try something without fear
- Use in the inclusive classroom.

Here are some basic guidelines to be followed in the classroom while using brainstorming:

- Make a small group of students. They are provided with a particular issue or topic.
- Ask the group members to think about the problem and give their ideas. They are advised to find as many ideas as they can. They are instructed not to criticize the others ideas. They are encouraged to put forward their suggestion without any hesitation even if they are thinking that they may be unusual.
- The idea of the students are to be listened and accepted patiently and the teacher or leader is not to pass any judgement or comment until the discussion is over.

These ideas can be the stimulus for a discussion to follow, topics for projects, topics with which students need assistance or some important points that might be included on an assignment later.

Thus, brainstorming promotes spontaneity and creativity, involves participants in ownership of ideas, is highly motivating, and increases task focus. The brainstorming sessions provide students with a platform where they can voice their thoughts without fear of failure. The sessions give the class a chance to tap into their provisions knowledge and form connections between the current topic and what they have already learned. The sessions can be in various forms as simple brainstorming, brainstorming in groups, paired brainstorming, pie method, care method, etc.

2. Collaborative Learning

Collaborative learning is an active learning strategy which involves grouping students to work together towards a common academic goal. It is based on the model that knowledge can be created within a group where members interact actively by sharing experiences and take on asymmetric roles. They remain active through face-to-face conversations and computer discussions. Collaborative learning activities can include collaborative writing, group projects, debates, study teams and other similar activities. Development of critical thinking is an important factor in collaborative learning. It is a fact that when individuals work in a group, they are able to achieve higher levels of learning and retain information for a long time.

In the modern era technology has become an important factor in it. Collaborative Networked Learning (CNL) is that learning which occurs via electronic dialogue between self-directed co-learners, learners and experts. Every learner remains accountable to each other for his/her success. Computer Supported Collaborative Learning (CSCL) is another paradigm within collaborative learning which uses technology to control and monitor interaction, to regulate tasks and to mediate the acquisition of new knowledge. Thus, collaboration is a critical skill for life. It is a powerful tool that enhances confidence and strengthens social skills. In the collaborative learning environment, the learners are challenged both socially and emotionally because they listen to different perspectives, are required to articulate and defend their ideas. The learners begin to create their own unique conceptional framework.

3. Peer Teaching

Peer teaching is not a single strategy but it is full of learning techniques that can help in enhancing students' achievement, content knowledge and students' engagement. It can be face-to-face or online. As a teacher you may think that it can be problematic because:

- My students are not experts. How can they teach one another?
- What if they teach and learn the information incorrectly?
- What if parents object at the idea of students learning from students when the stakes are so high for student assessment?

No doubt all the above concerns are valid and working of some debate but in reality peer teaching works in the present scenario where the teachers play the role of facilitator and motivator. Always encourage your students to help each other. There is a wealth of evidence that peer teaching is extremely effective for a wide range of goals, content and students of different levels and personalities. It is based on the belief that 'to teach is to learn twice'. Once when the student will prepare himself to teach, and the other when he will interact with the other student. Help from peer increases both for the student's being helped as well as for those giving the help.

The teacher, while using this strategy, should keep in mind that peer teaching does not mean a presentation or a lecture presented by the learner. The learners are the ones who are facilitating the session by engaging with fellow students. The facilitator ensures that the learning gets processed correctly. When your students help each other, they will feel more successful, empowered and confident about their learning.

Thus, peer teaching can enhance learning by enabling learners to take responsibility for learning, organizing and consolidating activity knowledge and material, understanding its basic structure, filling in the gaps, finding additional meanings and reformulating knowledge into new conceptional framework.

4. Problem Based Learning (PBL)

It is also an important and effective active learning strategy in which students learn about a subject through the experience of solving an open-ended problem. It does not focus on problem solving with a defined solution, but it helps in the development of other desirable skills and attitudes as knowledge acquisition, enhanced group collaboration, effective communication etc. It is based on constructivism. The role of teacher is to facilitate learning by supporting, guiding and monitoring the learning process. It helps in identifying what the students already know, what they need to know, how and where to access new information that may lead to solve the problem. It is focus on student's reflection and reasoning to construct their own learning. It is more nurturing and beneficial to the cognitive growth of the students. Some of the characteristics that make PBL an ideal for active learning, are as follows:

- Learner driven self identified goals and outcomes.
- The teacher enhances learner motivation by providing real life problems.
- Allows for knowledge acquisition through combined work and intellect.
- Enhances team work and communication, problem-solving and encourages responsibility for shared learning-all essential skills for future practices in employment as well as in real life.
- Learner identify, analyse, and resolve problems using knowledge from previous experiences and course rather than simply recalling etc.

The main focus of this strategy is to have an inter-disciplinary integrated development of deliverables, in order to improve the overall competency of the students. It is a structured activity that involves situated learning and constructivist learning strategies to encourage the culture of practice that would extend beyond the instruction to real life. The key advantage of this strategy is that it familiarizes students with real world problems and improve their confidence in solving these. The learners learn the value of team work.

An activity for PBL can be as follows:

- A problem is presented to students in small groups. They organize their ideas about the problem, evaluate it, define its nature and try to solve it with available knowledge.
- The learners discuss the problem and identify those aspects which need classification i.e. learning issues.
- They prioritise the issues and plan when, who, where and how these issues will be investigated.
- When the learners meet gain, they share and explore the knowledge gathered about the learning issues and use it to propose a solution to the problem. (If the solution is not satisfactory, they restart the cycle)
- After finishing work with the problem, the learners assess themselves, their group members and the process of the problem solving opined by them.
- Solutions may be demonstrated to the class.

PBL deals with ICEDIP

I — Inspiration
C — Clarification
E — Evaluation
D — Distillation
I — Incubation
P — Perspiration

Inspiration: Where you explore, generate ideas, have visions, brainstorm.

Clarifications: Where you discuss your aim, focus on your goal.

Evaluation: Where you assess which ideas have best potential and how to improve your work as it moves forward. What strengths can be enhanced? Here our mindset should be positive, critical and willing to learn.

Distillation: Decodes what ideas to work on. Choose your best ideas and expand them.

Incubation: We are bound to run into difficulties in coming up with solutions.

Believe in yourself that you will manage to find the way around those difficulties.

Perspiration: It is the final result of many drafts developed throughout all of the phases. Our perspiration mindset needs to be uncritical, enthusiastic and responsive.

Thus, with problem-based learning, students are in the driver's seat and take on a lot of responsibility. The problems must be complicated and do not typically have one solution. This is the main reason that PBL is different than case-based and project-based learning.

5. *Case study:* The case study is a participatory discussion-based way of learning where students gain skills in critical thinking, communication and group dynamics. It is a type of problem-based learning. Many students are more inductive than deductive reasoners, means may learn better from examples. It is a very effective strategy to learn commerce with examples by exploring the use of theory in practice. Cases come in many formats, from a simple 'what would you do in this situation?' questions to a detailed description of a situation with accompanying data to analyze. It depends upon the course objective that whether the teacher is using simple type case or a complex one.

How would you use case studies will depend on the goals as well as on the format of your course. Suppose you are teaching principles of marketing, then you may use the case of a particular company or product to explore marketing, issues and dilemmas in a real life context. If the size of the class is big, then you may break the class in 2 or 3 groups to discuss the relevant case. The following steps may be used while teaching with case study:

- The teacher should give ample time to read and think about the case.
- Clarify how you want students to think about the case.
- Create groups and monitor them to make sure everyone is involved. To get good results make the task of the group very concrete and clear.
- Ask groups to present their solution/reasoning. Write their conclusion on the board to forward the discussion.
- Ask students for clarification and to move discussion to another level.
- Synthesize issues raised.

Thus, case study, strategy is a partnership between students and teacher as well as among students. It promotes more effective contextual learning and long term retention. It involves trust that student will find the answer of the questions not only of 'how' but 'why'. It builds the capacity for critical thinking. It provides students to walk around the problem and to see varied perspective. The decisions are sometimes based not on absolute right or wrong but in relative values and uncertainty. As a result of interacting nature of this strategy, the teacher as well as the students remain active.

6. *Blended Learning:* Blended learning is a learning system that combine face-to-face instruction with computer mediated instruction. It allows students to work at their own. The learners have personalized experience because they can learn in their own time at home and time in class. It provides the necessary environment for learners to practice their skills. It is not simply adding computers to the classrooms. It represents, in many cases, a fundamental change in the way teacher and learners approach the learning experiences. It has already produced an offshoot—the flipped classroom—that has quickly become a distinct approach of its own.

It has three primary components:

- In-person classroom activities facilitated by a teacher.
- Online learning material.
- Structured independent study time guided by the material in the instructions and skills developed during the classroom experience.

Blended learning may also allow teachers to spend less time giving to whole-class lessons, and, more time meeting with students individually or in small group to help them with specific concepts, skills, questions or learning problems. The students would also be learning skills as self-discipline, self-motivation, and organizational habits they will need in adult life.

In blended learning, students can easily revisit the content anytime and anywhere with digital tools. They have more meaningful collaboration with peers. Group work will be possible without physical proximity and one to one interaction with the teacher. The students take ownership of their education and engage more deeply into course material.

Thus, blended learning, is not only based on theory but its application in real-life situation. By scheduling enough time in between classrooms sessions, the teacher can encourage the learners to learn by doing. And since the learners can see their own progress first hand, they are much more likely to adopt these new behaviour in their day-to-day work.

Other Learning Activities

One-Minute Paper—It is a highly effective technique for checking students' progress both in understanding the subject matter and in reacting to course material. Ask students to take out a blank sheet of paper, pose a question (either specific or open ended) and give them one or two minutes to respond. For example, what is trade? What is the most important point to keep in mind while making the advertisement for a product? Another good use of this strategy is to ask questions like 'what was the main point of today's class material?' It will help you to analyse that whether the students are attentive in the class.

Muddiest Point—This is a variation on one-minute paper. This technique involves students by asking them to write notes on the most unclear or most confusing element of a given home assignment, lecture, or class discussion. This exercise helps students to reflect on the lesson and identify concepts needing further examination or study. From teacher's point of view, the activity can serve as an insightful source of feedback.

Concept Map—A concept map is a way of illustrating the connections that exist between terms or concepts covered in course material. The teacher may ask the students to draw a concept map by connecting individual terms which indicates the relationship between each set of connected terms. Most of the terms in a concept map have multiple connections.

Game-based Learning—Sometimes a well conceived game is more fruitful than discussion or teaching in the class to make the concept more clear. Game-based learning add depth and differentiation to the educational process and allow students to work with their teachers to achieve their learning objectives.

For example, when students are introduced to the concept of 'Advertisement' and 'Effective Advertisement', it is hard is convey through lectures the mode of making the advertisement most effective. Instead, students play a couple of rounds to understand it in an effective way and then they can formulate their own principles to make an advertisement effective with the guidance of the teacher. Just don't forget to apply the three elements of gamification—achievement, competition and fun-1 into the endeavour.

Thus, active learning strategies are very beneficial to enhances and retention of the learning. While active learning places an emphasis on the learner's role in the learning experience, there is no doubt that the success of any active learning strategy starts with the thought and planning of a conscientious teacher. Teachers play an influential role in increasing student's situational interest in the active learning classroom. It occurs in the classroom where the teacher is committed to a learning environment that makes active learning possible. These strategies will keep building understanding rather than memorization of facts, develop confidence to apply learning to different situations and achieve greater autonomy over their learning.

This strategy will be more time consuming for the teachers as well as for the students. The teachers have to know their students more. The learners need to take more responsibility for their learning. The role as co-learners, guide and facilitator in the instruction of knowledge is one of the great challenges that PBL poses to teachers and institution.

Inspite of having these challenges, PBL strategy is a better way to learn as learners can discover new things using curiosity and they can drive their own learning as a result of problem presented. They become future ready for the job scenario.

10

Co-Curricular Activities in Commerce

"Co-curricular activities are an integral part of activities of the school like curricular work and their proper organisation needs just as much care as the curricular work. If properly conducted they can help in the development of valuable attitudes, interest and values." *–Secondary Education Commission*

Co-curricular activities form an integral part of the educational programme in the present times. In the present scenario, curriculum is not the teaching and learning in classroom. To attain the knowledge about the subject commerce, being a subject related with the study of business community, we have to move out of the four walls of the classroom and introduce some well organised and well planned programmes of co-curricular activities. The information gained through such programmes supplements the information gained through the regular teaching in the class.

Objectives of Co-curricular Activities

According to Tompkins we can divide the objectives in three groups. These are:

1. Individual Outcomes

(*i*) Constructive use of leisure time
(*ii*) Development of personality
(*iii*) Enriching of personality
(*iv*) Achieving self understanding.
(*v*) Taking initiative for individual responsibility and functioning.
(*vi*) Learning how to organise a meeting or conference and how one can participate in it.
(*vii*) Providing opportunities for self evaluation to the individual.

2. Social Outcomes

(*i*) Encouraging healthy teacher-student relationship.
(*ii*) Increasing business contacts.
(*iii*) Getting practice for working with others.
(*iv*) Developing the democratic responsibilities.
(*v*) Learning to practise good human relations.
(*vi*) Understanding group processes.
(*vii*) Providing physical and mental entertainment.

3. Civic and Ethical Outcomes

(*i*) Providing meaning to curriculum and diversifying it.
(*ii*) Putting national values and ideals in practical use.
(*iii*) Establishing the bonds of understanding of each other without any racial, religious, economic or intellectual differences.
(*iv*) Helping the students in their liking of the school.

Type of Co-curricular Activities

These can be divided into the following parts:

1. Academic or Scholastic Activities: Debates, declamation, symposium, extension lectures, story writing, reading newspapers and magazines, organising commerce club, etc.

2. Leisure Time Activities: Chart making, drawing cartoons to illustrate advertisement, visits to bank, transport offices, etc.

3. Projects: Running a cooperative store, co-operative bank, beautification of campus, alumni get-together, etc.

4. National Integration and International Understanding Activities: Celebration of national and international days, organisation of camps, educational tours and excursions, etc.

5. Cultural Development Activities: Preparation of charts and models related to different cultures, organising exhibition, dramatization, etc.

6. Civic Development Activities: Organising students' council, visiting civic institutions as gram panchayat, municipal committee, zilla parishad, high courts, celebrating religious festivals, celebrating social festivals, etc.

Principles Underlying Organisation of Co-Curricular Activities

Commerce teacher should try to involve the students in a variety of co-curricular activities by involving them in tasks which are of their liking and interest. No special emphasis be laid on any particular activity and should also not neglect any activity. It would be desirable if the maximum number of students are asked to participate in the activities. In organizing these activities the following principles should be kept in mind:

1. The activities should be selected according to *the needs and interests* of a large number of students. The opportunities should be provided in such a way that maximum number of students can participate in one or the other activity.
2. *Educationally relevant* activities should be set.
3. From economic point of view the activities *should not be too expensive.* They should not put much financial burden on the students.
4. The *mental level* of the students should always be kept in mind.
5. Activities should be selected as *means to the end* (educational goal) and not ends in themselves.
6. Pupils should be free to make a choice of the activity he\she wants to participate in. These should *not be put too much burden* on the students by making it compulsory for them to participate in too many activities.

7. The programme of co-curricular activities should be *introduced gradually* depending on the resources available.
8. The activities which are selected by the teacher should be *constructive* with aim at development of higher level objectives, which are not attainable through regular classroom teaching.
9. The activities selected should be *executed* with the active and willing co-operation of the students, staff and school management.
10. The teacher should keep *a balance* between the activities of each individual student and the programme of the commerce department as a whole.
11. As far as possible school building and games field should be the *venue* of all the activities.
12. They should take *place within* school timings. As Mohiyud-din has remarked, "By inclusion of these activities in the regular time table of our school, not only opportunities would be provided for all pupils to participate in social experience and gain valuable training in the practical art of citizenship, but the status of these activities would also be raised to the level of curricular pursuit."
13. Every co-curricular activity should be *so organised* that through it the students' mental, social and moral development can take place.
14. These activities are to be *systematically organised* and *properly supervised.* They should be supervised by the teacher and the teacher's work be supervised by the head of the institution.
15. The aim of each activity should be *clearly defined* in specific and definite terms.
16. *The permission* of head of the institution must be obtained before introducing any activity.
17. The principal should have a *right to stop* any co-curricular activity if he feels that it is not in the interest for the students.
18. *The expenditure* on these activities should be properly audited.
19. *Leadership* should be provided rotationally and maximum number of students should get an opportunity to conduct the activity.
20. The role of the teacher should be like an *observer, supervisor, guide and facilitator*. He should inspire respect and confidence among the pupils.
21. A record of each activity should be maintained. The teacher should enter the detail in a register.

The diagram 15.1 summarizes the main principles which need to be kept in mind while organising these activities.

Thus by planning a coherent programme of different activities, rich in stimuli, the school will not be frittering away either the time or the energy of the pupils but will be heightening their intellectual powers which also side by side train them in other fine qualities. These activities should be organized as the resources of the school permit.

Need and Importance of Co-curricular Activities

Co-curricular activities have an important place in the curriculum. They have a number of values as educational values, development of social spirit, aesthetic

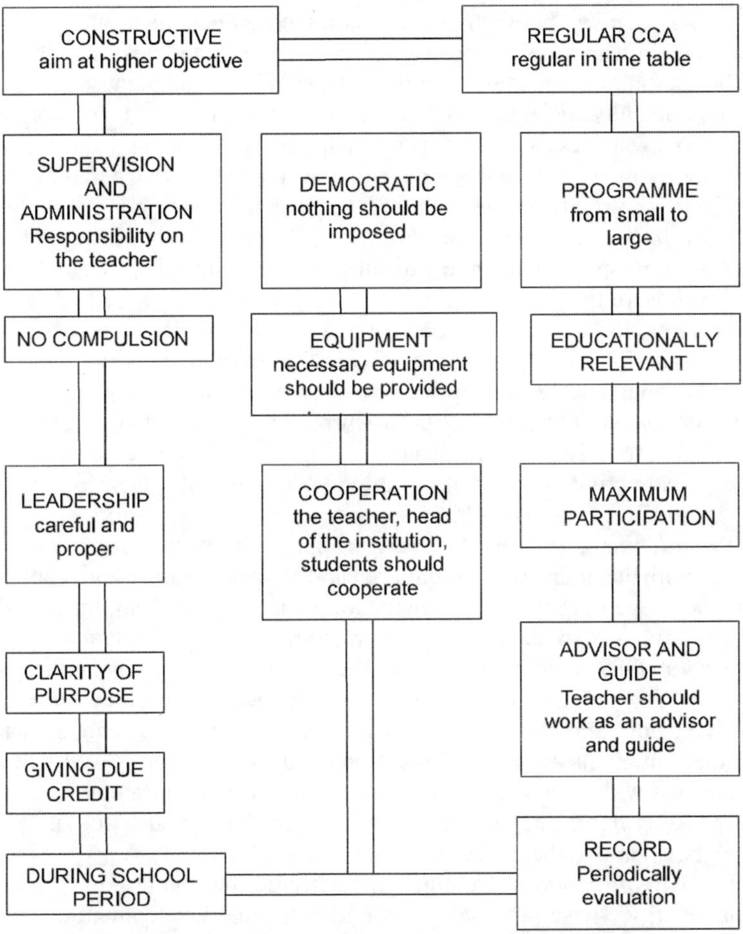

Fig. 10.1: Principles of Organising Co-curricular Activities

development and development of cultural values. They are of immense value to the students, teachers as well as school administration. They are as:

1. Development of Democratic Spirit: Through co-curricular activities the students develop the democratic spirit. They learn the importance of democratic living and become aware of their rights and duties. These activities develop the virtues connected with democracy and prepare the children for citizenship of a progressive nation.

2. Development of Capabilities and Talents: When the students participate in various activities according to their interest and aptitudes, their capabilities and talents developed to the maximum like library reading, dramatization, role playing, organising different activities, etc.

3. Development of Abilities of Leadership: Co-curricular activities help in the development of abilities of leadership. The students learn about the qualities of a good leader and his role in the society. The leadership qualities in the pupils are also allowed to flourish through these activities.

4. Learn to Adjust: These activities develop such temperament among the pupils which help them lead a better social life. These develop the qualities like fellow feeling, brotherhood, sympathy, sincerity and discipline — all of these are essential features for a healthy social life. These also develop the habit of team work which is essential to do business activities. Through these activities, pupils learn to adjust in social environment. The students develop the spirit of service and they learn to act in a friendly spirit. These are the media to provide civic training to the youth.

5. Learn to Spend Leisure Time Fruitfully: The pupils with the help of these activities learn to spend their time fruitfully and meaningfully. These days wise spending to leisure time is a big problem. The people have developed sedentary habits and remained glued to the television. The participation in games, cultural activities, excursions, etc. trains the pupils in the ways of spending their leisure time most advantageously for themselves as well as for the society.

6. Development of Sound Health: Co-curricular activities have proved to be a potent means of sound mental health and development. The participation in games, sports, physical activities, etc. help in the development of good physical health among the students. Healthy children are in fact assets to the nation.

7. Provide Pleasure and Relaxation: These activities are organised in accordance with the interests of the children and provide pleasure and relaxation to them. These prove helpful in the satisfaction of interests and aptitudes and thus reduce the chances of dissatisfaction and frustration to a great extent.

8. Develop Interest Towards School: These activities develop interest towards school and its functioning among the students. The pupils when they participate in competitive games and other activities with the pupils of other schools then they develop the sentiments of love and affection towards their own school. They start feeling oneness with their schoolmates and try their best to present their school in the best possible light. They do not involve themselves in such activities which may bring bad name to their school.

9. Training of Emotions: Co-curricular activities help in providing outlets to emotional energy. These provide opportunities for the development of emotion. When pupils are engaged in co-curricular activities their bad spirits change into brotherhood spirit and their energies are directed in the right direction.

10. Development of Interests and Hobbies: The co-curricular activities provide an opportunity to the child to develop his interests and hobbies. A child interested in music or having a hobby of painting gets an opportunity to participate in co-curricular activities which are in accordance with his interests.

11. Moral Development: The children get moral education through these activities. They learn to be honest, just, unselfish, pure, etc. through morning assembly, celebration of birthday of great men and social service activities. In games they learn to play with self-control.

12. Better Understanding of the Culture: Different activities like drama, excursion, visit to museum, exhibitions, etc. portray our cultural heritage. These provide better understanding of the culture. These help in preserving the culture.

13. Development of Aesthetic Sense: The development of aesthetic sensibility is one of the chief objective of education. Co-curricular activities like preparation of charts and models, excursions, etc. help in the development of aesthetic aspect of the personality.

14. Proper Channelization of Surplus Energy: These activities help the adolescent release their surplus energy. If this release is not in the proper direction and it is repressed then the energy bursts forth in undesirable activities. The adolescent may develop sexual deviations. He may involve in sexual crimes. Co-curricular activities act as safety valves through which the extra energy of the adolescents gets the medium of release.

15. Recreational Value: These activities provide enjoyment and healthy recreation. If the students are involved only in theory classes, the classroom environment becomes dull and monotonous. These activities provide recreation which is conducive to mental, emotional and moral health. Learning becomes effective as a by product of interesting activities.

Thus, all the above points show the importance of co-curricular activities. It has been established that these activities must occupy a vital place in the school curriculum. No system of education is complete in their absence. In those schools where there are no adequate arrangements for games, sports and other activities quality of education suffers. In these schools, the children fail to develop their social, moral, cultural and physical health. It is said that without these activities *the schools are reduced to teaching shops, the teachers become information managers, the pupils become book-worms* and *education narrows down to mere cramming.* These activities play an important role for the development of child's personality, draw out the latent powers and abilities of the children of different temperament, supplement academic work, develop social and civic sense. If there is lack of these activities, the students will not be able to utilize the subject of commerce fully which is of much importance to understand the society.

Role and Organisation of Some Co-curricular Activities in Teaching of Commerce

1. Commerce Club

The organisation of commerce club may be given an important place in the school's co-curricular activities. The club may be constituted for the development of the interests of the students. Every class must have a definite aim that will contribute in the welfare of the pupils, teachers, school, home and society.

Objectives/Values

1. To provide opportunities for creative activities and for the development of leadership qualities to the students.
2. To help in developing positive outlook towards different occupations.
3. To learn public speaking, participation in debates and other literary activities.
4. To provide opportunities to the students to organise functions cooperatively.

5. To provide opportunity for self expression and performance in public which develop self confidence among students.
6. To win over the shyness and stage-fear through the participation in different activities.
7. To provide opportunities for the development of abilities and capacities of the pupils.
8. To furnish constructive use of leisure time.
9. To identify the needs and problems of the society and finding their solutions.
10. To develop the qualities of democratic citizenship.
11. To provide opportunities to the students for enriching their experiences.

Organisation of Commerce Club

Every commerce club should be organised on the basis of some rules and regulations and every member should strictly abide by it. Its organisation may be as follows.

1. Patron: The head of the institution should work as the patron of the club. All types of cooperation and facilities should be provided by him for the successful execution of the club.

2. Incharge: A senior commerce teacher should be the incharge of the club. He should work as a guide. He should be intellectually sound and educationally well informed. He should behave in friendly manner with other members of the club and not as a dictator. He/She should have the following qualities:

(*a*) He must be democratic in spirit.
(*b*) He must possess sense of humour.
(*c*) He must be friendly and cooperative to other members of the club.
(*d*) He must be enthusiastic.
(*e*) He must be a guide.
(*f*) He should provide constructive suggestion for the running of the club successfully.
(*g*) He must be willing to give time in making the work of the club a success.
(*h*) Careful preparation or planning of the activities.

3. Members: If it is possible, all the students should be members of the club but it should not be imposed on them. It should be open not only to the students of Commerce alone but others also. A nominal membership fee should be charged from every member. All the teachers related to the subject of Commerce should also be the members of the club.

4. Organising Committee: A committee should be formed amongst the students, which should formulate the constitution of the club.

5. Constitution of the Club: The constitution of the club should include the following aspects:

(*i*) Name of the club.
(*ii*) Objectives of the club:
  (*a*) To broaden the outlook of the students.
  (*b*) To understand the importance of Commerce in our daily life.
  (*c*) To impart knowledge of new discoveries and inventions of Commerce to the community.

(*d*) To increase the knowledge of Commerce.
(*e*) To know the problems and needs of the business and to conduct workshops and seminars to search solutions.
(*f*) To publish different bulletins and magazine related to Commerce.
(*g*) To provide leadership to the students.

(*iii*) Conditions and procedure of becoming the member:
(*a*) Any student who is interested may become a member of the club.
(*b*) All the members have to attend the meetings regularly.
(*c*) Those students who are studying other subjects related to Commerce can become the members.

(*iv*) Means to finance the club –
There should be clear cut instructions as from where the finances for the various activities of the club will be obtained. Membership fee of Rs ____ shall be paid annually in the beginning of the school year. It should also be planned that how much will be collected as membership fee in the financial year and how and where the money will be used/kept.

(*v*) Selection of office bearers
The following shall be the office bearers of the club:
(*a*) Patron
(*b*) Teacher-in-charge
(*c*) President
(*d*) Vice-president
(*e*) Secretary
(*f*) Joint Secretary
(*g*) Treasurer
(*h*) Editors
(*i*) Store-keeper
(*j*) Publishing in-charge
(*k*) Recorder
The office bearers shall be elected by the majority of the members. The election should take place at the first meeting of the each session. Any office bearer may resign at any time by giving written notice to the secretary. The duties and responsibilities of all the office-bearers should be clearly defined. Any officer bearer may be expelled for inefficiency, negligence of duties or for doing such activities that will discredit the club by the 3/4 members of the club.

(*vi*) Meetings–
(*a*) Regular meeting should be held.
(*b*) Special meeting may be called by the Patron/teacher-incharge/ president at any time.
(*c*) Agenda for each meeting shall be planned by the office bearers.
(*d*) Venue and times shall be well informed.
(*e*) The number of members presented in the meeting should be clearly mentioned.

(*v*) Amendments – The constitution may be amended by a 3/4 vote of all the members of the club.

6. *Activities:* The following type of activities can be organised by the club:
(*i*) Conduct Meetings.
(*ii*) Tours.
(*iii*) Organisation of fairs and exhibitions.

(*iv*) Arranging extension lectures of learned personalities in the field of business.
(*v*) Visit to industries.
(*vi*) Drawing of charts, pictures, posters, etc.
(*vii*) Preparation of models.
(*viii*) Publish magazine.
(*ix*) Organisation of debates, oration and essay competition.
(*x*) Preparation of slides and film strips.
(*xi*) Collecting and preparing material for Commerce room.
(*xii*) Adult Education programme.
(*xiii*) Various subject related demonstrations.
(*xv*) Film shows.

Thus, the proper planning and functioning of Commerce club will induce self-confidence among the student to choose scientific occupations and make fruitful decisions in their happy and fruitful future. In this way with the use of appropriate materials under the able guidance of the teachers these clubs give the students real training for their future and thus make a great contribution in building a healthy society and self-sufficient nation.

2. Debate

A debate is a form of literary discussion rich in arguments in which one or more students present their views for and against a particular problem. The debate has been used as co-curricular activity from the days of early Greece down to the present times. A debate on a trading issue often has great value, but the discussion of a problem that has a practical bearing on everyday life is usually more effective. Topics such as *'E-banking' is an 'effective business service', 'Role of women entrepreneurs in business',* can be debated with success, interest and much value. But a debate on our relations with developed countries, on the success of woman suffrage, on the effects of certain laws, on a community problem such as the attributes of worthy citizenship is usually more vigorous and stimulating.

Role of Debate in the Commerce

The debate has a great value in proper understanding of society. M.C. Cown has expressed the importance of debate in the following words:

"As a developer of intellectual interests and capacities, fluency to expression, clear and discriminate thinking and increased ability to appreciate the important affairs to modern life, good sportsmanship, self-reliance, self confidence, poise and similar desirable qualities."

It has certain values as:

1. It trains the pupils in the art of fluent expression.
2. It develops self-confidence.
3. It helps in the development of self-control.
4. It develops reasoning power and judgement.
5. It affords the pupils a knowledge of parliamentary procedure.
6. It develops the problem solving attitude and the tolerance to hear one's own criticism.

7. It broadens the outlook.
8. The higher order cognitive and affective objectives of teaching are achieved.
9. It develops the creative ability and thinking among pupils.
10. It has the greater scope of criticism of incorrect approaches, ideas and concepts.

Organisation of Debate in Commerce

The organisation of debate is not a simple task. It needs complete planning.

1. Selection of the Topic: The teacher should make a judicious selection of interesting and useful topic. The topic should emerge out from the course of study. It should be capable of stimulating the thoughts. It should give rise to controversial arguments, but it should not be controversial.

2. Planning of the Debate: The teacher should announce the topic of the debate well in advance. He must specify the number of speakers and the time allotted to each speaker, the place and date of holding the debate. The teacher must explain to the participants all the technical points such as how to open and conclude the debate. The teacher must guide the speakers and help them to consult source material, to proper arguments, guess counter arguments by opponents and remain prepared for answering those counter arguments instantaneously.

3. Preparation for the Debate: The debators should be trained to speak freely. The style of the speech should be brisk and effective. Humour and light ridicule is the sauce of such speeches. Cramming and reading written text papers should be disallowed. While preparing for the debate the participants should always be guided at each and every step by the teacher. Judges must be appointed and all the required information should be provided to them before the start of a debate.

4. Conducting the Debate: The number of speakers, their sequence and the time allotted may be written on the blackboard so that it is perceptible to all. The responsibility of conducting the debate should be shared by the teacher-in-charge with some students. The debate should be conducted with integrity. The theme should be clear-cut. No opponent should be insulted. It should be properly concluded.

5. Evaluation of the Debate: The debate must be properly evaluated in its proper perspective. It should be evaluated objectively as: Did the speaker stick to the topic?; Were the speakers objective in their arguments?; Did the topic covers all the points?, etc.

Suggestions to Make the Debate Effective

1. The work of obtaining material in preparation for the debate should be divided among the pupils, as far as possible.
2. Not to select topics beyond the grasp of the pupils.
3. The material involved in debate must not be beyond their comprehension.
4. Pupils must be systematically trained in the methods of getting material for debate. This naturally involves the judicious use of reference books and periodicals.
5. Direction and planning on the part of the teacher should be effective.
6. As many pupils as possible should be encouraged to participate in the debates.

7. The debate must be objective in their arguments.
8. After the debate, the listeners should be encouraged to ask questions from the debators to make them active.
9. The true spirit of debating must be inculcated.
10. The debate should be conducted more formally.

Thus, debate develops the habit of independent study and is extremely valuable from many points of view. It demonstrates clearly to the pupil the value of accurate facts, shows him the unreliability of many newspaper assertions, and releases him from the bondage to the printed page.

3. Field Trips or Excursion

'Field trips correlate and blend school life with the outside world, providing direct touch with person and with community situations.'

A class room has a limited space. The limited equipment of the classroom has no comparison to the bountiful resources of nature outside the classroom. Nature can serve as a laboratory where the teacher and his pupils can carry out unrestricted experiments upto any length of time. Field trips are, therefore, useful as they permit first hand study of actual object and societal situations. It is an important way to utilize many community resources. This plan can be used at any grade level, and yields valuable returns when the teacher takes the necessary precautions.

A careful planned field trip involves:

(*a*) Adequate preparation of the class.
(*b*) Arrangements when necessary with those incharge of the 'place to be noted'.
(*c*) A planned procedure during the visit.
(*d*) Checking and synthesizing the results into the larger pattern of instruction.

Places to Visit: Within the limits of the resources available, each teacher must decide which trips are practicable and fruitful. These places can be economic resources, geographical resources, political resources, cultural resources, etc. The following list may prove to be suggestive:

Possible Field Trips

Factories	Insurance offices
Newspaper plant	Markets
Bakery	Corporate Office
Steel plant	Court
Bank	Packing plant
Television studio	Brickyard
Automobile Assembly Plant	Hydro electric plant
Dairy	Trade Fair
Farm	Advertising Companies
	Greenhouse

All communities, however, regardless the time of their origin, have some business concerns that is more or less important. Pupils should be encouraged to explore different sites and places, and if possible, organized groups under the supervision of the teacher should visit new sites.

Planning the Visit: The trips have to be undertaken outside the regular school periods only. When a trip to a business place is arranged, careful planning should be made beforehand. The teacher or a student who has already visited the place may give a general description. Pictures, articles, concerning the industry, place or institution may be utilized. The object is to arouse interest and to prepare the students so that they will actually observe and are benefitted from it. Some teachers find it helpful to raise a series of questions requesting that each student be prepared to ask one pertinent question. Sometimes it is better to assign special aspects to designated group of pupils. The pupils must know the objective of the field trip. In the description given by the teacher, the pupils neither be confused by a multitude of details, nor should they be required to hurry. If each student feels the responsibility of learning at least one point, he will not regard the trip as a mere excursion.

While visiting a bank, store, factory, the teacher should make arrangements with their in-charge. This precaution will avoid disappointment and will ensure a welcome reception for the class. Previous arrangements also ensure that the person in-charge of the place will have some appreciation of the purpose of the teacher.

It is also to be kept in mind that no teacher will take the class off the school without the permission of the principal. He in turn will usually want to secure the consent of the parents. Sometimes the teacher can make arrangements with the parents to provide transportation. Having taken these precautions, the teacher will also do well to describe the route and to emphasize the proper conduct during field trips.

These precautions are necessary for safety as well as the best returns from the field trip. If the class is large enough, it should be accompanied by more than one teacher.

Execution: After planning, the teacher is to execute it in reality. The trip itself should allow ample time for necessary questions, explanations and observations. The teacher should assist the students in seeing the relationship between different parts and their importance.. Thoughtful questions and observations should be encouraged and efforts made to ensure that the students have a meaningful visit and experience.

Evaluation of the Field Trip: The results of the visit should be ascertained formally and informally if a test or written report seems feasible. Letters of appreciation to those who welcomed them, reports to parents or to the principal, oral reports to the class or in assembly, and additional projects of related nature are some of the form that may be utilized in checking and synthesizing the results of a field trip. If the visit is successful, it will enrich the recitation, illuminate the topic and provide material for projects.

Preparing the Report: Many of the above items with regard to field trips can be conveniently summarized in a file. Part of the information is filled out prior to making the trip and a brief entry is also made upon the return from the trips.

Example

Insurance Office

1. Location
2. Telephone
3. Contact
4. When to call
5. Length of visit – Half day or longer

6. Number of students
7. Material available
8. Service available:
(*i*) Will grant interviews.
(*ii*) Will arrange to have group discussions with officers.
(*iii*) If possible, will arrange to have one of the officers address the group.
9. A brief description of what was seen and done. Trip outline for_________ date ______
10. Comments __________ Teacher's impressions and reactions.

Follow Up Work for Field Trip

The follow-up work of the field trip is equally important. It consolidates the educational gains acquired during the visit. As the students return from the field trip, they may be asked to write a fruitful account of the trip. Preparing scrap-book, or holding power-discussions, verbal description of the places visited, and the knowledge gained can be correlated with the content matter of Commerce.

Thus, with the proper arrangements field trips can be organised and executed fruitfully.

Importance of Field Trips

The proper visits will generate some pride in the past achievements and a reasonable degree of faith in its future possibilities. Field trips help in extending the curriculum in to the community in order to give the children increased experience with things related with the curricular plan.

1. Unique Source of Knowledge: Generally the students get the knowledge through reading or listening but with the help of field trips they get the real knowledge about the society. It is a general belief that the knowledge gained through the eyes remains permanent.

2. Spontaneous Way of Effective Teaching: In the society, a child develops concepts of transportation, communication, government and other aspects of living. It is an effective way of teaching because it is the subject which directly relates with society.

3. Supplement the Work of Classroom Teaching: Visits to business concerns are an aid to the study of commerce. Classroom teaching provides the artificial environment to the teaching.

4. It Helps in All Round Development of the Child: An important aim of education is the development of all round personality of the child. The classroom teaching does not help in fulfilling this aim because it lays more stress on mental development only and the other aspects of the personality are to some extent remain neglected.

5. It Provides Education for Effective Social Living: Man is a social animal. He is to live in the society. Social development is essential for individual development. By arranging and participating in field trips the feelings of cooperation, brotherhood, tolerance, etc. are developed among the students which help in effective social living.

6. Helps in Getting Knowledge About the Culture of the Society: Education not only provides the knowledge about the culture but it also helps in enriching the culture of the society. With the help of field trips the students will get the knowledge about the pros and cons of their culture and will help in bringing improvement in it.

7. Growth of New Interests: Psychologists agree that to some extent interests are inherited but they need the environment to come out. Field trips provide the opportunities for the growth of new interests which are natural and creative, not imposed from outside, but develop from within.

8. Help in Developing Skill and Attitudes: By field trips, the students will not only get the knowledge but they will also be able to think of solving the problems of their society. They become responsible citizens of the society as well as of the nation. Different skills are fostered and a sense of security gives students that pride which everyone should possess in his society.

9. Knowledge About the Effect of Science and Technology on Business Activities: While going to different places, the students will understand the good as well as the bad effects of modern science on the working, attitudes, thinking of the people. They can judge whether science is a blessing or a curse for the society.

10. Direct Experiences: Students will come in to direct contact with the resources of the community and get direct experiences. Proceeding from the known to the unknown and from near to the distant it is a natural process of establishing relationship, particularly suitable to young students.

Thus, field trips are very valuable for learning. During fieldwork all senses are actively functioning and the observation power is much emphasized because of direct contact with things. These first hand experiences are accurate and lasting. Field trips for younger pupils can be arranged with in the vicinity of the school because long trips require use of transport and money and involve many administrative problems. Occasionally, long trips may be arranged for senior students, as they will be capable of planning trips better.

A word of caution is necessary in discussing the field trips by the school. It is true that one learns best by first hand experiences. However, life has become so complex that children must be taught many things, not by actual experiences but through vicarious experiences. No one doubts the efficacy of the first hand information but time is a crucial factor. In planning a trip, the teacher must take into account the entire school programme and ask himself if the time taken for it is of greater value than the loss of time taken from the school subjects. Trips may be an aid to education but they can never take the place of the school.

The school can be made a dynamic or multi-dimensional affair. If suitable curricular and co-curricular activities are organised in a school as well as out of school in which each student of commerce participates, contributes his maximum and prepares himself for becoming a good citizen of the society, then these will be more fruitful and meaningful. The activities should be such that they help in achieving goals of education, make students enthusiastic, develop leadership qualities, develop sociability and enhance their learning abilities.

11

Commerce Teacher

"The teacher's place in society is of vital importance. He acts as the pivot for the transmission of intellectual traditions and technical skills from generation to generation and helps to keep the lamp of civilization burning."

–*Dr. Radha Krishnan*

It is very rightly said that the teacher is the pivot around which the whole education system revolves. The child from the Hindu standpoint, receives second birth at the hands of the teacher. It is the teacher who plays the most prominent role in moulding the habits and character of the pupils. Books may teach a child but a teacher educates him.

The success or failure of any education system depends upon the teacher. If the teachers are well educated and if they are intellectually alive and take keen interest in their work, then only success is ensured. But if on the other hand, they lack training in teaching and if they cannot give their heart to their profession, the system is designed to fail.

God created man in the shape of his own image, the teacher fashions the child in the shape of his own image. Hence, it is said, as the teacher, so is the child. A teacher is the 'Architect of the Nation', 'the Harbinger of the progress of the culture', 'the maker of the man', and the 'maker of history'.

Manu, "The teacher is the image of Brahma."

Swami Vivekanand, "The true teacher is he who can immediately come down to the level of the student, transfer his soul to the student's soul and see through and understand through his mind. Such a teacher can really teach and none else."

Henry Adams, "A parent gives life, but a parent gives no more. A murderer takes life and his deed stop there. A teacher affects eternity, he can never tell where his influence stops."

If commerce is to help pupils to understand the economy, the business in which there is much scope of occupation, in order that they may better adapt themselves to it and prepare themselves for an intelligent citizenship, does this not require a well-trained and a supervisor type of teacher?

In the report of Education Commission "Of all the different factors which influence the quality of education and its contribution to national development, the quality, competence and character of teachers are undoubtedly the most significant."

Qualities of a Commerce Teacher

In the words of Joad, "Teaching is not everybody's cup of tea." To become a teacher, both learning, passing the examination and his ability to instruct are not enough. The quality and effectiveness is very necessary for a subject teacher. He should possess a sterling character and certain physical, intellectual, social and professional qualities which are prerequisite for success in teaching.

The qualities can be expressed in the form of an abbreviation:

Traits of a Good Commerce Teacher

T = Thoughtful	G = Gregarious	T = Thoughtful
R = Reliable	O = Originality	E = Ecumenical
A = Abilities in leadership	O = Orator	A = Amiable
I = Integrity	D = Discernment	C = Convival to students
T = Tactful		H = Healthy (physical and mental)
S = Sense of humour	C = Cooperative	
	O = Optimistic	E = Efficient
O = Objectivity	M = Mastery over the subject	R = Resourcefulness
F = Fluency	M = Man in child psychology	
	E = Expositor	
A = Ability to do creditable institutional work	R = Recitative	
	C = Conscience	
	E = Enthusiasm	

Teaching is not like other profession. As a teacher, you will wear many hats. You will, to name but of a few of the roles teacher assumes in carrying out these duties, be a communicator, a disciplinarian, a conveyer of information, an evaluator, a classroom manager, a counsellor, a decision-maker, a role model, and a surrogate parent. Each of these role requires practice and skills that are often not taught in teacher preparation programmes.

Since the birth of civilization, teachers have been the pillars of society. Staying in this background, at least for most of the time, they have been indirectly responsible for the advancement of the race. Often, it is their lot to go unnoticed. But time and again, all great men and women have been unsparing in their praise of teachers. This is by far their greatest responsibility. Teachers are the ones who guarantee that our tomorrows will be as good as, if not better than, our today. By shaping character and instilling knowledge, they ensure that the world continues to be.

1. Qualities Pertaining to Personality

(*i*) *Personal Appearance:* In appearance the teacher should look like a teacher. Here we can't limit down his physique and status.

(*ii*) *Sound Mind:* The teacher should have an alert and sound mind and this is possible only with sound health.

(*iii*) *Voice and Pronunciation:* The teacher should have a clear voice with good pronunciation.

(*iv*) *A man of Character:* The teacher should not be a slave of passions and emotions. He should be a man of high moral character.

(*v*) *Qualities of Leadership:* The teacher should lead his students in every respect.

(*vi*) *Humours Temperament:* The teacher should always have a smiling face and good gesture which will help in creating suitable environment in the classroom.

(*vii*) *Patience and Self Confidence:* The teacher of commerce should have the patience and confidence to teach the required subject matter. "To teach is to first understand purposes, subject matter structures and ideas within and outside the discipline." The teacher must consider the relevant aspects of students' ability, gender, language, culture, motivation, or prior knowledge and skills that will affect their responses to different forms of presentation.

(*viii*) *Positive Attitude:* Good teachers always have positive attitude. Cynical people usually create a negative attitude in students since they are in a raw state of gaining and developing attitude.

(*ix*) *True Compassion:* The good teachers care about their students as individuals and want to help them. They have a sixth sense to judge when a student needs extra attention and give it gladly. They don't expect students to leave extra thoughts of the outside world at the door to the classroom. They give time to discuss subjects outside their teaching, knowing that sometimes lessons can still be taught without following the textbook.

(*x*) *Industrious:* The teachers are always hard workers. They have large aims in their life and work diligently to accomplish those aims.

2. Professional Qualities

(*i*) *Dedication to Excellence:* Good teachers want the best from their students and themselves. They don't settle for poor graders, knowing it reflects upon their ability to teach just as much upon a student's ability to excel. The teachers encourage the sharing of ideas and offer incentives to get students to think outside the box. They encourage students to be good people, not just good memorizers of text. They want students to learn and be able to apply what they learned, not just be able to pass tests.

(*ii*) *Unwavering Support:* The teachers know that everyone is able to do well if they have the right teachers. They don't accept that a student is a lost cause. They stand up for individuals against other students.

(*iii*) *Willingness to help student achieve:* The good teachers are those that don't stop teaching when the bell rings. They know that some need extra attention or assistance, and they don't act like it's not their job. They realise that achievement is not just a good grade on a test, but a feeling of accomplishment with mastering a subject, they are willing to work with a student for that feeling.

(*iv*) *Pride in Student's Accomplishments:* The good teachers celebrate the accomplishment of everyone, knowing that everyone is capable of doing well. They are upbeat and positive, focusing on how a student did well, not how well they taught. They may know that it was the strengths of their teaching that helped a student to achieve, but they act as if the student is completely responsible.

(*v*) *Professional Attitude:* A teacher must know his profession thoroughly. He must know his subject of commerce thoroughly. He needs to be an expert in his field. For example, if he is teaching accountancy, he should know all the accountancy related fields and careers out there. He should also be able to relate how accountancy is related to our everyday life, and not some abstract concepts and theories. The teacher needs to translate those abstract concepts and turn them into interesting things that the students can relate in their everyday life.

(*vi*) *Sound Professional Training:* Knowing his subject is of no use if he does not know how, or does not bother to teach most effectively to his students. Many times we have seen scholars-turned-teachers fumbled when they started their teaching career. The teacher should have sound professional training.

(*vii*) *Knowledge of Psychology:* Commerce teacher should have the knowledge of psychology because it helps the teachers in understanding the child psychology, individual differences, stages of mental and physical growth, etc.

(*viii*) *Knowledge of Different Teaching Methods:* The teachers should have sound knowledge of different teaching methods so that he may show awareness in teaching activities, that learning is a process which transforms and changes learners. He should encourage pupil participation. He should integrate appropriate teaching methods and technologies, tailored to course goals and learning outcomes, and facilitates student participation.

(*ix*) *Respectful for diverse talents and learning styles of students:* For the development of all the students, he should promote a stimulating learning environment. He should have the knowledge about different learning styles so that he may be able to recognize and accommodate different learning style.

(*x*) *Knowledge of Current Affairs:* The present age is the age of science. The age of science is the epitome of newness and change. Commerce provides base for the newness. Commerce teacher should have the knowledge of current affairs. If he does not have the knowledge, he will not be able to evaluate the current economic situation of the world. It is he who interprets the present, ever changing complex world to the pupils.

(*xi*) *Knowledge of Economic Problems:* Commerce education is that part of the educational process which on the one hand relates with the occupational preparation and on the other hand relates with the information regarding business/trading activities which is important for every student to understand the business environment and economy on day-to-day life. Commerce teachers should also have the knowledge of economic problems.

3. Qualities Related to Classroom Procedure

- Use of different methods and technologies
- Use of different skills
- Proper use of chalk board
- Well planned teaching
- Well distributed questions
- Proper use of instructional aids
- Class discipline
- Carefully planned assignment
- Pupils well motivated for study
- Resourcefulness in the class

4. Relationship of Teacher

Teacher and his Pupils

The relation between the teacher and the pupil in one phase must be that of a parent and the child. He must know the child well and discover his abilities, interests, attitudes, likes and dislikes. For this he may have to come down to the level of the pupil. He must respect the child, sympathise with his instinctive needs and take genuine interest in him. He must be easily accessible to pupils and must bear a democratic attitude. His behaviour should be exemplary. He must act as their model and must do nothing himself that he forbids the pupils to do. He must not be a hypocrite. His behaviour has a direct influence upon the pupils. He must be free from prejudices or any communal bias. Any display of favouritism on the part of the teacher is detrimental to the best interests the pupil thus favoured and may stimulate group resentment. He must remain calm and judicious in difficult situations. His behaviour should, therefore, be sympathetic, friendly and just. As remarked by Aurobindo Ghosh, "The teacher is not an instructor or task-master. He is a helper and guide. His business is to suggest and not to impose." The teacher should be objective and refrain from flattery. He must know when and how to exercise his authority.

The Teacher and the Faculty

The entire faculty has a common task and the need is the unity. As teaching in the school is a cooperative enterprise so a teacher attitude towards his faculty members should be that of a member of the same family. He should avoid back biting and unnecessary interference in the task assigned to others. He may learn much more about the pupils and problems of the school if he will discuss them with faculty members. He should not criticize the school system in which he works. A closely knit and friendly faculty is a sure means of developing school loyalty and general friendliness among pupils. Rifts in the faculty members have a detrimental effect upon the school discipline.

The Teachers and Community Relations

The school springs from the community and works for the enrichment of the community. The teacher should, therefore, establish good contact with the community. He should make the school a community centre. The home and school meeting is a valuable aid in promoting this. The better he understands and serves the community and its people, the better he will be as a teacher. It is only through social interaction that he will be able to find for himself a status and a respected place.

Role of the Teacher in Teaching Commerce

The teacher is the pivot around which the whole teaching learning process revolves. He has to play the several roles:

1. As a Guide: The teacher as a guide helps the students in their personal and learning problems. He is to guide the students in their professional career also.

2. As a Researcher: The teacher should be the master of the subject. He should have the knowledge and skill for using action research. Sometimes students feel boredom in the subject of commerce, so he should apply other tactics to make it interesting. Classroom problems can be solved with the help of action research projects.

3. As a Manager: The teacher's role is to manage the class properly. The main functions of a manager are planning, organising, supervising, directing, coordinating the teaching process.

4. As a Leader: The teacher is the leader of the class. He should be sensible enough to take independent actions in case of emergency as and when the occasion demands. He should have the ability to direct his plans in actual practice. He must be a person of wisdom and vision. If he works as a good leader, he can develop the qualities of leadership among his students.

5. As a Teacher: The teacher is an ideal for the students. He must know the entrybehaviour of the students and should try to achieve the desired outcomes.

6. As a Planner: Every successful teacher for effective teaching has to plan his teaching process. He plans the curriculum of commerce day wise, week wise, month wise and year wise according to the topics and units. He plans where to use different audio-visual aids in teaching process. He also plans about the co-curricular activities relating to the subject of commerce.

7. As an Organiser: The teacher is to organise different activities relating to his subject. He has to organise various curricular and co-curricular activities, library work of the pupils, instructional process, giving assignments, evaluation of the students in social studies, etc.

8. As a Supervisor: The teacher has to supervise the activities of the students in the classroom as well as out of the classroom. He has to maintain discipline in the class. He has to supervise the written work of the pupils.

9. As a Recorder: The teacher is to keep the record of the activities of the student so that he may inform the parents accordingly about the participation of the students.

10. As an Evaluator: It is the most important role the teacher has to play. He is not only to educate the students but also to evaluate the achievements of them from time to time. With the help of evaluation, he diagnoses the weaknesses of the students and tries to remove them with the help of remedial teaching.

11. As a Reader/Scholar: Reading is a means of self-improvement that all teachers can use. He becomes familiar with the best books and magazines in the field. Many professional periodicals of a general nature prove helpful to the teacher. If he reads good books, he can impart best knowledge to the students.

Thus, in the modern society the teacher has to play several roles to fulfil his responsibilities as the society is becoming more complex day by day. The teacher should constantly strive to improve those traits and abilities which lead towards success. He should enjoy academic freedom but should be careful not to do anything that will reflect on his position as a teacher. The teacher of the commerce deals with the attitudes, ideals and appreciation to a larger extent than is the case in other branches of study. For the new paradigm in education, as described in NEP 2020, the high respect for teachers and the high status of the teaching profession will be restored, which will inspire the best persons to enter the teaching profession. The motivation and empowerment of teachers is required to ensure the best possible future for our children and our nation. School complexes will be encouraged to hire local eminent persons or experts as 'master instructors' to benefic students and help preserve and promote local knowledge and professions. The teachers should be recognized for novel approaches to teaching and improve learning outcomes in their classrooms. They should be given continuous opportunities for self-improvement and to learn the latest innovations and advances in their professions. These can be offered in multiple modes including in the form of local, regional, state, national and international workshops as well as online teacher development modules. Continuous professional development should cover the latest pedagogies regarding formative and adaptive assessment of learning outcomes, competency based learning and related pedagogies as experiential learning.

12

Construction of Tests in Commerce

Every subject has three important aspects as — goal, curriculum and evaluation.

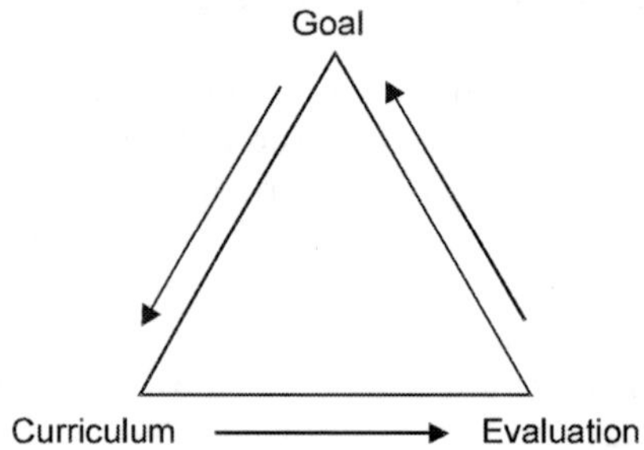

Achievement test plays an important role in the evaluation of students.

ACHIEVEMENT TEST

The term 'intelligence', 'aptitude' and 'achievement' are commonly used in the field of psycho logical and educational testing. Achievement refers to what a person has acquired or achieved after the specific training or instruction has been imparted. In other words, achievement tests are primarily designed to measure the effects of a specific programme of instruction or training. Thus the performance on the achievement test indicates the performance under known and controlled conditions because the performance is the outcome of specific training given in a specific field.

Achievement test, also known as proficiency test, is one which measures the extent to which a person has acquired or achieved certain information or proficiency as a function of instruction or training. Achievement tests are present and past oriented. The primary purpose of an achievement test or proficiency test is to evaluate what a person has learned. These tests are edumetric tests. An edumetric test is one whose major intention is to measure the gain or growth of individuals such as measurement of skills, proficiency and achievement.

Achievement is which measured with the help of achievement tests. Achievement tests are important frequently used tools in the field of educational evaluation. Achievement tests help in adapting the instruction to the individual need of the learners. The performance on the achievement tests directly reveals the need for further guidance to be given to each learner and accordingly, the instruction can be modified to suit the individual need. These tests are also effective in the formulation of educational goals and provide a very easy means of critical examination of the content and methods of instruction. A well-constructed achievement jest is an effective way of producing and illustrating the major changes in any educational goal, which is often understood in terms of some commonly agreed methods.

Thus, the tests are expected to yield information on the performance of individual students who are tested as well as the performance of the group of students as a whole. In school, the examinations conducted at the end of the term or semester are meant for measuring students' achievement on the basis of which, a student is either promoted to the next grade or detained in the same grade. Apart from the school level examination in which question papers prepared by the teachers of school are used, there are Board examinations in which all the students who have completed a given course while studying in a certain school system or through distance education mode, are tested together. The Board examinations are meant for certification of students and showing the level of achievement of each student who is examined as well as collectively for all the examinees, in terms of norm groups.

Definition

To clarify the meaning of achievement test, different educationists have given the following definitions:

"Achievement test is a test designed to measure knowledge, understanding and skills in a specified subject or group of subjects." —*Freeman*

"An achievement test is used to ascertain what and how much has been learnt or how well a task has been performed." —*Super*

"A general achievement test is one designed to express in terms of a single score a pupil's relative achievement in a given field of achievement".

—*Lindquist and Mann*

"Achievement test is a test, often in a standardised format for measuring a student's mastery of a given subject or skill." —*Webster Dictionary*

"Achievement test is a type of psychometric test which measures what a person already knows and can do at the time of testing." —*Business Dictionary*

"The achievement test focuses upon an examinee's attainment at a given point in time." — *Popham*

"An achievement test is a systematic procedure for determining the amount a student has learned through instruction." —*Gnonlund*

"An achievement test is one designed to measure a student's grasp of knowledge or his/her proficiency in certain skills." — *R.J. Ebel*

On the basis of above definitions, it can be said that achievement test is the test of knowledge or developed skills. In educational system, the scores of achievement tests are used usually to determine the levels of instructions with the help of which the students are prepared. High achievement scores usually indicate that the students have already acquired the subject matter of that level and they are ready to acquire the instructions of high level. Low achievement score indicates that there is need of change in the process of teaching and learning.

Thus, achievement test is a test through which the knowledge and understanding of the student in a specific subject or in different subjects are measured after the teaching-learning process for a definite time period. These are generally used by every school for the measurement in all the subject because the main objective of these is to do prediction in educational area as well as measurement. When the educational achievement of a student is measured then on the basis of this measurement the students can be motivated to learn more, their achievement level can be maintained, teaching methodology can be improved and efforts can be made to provide proper learning environment. The outcomes of the achievement test not only help in providing guidance to the students but the students can be motivated to reach at the highest level of the progress.

Characteristics of Achievement Test

1. Achievement test is the means to measure educational achievement of the students.
2. It has a description of measured behaviour.
3. It contains a sufficient number of test items for each measured behaviour.
4. It is divided into different knowledge and skills according to behaviours to be measured.
5. Its instructions with regard to its administering and scoring are so clear that they become standardised for different users.
6. It is objective oriented.
7. It is accompanied by norms which are developed at various levels and on various age groups.
8. It provides equivalent and comparable form of the test.
9. It has vast subject matter.
10. The subject matter of the test is according to the level, ability, interest and potentiality of the students.
11. It provides base to the teacher to plan his teaching.
12. A good achievement test is tried out and selected on the basis of its difficulty level and discriminating power.
13. It carries with a test manual for its administering and scoring.
14. It is made to test teaching learning process.
15. It has intimate relation with educational objectives.
16. There is close relationship between instructional objectives, teaching process and achievement test.

Purposes of Achievement Test

To begin with, the purpose for which an achievement test has to be constructed need to be spelled out clearly. Every teacher should keep in mind the following purposes:

1. To test the learning gained by the students.
2. To provide feedback to the students in their learning process.
3. To provide feedback to the teacher in teaching process.
4. To measure the effectiveness of units and their organisation.
5. To bring improvements in instructional strategies on the basis of outcome of achievement test.
6. To classify goals of school.
7. To evaluate, revise and improve the curriculum.
8. To diagnose backward children.
9. To plan remedial measures.

10. To diagnose needs and abilities of the students.

Uses of Achievement Test

The teaching process of the teachers and learning of the students are evaluated by achievement tests. Achievement tests are very useful in the following ways:

I. From Administrator Point of View

- Tests help to *classify* school objectives.
- Achievement test helps to *select talented pupils* in different areas.
- They help in *deciding proper classification* of pupils.
- They help to *evaluate the extent* to which the objectives of commerce teaching are being achieved.
- Tests discover the *type of learning experiences* that will achieve these objectives with the best possible results.
- They help to *evaluate*, *revise* and *improve* the curriculum in the light of these results.
- They help to *discover backward children* in commerce who need help and to plan for remedial instruction for such students.
- They help in *providing better understanding* of the needs and abilities of pupils.
- They help in *selecting pupils* for the award of special merit or scholarships.
- They help in *grouping pupils* in the class on the basis of individual differences.
- They help in determining the *general level of achievement* of a class in commerce and thus to judge the teaching efficiency of the teacher.
- They help the parents in recognising the *strengths and weaknesses* of their children, so that they are able to direct their energies on suitable goals only and do not put heavy demands on them.
- The help in *comparing* the efficiency of one school with the other.

II. From Teachers' point of view:

Achievement tests will be helpful for the teachers in the following ways:

- The teacher will *spot out brilliant* and *backward* children in the subject of commerce.
- The teacher will come to know the *general range of abilities* of students in Business Studies as well as Accountancy in the class.
- In the light of the above, he will *select appropriate materials* of instruction so that all individuals benefit from instruction to the maximum.
- Achievement tests will help the teacher in *diagnosing* the *weaknesses* of students in Business Studies and Accountancy.
- He will determine the *progress of the students* in a particular subject over a period of time.
- On the basis of outcomes of achievement tests, the teacher can *determine* whether or not the students are working at their maximum capacity.
- Achievement tests help the teacher in *testing the fulfilment of objective* of different subjects of commerce.

Scope/Areas of Achievement Tests

Achievement test measures educational outcomes or learning outcomes. Its scope is very wide because it includes the following areas:

- Cognitive outcomes of education — knowledge, understanding, application, analysis, synthesis and evaluation.
- Non-cognitive outcomes of education — flexibility in thinking, balanced decisions, cultural awareness, critical outlook, analytical and synthesis abilities, etc.

Types of Achievement Test

Achievement test can be categorised as follows:

1. Standardised Tests

Standardised tests are those tests which are prepared carefully by experts by keeping in mind their objectives; in which the administration process, scoring process and interpretation of scores process are standardised, anybody can give this test at any place, the outcomes of which are comparable and in which norms for class level and age level are determined in advance.

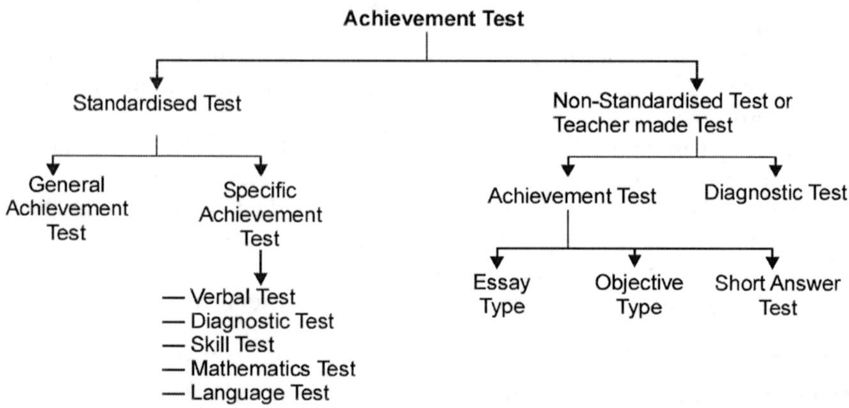

2. Teacher-made Tests

Teacher made tests are those which are constructed by the teachers themselves. While constructing these tests the general objectives are kept in mind. These tests are also good and objective. The construction procedure of these tests is similar to standardised tests but these can't be applied to whole population.

Difference Between Standardised and Teacher Made Achievement Test

Although the teacher-made tests and standardised tests use similar type of test papers and both of them can be constructed on knowledge aspects yet there are some differences among these as:

Standardised Tests	Teacher-Made Tests
1. These tests are based on the same curriculum taught in different schools of the state/ country	1. These tests are made by the teacher for a specific class on the basis of specific school's syllabus.
2. The norms are provided in these tests which generally represent the achievement or work at a specific level in the whole country/state.	2. These tests do not provide such type of criterion for comparison.
3. These tests are generally based on the testing of complete knowledge or ability.	3. These tests are related to the area of limited or specific knowledge or ability.
4. These tests are developed by trained constructors and editors of tests.	4. These are developed by teachers.
5. These tests are helpful in the comparison of different groups.	5. These tests are used generally to know the attainment of the knowledge of the child in a specific area.
6. On the basis of these tests, the comparison can be made of the achievement.	6. It is not possible through these tests.
7. The knowledge gained in different areas can be compa-red.	7. The attainment of specific objectives of education can be known.
8. The comparison of different schools and classes can be made.	8. The students of a class can be classified on the basis of these tests.

Construction/Preparation of Achievement Tests

An easy and simplified technique for measuring cognitive development is – written test which is being utilised for class test, annual test and an achievement test. Before discussing the procedure, let us discuss some major considerations to be kept in mind while constructing any test. These are:

Deciding the Purpose of Testing

To avoid the inappropriate use of test, it is essential that the purposes of testing should be determined in advance. Purposes are different from objectives. Objectives are related with curriculum whereas purposes are related with the use of test as test is for selection or for diagnosis or for promotion, etc.

Purpose of Testing Students in a Class

A teacher-made unit test or tests in commerce used in the classroom from time to time are essentially for monitoring the progress of students in the subject of commerce and taking remedial actions in the areas in which students perform badly. Such testing is a part of formative evaluation of students. The tests used in semester or term examinations are generally meant for deciding whether the student is fit for promotion to the next grade or not. Such tests are summative in nature.

Purpose of Testing Students in Board Examinations

The main purpose of this examination conducted by Board of Examination is classification. These examinations also help in classifying the students in different subjects on the basis of their achievement as well as on the whole.

Purpose of Testing Students in an Achievement Survey

Specifically the objectives of a large scale achievement survey in one or more subjects at a particular level of education are:

- To identify the levels of achievement in different types of schools or school system in the whole country or in a state or a district.
- To provide feedback to curriculum developer and organisers of in-service and pre-service teacher training in the subject of commerce for improving the curriculum and training programmes.
- To estimate the change in performance in commerce over time.
- To identify the school, teacher variables and the inputs or combination of inputs that affect achievement in different subjects of commerce as Business Studies, Accountancy, etc.
- To determine the percentage of students according to the performance at different achievement levels (e.g. pre-determined minimum level, mastery level, etc.)

Coverage of Assessment Objectives

Every good curriculum framework in the subject of commerce provides curriculum objectives for Business Studies, Accountancy and other branches. When an achievement test is to be prepared for the subject of Commerce, one has to be well aware of the assessment objectives to be tested. Commonly used assessment objectives are *knowledge*, *Understanding* and *Application*. For proper coverage of assessment objectives, the achievement test constructor should be familiar with the implied competencies under each objective (for details refer to Chapter 4). Proper coverage of these abilities is important. Therefore, giving weightage to these assessment objectives in terms of marks is the first significant step in developing an achievement test as:

Objectives / **Topic S. No.**	**Knowledge**	**Understanding**	**Application**	**Analysis**	**Skill**	**Total**
1						
2						
3						
4						
5						
6						
Total						

Coverage of Prescribed Syllabus

While constructing any test every constructor is to ensure that the prescribed syllabus is adequately covered. Poor coverage of the content is one of the major shortcomings of achievement test. To overcome this, it is necessary to take the following steps:

(i) Identify the content areas to be covered.

(ii) Determine the weightage in terms of marks to be assigned to each content area.

It is difficult to cover whole syllabus by giving weightage to every topic in an annual examination. In a semester, it is relatively easier to cover most of the syllabus since the course content is limited. It is even more difficult to cover all the topics or chapters of the subject in a single question paper.

Pre-requisites of a Question Paper

Before setting a question paper it is necessary to decide the type of questions to be included in the test, the number of questions of each type, the time allowed for answering the questions, the total marks and distribution of marks over the questions and special instructions, if any, to be given to the examiners and evaluators.

Types of Questions: Broadly speaking, there are two types of questions:

- Selection type, requiring recognition responses i.e. the examinee has to choose the correct answer out of some given alternatives.
- Free-response or supply type requiring constructed responses, i.e. the examinee writes the answer in his/her own way.

The later are more suitable for testing higher order abilities such as "expression of ideas, ability to analyse and ability to synthesise, drawing conclusions and evaluating given information. There is, however, no hard and fast rules. The common selection type items are:

- Multiple choice
- True-false
- Matching type
- Classification
- Fill in the blanks

The common supply type questions are:

- Essay type
- Short answer type
- Very short answer type
- Completion type

Thus, in the achievement test of Commerce following types of questions can be included:

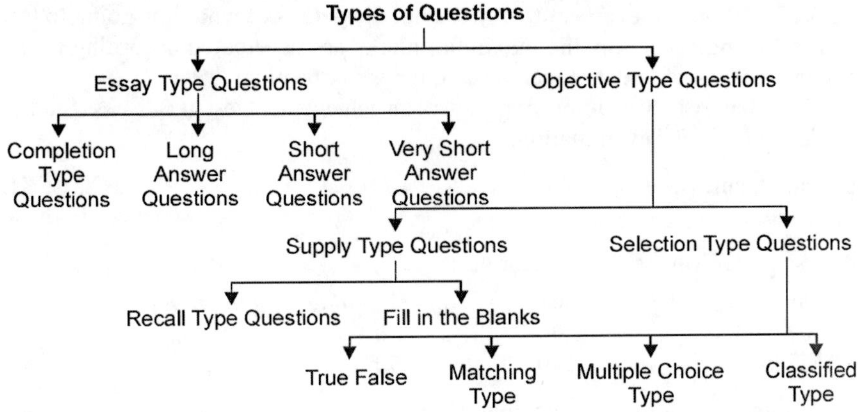

A balanced test paper should have different types of questions in pre-determined proportions.

Time to be Allowed for Answering Questions

Generally, in semester or annual examinations, time allowed for answering question paper in Commerce is two to three hours. The focus group on Examination Reforms set up by NCERT in 2005 has suggested that the question paper in Board Examinations should be ideally of only 2½ hours duration in senior secondary examination, so that, students are not over-burdened and examination stress will be less. It has also been suggested that 10 to 15 minutes extra time should be allowed only for reading of the question paper.

The achievement test constructor should estimate the time that an average student will require for answering each question and include only as many questions as can be answered easily within the allocated time for the paper. Some experts feel that the length of a question paper should be such that 95 per cent students are able to answer it within the allotted time.

The following factors should be kept in mind while deciding the time for answering a question paper:

- Availability of resources
- Class for which testing is to be done
- Content to be covered
- Number and type of questions to be included

Allotment of Marks to Question Paper and Questions within a Test

The maximum marks of each test have to be decided in advance. In a unit test, it may be just 20 or 25 marks and in annual test, it can be 50 or 100. If the content to be covered is large, the test has to include more questions. On the other hand, one has to decide how much weightage is given to each objective in term of marks out of the total marks of the achievement test. The design of the question paper should indicate the distribution of total marks over the different content areas, different assessment objectives and for various types of questions.

Developing the Design of an Achievement Test

The design of an achievement test spells out the details of what it is going to test and how. It indicates how the maximum marks are distributed according to the content areas, assessment objectives and types of questions.

Given below is an example of design of an achievement test in Business Studies for Class XII annual examination.

Subject: Business Studies — Class: XII
Time: 3 hrs. — Marks: 100

(a) Assigning weightage to objectives:

Objectives	*Knowledge*	*Understanding*	*Application*
% of marks	40	50	10
Marks	40	50	10

(b) Assigning weightage to content areas:

	Topics	*Marks*
1.	Nature and significance of management	07
2.	Principles of management	07
3.	Planning	07
4.	Organising	10
5.	Staffing	10
6.	Directing	12
7.	Controlling	07
8.	Financial management	12
9.	Financial markets	08
10.	Marketing	14
11.	Consumer protection	06
	Total	100

(c) Assigning weightage to different types of questions:

Type of questions	MC	VSA	SA	LA	Total
No. of questions	10	8	16	3	37
Marks allotted	10	8	52	30	100
Estimated answer time (in minutes)	20	20	60	80	180

While MC and VSA type questions carry 1 mark each, SA and LA questions are of 2 to 4 marks each and LA questions are of 10 marks each.

(d) Assigning weightage to difficulty level:

Easy	25%
Average	50%
Difficult	25%

Preparation of Blueprint

A blueprint is essentially a table of specifications in which it is specified what the test should cover. It helps in preparing an achievement test according to a given design. It is in a tabular form which allows questions of the test to be placed in appropriate cell in such a way that the test is according to a pre-determined design. It is also called three-dimensional chart, because it depicts distribution of questions with marks and number of different type of questions to be set in relation to different units of prescribed syllabus, testing different objectives in terms of total marks, time allotted and total number of questions.

The following steps are followed for preparing a blueprint:

(a) Transfer the total marks to each content area and to each objective from the design to the blueprint.

(b) If essay type questions are included, decide first about the units that suit better and have appropriate weightage for accommodating ETQ.

(c) Distribute the marks over the different cells and show the number of questions to be included (within brackets) and the marks allotted to these questions.

(d) Insert row-wise and column-wise sub-totals, indicating the number of questions and the total marks for those questions. Check the total.

Blueprint of Achievement Test Based on Design

Objectives	Knowledge			Understanding			Application			Skill			Total
Form of Question	LA	SA	Obj.	LA	SA	Obj.	LA	SA	Obj.	LA	SA	Obj.	
Subject Matter													
Sub-total													
Total													

LA = Long Answer; SA = Short Answer; Obj. = Objective Type.

It may be noted that there is no rigidity in setting the questions strictly according to the blueprint. Some minor deviations are generally permitted. The teacher has to prepare a balanced question paper based on a rough blueprint for testing what has been taught in the class.

Framing of Questions

In this step, the test constructor writes the question according to the blueprint. While framing the questions the learning objectives, subject matter, circumstances etc. are to be kept in mind as:

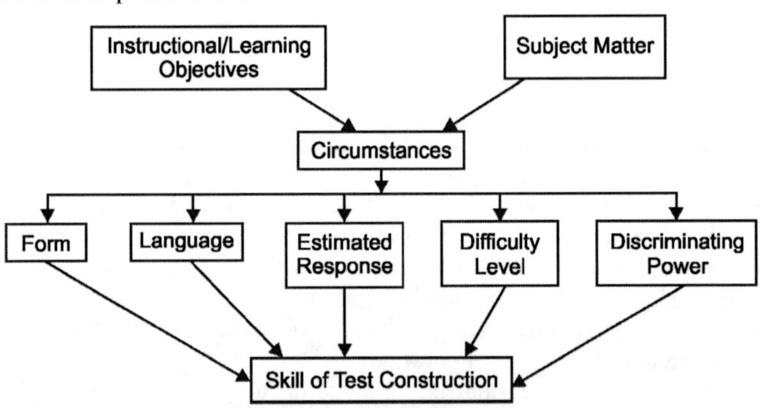

(i) The preliminary form of the test should be made according to the blueprint.
(ii) Different types of items should be included.
(iii) Number of items should be more in preliminary test because some may be deleted due to discriminating power and difficulty level.
(iv) Language of questions should be simple, concise and clear. They should not have double meaning.
(v) Questions should be framed such that there is no clue of answer.
(vi) The order of the given answers should not be such that the students may understand the order and give answers accordingly.

(vii) Question from the textbooks should not be included i.e. the test constructor should frame the questions in his own sentences.
(viii) Such type of questions should not be included in which guesswork is possible.
(ix) 'Never' should not be included in MC questions because it reduces the reliability of the questions.
(x) The items should be in the limit of the subject matter.
(xi) There should not be any doubt, grammatical error or incompletion of the sentences.

Selection of the Item

After framing the question in preliminary form, the test constructor tests the questions. It is done at two levels — Pre-tryout stage and actual-tryout stage. In pre-tryout stage the test is given to some related students to answer it. So the questions, in which there is no clarity, are omitted and difficulty faced in the administration is corrected. After modification the test is sent to some experts for their suggestions. After that the test is again given to some related students i.e. actual-tryout stage. Item analysis process is applied to find out the difficulty level and discriminatory power of each item and to find the reliability and validity of the test. Questions that are too easy or too difficult may be omitted.

Item Analysis

After the items have been written, reviewed and carefully edited, they are subjected to a procedure called item analysis. Item analysis is a set of procedures, that is applied to know the indices for the truthfulness of items. Items can be analysed qualitatively, in terms of their content and form, and quantitatively, in terms of their statistical properties. Qualitative analysis includes the consideration of content validity and the evaluation of items in terms of effective item-writing procedures. Quantitative analysis includes principally the measurement of item difficulty and item validity.

Item analysis is a technique through which those items which are valid and suited to the purpose are selected and the rest are either eliminated or modified to suit the purpose. The validity of the whole test is dependent upon the validity of each individual item.

Meaning of Item Analysis

"In a narrower sense, the term (item analysis) will be used specifically for an assessment of how effectively each individual item contributes to the overall validity of the test." — *A.S. Reber*

"The term 'item analysis' refers to a loosely structured group of statistics that can be computed for each item in a test." — *Murphy and David Shofer*

"The procedure used to judge the quality of an item is called item analysis." — *Lamark*

"Item analysis is the process of evaluating single test items by any of several methods. This usually involves the determination of how well an individual item separates examinees, its relative difficulty value, and its correlation with some criterion of measurement." — *Dictionary of Education*

"In psychological testing, analysis based on the responses to individual question is referred to as an item analysis." — *Dictionary of Statistical Terms*

"Item analysis refers to the determination of any item characteristic, such as difficulty, level of ambiguity, time limits etc." — *J.P. Chaplin*

Thus, item analysis is that process or technique through which the effectiveness of each item is studied.

Purpose or Need of Item Analysis

The main purpose of item analysis is to select those items of the test which are valid, reliable and appropriate for that class of students or people for whom the test has been constructed. A good test should comprise of good items. If the item of a test are purposeful as well as valid and reliable, that test is considered useful. The purposes of item analysis are as follows:

1. *To know the difficulty level of an item*: The main objective of item analysis is to find out the difficulty level of each item. In other words, it indicates which items are difficult, easy, moderately difficult or moderately easy.
2. *To know discrimination power of the item*: The second purpose of item analysis is to find out the discrimination power of each item. It provides indices of the ability of the item to discriminate between inferior and superior. It is also known as item validity.
3. *To indicate the effectiveness of distracter analysis of an item*: The third purpose of item analysis is to indicate the effectiveness of distracter analysis in multiple-choice items. For example, if an item has four alternate responses as — a, b, c and d and in them option 'b' is correct answer and other three are incorrect. Thus, these three are distracters. Item analysis is done to indicate the extent to which the distracters or fools are effective in each item.
4. *To modify the item*: Sometimes item analysis also indicates why a particular item in the test has not functioned effectively or what is the error in it. In other words, the purpose of item analysis is to know that how this item might be modified so that its functional significance can be increased.

Thus, item analysis carried out on the data of trial testing provides difficulty and discrimination indices that help in judging whether a particular item should be accepted or rejected. It can also be carried out on the test data generated by administration of a test in an achievement survey or in an examination where the purpose is not to select good items but to find out how the items behaved when the test was administered to a given population or sub-population of the students.

It should now be clear that the main purpose of item analysis is to provide indices of item difficulty and item discrimination on the basis of empirical data obtained from trial of the test on a representative sample of the students for whom the test is meant.

Methods of Item Analysis

The process of item analysis includes three stages as:

1. Distracter analysis
2. Item difficulty or facility index
3. Item discrimination

1. Distracter Analysis

The first step of item analysis is distracter analysis. In the multiple-choice items there are different answers in which one is correct and others are wrong. The wrong answers are known as distracters. Usually the number of examinees answering each distracter of an item in both the upper group and the lower group is counted. Ordinarily, any distracter to be called a good distracter must be answered by more examinees of the lower group. If this happens, a distracter is retained in the form it was presented in the item. But if a distracter is answered by more examinees of the higher group than the examinees of the lower group, the distracter is regarded to be of poor form. A test constructor may find some non-functional distracters, which, by definition, are those that contribute nothing to the test. Such distracters are not chosen by any examinee in the upper as well as in lower group. The test constructor often drop such type of distracters from items or carefully modifies them. There are also distracters which are equally attractive to both upper and lower class, such distracters also need suitable modification.

Suppose there are 100 examinees who answer to a particular four option multiple choice item. Suppose on this item 55 responded to 'a', 15 to 'b', 23 to 'e' and 7 to d (a is the correct response). It means that 45 examinees answered the item incorrectly.

$$\text{Number of persons expected to choose each distractor} = \frac{\text{Number of persons answering item incorrectly}}{\text{Number of Distractor}}$$

We should, therefore, expect 15 examinees to choose each distracter. In fact 15 examinees chose distracter 'b', more chose 'c' than expected, and fewer chose 'd'. When the number of examinees choosing a distracter exceeds the number expected, there may be two possibilities. Firstly, it is just possible that the choice may reflect partial knowledge, secondly, the item is poorly constructed. But one thing should be kept in mind that distracter analysis is needed if the items are multiple choice type, otherwise not.

2. Item Difficulty

In item analysis, the next step is to find out the difficulty value of the item or the index of difficulty of an item.

In the words of Chaplin, "item difficulty is the difficulty level of a test item as measured by the frequency with which the item is passed (or failed)".

In the words of Anastasi, "The difficulty of an item is defined in terms of percentage of persons who answer it correctly."

On the basis of above definition we can say that difficulty value of an item is defined as the percentage or proportion of the examinees or individuals who answer the item correctly. This percentage or proportion is known as the index of difficulty of an item. The proportion passing an item is inversely related to the difficulty of an item. The difficulty level can be calculated with the help of following methods:

I. Empirical method

The empirical method is the basic and scientific method of determining the index of difficulty of an item, also known as statistical method. The following are different methods of securing difficulty value of an item as:

(i) *27 per cent Upper and 27 per cent Lower Group Method*: Before analysing the items the test should be given to a representative sample of 200 individuals. The scores of the items are calculated. The total scores of every individual is calculated. The total scores and the answer sheets are to be arranged in ascending order. The total answer sheets are divided into two parts — upper group and lower group. In the upper group the answer sheets of top 27 per cent individuals and in the lower group lowest 27 per cent of the answer sheets are selected. Thus, we have the answer sheets of 54 per cent individuals. After dividing the students in upper and lower group RH and RL are calculated. RH means the right answers given by the individuals in high or upper group for every item. RL means the right responses of lower group individuals for each item.

$$\text{Difficulty Value (D.V.)} = \frac{RH + RL}{2n} \times 100$$

Where

RH = Right response for an item in upper group

RL = Right response for an item in lower group

n = Total number of students in the group giving right responses.

Thus, we get difficulty value in percentages. To illustrate suppose N1 = 200, N2 = 200 and RH = 150 and RL = 50 for a particular item in a test then its difficulty value will be:

$$\text{D.V.} = 100 - \frac{150 + 50}{2 \times 200} \times 100$$

$$= 100 - 50 = 50 \text{ per cent}$$

The item with high difficulty value will be much difficult. The item with 50 per cent difficulty level is considered good. In the words of Anastasi, "It is best to select items with moderate spread of difficulty level, but whose average difficulty is 0.50".

(ii) *Harper's Facility Index*: Harper also followed the method of right responses given by 27 per cent upper and 27 per cent lower group.

The formula is:

$$\text{F.I.} = \frac{RU + RL}{2E} \times 100$$

Where

F.I. = Facility Index

RU = Number of correct responses in upper group

RL = Number of correct responses in lower group

E = Total number of students in each group

With the help of above example the facility index will be:

$$\text{F.I.} = \frac{150 + 50}{2 \times 200} \times 100 = 50\%$$

Harper view is that if F.I. is between 35 per cent to 85 per cent then the item's difficulty value is good. The items having less than and more than that should be dropped.

The difference between the Harper and the previous formula is that if the value of F.I. is high it means the item is very easy whereas in the previous formula if D.V. is less, the item is easy.

(iii) *50 per cent Above and 50 per cent Below Right Response Method*: In this method the respondents are divided in upper and lower group on the 50-50 per cent basis.

Student/Items	1	2	3	4	5	6	7	8	9	10	Score	U&L Group
1	√	√	√	√	×	√	√	×	√	√	8	U
2	√	√	×	√	√	×	×	√	√	×	6	U
3	×	×	√	√	√	×	×	×	√	√	5	U
4	√	√	√	√	×	×	×	√	√	√	7	U
5	×	×	×	×	√	√	√	×	×	×	3	L
6	√	√	√	√	×	×	×	×	√	√	6	U
7	×	×	√	√	√	√	×	×	×	×	4	L
8	×	×	×	×	×	√	√	×	×	×	2	L
9	×	×	×	×	×	×	×	√	√	√	3	L
10	×	×	×	×	×	×	√	√	×	×	2	L

$$\text{Difficulty Index} = \frac{R_U + R_L}{2}$$

Where

RU = Right response in upper group

RL = Right response in lower group

Difficulty Index Table

Item No.	*Upper Group*		*Lower Group*		*Difficulty Level*	
	No. of Right Responses	R_U	*No. of Right Response*	R_L	R_UTR_L	$R_UTR_L/2$
1	4	$\frac{4}{5}=.8$	–	–	.8	.4
2	4	.8	–	–	.8	.4
3	4	.8	1	$\frac{1}{5}=.2$	1.0	.5
4	5	1	1	.2	1.2	.6
5	2	.4	2	.4	.8	.4
6	1	.2	3	.6	.8	.4
7	1	.2	3	.6	.8	.4
8	2	.4	2	.4	.8	.4
9	5	1	1	.2	1.2	.6
10	4	.8	1	.2	1.0	.5

In the above table, the item with difficulty level.6 is easiest and difficult with difficulty level of.4.

D.I. in Speed Test. In a speed test many examinees never reach the end of the test not because of their intrinsic difficulty but because of their position in the test. Hence the usual way to determine the index of difficulty as in power test would be misleading. So, the formula for the index of difficulty becomes—

$$P = \frac{R}{N_r}$$

Where

P = Index of Difficulty

R = No. of examinees who gave the right response

N_r = No. of examinees who actually reached or answered (right or wrong) that item.

Illustration. Suppose that a test consists of 40 items. Of these the first 30 items were answered by all examinees (N = 80) but the remaining 10 items were answered by only a few. Further suppose that item 38 was answered only by 60 examinees out of which 20 answered it correctly. What will be the index of difficulty of item 38.

Solution. Index of difficulty of item 38 = $\frac{20}{60} = 0.33$.

Correcting Difficulty Index for Chance Error. In multiple choice items, always there is possibility of answering the items by guess work. So, we have to use correction formula as:

$$P_c = \left(R - \frac{W}{K-1}\right)\frac{1}{N} \text{......(Guilford)}$$

Where

P_c = Percentage of individual who really give right response

R = Percentage of those who give right response

W = Percentage of those who give wrong response

K = Number of options or choice

Illustration. Suppose in a sample 500 examinees, an item was correctly responded by 350 individuals and every item has 5 choices. What will be difficulty level of that item?

Solution.

$$P_c = \left(350 - \frac{150}{5-1}\right)\frac{1}{500}$$

$$= (350 - 37.5)\frac{1}{500}$$

$$= 312.5 \times \frac{1}{500}$$

$$= .625 = .625 \times 100 = 63\%$$

But sometimes it has been observed that some students don't try to solve the items. The reason may be shortage of time or more difficult item or other cause. Then items remain unattempted or unreached. For example, in a test of 50 items an examinee solve 1 to 25 questions and 26th and 27 are left unsolved and then 28 to 40 are solved and afterwards no item was solved. In this situation items 41 to 50 are unattempted but 26 and 27 are not. The group will be divided in three as — group giving correct responses, group giving wrong responses and group with unattempted items.

In such a situation the formula will be:

$$P_c = \left(R - \frac{W}{K-1}\right)\frac{1}{N - NR}$$

Here NR = No. of those students who don't try to solve the items.

Illustrations. A test of 200 items was given to 300 examinees. Every items has 5 alternate responses, 150 gave correct response, 120 gave incorrect response and 30 students were with unattempted questions. What will be the difficulty level of that item?

Solution.

$$P_c = \left(150 - \frac{120}{5-1}\right)\frac{1}{300-30}$$

$$= \left(150 - \frac{120}{4}\right)\frac{1}{270}$$

$$= 120x\frac{1}{270} = .44 \text{ or } 44\%$$

Kelley's Formula

When the number of examinees is larger than this method is useful.

$$P_c = \frac{1}{2}\left[\left(R_H - \frac{W_H}{K-1}\right)\frac{1}{N_H - NR_H} + \left(R_L - \frac{W_L}{K-1}\right)\left(\frac{1}{N_L - NR_L}\right)\right]$$

Where

RH = No. of examinees giving exact right responses in upper group.
WH = No. of examinees giving wrong responses in upper group.
NH = Total number of examinees in upper group.
NRH = No. of examinees who don't try to solve the items in upper group.
RL = No. of examinees giving exact correct responses in lower group.
WL = No. of examinees giving wrong responses in lower group.
ML = Total number of examinees in the lower group.
NRL = Total number of examinees who don't try to solve the items in lower group.

II. Method of Judgement

In this method the difficulty value of an item is determined on the basis of judgement of experts. Items are given to experts, with the instruction to rank the items in their increasing order of difficulty. Sometimes the test constructor himself takes the decision on the basis of total time taken by the examinees in its solution. This method is not considered good because it lacks reliability and objectivity.

Some experts have suggested that inter-correlations of all items should be computed because it gives an indication regarding the distribution of item difficulty, which, in turn, helps in the process of the selection. The best index of item inter-correlation is the phi-coefficient of the items are scored as either +1 or 0. When the items are nearly equal in difficulty, their inter-correlation is high but when items vary in the indices of difficulty, such items don't yield high inter-correlation and this depicts a low reliability of a test.

III. Normal Curve Method

The difficulty level of an item of a test can be measured with the help of sigma distance in normal curve. This is calculated by standard deviation of the normal curve.

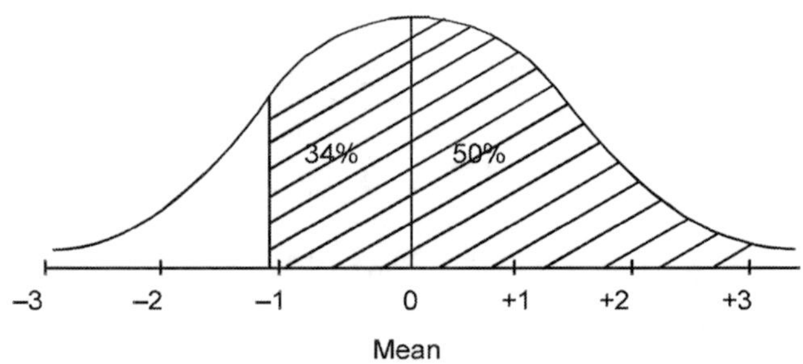

The figure indicates the difficulty level of an item passed by 84 per cent of the cases. The item falls below 1s below the mean. An item passed by 16 per cent of the cases (50 – 34 = 16) fall 1s above the mean. The more difficult items have plus values, the easier items minus values. The difficulty value corresponding to any percentage passing can be found by reference to a normal curve frequency table. With this method the difficulty value will be in quantitative form and that is why this method is known as scientific method. The comparison of difficulty value of different item is also possible with this method.

Optimal Difficulty Value for a Reliable Test

Most test constructors mean that optimal level of difficulty is one which produces maximum item inter-correlations and thereby maximum item-total correlation is also a higher reliability of test scores. So, the optimal level has a direct link with the reliability of the test scores. Lord has suggested that optimal level of difficulty for the alternate item is 0.85, for three alternative items is 0.77, for four alternative items is 0.74 and for five alternative items is 0.69.

3. Item Discrimination

Discrimination power or discrimination value of an item is known as item validity. It is that ability of the item on the basis of which the discrimination or distinction is made between superiors and inferiors.

In the words of Marshall and Hales (1972:81), "The discriminatory power of validity of the item may be defined as the extent to which success or failure on that item indicates the possession of the trait or achievement being measured."

In the words of L.R. Gay, "Discrimination power refers to the degree to which an item discriminates between high and low achievers on the test."

There are several ways of determining the index of discrimination. We will discuss the important ones as follows:

(i) *Johnson Method*: Johnson has suggested a very simple and quick method of determining the index of discrimination. In this method, the examinees are grouped in two extremes i.e. upper 27 per cent and bottom 27 per cent. The number of students will be same in both the groups. The formula is:

$$\text{D.I.} = \frac{R_U - R_L}{E}$$

Where

D.I. = Discrimination Index
RU = Number of correct responses in upper group
RL = Number of correct responses in lower group
E = Number of students in each group

Example. Suppose that in a group of 200 students 49 students gave correct response in upper group and 24 in the lower group. Find D.I. of that item.

$$\text{D.I.} = \frac{R_U - R_L}{E} = \frac{49 - 24}{54} = \frac{25}{54} = 0.46$$

Johnson said that D.I. above 0.40 is good. Some educationists say that 0.50 and above the value of D.I. is good. Sometimes those items are also selected who have D.I. = 0.30. Generally, the items with high D.I. have to be selected.

(ii) *Correlation Method*: When the correlation between the total score and the individual item score is computed as a measure of the discriminative power of the item, it shows how well the item is measuring that function which the test itself is measuring. Five common measure of correlation as product moment, bi-serial r, point bi-serial r, tetrachoric and phi-coefficient are frequently applied. When multipoint items are there in the test, product moment correlation is the most appropriate one. When items are in two-alternative responses i.e. when the dichotomous items are, bi-serial or point bi-serial correlation is the most preferred. When the total score is also dichotomous, as the response items, the tetrachoric or phi-coefficient of correlation are used.

Flangan was the first person to provide a short cut to these correlation coefficients especially the bi-serial r. He prepared an abac table from which one can directly read the value of bi-serial correlation provided one knows the proportion of examinees passing an item is the upper 27 per cent criterion group. In each extreme group, N should not be less than 100, which means that the total number of examinees should be 370.

Item No.	*N = 100 Proportion Correct in Upper 27%*	*N = 100 Proportion Correct in Lower 27%*	*Index of Difficulty*	*Index of Discrimination*
1	0.80	0.20	0.50	0.60
2	0.65	0.35	0.50	0.30
3	0.90	0.40	0.65	0.50
4	0.40	0.60	0.50	– 0.20*
5	0.65	0.85	0.75	– 0.25*
6	0.55	0.25	0.40	0.30
7	0.50	0.50	0.50	0.00*
8	0.70	0.70	0.70	0.00*
9	0.75	0.05	0.40	0.70
10	0.95	0.90	0.92	0.05*

* Items should be dropped or modified

In this table the difficulty value has been calculated as the average of upper group and lower group (0.80 + 0.20 = = 0.5). The index of discrimination of each item which exhibits bi-serial r real directly from the Flangan abac table. In the table items 1, 2, 3, 6 and 9 have positive bi-serial correlation co-efficient indicating that the items are discriminating. When all the items have got correlation coefficient, then they are selected from highest to lowest. In general, the correlation coefficient of 0.20 or above are selected for final inclusion in the test.

(iii) *Symond's Method*: This method is very easy and simple method for finding the validity of the item but not more reliable. Two groups are taken, one is brilliant group and the other is weak group. The correct responses for every item in each group are calculated and then the difference is calculated. This difference is known as the index of discrimination.

Item	*25 Brilliant Student Group (Correct Response)*	*25 Weak student Group (Correct Response)*	*Difference*
1	20	14	6
2	22	18	4
3	25	25	0
4	09	06	3
5	22	08	14

In Symond's method the range of index is ±0 to ±20. The items having less than 14 index are understood weak. Thus, in the above table only one item 5 has discrimination power.

(iv) *Simple Analysis with Small Group*: Item analysis may be done in still more simplified and convenient way without using any of the above methods. Suppose that in a class of 80 students we have chosen 26 students (33 per cent) with the highest and 26 with the lowest scores. We now have three groups – upper (U), Middle (M) and lower groups. First we need to tally the correct responses to each item given by students in each group. A rough index can be prepared as:

Item	*U (26)*	*M (28)*	*L (26)*	*Difficulty (U+M+L)*	*Discriminati on (U-L)*
1	15	9	7	31	8
2	18	18	10	46	8
3	22	20	9	51	13
4	25	22	16	63*	9
5	20	17	22	59	–2*
6	11	9	11	31	0*
7	16	10	0	26	16
8	07	02	04	13*	3*
⋮					
80					

The table reveals 5 questionable items that have been identified for further consideration. Items 4 and 8 have been singled out because it seems to be very easy and others very difficult. Items 5, 6 and 8 while satisfactory with difficulty but show a negative and zero discrimination value respectively. For discrimination we will consider item 8 also. With larger group, we would expect larger difference to occur by chance in a non-discriminating item.

Relation between Difficulty Level and Discrimination Power of an Item

There is a close relationship between the difficulty level and discriminating power of an item of a test. It has been observed that the item which is too easy or too difficult can't discriminate the students/respondents. In other words, we can say that this item has less discriminating power. It is not necessary that an item with discriminating power of.50 will also have the difficulty level of.50 and vice versa.

Factors Influencing the Discrimination Power and Difficulty Level

After trial testing and item analysis of the data obtained from it, one has to make decisions about items that should be retained, rejected or modified. One has to keep in mind that enough items of different difficulty values are left. When we find that an item is too easy or too difficult or not sufficiently discriminating, then we have to look for the possible reasons before accepting or rejecting it or modifying it.

If an item is too easy, the possible reasons may be:

- The distracters are not plausible.
- Most students have the knowledge of what the item is testing. In achievement testing it may be an item fit for a lower class.

If an item is too difficult, the possible reasons may be:

- The correct answer is actually incorrect.
- The item has more than one correct answer.
- The language may be misleading or ambiguous.
- The length of the test.
- The item is readily complex and assesses higher level ability.
- Non-familiarity of the examinee with the content of the item.

If an item is not sufficiently discriminating, the possible reasons may be:

- The 'correct' answer is wrong or there is more than one correct answers.
- The item is ambiguous, the task is not clearly spelled out.
- The correct answer is too obvious; the item is very easy.
- The item is something different from what the test is supposed to test.
- The better students were somehow ill-informed or wrongly taught.
- Only the weak students were taught properly, as it was assumed that the abler students knew the subject well and hence were ignored.

Thus, while analysing the items these reasons should be kept in mind. Each item has to be reviewed carefully so that no flaws are left in its content or wording, and the alternatives.

Criteria for Item Selection and Rejection

1. The item which has high difficulty index or low difficulty index is rejected. Such type of items if included in the test do not fulfil any objective.
2. The items which have negative or zero discriminating power, those are also rejected, because these are not considered appropriate for the test.
3. The items with difficulty index of.40 to.70 and positive discriminating value are selected.
4. The items are not selected only on the basis of index. While selecting the items both difficulty index and discriminating index are kept in mind. For example, if an item has.50 difficulty index and zero discriminating index, that item is also rejected.

Thus, it is not necessary that we can find the items with item analysis once upon a time. We are to modify the items again and again.

Problems of Item Analysis

Item analysis is a complicated process. Despite the fact that test technicians have devised numerous methods of item analysis so that a test constructor may not face any difficulty or problem, though some basic problems remain constant as:

1. *Problem of guessing or chance success*: If the items have two alternative options, the guessing or chance success increases too much. In the multiple choice items chance of guessing is minimised, though not fully eliminated. Some test technicians have given the correction formula for this problem but some of them oppose this idea on the ground that guessing does not necessarily reveal the lack

of real knowledge being measured by the item. Thus, the following measures or solutions can be opted for this problem as – guidance from the experts, use of multiple choice item instead of two alternatives, if possible give instruction that if the student gives response on the basis of guessing there will be negative marking etc.

2. *Problem of spurious correlation*: The practice of rejecting items that have low correlation with total score provides a means of purifying or homogenising the test. By such a procedure, the items with the highest average inter-correlation will be retained. This method of selecting items will increase test validity only when the original pool of items measure a single trait and when this trait is present in the criterion. Most tests developed in actual practice, however, measure a combination of traits required by a complex criterion. The solutions for minimising the extent of spurious correlation are – the number of items should preferably be large in the test and as the items having 0.5 as difficulty index have more of a spurious element than items of extreme indices of difficulty, such extreme items should also be included in the test.

3. *Problems related to dichotomous items*: By dichotomous items we mean the items whose responses are in yes/no, right/wrong, true/false, agree/disagree etc. Generally, it has been observed that the test constructor gives +1 for yes or true or agree and –1 for no, false or disagree. If the test has half positive and half negative questions then the correlation of each items with other items will be very close to zero and therefore, all item total correlation also be very close to zero. Moreover, all positive statements would correlate negatively with the negative statements. In such a situation, where the item – total correlation for all items approaches either near zero or becomes negative, items can't be selected on the basis of the item – total correlation. The solution for this problem can be that the test constructor should prepare the scoring key as to give +1 to all the positive statements when agreed and to all negative statements when disagreed. As a result, most of the items on total correlations will be +ve and items can be selected on the basis of the correlation of an item with the total score.

4. *Problem of controlling unwanted elements*: Ideally in homogeneous tests, all items should measure only one attribute and not other, but in practice, items also tend to correlate with a factor or factors, which are not wanted. For example, the items of a numerical aptitude test not only measure quantitative aptitude but also measure the factor of verbal comprehension because items also involve the comprehension of words and sentence used in items. In such a situation, the items would also tend to correlate with the unwanted factor of verbal comprehension. The solution for this type of problem is that the test constructor should frame four times the actual number of items to be retained in the final form.

5. *Problem of the examinee not reaching to the last item*: As it has been said that in reality no test is power test. Every test has time limit. So, they are speed tests. In the limited time, the examinee can't reach to the last item. If adequate time is given then this problem can be solved.

6. *Problem associated with difficulty level and discriminating power*: Generally it has been seen that as the difficulty level of the test increases, in the same way the

discriminating power of that item also increases. But sometimes it has been seen that an item which has difficulty level of.50 or near to it but its discriminating power is very much less. For solving such type of problems we should keep the items in the test with appropriate difficulty level.

The difficulties encountered in the item analysis of speeded test are fundamentally similar to the above discussed. Various solutions, both empirical and statistical, have been developed for meeting these difficulties. One empirical solution is to administer the test with a longer time limit to the group on which item analysis is to be carried out.

Marking Scheme

In order to help the examiner in evaluating the answers objectively, it is necessary to develop a marking scheme which shows how marks are to be awarded for each question. A detailed marking scheme is needed particularly for examination in which several evaluators are required. In the case of multiple choice or other objective type questions and also very short answer type questions there is unique correct answer or a model answer, and hence, the variations in marking can be avoided. Every examiner will score the answer in exactly the same way. But in short answer or essay type questions, the marking scheme should show the marks allotted to different value points expected to be covered in the answer as well as marks to be deducted (if desired) for errors or poor quality of an answer. In the questions which have two or more parts, the marks for each part should be shown.

Preparation of the Final Test

Now the achievement test is prepared in the final form according to the blueprint.

Editing or Formatting of the Achievement Test

Now the questions are arranged and edited according to the above written plan.

(i) *Section scheme*: The teacher should keep in mind that every type of question should be kept in different section as essay type in one section, short type in one section and objective type in one section.

(ii) *Directions*: The directions should be provided in a proper way i.e. length of the answer, method of answering, time limit, marking scheme, marks for clearing, etc.

(iii) *Organisation of questions*: The questions should be organised in the section based on the maxim of simple to complex.

(iv) *Final form of the test*: The test should be given final form i.e. it should include following features like name of subject or course and its code, if any, year or month of examination, maximum marks, time allotted for answering, special instructions, if any, for the examinees, questions written in a pre-determined order, marks in the margin against each question.

Examples of an Achievement Test

Example 1: Business Studies – XI

Time 3 Hours **M.M.: 100**

All Questions are compulsory

1. The minimum number of Members for the formation of Private Company is:
   1. 2 2. 5
   3. 3 4. 7
2. Equity shareholder is to be called:
   1. Owner of company 2. Officer of company
   3. Partner of company 4. Guardian of company
3. In small scale industry investment limit is:
   1. Upto one crore 2. Upto three crore
   3. Upto two crore 4. Upto ten crore
4. Internal Trade means:
   1. Trade within boundary of a country
   2. Trade within two country
   3. Trade with one foreign country
   4. At the world level
5. .... can place sample on his shop
   1. Company 2. Wholesaler
   3. Retailer 4. All
6. .... can deal in many things
   1. Retailer 2. Wholesaler
   3. Broker 4. Agent
7. Automatic vending machine can be used for
   1. Cigarette 2. Cold drink
   3. Both 4. Car
8. What complexity is involved in international business:
   1. Language difference 2. More risk
   3. Government control 4. All of these
9. What is the advantage of Malls
   1. Easy selection 2. High prices
   3. More running cost 4. Huge capital investment
10. Producer-wholesaler-retailer-consumer is the example of...............
    1. Retail trade 2. Wholesale trade
    3. Direct trade 4. Indirect trade $1 \times 10 = 10$
11. Who is promoter?
12. Write the names of two documents to be filed with Registrar.
13. What is tiny sector?
14. Write two features of wholesale trade.

15. Who is pavement trader?
16. Write the names of two things sold by automatic vending machine.
17. Mention two document used in import trade.
18. What is project work? $1 \times 8 = 8$
19. Write two features of Business Finance.
20. Write two differences between wholesaler and retailer?
21. Write two problems of small business in India.
22. What is indent or placing an order in terms of import trade?
23. Write two features of Export Processing Zone.
24. Write two features of American Depository Receipt? 2×6=12
25. Write four importance of project work.
26. Write four incentives available for export promotion.
27. Write four features of international trade.
28. Write four disadvantages of mail order business.
29. Write any four services of retailer towards consumer.
30. Write four services of wholesaler towards manufacturer.
31. Write four advantages of direct trade.
32. Differentiate between equity share and preference share. (Any four)
33. What is prospectus? Also write its two objectives.
34. Write four demerits of multiple shops? $4 \times 10 = 40$
35. What is international trade? Write its eight features.

    or

    Write five advantages of mail order business to consumer and seller.
36. Write the meaning of departmental store? Write its four merits and demerits.

    or

    Write eight differences between departmental store and multiple shops.
37. What is equity share? Write any four merits and demerits of equity shares to company.

    or

    Write six difference between memorandum of association and articles of association. $10 \times 3 = 30$

Example 2: Accountancy-XI

Time: 3 Hours **M.M.: 100**

All questions are compulsory

1. What do you mean by Accounting? What are the functions or objective of Accounting? 8
2. What do you mean by different accounting terms: Capital, Income, Stock, Drawing, Discount. 8

3. What is the difference between Provision and Reserve? 8
4. What do you mean by Profit and Loss A/c? What is the need and importance to prepare it? 4
5. What is the difference between Bills of Exchange and Promissory Note. 6
6. What is depreciation? What are features of depreciation? 4
7. There was a difference of Rs. 430 in a Trial Balance it was placed on the debit side of Suspense A/c. Later on the following errors were discovered. Pass rectifying entries and prepare Suspense A/c.
   1. Purchase Book was overcast by Rs.100.
   2. Sales Book was overcast by Rs.1000.
   3. Goods for Rs.800 purchased from Umakant, though entered in the Purchase Book, has not been posted to his account.
   4. An amount of Rs. 500 has been posted to the credit side of Commission account instead of Rs.570.
   5. Goods sold to Bharti for Rs.4,400 has been posted to her account as Rs.4,000.
   6. Goods sold to X for Rs.750 was recorded in Purchase Book. 10
8. Raja Textiles Co. which closes its books on 31st December, purchased a machine on 1.1.1988 for Rs.50,000. On 1.7.1989, it purchased an additional machine for Rs. 30,000. The part of the machine which was purchased on 1.1.1988 costing Rs.10,000 was sold off for Rs.3,600 on 30th June 1991. Prepare the Machine A/c for four years, if depreciation is provided, at the rate of 10 per cent PA on diminishing Balance Method. 10
9. Calculate cost of goods sold by the following:

	Rs.
Opening Stock	100000
Closing Stock	70000
Purchase	50000
Direct Exp.	60000
Return Outwards	5000

4

10. Jitendra keeps his books by single entry system. His position was as follows:

	1 Jan 1980	31 Dec. 1980
Cash in hand	200	300
Cash at Bank	3000	2000
Stock-in Trade	20000	19000
Sundry Debtors	8500	14000
Plant & Machinery	15000	27000
Fixture & Fitting	1800	1500
Sundry Creditors	22000	29000

During the year, Jitender introduced Rs.5000 as further Capital in the business and withdrew Rs.750 per month. From the above information, show profit or loss for the year ended 31st December 1980. 8

11. A sells goods for Rs.3000 to B on 1st January 1986 and on the same day

draws a bill on B at three month for the amount B accepts it and return it to A, who discounts it on 4th February, 1986 with his bank at 18 per cent PA. The acceptance is dishonoured on the due date, the noting charge paid by the bank being Rs.20.

On 4th April, 1986, B accepts a new bill at two months for the amount then due to A together with interest at 12 per cent per annum.

Make journal entries to record these transaction in the books of A and B. 12

12. Prepare Trading and Profit & Loss Account for the year ended 31st Dec. 1985 and Balance Sheet as on that date from the following Trial Balance.

	Dr.	Cr.
Capital		10,000
Cash	1,500	
Bank Overdraft		2,000
Purchase and Sales	12,000	15,000
Return	1,000	2,000
Establishment Exp.	2,200	
Taxes and Insurance	500	
Bad-debts	500	
Provision for Bad Debts	700	
Debtors and Creditors	5,000	2,000
Commission		500
Deposits	4,000	
Opening Stock	3,000	
Drawings	1,400	
Furniture	600	
B/R and B/P	3,000	2,500
	34,700	34,700

Adjustments:

(i) Salaries Rs.100 and Taxes Rs.200 are outstanding but insurance Rs.50 is prepaid.

(ii) Commission Rs.100 is received in advance for next year.

(iii) Interest Rs.210 is to be received on deposits and interest on Bank Overdraft Rs.300 is to be paid.

(iv) Bad debts provision is Rs.1000.

(v) Depreciate furniture by 10 per cent.

(vi) Closing stock Rs.4500. 18

UNIT-TEST

"A unit in commerce may be defined as a carefully developed series of child like experience, related to a particular topic and designed to contribute to the achievements of purposes of commerce."

— *Michaelis*

The word 'unit' is sometimes used as an equivalent to a topic or a combination of two or more topics that are related. It is better to relate a unit of teaching to related learning experiences that involve unitary organisation of experiences rather than combination of two or more topics. Since subject matter is the recorded experience, the dichotomy between the two is not possible. Of course, one has to utilise some source of unity around which learning experiences may be organised.

In the words of Hanna, Hageman and Potter, "A unit can be defined as a purposeful learning experience focussed upon some socially significant understanding which will modify the behaviour of the learning and enable him to adjust to a life situation more effectively."

The vast subject matter of commerce has to be organised in large divisions, each sub-division is called a unit. The units demand the selection of material should be on the basis of its contribution in promoting understanding. It is based on the belief that there is a need for the gradual growth of the individual pupil through participating in experiences that are continuous, integrated and unified around a large topic. A unit is, therefore, more than a lesson, an activity, an arbitrary division of subject matter or the learning experiences.

Meaning of Unit Test

A unit-test is a written oral or practical exercise based on the content of the unit and the unit-objectives, administered after the completion of the unit as a formal device for measuring the students' achievement in order to get feedback on their learning and use it for further improvement of their achievement.

A unit-test is basically a miniature test. In a unit-test the coverage of content is intensive and selected in a full fledged question paper. It may be based on one or two objectives. As after the teaching of a lesson, the teacher tests the learning of the students with the help of a short test, in the same way, after the completion of a unit, the teacher is to test the gained knowledge of the students and that test is known as unit test. It may include one form of questions or all the forms, as we usually have in any annual question paper. The time period may be of 30 or 40 minutes depending upon the scope of a unit-test. Usually the class period is taken as the time frame. The learning that takes place is assessed or evaluated not only for the learning benefit but also for the teacher to evaluate his work. At the end of the unit, the teacher needs to get feedback as what the learner has achieved, as a result of teacher's efforts and also indirectly to assess her own achievements as a teacher.

The results of a unit-test are normally used for diagnosing the pupils' adequacies and inadequacies in learning. Focus of unit testing is not on measuring and grading but on improvement of pupils' achievement through regular feedback.

Purpose of Unit-Test

1. To ascertain the effectiveness of teaching.
2. To utilize for remedial work.
3. To identify the students' learning difficulties-whether persistent or recurring.

4. To assess the students' learning and to provide feedback to students and teachers for teaching learning process.
5. To motivate the learners.
6. To serve as self-evaluation device.
7. To find out strength and weaknesses of individual student.
8. To measure whether the students have achieved the objectives of planned instruction.

Construction of a Unit-test

There are several steps involved in the construction of a unit test as:

1. Determination of Objectives: The first and the most important step in planning the construction of a unit test is to determine the instructional objectives. In commerce, the major objectives are categorised as knowledge, understanding, application and skill. These objectives are termed in the form of behavioural changes from the viewpoint of learners.

2. Designing the Unit-test: The second step is to make a design which includes the following steps.

(*i*) Delineate the unit content to sub-units, keeping in view the integrated chunk of content that can be taught almost independently. Depending upon the scope of the unit, we can divide the content of the unit into 3 to 5 sub-units.

(*ii*) Give proportionate weightage to each sub-unit.

(*iii*) Undertake content analysis like new terms, concepts, principles etc.

S. No.	Unit & its Sub-units	Marks	% of Marks
1			
2			
3			
4			
5			
Total			

(*iv*) Assign proportional weightage to each of assessment objectives identified under step (*i*).

S. No.	*Objectives*	*Marks*	*% age of Marks*
1.	Knowledge		
2.	Understanding		
3.	Application		
4.	Skill		
Total			

(*v*) Decide the number and forms of questions to be included in the test and give proportionate weightage to each type depending upon the nature of content of the unit and familiarity of students with one or the other form. A unit test may have one or more types of questions, with variation of weightage to each type in different units.

S. No.	*Forms of Questions*	*Marks*	*No. of Questions*	*Total Marks*
1.	Essay type			
2.	Short Answer			
3.	Very Short Answer			
4.	Objective Type			

(*vi*) Decide appropriate time to be allotted to the unit-test. It can vary from 30 minutes to 1 hour, preferably a period of 40–45 minutes, depending on the size of the unit (5 to 10 teaching periods).

(*vii*) Decide the total marks to be allotted to the unit-time keeping in view the time fixed for the unit-test and the form of questions to be included.

(*viii*) No option to be given and all the questions would be compulsory. Even internal options should not be there because the purpose of unit-test is not only measurement of students' achievement but to discover the inadequacies in learning also.

These are not the compulsory steps to be followed because the design can change as the weightage given to assessment objective sub-units and form of questions would vary from unit to unit, depending upon the nature, scope and potential of each unit in terms of cluster of content elements it is composed of.

Preparation of Blue-print

A blue-print reflects unit-wise distribution of different types of questions along with the allocation of marks in different sub-units testing different objectives of the unit, which may vary from unit to unit. It is also called three dimensional chart. The decision in the design of the unit-test is reflected in to action through the blue print. Let us suppose that a unit-test of 30 marks with 40 minutes duration is to be prepared for class XII based on a unit of teaching on 'Oraganisation'.

Procedure\Steps

(*i*) Insert total marks 30 in the total column.

(*ii*) If essay type question is included, decide first about the sub-unit that suits better and have appropriate weightage for accommodating ETQ.

(*iii*) Decide about the objective type questions testing knowledge, understanding, application and skill objectives related to different subunits.

(*iv*) Make necessary adjustments, if needed, under knowledge and understanding objectives, without disturbing application and skill objectives.

(*v*) Insert row-wise and column-wise subtotals, indicating the number of questions and the total marks for those questions. Check the total.

(*vi*) Check whether in the blue print the questions are well spread over various parts of the unit and are not crowded at one place.

The format can be as follows:

Sample Blue Print

Subject – Business studies | Class – XII
Unit – Organisation | Time – 40 minutes
Max. Marks – 30 | Min. Marks – 10

Objectives	*Knowledge*			*Understanding*			*Application*			*Skill*		*Total*
Forms of Questions	*E*	*S*	*O*	*E*	*S*	*O*	*E*	*S*	*O*	*E*	*S*	*Sub-unit wise*
Sub-units												
1. Meaning of Org.	-	2(1)	-	-	-	1(1)	-	-	-	-		3(2)
2. Importance of Org.	-	-	1(1)	-	-	2(2)	-	2(1)	-	-	2(1)	7(5)
3. Types of Org.	-	2(1)	1(1)	-	2(1)	-	-	-	1(1)	-	-	6(4)
4. Principles	4(1)	-	-	-	2(1)	2(2)	-	2(1)	1(1)	3(1)	-	14(7)
Sub totals	4(1)	4(2)	2(2)	-	4(2)	5(5)	-	4(2)	2(2)	3(1)	2(1)	30(18)
Total	10			9			6			5		30

Note: figure with in brackets indicate the number of questions and figure outside the bracket indicate marks.

This blue print is just for illustration purpose to understand how it is developed. Different blue prints on the same unit may be possible because different teachers in different schools may provide different weightage to assessment objectives, subunits and form of questions. When remedial teaching is undertaken on a unit, it is possible to retest the students on the same unit, using in parallel unit test. We can find out the *reliability* of the unit test also by analysing the performance of the students on both the parallel unit tests. Due weightage to different sub units and assessment objectives ensures curricular validity of the unit test. Study of blue print of different teachers on various units, if done from time to time, throw light on the instructional strategies of the teachers regarding emphasis being laid on different instructional objectives and type of questions used. A blue print of a unit test provides scientific basis for the constructions of a unit test as it takes care of adequate coverage of content and objectives to ensure the needed validity. A question bank can also be prepared with the help of the different unit tests prepared by different teachers from different schools.

Preparation of Questions

Next step after making blue print of the unit test is writing appropriate questions of various types in accordance with the broad parameters set out in the blue print. This can be done starting with essay type questions followed by objective type and then short answer questions. Quality of these questions is to be maintained as described in the chapter of evaluation. The questions then have to be arranged in a logical sequence.

Editing of Questions

Before finalising the unit test, each question must be edited. It should meet the requirements of the blue print and should be relevant to the model answer or key prepared while writing the items. The best way is to use question wise analysis which requires verification of each question in terms of –

- Intended assessment objective it tests
- Content area or concept tests
- Suitability of form of question
- Appropriateness of the language used
- Correctness of the answer
- Estimated difficulty level
- Time required to answer

With the help of this process, we can identify if certain questions are to be moderated for further improvement.

Consolidation of Questions or Final Drafting

Now the step is to consolidate the questions in the form of a test. The objective type questions should be provided in the beginning starting from knowledge based items followed by understanding, application and skill based items. These may be followed by short answer type question in increasing order of complexity. At the end or in the last section, there may be long answer questions.

Preparation of Marking Scheme

In this step, marking scheme is to be prepared. It helps preventing inconsistency in judgement. In this possible responses to items in the test are structured. The various value points for response are graded and the marks allowed to each value point indicated. The marking scheme ensures objectivity in judgement and eliminates differences in score, which may be due to the individual differences of the evaluators.

Writing Instructions for Examinees

Last step is to write instructions regarding questions to be attempted, mode of indicating correct answer in case of OTQ and other guidelines for them to write answers, time factor etc. that facilitate writing of the intended answer.

Uses/Advantages/Merits of Unit Test

1. When unit tests are given at regular intervals, they act as good incentives for students to evaluate their progress regularly and also improve their performance further.
2. Every unit test carries with it the key to objective type questions and outline answers to SAQ and LAQ. Students can make use this for self evaluation, if made available to them. For this school has to maintain a library of unit tests.
3. Well planned unit tests used at regular intervals discourage selective study on the part of the students.

4. It provides useful hints for remedial measures.
5. Some questions can be utilised by the teacher as an instructional aid.
6. On the basis of test results it is possible to locate certain areas where better achievement is possible and the teacher can concentrate on those areas.
7. It is possible to diagnose the students' weaknesses in certain content areas by an individual or group of individuals on the basis of analysis of test results.
8. These help the teacher to know the progress of students as well as the extent of attainment of objectives of the unit.
9. Feedback of results helps both students and teachers to improve their learning and instructional efficiency.
10. A large pool of items or questions can be developed with the help of unit tests year after year.

Criteria of a Good Unit-Test

1. It should have discriminating value.
2. It should be a power test rather than a speed test.
3. It should be comprehensive.
4. The objectives should be clear-cut.
5. It should be free from biasness.
6. It should be based on psychological principles of learning.
7. Each question of the unit test should be so worded that its whole content, rather than only a part of it, functions in determining the answer.
8. The direction to the pupil as well as the instructions for the examiners should be clear, precise and complete.

Thus, unit test is indeed the sine qua non of classroom testing. It is an indispensable tool of evaluation both for students and teachers. With the help of these, students not only know about their performances but also about their progress, inadequacies in learning and developing good study habits. Teachers get feedback about their instructional efficiency, areas of remedial instructions and improving their instructional strategies. Of course, a unit test must be planned properly and developed scientifically, through proper designing, blueprinting, framing, editing and consolidation of questions.

UNIT TEST - I

Time - 40 minutes **Subject - Commerce** **Marks - 30**

Objective Type Questions: (Each 1 mark)

(1) Bank means an ________ which transacts in ________.
(2) Find the odd ones -
 (*a*) Electronic Fund Transfer, (*b*) Automatic Teller Machine,
 (*c*) Debit Card (*d*) Overdraft
(3) Private Sector Banks are those banks which are owned and controlled by ____________.

(4) 'Accepting deposit' is which type of function of banks?

- (*a*) Primary Function
- (*b*) Secondary Function
- (*c*) Social Function
- (*d*) None of the above

(5) Classification Base Bank

(*i*) Ownership	(*a*) Commercial Banks
(*ii*) Functions	(*b*) Central Bank
(*iii*) Agriculture	(*c*) Public Sector Bank
(*iv*) Apex Banking	(*d*) Land Development Bank

(6) True / False

(*i*) Bank charges interest on time deposit account. [ ]

(*ii*) Demand loans are provided against the security of fixed Deposit, Security, Policies, etc. [ ]

Short Answer Type Questions: (30 to 40 Words each 2 marks)

(*i*) What do you understand by Commercial Bank?

(*ii*) Write two functions of NABARD.

(*iii*) What is Tele-Banking?

(*iv*) What is difference between Demand loan and Term loan?

(*v*) What are the advantages of Electronic Fund Transfers?

Long Answer Type Questions: (Each 5 marks) Do any two.

(*i*) State the various types of Banks on the basis of functions.

(*ii*) Define Bank. State the various types of Banks.

(*iii*) What are the role of Banks in Economic Development?

13

Pedagogical Analysis in Commerce

"Pedagogy is an art or science of teaching, especially instructions in teaching methods."
– *Webster Dictionary*

Pedagogy is the art or science of being a teacher. The term generally refers to strategies of instruction or a style of instruction. It is also sometimes referred to as the correct use of teaching strategies. For example, Paulo Freire referred to his method of teaching adults as 'Critical Pedagogy'. In correlation with those teaching strategies the instructor's own philosophical belief of teaching are harboured and governed by the pupil's background knowledge and experiences, personal situations and environment, as well as learning goals set by the student and teacher.

The word 'Pedagogy' comes from the Greek word 'Paidagoged' literally meaning 'to lead the child'. Webster Dictionary of education refers to the whole content of instruction, learning and the actual operations involved therein, although both words have roughly the same original meaning. In the English-speaking world the term pedagogy refers to the science of theory of education.

However, when teachers take an analytical approach to teaching and actually take time to examine the nature of teaching/learning instruction, they get a glimpse of its complicity. Effective activity prior to teaching should not only improve the teaching itself but also facilitate appraisal after teaching. It is possible for teachers to ensure effective prior activity of this type through the procedures of pedagogical analysis. These procedures start from the premise of teaching's being a highly complex skill demanding a high level of problem solving ability by teachers.

Pedagogical analysis involves making a systematic examination of a teaching task so as to reveal its essential elements. The outcome of this analysis is a plan for the teaching of the lesson or lessons. It is very important to note that the plan resulting from pedagogical analysis is not a conventional lesson plan. Lesson plan typically resembles scripts or directions detailing lines to be delivered or steps to be taken. Pedagogical analysis produces guides to action in a specific piece of teaching that will take into account such things as the conceptual structure of *what is to be taught, what we know about human learning that might enhance the learning and the experiences teachers have had in past teaching.*

In its simple meaning, the term pedagogical analysis (is composition of two words) stands for a type of analysis based on pedagogy. Analysis, as a term stands for the process of breaking or separating a thing into its constituents or elements. In teaching, we break a teaching unit into subunits, topics or single concept, etc. through the process of unit analysis.

Aspects of Pedagogical Analysis

1. Content Analysis: In this process, the content of prescribed unit or topic is analysed in to various constituents – major and minor, sections and subsections, topics and subtopics known as content analysis. On this basis, the teacher determines teaching points. While selecting teaching points, the attitude of the teacher should be skillful and intellectual. These teaching points provide direction to the teacher. Teaching is based on teaching points. While analysing the content the teacher should keep in mind the following points.

- Knowledge of maxims of teaching.
- Knowledge of principles of teaching.
- Knowledge of subject matter.
- Knowledge of important points of subject matter.
- Knowledge of sequence of subject matter.
- Knowledge of level of students.

With these points, the teacher can determine that on what parts of the topic the stress should be given.

2. Determination of Objectives: After content analysis, the teacher determines the desired change in the behaviour of the students with reference to cognitive, psychomotor and affective aspects. The teacher enlists the objectives. Teaching objectives determine learning outcomes. The knowledge of level of teaching helps in making teaching objectives in behavioural terms.

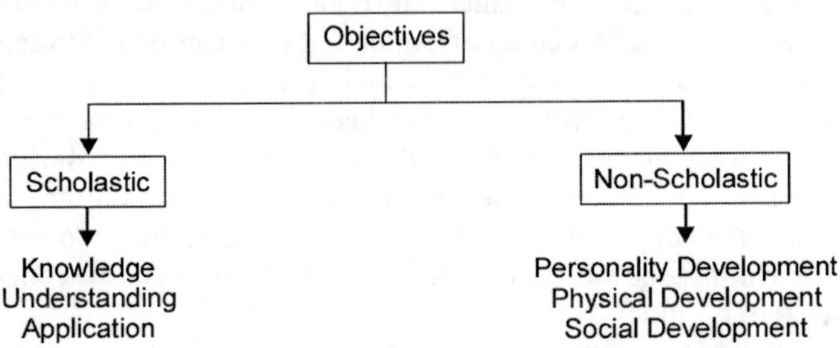

3. Teaching Learning Experiences: It is the most important part of pedagogical analysis. Considering the nature of the learning involved in relation to the analysis of conceptual content is integral with the planning of type of examples to present to the learner. Conceptual learning will be difficult and in some cases impossible if the teacher's talk is the learner's sole experience in new learning. Speech and experience must be integrated. In the case of learning psychomotor skills, explaining and demonstration may provide some basic information if the learners are familiar with the concepts used in the explanation. Introducing a wide variety of examples of the skill involved through the use of different media such as diagram, pictures and films, and by observing a variety of people practising the skills, not just experts, would be more effective. The teacher's talk is the most pervasive medium for presenting examples.

The consideration of the nature of learning involved in specific teaching situations will guide a teacher in identifying modes of structuring the learning environment so that it contains more than just a teacher talking. For any type of learning to take place there must be a response from the learner to a particular event or series of events in the environment. Experienced teachers may be able to detect from non-verbal cues whether or not any inner activity is taking place while they are addressing their pupils. It is a vital part of learning for the pupils and it provides feedback to the teacher about the effects of the way the teaching has been structured.

The learning activities should include such teaching methods and techniques which determine the fulfilment of teaching objectives as:

Techniques

- Illustrations
- Description
- Exercise
- Assignment
- Home work
- Questioning, etc.

Methods

- Lecture method
- Discussion method
- Project method
- Problem solving method
- Inductive deductive method

Thus, while preparing the process of teaching, we should determine how we should discuss about that subject matter, which methods should be used, what type of teaching material should be used with which the teaching and learning can be made effective, the students can be motivated to study, the teaching can be made interesting and the analytical and synthetically thinking of students can be developed.

4. Evaluation: The best method of evaluating new learning is to see if it is of use in circumstances other than those in which it took place. To evaluate pupils' learning of concepts it is best to avoid asking them just to state the general principles they embody, as in a dictionary definition. Presenting novel problems which depend on having learned the concept is the best way of making certain that conceptual learning has taken place. It should also be possible for a person who has learned a concept to discriminate between examples and non-examples of the concept with a very high level of accuracy.

Many techniques are available for the evaluation of teaching and students' learning, but before that the teacher should try to find out the answers of the following questions:

- What is our aim?
- What are we doing in real?
- What is the availability of means in comparison to our goals?
- For the fulfilment of goals, how can we bring improvement in the process?

Different techniques can be used for the evaluation in different areas as:

(*i*) *Evaluation of knowledge and Information:* For this we can use oral tests, essay tests, objective tests and class work.

(*ii*) *Evaluation of Skills:* For this the teacher can use homework and assignments.

(*iii*) *Evaluation of Attitude's, Interests and Values:* For this we can use observation, anecdotal records, rating scale, interest inventories, diagnostic tests, etc.

In teacher training institutions, while much attention may be given to the preparation for teaching by student teachers, much less is given to retrospective analysis. But, this is the most important aspect of the teaching cycle. The self appraisal guided by knowledge about the processes of concept learning enables the teachers to detect critical incidents in their teaching where their plans went astray and they misled their pupils. The outcomes of their self-appraisals fed back into the teaching system to be incorporated in future planning.

The principle of systematic variation is of great importance in the presentation of examples. The pedagogic art is to provide interesting examples that introduce all the criterial attributes with maximum efficiency and maximum economy. The structure of the heuristic provides a framework and a reminder of things to bear in mind. Teachers' imaginations provide the way in which the pedagogic principles and their own knowledge of the field of study come together to provide elegant solutions to teaching problems.

Utility of Pedagogical Analysis for Commerce Teachers

- Clarity of subject matter.
- Clarity of Objectives.
- Pre-preparation of teaching aids.
- Pre-preparation of teaching methods.
- Fixation of evaluation techniques.
- Systematic development of subject matter.
- Knowledge of different skills to be used in teaching in advance.
- Proper analysis of subject matter.
- Knowledge of important aspects of the subject matter.
- Knowledge of teaching maxims.
- Selection of suitable teaching methods, teaching techniques and aids according to the level of students.

Example: The topic is Bank

BANKS

In modern age banking has become the foundation of economic development. The word 'Bank' is desired from *'Banchi'* or from the Greek word '*Banque*'. In the olden days, the traders of Italy who performed the job of exchanging money were known as *Banchi* or *Bancheri*.

In common parlance, Bank means an organisation which transact in money. Nowadays, except the work of transacting in money, bank performs many other functions also as credit creation, agency functions, general services, etc. Hence, *Bank is an organisation, which accepts deposits, lends money and performs other agency functions.*

Definition

In the words of Whitehead, "A Bank is defined as an institution which collects surplus funds from the public, safeguards them, and makes them available to the true owner when required but also lends sums not required by their true owners to those who are in needs of the funds and can provide security."

According to Banking company Act, "Banking company is one which transacts the business of banking which means the accepting for the purpose of lending or investment of deposits of money from the public payable on demand or otherwise and withdrawable by cheques, draft, order or otherwise."

Types of Banks

Banks can be classified on the following basis:

1. Classification on the basis of Ownership

Banks can be classified on the basis of ownership in following way:

(*i*) *Public Sector Banks:* These are owned by government. In India 14 banks were nationalised in 1969 and six in 1990. Their main objective is social welfare. After merging of New Bank of India in Punjab National Bank, number of nationalised banks is now 19. The subsidiaries of State Bank of India are also included in it, which are eight in number.

(*ii*) *Private Sector Banks:* These are owned and controlled by private sector or individuals. Their main objective is to earn profit.

(*iii*) *Cooperative Banks:* These are governed by a group of individuals. The main objective of these is to help its members.

2. Classification on the basis of Functions

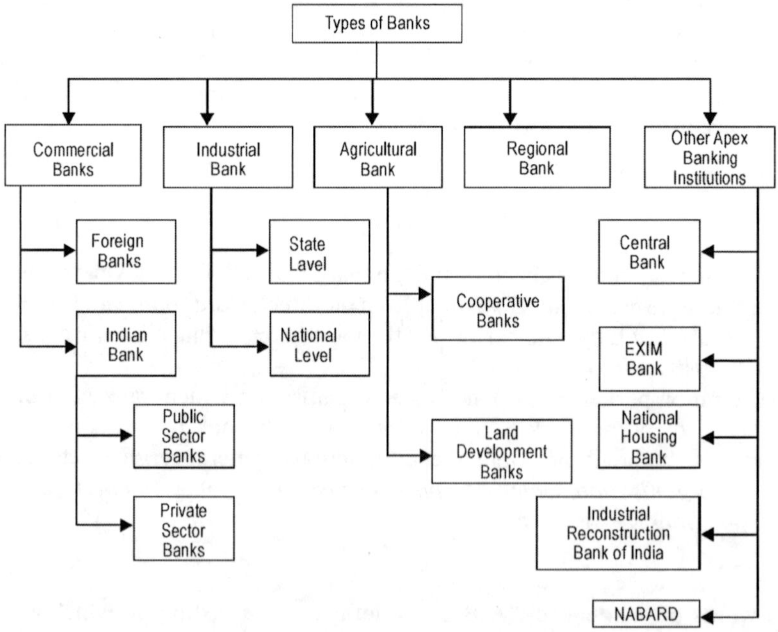

(*i*) *Commercial Banks:* These banks accept the deposits from general public and provide short term loans to manufactures and traders. In India, there are two types of Commercial Banks:

(*a*) *Foreign Commercial Banks:* Those banks which are based in some foreign country but have a branch in India, are called as foreign commercial banks. Examples are Chartered Bank, Bank of America, etc.

(*b*) *Indian Commercial Banks:* These banks are based in India.
- Public Sector Banks: These are governed by government. They are 27 in number.
- Private Sector Banks: These are governed by private sector.

(*ii*) *Industrial Development Banks:* These banks give medium term and long term loans to industries. They usually provide loan for purchasing land, plant, machinery, etc. These can be classified in two categories:

(*a*) *National Level:* There are four banks which provide loans for industrial development:
- IDBI
- SIDBI
- IFCI
- ICICI

(*b*) *State Level*
- SFC
- SIDCs

(*iii*) *Agricultural Banks:* These Banks provide loans for agricultural works. These can be classified as:

(*a*) *Cooperative Banks:* These banks provide short term loans to agricultural sector. These are as:
- State cooperative banks.
- Central cooperative banks.
- Primary cooperative societies.

(*b*) *Land Development Banks:* The main function of these banks is to provide loans on security of land. These provide long terms loans. They are as:
- State Land Development Bank.
- Primary Land Development Bank.

(*iv*) *Regional Rural Banks:* These were established in 1975 to enhance the banking facilities in rural areas. The main function is to provide loans to small farmers, small traders and for the development of agricultural activities.

(*v*) *Other Apex Banking Institutions:*

(*a*) *Central Bank:* It is the most important bank of the country. The main function of this bank is to maintain the economic stability of the country and in reference to underdeveloped countries. In India — Reserve Bank of India, in England — Bank of England, in America — Federal Reserve Bank are the central banks.

(*b*) *EXIM Bank:* This bank was established on Jan.1, 1982 to expand foreign trade. The main objective of this was to provide assistance to traders engaged in import and export.

(*c*) *National Housing Bank:* It was established is 1988. This bank provides the facility of refinancing on housing loans extended by financial institutions and commercial banks.

(*d*) *Industrial Reconstruction Bank of India:* The main objective of this bank is to rehabilitate the industries.

(*e*) *National Bank for Agriculture and Rural Development (NABARD):* The main objective of this bank is to develop agriculture and rural areas.

Functions of Commercial Banks

Commercial banks have emerged as the single most important source of institutional credit. The functions of commercial banks have been classified in four categories:

I Primary Functions.
II Secondary Functions.
III Social Functions.
IV Electronic Banking Services.

I. Primary Functions

1. Accepting Deposits: The bank accepts the deposits from public. People deposit their money as per their convenience and capability, into following accounts.

(*i*) *Fixed or Time Deposit Account:* Money is deposited in this account for a fixed period. Longer the period of deposit, higher will be rate of interest on deposit. Money deposited in this account is also known as Time Liability of Bank.

(*ii*) *Current or Demand Deposit Account:* In this account, depositor can deposit the money any number of times and can withdraw the money as and when he requires. Generally, bank does not pay interest on this deposit. Business houses deposit the money in it. Money deposited in it is known as Demand Liability of Bank.

(*iii*) *Saving Deposit Account:* This account is to encourage the small savings and bank pays interest on this account which is less than that of fixed deposit account.

(*iv*) *Recurring Deposit Account:* In it, depositor deposits a fixed amount of money for a fixed period. The money cannot be withdrawn before expiry of a fixed term except in certain conditions.

2. Advancing of Loans: Another main function of bank is to advance loans to other persons. The banks generally provide loans for production work and while doing so, they demand for a proper security. Banks advance loans of the following types:

(*i*) *Cash Credit:* Under this, borrower is allowed to withdraw a specific amount on the basis of a specific security. The borrower withdraws the money within this specific limit only.

(*ii*) *Overdraft:* The customer who maintains a current account with the bank, takes permission from the bank to withdraw extra amount than deposited amount in account. The extra money withdrawn is called as overdraft.

(*iii*) *Demand Loans:* These loans are provided by the banks against the security of Fixed Deposit Receipt (FDR), Government Securities, Life Insurance policies, etc. These are called demand loans because bank can demand them at any time.

(*iv*) *Term Loans:* These loans are extended by the banks to their customers for fixed period to purchase machinery, car, House, etc.

(*v*) *Discounting of Bill of Exchange:* Under this, bank gives money to its customers on security of Bill of Exchange before the expiry of bill if need arises for the customer.

II. Secondary Functions

1. Agency Function

(*i*) Collection and payment of various items
(*ii*) Purchase and sale of securities
(*iii*) Trustee and Executor
(*iv*) Remitting of Money.
(*v*) Purchase and sale of foreign exchange.
(*vi*) Letter of Reference

2. General Utility Services

(*i*) Locker facilities
(*ii*) Traveller's cheques and letter of credit.
(*iii*) Business information and statistics.

III. Social Functions or Role of Banks in Economic Development

(*i*) *Capital Formation:* The banks collect the idle savings of general public and invest them in production works.

(*ii*) *Role in the Development of Rural Sector:* The banks provide loans to farmers at lower interest rate for purchasing land, equipment, etc.

(*iii*) *Helpful in pushing up the Demand:* Banks provide consumer's credit to their customers to purchase durable consumer items.

(*iv*) *Monetary Policy:* These banks extend or contract the credit as per the instruction of central bank.

(*v*) *Employment:* Commercial banks help in increasing the chance of employment. Unemployed youth can take loan from these banks at reasonable rate of interest and arrange self-employment.

(*vi*) *Inducement to Innovation:* By providing credit to entrepreneurs, bank induces the innovations.

IV. Electronic Banking Service/E-Banking

The chief electronic services are as:

1. Electronic Fund Transfer
   (*i*) Direct credits
   (*ii*) Direct Debits
2. Automatic Teller Machine (ATM)
3. Debit Card.
4. Credit Card.
5. Tele-Banking.

Content Analysis

The content of bank can be analysed in two parts:

(*a*) *Major Concepts*

– Meaning of Banks

- Features of Banks
- Classification of Banks
- Functions of Banks

(*b*) *Minor Concepts*

- *Classification on the basis of Ownership*

(*i*) Public Sector Bank
(*ii*) Private Sector Bank
(*iii*) Cooperative Bank

- *Classification on the basis of functions*

(*i*) Commercial Bank
(*ii*) Agricultural Bank
(*iii*) Regional Rural Bank
(*iv*) Industrial Development Bank
(*v*) Other apex.
Primary Functions
Secondary Functions
Social Functions
Electronic Banking Services

Behavioural Objectives

After learning about banks the students can:

- Recall the meaning of bank.
- Define the term bank.
- Classify the bank.
- Explain the objectives of public sector banks.
- Illustrate the public banks.
- Discuss about the functions of bank.
- Label different types of bank.
- Cite some examples to define cooperative banks.
- Generalise the functions of commercial banks.
- Relate the functions of bank to their daily needs.
- Classify the functions of bank according to preference of work.
- List the functions of bank.
- Recognise the ability of bank in the development of the nation.
- Differentiate between different types of banks.
- Analyse the functions of bank.
- Summarize the content of banks.

Teaching Learning Activities

The teacher will use various teaching methods, strategies, skills, techniques to make teaching learning process effective as –

- The teacher tells about the need of capital by every trader, manufacturer as availability of finance for the uninterrupted flow of goods and service from producers to manufacturers, and manufacturer to the wholesaler, retailer and to the ultimate user *i.e.* consumer is the most essential aspect of business and banks help them in meeting their financial requirements. The teacher asks some questions about the need of capital for a businessman.

- The teacher attracts the attention of the students towards the model of the bank and starts asking about different cabins in the model.
- The teacher tells about the types of banks by illustrating some examples of banks in India with the help of following chart:

Types of Banks

- On the Basis of Ownership
  - Public Bank
  - Private Bank
  - Cooperative Bank
- On the Basis of functions
  - Commercial Bank
  - Industrial Development Bank
  - Agricultural Bank

- The teacher asks some questions to recall the meaning of bank as
  - Where do we deposit money?
  - Why do we deposit money?
  - If we are in need of lakh of rupees to purchase a house, from where we can get it?
- The teacher takes the students to nearest bank to show the functions of bank and show some forms which are of daily use as–
  - Deposit slip (cash, cheque)
  - Cash withdrawal form
  - Opening account form (saving, RD, FD, etc.)
  - Cheque Book
- The students may understand the electronic functions of Bank, teacher shows samples of credit card, Debit card, ATM Booths and tell the functioning of ATM that how to draw money from ATM, what type of security we should keep in mind while withdrawing money from ATM.
- The teacher while teaching writes main points related to the subject matter on the chalk board and asks students to write down those in their note books.
- The teacher summarizes the subject matter and asked about the problems of the students.
- The teacher says to the student to talk to their elders at home or in society and make the list of banks in their city and their functions.

Thus, different activities can be done to make teaching learning more interesting.

Evaluation

Answer in one word:

Q. Name the organisation which transacts in money.

Q. From which Greek word the term Bank has been originated?

Q. How many banks were nationalized in 1969?

Q. What is the main objective of private sector bank?

Fill in the blanks

1. ________ banks are owned by government.
2. Jammu and Kashmir bank is a ________ bank.
3. ________ banks were established is 1975.
4. _________ bank is the apex bank.

Match the following

IRBI	Provide housing loans
NABARD	Rehabilitate the Industry
EXIM BANK	Development of agriculture
National Housing Bank	Assistance to traders engaged in export and important.

True / False

1. Bank receives money through deposits.
2. The customer who maintains a current account with the banks can withdraw extra money than deposited in his account at his will.
3. ATM has increased the work of an employee.
4. The term bank is derived from the word bench.

Choose the Correct Answer:

1. Which bank is known as 'Apex Bank' of India?
   (*a*) State Bank of India (*b*) Reserve Bank of India
   (*c*) Central Bank (*d*) Bank of India.
2. Which of the following do not come under E-Banking?
   (*a*) Electronic fund transfer (*b*) Automatic Teller Machine
   (*c*) Debit Card (*d*) Overdraft.

Short Answer Questions

1. Classify the banks on the basis of ownership.
2. Name the four National level Banks which provide loans for industrial development.
3. What is credit card?
4. What is Tele Banking?
5. Write three functions of NABARD.

Long Answer Questions

1. Define bank. State the various types of Banks.
2. What do you mean by commercial Banks? What are their functions?

14

Assessment, Evaluation and Grading in Commerce

"Evaluation is the process of gathering and interpreting evidence on change in behaviour of all students as they progress through school."
—*Hanna*

Concept of Assessment

The term assessment covers activities included in grading (formal and non-formal), examining, certifying, and so on. An applicant's attitude for a particular job may be assessed. Throughout the world most educational system find it appropriate to record student's achievement in some way, whether with a number, a letter code, or a comment such as satisfactory or needs improvement.

Radhakrishnan Commission, Mudaliar Commission and Kothari commission laid great emphasis on the need for revamping students' assessment through examination for bringing quality and confidence in the system of education.

Assessment is a process by which information is obtained relative to some known objective. Good assessment is a broad term that includes testing. A test is a special form of assessments. Tests are assessments made under contrived circumstances especially so that they may be administered. In other words all tests are assessment, but not all assessments are tests. We test at the end of a lesson or unit. We assess progress at the end of a school year through testing, and we assess verbal and quantitative skills through different instruments whether implicit or explicit. Assessment is most usefully connected to some goal or objective for which it is designed. Assessment of skill attainment is rather straight forward. Either the skill exists at some acceptable level or it doesn't. Skills are readily demonstrable.

Assessment of understanding is more difficult and complex. Skills can be practised; understanding cannot. We can assess a person's knowledge in a Variety of ways, but there is always a leap, an inference that we make about a person does in relation to what it signifies about what he knows. From this point of view, to assess means to stipulate the conditions under which the behaviour specified in an objective way be ascertained.

In the words of Linn and Gronlund, "Assessment is a term that includes a lot of procedures used to gain informations related to student learning and formation of some value judgements about learning progress."

University of *Oregon* defines assessment as, "It is the process of gathering and discussing information from multiple and diverse sources in order to develop a deep understanding of what students know, understand and can do with their knowledge as a result of their educational experiences."

A critical Dictionary of Education (1982) describes that in education assessment is the process by which one attempts to measure the quality of learning and teaching using various assessment techniques, assignments, projects, continuous assessment, objective type tests.

Educational assessment has two main purposes: The first is to help teachers to design the instruction while the second is to contribute to learners in their progress. Baker and Piburn used the terms: traditional assessment and constructivist assessment. In traditional assessment, students' cognitive knowledge is determined by using a teacher made or standard test such as multiple-choices, true-false; fill in the blanks and short answer questions. In constructivist assessment, however, essay test, practical examinations, papers, projects, questionnaires, inventories, checklists, portfolios, teacher observations, discussions and interviews are preferred for that purpose.

National Education Policy 2020 emphasizes on transforming assessment for optimizing learning and development of all students with a focus on:

- Regular
- Formative and competency based
- Promoting learning
- Assessment for learning
- Test higher order skills i.e., analysis, critical thinking, conceptual clarity etc.
- Help in revising continuously teaching-learning processes to optimize learning

In this way it is transforming the culture of assessment-

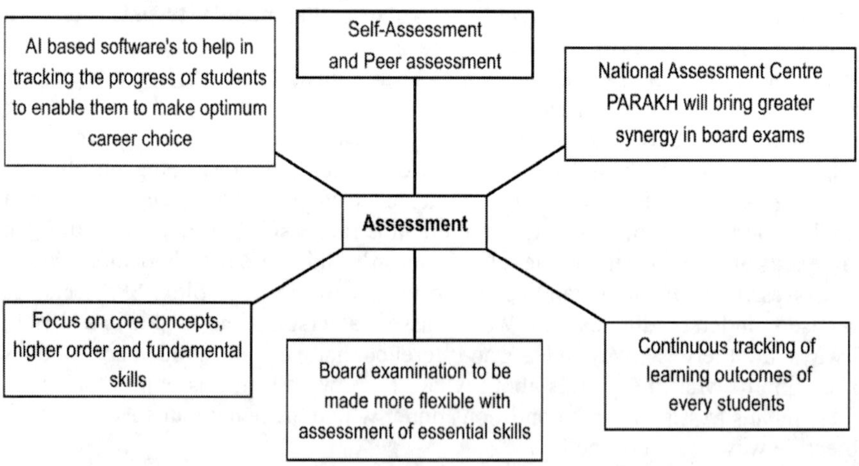

Characteristics of an Effective Comprehensive Assessment

1. It is directly linked with course, daily outcomes and standards.
2. It includes opportunities for self-assessment, goal-setting, and personal/professional development through reflections.

3. It includes a variety of tools which take into consideration the characteristics of the learners and the structure of the content.
4. It includes opportunities for reproduction of factual knowledge and application of skills.
5. It includes performance based tasks related with real life.
6. It provides specific feedback to the students about their strengths and areas for improvement.

Thus, we can say that assessment is comprehensive. In it the students are situated in the real life context and while they are struggling with the problems they encounter, they are observed. Besides this, it is explicit that students should be assessed individually rather than collaborately.

Types of Assessment

For the purpose of classroom instruction, assessment procedures which are used can be classified in terms of their functional roles as:

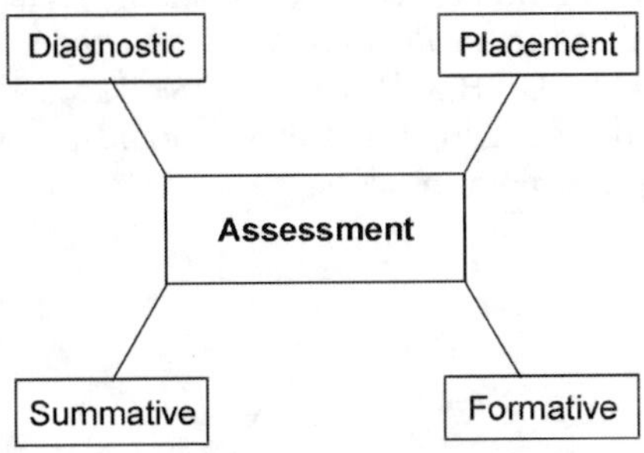

Types of Assessment

1. Placement Assessment: In this assessment a teacher determines pre-requisite skills, course goals, and the best form of learning.

2. Formative Assessment In this assessment, the teacher determines the learning progress, provides feedback to reinforce learning and corrects learning errors. It is also important for a teacher to critically examine and systematically look at the phenomenon that appears in the classroom.

3. Diagnostic Assessment: In this assessment, the teacher determines the cause i.e. intellectual, physical, emotional and environmental, of persistent learning difficulties.

4. Summative Assessment: In this assessment, the teacher determines end of course achievement for assigning grades or certifying mastery of objectives. It is clear that the recorded phenomena concentrate on describing incidents of student performance over a period of time. However, the sequence of phenomena can serve as a record of the student's own development toward long-term goals such as lifelong learning, self-concept, cooperative learning, skill development, study skills, knowledge development and interest.

Concept of Evaluation

The word 'evaluation' means — value judgement or an observation. When we use this term in education, it implies to evaluate the teaching of the teacher and to inform him whether the behavioural changes occurred in the pupils are with the reference to the predetermined learning objectives or not. If suitable desirable change occurred then up to what level and if not then what steps should be taken to achieve the predetermined learning objectives or not. Thus, evaluation is the scheme of collecting evidences of behavioural changes and finding the direction and extent of such things. This necessitates a clear understanding of the objectives of teaching, both for the purpose of providing worthwhile learning situations and for testing.

Before the existence of the term 'evaluation', the term 'test' was used to assess the acquired knowledge of the pupils. The written examination came into existence in 1702 as a result of the sincere efforts made by Cambridge University of England, but the problem was to assist the students' personality, interests, attitudes, etc. through the written examination except to evaluate the style, language, thoughts, etc. of the pupils. Then the term '*evaluation*' was developed in America and through the sincere efforts made by Dr. B.S. Bloom in 1958. His main emphasis was that testing should be based on teaching and these should be objective centred. He states that education is a tri-polar process.

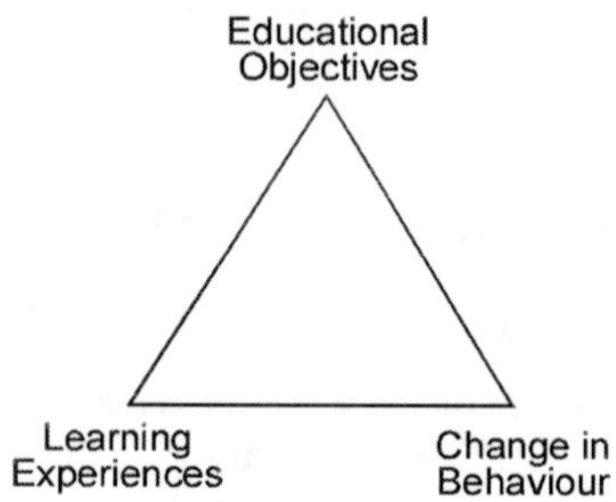

The effectiveness and appropriateness of educational process is ascertained by evaluation approach.

"Evaluation is the process of gathering and interpreting evidence on change in behaviour of all students as they progress through school".– *Hanna*

Evaluation has been concerned with human's curiosity since the time immemorial, by which he went on assessing the result of his performed actions through various devices of evaluation. During the last five decades of examination reform programmes in India and abroad, the concept of examination has changed with that of evaluation, because of the changing emphasis in the nature, purpose and scope of examination. This has led to the emergence of new term related to the process of examining student and certifying them in a more meaningful manner.

Evaluation quite often is regarded as an end of the course activity rather than an integral part of the total curriculum, because of the narrow concept of the curriculum conceived by most of the teachers. It is like one's destination in terms of Brubacher. From this definition one can identify the following five questions that every teacher must ask himself /herself before becoming a successful teacher:

(*i*) What for should I teach a particular subject?
(*ii*) What should I teach in that subject?
(*iii*) How should I teach well or how best the students can learn?
(*iv*) How best I have taught or how best the students have learnt?
(*v*) In what way can I improve my teaching or students learning?

From the above five questions raised, first question refers to *instructional objectives*, second relates to selection of *content*, third reflects the use of *teaching learning strategies*, the fourth concerns the mode of *performance assessment of students* and the last relates with *feedback* of evidences to improve the students' learning or achievements by adopting the effective teaching learning testing strategies thereby attempting to validate the curriculum. The relationship among all the five concepts is depicted as under:

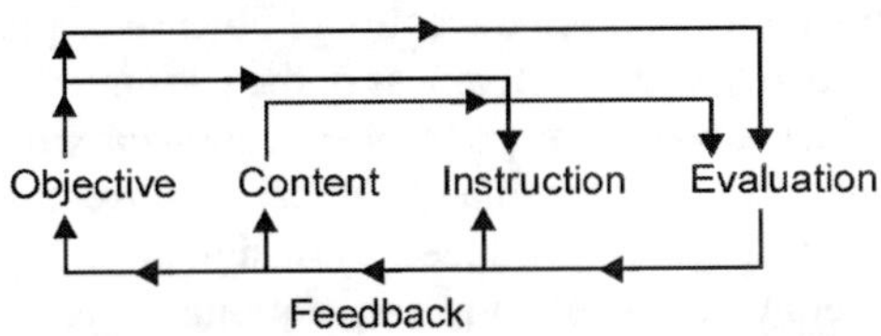

Fig. 15.1: Basic Teaching-learning Model

Source: Handbook of Measurement and Evaluation, Singh (2005)

Now let us examine how evaluation is integrated with other components.

(*a*) *Instructional Objectives*: Instructional objectives or intended learning outcomes represent the nature, desirability, and the aims of teaching learning process. In a way, they form the philosophical basis of this model. Evaluation, therefore, has to be objective based or objective focused without which it will not be possible to know whether the intended learning outcomes have been achieved or not.

(*b*) *Content of Learning*: The content of learning or the syllabus represents the medium through which the intended outcomes are to be achieved. It is assumed that content elements reflect learners' and social needs. Here again evaluation has to be content oriented.

(*c*) *Teaching Learning Strategies*: The teaching learning strategies represent the mode of transacting the teaching learning activities related to content of learning in a given subject. These include instructional strategies, use of textual material and manuals of teaching and other teaching learning activities carried and to achieve the intended outcomes of learning. Here again evaluation has to be integrated with these activities by using it as an integral part of teaching like use of questioning, review, project work, etc.

(*d*) *Evaluation*: Evaluation refers to diagnostic, formative and summative judgements and decision taking.

(*e*) *Feedback*: It refers to feedback of evidence for students, teachers and evaluator himself/herself. Evaluation provides evidences on students' performance, instructional efficiency and quality of test itself. Feedback refers to adapting and improving the objectives, content selection, instruction and even evaluation process.

Thus, we can infer that evaluation is an integral part of the teaching learning process and is one of its significant components. It provides a lot of information about pupils' learning, instructional impact and quality of the evaluation instrument itself. It can play a significant role for validating the whole educational process. Thus, evaluation is an important part of the whole programme of education and attempts to measure a comprehensive range of objective.

Definition

The term evaluation can be elucidated more with the help of definitions as given below:

1. National Council of Educational Research and training (NCERT), "Evaluation is any systematic, continuous process of determining.

(*i*) The extent to which specified educational objectives previously identified and defined are attained, (*ii*) The effectiveness of the learning experiences provided in the classroom and, (*iii)* how well the goals of education have been accomplished."

2. Wrightingstone in Encyclopaedia of Educational Research, "Evaluation is relatively a new technical term introduced to designate a more comprehensive concept of measurement that is applied in conventional tests and examination."

3. Goods, "Evaluation is the process of ascertaining or judging the value or an amount of something by careful appraisal."

4. Wile, "Evaluation is a process of making judgements that are to be used as basis of planning consists of establishing goals, making judgements about the evidences and revising procedure, and goals in the light of the judgements. It is a procedure for improving the product, the process and even the goals themselves."

5. James M. Lee, "Evaluation is the appraisal of pupil's progress in attaining the educational goals set by school, the class and himself. The chief purpose of evaluation is to guide and further the student's learning. Evaluation is thus a positive rather than a negative process."

6. John U. Michaelis, "Evaluation is the process of determining the extent to which objectives have been achieved. It includes all of the procedures used by the teacher, children, principle and other school procedures to appraise outcomes of instruction."

7. One of the best definitions given by Clara M. Brown, "Evaluation is essential in the never ending cycle of formulating goals, measuring progress towards them and determining the new goals which merge as a result of new warning. Evaluation involves, measurement which means objective quantitative evidence. But it is broader than measurement and implies that consideration has been given to certain values, standards and that interpretations of the evidence have been made in the light of the particular situation."

Thus, on the basis of above definitions we can say that evaluation is an important part of the activities done by the teacher. It not only measures the educational achievements of the students but helps in the growth of them. It includes all those changes or modifications which are helpful in the development of balanced personality.

National Policy of Education (1968) recommended for a shift in the focus of evaluation from certification to improvement in learning.

Characteristics of Evaluation

1. There is a close relationship between the objectives and process of evaluation.
2. Evaluation helps in the comparative study of different behaviours.
3. It is completely an objective oriented process.
4. It is an organised process.
5. It is a comprehensive term which includes measurement as well as testing.
6. The scope of its process is very comprehensive.
7. It is a decision-making process.
8. It not only measures the educational achievement, but helps is their progress also.
9. There is a close relationship between instructional objectives, teaching process and evaluation.
10. It provides reliable and objectives information about the abilities, capabilities and potentialities of the students.
11. It is a dynamic process.

Objectives/Purposes of Evaluation in Commerce

Evaluation has varied purposes. Every teacher should keep before him the objectives/ purpose of evaluation. The main objectives are:

1. If the purpose is to stimulate teachers to improve their techniques of classroom instruction, evaluation must concern itself with ascertaining the extent to which such improvement is being affected.
2. If the purpose is to enrich and visualise the course of study, evaluation must seek to determine whether the pupils are deriving greater educational value from the 'enriched' and 'vitalized' programmes than they did formerly.
3. If the purpose is to re-establish faculty 'espirit decorps' and school morale, the objectives of evaluation will be as to assess in various ways the degree of improvement in personal and professional attitude, in human relations and ultimately therefore in efficiency of teaching and learning.
4. If an important purpose of the supervisory programme is to promote greater educational attention to the individual needs of pupils, evaluation will necessarily concern itself with estimating the success with which guidance procedures, differentiated programmes of study, course and units of learning experiences, individualised teaching and learning procedure, and other educational measures designed to achieve greater satisfaction of individual need are operating.

The other objectives are:

1. To prepare remedial measures for revising the weaknesses and difficulties of the students.
2. To improve the testing system of the subject.
3. To provide basis for admission not only in the schools and colleges but also to the institutions of vocational training and business concerns.

4. To serve as a method of improvement.
5. To relate measurement to the goals of the instructional programmes.
6. To aid pupils-teacher planning.
7. To appraise the status of and changes in pupil's behaviour.
8. To strengthen motivation.
9. To justify the school programme to the community.
10. To judge the efficacy of units and unit organisation.
11. To help the teachers in directing the intellect and emotions of his pupils in such a manner that they will not possess undesirable traits like narrow prejudices, selfish motive, jealousy and ill-will, etc.

Thus, evaluation is necessary in order to check the effectiveness of each element in a process.

Need and Importance of Evaluation

Education is a process which works out changes in children. By using appropriate evaluation techniques, the teacher can determine how much information the students have acquired, how much they have changed their attitudes, how much they have improved in their working, how reasonable a new unit proved to be, and, how effective a new method was and what type of improvements are needed in the instructional methodology. Evaluation is of much importance because it:

1. Helps in Clarifying Objectives: An important aspect of the education system is the setting of the objectives and the other aspect is evaluation. Evaluation is based on objectives. The teaching learning process depends upon the realization of these objectives. The teacher tries to understand the objectives of every topic of the subject in the light of their utility in education.

2. Provides Knowledge About the Progress of the Students: Evaluation is of great importance because it indicates the progress of the students regarding their acquired knowledge through teaching learning process. The teacher, on the one hand, come to know the strengths and weaknesses of the students and on the other hand students come to know where they are and how far their efforts have been successful.

3. Basis of Guidance: Evaluation helps the teacher in recognising individual difference i.e. in abilities, aptitudes, interests, achievements and other aspects of the personality. On the basis of the students' progress in different fields through different tests, educational and vocational guidance can be given to the pupils.

4. Helps in Classification of the Students: Evaluation helps the teacher to know about the capabilities of the students and he can classify them according to their achievements in different tests. It will also help him to choose the right instructional procedure. It will ensure the uniform progress and avoid educational wastage.

5. Basis of Admission: Evaluation helps in finding the capacity, ability and achievement of students in different fields through different tests. On the basis of the result, admission is given to them in the next class. It provides the minimum essential achievements necessary for a particular course of study being an efficiency bar to be crossed at a particular stage.

6. Basis of Planning of Education: With the help of evaluation, we can judge that to what extent we have been able to achieve the objectives of the subjects. It will help in further planning of the education system that where is need of change in it.

7. Helps in Providing Incentives: Evaluation helps in providing incentives for the students as examination sets a clear cut goal to achieve before the students. They make great efforts to reach the highest level of achievement. When they are able to get it, it stimulates them for harder work.

8. Helps in Testing the Efficiency of the Teacher: Evaluation helps in testing the effectiveness of the methodology of the teaching adopted by the teacher to teach the students. If the results are not good, it shows that there is need to bring the change in the teaching methodology. The teacher can assess the success of his teaching through evaluation.

9. Helps in Awarding Scholarships: Evaluation helps in judging the progress of the students and to give them motivation. The Government of India, State Governments select some students for the award of scholarships on the basis of achievement and intelligence test.

10. Helps in Bringing Improvement in the School Programme: Evaluation helps in knowing the strength and weaknesses of school programme. We can compare the programme of different schools with the help of evaluation. This comparison helps in making improvements in the functioning of the school.

11. Promotion of Better Learning: Evaluation signifies a wider, comprehensive and continuous process of assessing the progress of students with the help of different tests. In addition to the acquisition of different amount of formal knowledge they will also develop proper attitudes, skills, habits, appreciation and understanding. They will promote better learning to the development of better personalities of the students.

12. Helps in Bringing Change in Curriculum: Evaluation is based on objectives and objectives are based on the needs, interests of the child and the psychology of learning. It leads to changes in the curriculum to enable it to keep pace with the demands of a rapidly changing and complex society.

Thus, evaluation helps in bringing improvement in methods, making the curriculum more and more effective and justify the school programme to community.

Methods of Evaluation

Evaluation methods are the means by which the teacher obtains information of student's progress and the effectiveness of instruction. These includes qualitative and quantitative measures, objective measures and subjective measures. There are different areas which can be evaluated through different techniques:

(*i*) Observation Techniques

(*ii*) Testing Technique

(i) Observation Technique: One of the most pervasive activities of our life is observation. This technique is indispensable in evaluation. It is used at all stages of education. It becomes more scientific if planned systematically and recorded accordingly. It is most commonly used for observing the behaviour and activities of the students. It is used for evaluating cognitive, affective and psychomotor

objectives. By this method we can record the behaviour of the students as it actually occurs. This method is quite useful to evaluate the achievements of the students. The classroom interaction can also be evaluated through this technique.

(ii) Testing Technique: This technique is used commonly for testing in the field of education. It is also called examination. Examination is an attempt to evaluate the students' achievement. It is highly reliable and valid. This can be classified in three types: (*a*) oral, (*b*) written, and (*c*) practical.

Types of Evaluation

1. Formative Evaluation

Formative evaluation seeks to identify the learning difficulties prior to the completion of instructions as a unit. This is intended to facilitate learning mastery by providing information which can direct the remedial instruction to be followed to enable students to overcome the learning difficulties. Formative tests are used to make teaching learning more effective. With formative evaluation, the question is: During a period of study, how well is the student progressing towards mastering the various learning objectives? The results are typically used for giving the students and teachers feedback on the students progress and consequently, for locating errors in terms of the structure of a study so that remedial alternative instruction techniques can be adopted.

According to Tanner, "Formative evaluation refers to the use of tests and other evaluative procedures while the course and instructional programme is in progress."

Groxlund pointed out that the specific use of formative evaluation is to plan corrective action for over coming learning difficulties or deficiencies, to aid in motivating learning and to increase retention and transfer of learning. Needs of classroom group and correction in learning deficiencies are made through periodic testing and evaluation of pupils during the instructions.

Both criterion reference and norms reference tests are designed in formative evaluation to mastery in contents. These are the tests given at the end of learning unit, such tests are also called interior tests, unit tests, learning tests and quizzes.

Features of Formative Evaluation

1. In formative evaluation a particular unit of learning is selected.
2. The components of the unit are analysed as:
   (*i*) The content, (*ii*) The behaviour of the pupil, and
   (*iii*) The objectives to be achieved in relation to the content.
3. It seeks to identify learning difficulties.
4. It includes new terms, new relations and new procedure.
5. Each item of the test indicates student's mastery of the unit element.
6. It provides remedial instructional material in the form of textbooks, work books, programmed instructions and films.
7. It provides opportunity to students to get mastery in the content.
8. More emphasis is given on the achievement of objectives.
9. It serves to reinforce the learning.
10. It provides motivation to learning.
11. It makes teaching-learning more effective.

Uses/Merits of Formative Evaluation

1. Helpful in Pacing Students Learning: Frequent use of formative evaluation during a course may be effective in pacing student learning. In highly sequential learning, it is of utmost importance that student master one learning task before another if he is to be successful in mastering the task in a course. The use of formative evaluation after each unit or task in the learning process can help to motivate the students to the necessary effort at the appropriate time.

2. Provides Feedback to the Teacher: Formative evaluation provides feedback to the teacher after the completion of each unit in the sequence of instruction. If a significant proportion of the students have made particular error or have had difficulty with a learning tasks, the teacher should consider it as an evidence of weakness in the instruction.

3. Helps in Setting the Goals: Formative evaluation helps in setting goals for student learning. For attaining the goal the time can also be decided.

4. Helps in Framing Sequence of Learning: It can also help students in dividing the entire learning sequence into smaller units. The students can make thorough preparation while they are learning a particular unit.

5. Provides Feedback to the Students: Formative evaluation provides feedback to students in their mastery of objectives learning tasks of an instructional unit. If a student knows that he has mastered all or most of the items in a formative test, this awareness can assure him that his learning is sound and that he should continue his present learning procedures.

6. Provides Reinforcement: The results of the formative evaluation can serve to reinforce the learning and can help to decrease the student's anxiety about his learning. The repeated evidence of mastery is a powerful reinforcement.

7. Helps in Diagnosing Learning Difficulties: For non-masters of a particular unit of learning, the formative evaluation can indicate precisely the specific areas of difficulty. If the non-masters can be motivated to correct their learning difficulties and if appropriate instructional material and procedure are made available to them, it is most likely that the majority of them can achieve mastery over each unit in a course.

Thus, the use of formative evaluation suggests that evaluation in relation to the process of learning and teaching can have strong positive effects on the actual learning of students as well as on their motivation for the learning and their self concept in relation to school learning. Formative evaluation is primarily useful in identifying learning errors, planning corrections for overcoming learning deficiencies, motivating learning process, providing practice, minimising test anxiety and to enhance the academic achievement of children at the stages of summative evaluation.

2. Summative Evaluation

When formative evaluation takes its last step, there is an urgent need of summative evaluation. Hence, it can also be said that summative evaluation is a later process to occur in the end of a session or term to measure the achievement of pupils. This sort of evaluation helps in obtaining the overall results of teaching learning process. In simple words, we can say that where class tests, unit tests, quizzes and learning tests are the techniques of formative evaluation, Term tests, Annual tests and External examination conducted by school, universities, board or pupils agencies are the essential parts of summative evaluation. So, summative evaluation may be either external type or internal type evaluation.

As summative evaluation assesses student's achievement at the end of instruction, it invariably covers relatively large blocks of instructional material. The instruments used for the purposes are usually paper and pencil tests designed to appraise the extent to which the larger, more general objectives have been attained. These instruments are constructed to measure the pre-defined objectives related to specific subject area. The standard set prior to the summative evaluation serves as the sole criterion against which each student's performance is judged.

Summative evaluation may be seen in three different ways (National Curriculum Frame work for school education, 2000); the three ways are known as follows:

- By assessing the progress of students with reference to their ownselves (self Referenced)
- By assessing the progress of students with reference to criteria set by their teacher (Criterion-Referenced)
- By assessing the progress of students with reference to the progress made by their peer group (Norm-Referenced)

Characteristics/Features of Summative Evaluation

1. The primary purpose of summative evaluation is to grade students according to their achievement of course objectives.
2. It takes place at the end of the term, course, programme semester.
3. It is the accurate and reliable means of grading the student achievement.
4. It is designed to evaluate the progress of the student.
5. It is used to judge the effectiveness of the teacher, curriculum and educational plan.
6. It is used to promote the students to next class.
7. It does not provide feedback.
8. It provides the over-all results of teaching learning process.
9. Its results are used for classification, placement and prediction for future success.

Uses/Importance of Summative Evaluation

Bloom and others have given the following uses of summative evaluation:

1. Basis of Assigning Grades: The primary purpose of summative evaluation is to assign the grade to students according to their achievement of the course objectives. Grading helps in classifying the pupils according to their performance.

2. Basis of Certification: Summative evaluation gives birth to a certificate that bears the whole year work out.

3. Knowledge of Progress: Summative evaluation helps the pupils in knowing their progress. It is identification document of failure and success of the student.

4. Basis of Guidance: With the help of summative evaluation, an evaluator knows about the subsequent areas of success and it serves as the basis of providing guidance to the pupils.

5. Helps in Comparison of different Groups: On the basis of summative evaluation we can compare the outcomes of different groups taught by different teachers, which helps in evaluating the effectiveness of teaching-learning process.

6. Basis of Promotion: Summative evaluation occurs at the end of the academic year session, helps in promoting the student in the next class.

Summative evaluation, though, is an efficient, usually accurate and reliable means of grading student achievement but it does not serve the purpose of diagnosing learning difficulties, during instruction, to provide any remedial instruction prior to grading. For this there is need of formative evaluation. Both the evaluation types are complementary to each other. Both bring a great change in educational system.

Difference between Formative and Summative Evaluation

	Formative Evaluation		*Summative Evaluation*
1.	Formative evaluation seeks to identify learning difficulties prior to the completion of instruction on a unit.	1.	It seeks to identify student's achievement after the completion of the instruction.
2.	The purpose is to diagnose the strength and weaknesses of the students.	2.	The purpose is to classify and promote the students.
3.	Its central point is the improvement of student's achievements.	3.	Its central point is the measurement of student's achievements.
4.	It is an integral part of teaching-learning process.	4.	It is treated as an end of course activity.
5.	It helps in providing feedback to both student and teacher.	5.	It does not provide feedback.
6.	It refers to continuous evaluation by means of unit tests, assignments, etc.	6.	It refers to paper-pencil tests as term, tests, annual examination, etc.
7.	It results in further improvement of instructions.	7.	Its results are used for certification.
8.	No standard is set prior to formative evolution.	8.	The standard is set prior to summative evaluation.
9.	Its results are used for remedial measure.	9.	Its results are used for predictions for future success.

3. Process Evaluation

We have already indicated that instructional evaluation is concerned with the achievement of goals of instruction and learning. Social needs and preferences determine broad goals, while the specific objectives are determined by the students. The students seek to become educated persons, capable of earning a living and contributing to society. *Evaluation programme when is directed towards the analysis of needs and goals and is designed to expedite the production of outputs in the most efficient and effective manner is the process type of evaluation.* The evaluation provides evidence in the exact state of affairs and suggests the adjustments or changes which are required.

Process evaluation provides continuing or periodic feedback so that those responsible for programme, planning and operation can review and possibly alter earlier decisions. The process evaluation is thus concerned with the identification of the defects and drawbacks in the instructional procedural design, particularly in the sense that planned elements of the instructional programme are not being implemented as they were originally conceived.

The process evaluation monitors the actual instructional procedures in order to help the instructional decision-makers to anticipate and overcome procedural difficulties. In this way process evaluation relates with the evaluation of instructional process.

4. Product Evaluation

Product evaluation attempts to measure and interpret the attainment achieved by an instructional programme. This may be done at the conclusion of the instructional programme or during the continuation of the programme itself. The emphasis in product evaluation is on terminal behaviour but this terminal behaviour may be evaluated after the completion of every unit of the programme. The outcome of the programme must be evaluated in terms of the objectives of the programme.

The product evaluation helps others to decide whether to continue, terminate, modify or refocus an instructional programme.

The product evaluation includes:

1. The assessment and identification of the discrepancies between original objectives and actual attainments.
2. Identification of unintended results. It means those results or behavioural outcomes which are not sought to be achieved by instructional programme.
3. Provision of information and of suggestions for decisions to alter or replace previous planning, input and process decision.
4. Provision for quality control by recycling the programme to achieve those objectives which have not been achieved by the instructional programme.
5. Provision of basic information and suggestions for continuing, modifying or terminating the programme.

5. Oral Evaluation

In Oral evaluation the student is either asked certain questions verbally which he has to answer or asked to discuss a topic in the group or to express his opinion about any issue related to the business programme.

This is used to measure skills, which cannot be measured by written evaluation. In it thought provoking questions provide incentives to the pupils.

It is done for the purpose of assessing student's:

- Verbal expression
- Expressing of views and opinions about some vital issues.

- Arguing and supporting one's views or opinions in discussing a topic.
- Leadership Traits
- Educational stability
- Quick thinking
- Understanding and solving certain problems.

The important techniques of oral evaluation are:

- General Conversation
- General Questions
- Reading aloud
- Conversation on the prepared topics.

Oral evaluation has the advantages of comprehensive evaluation as:

1. Helpful in developing the expressing ability of the students.
2. Helpful in knowing the thinking ability of the students.
3. Economics.
4. Helpful in providing incentives to the students by the personal presence of the teacher before them.
5. Helpful in providing instant feedback.

6. Written Evaluation

The written tests are by and large the most common methods of evaluation. The teacher may develop many types of written tests such as quizzes, comprehensive midterm and final examinations, as well as tests to detect the problem restricting the learning of the students. The following steps are to be followed in conceptualizing and producing a classroom written test:

Step 1. Determine How Results of Test will be Used: One of the important uses of classroom test is to obtain a measure of student's achievement at various points in a course. The results of the test may be used to estimate instructional effectiveness and the basis on which to assign grades. Another use of tests is to inform students how they are doing in various skill areas. The feedback provided by these tests may helps the students to improve their skills.

Step 2. Determine the Nature of Skills to be Measured: The essay and objective type tests can directly or indirectly measure higher cognitive skills. The essay types tests can also directly measure student's ability to organise and express ideas in writing.

Step 3. Determine the Type and Number of Items to be Used: At this step the specific type and number of items must be determined. A written test may contain a mixture of item formats. The number of items included in a test is limited by the amount of time available to administer the test.

Step 4. Determine the Number of Items to be Associated with Each Objective: At this step, the number of items used to assess each skill is to be determined. This is done by developing a table of specifications or by deciding how many items should be used with each performance objective.

Step 5. Prepare the Required Test Items: This step is time consuming. To save time relevant items may be chosen from the books or manuals. It is better if all the items needed for one skill are established before moving to the next skill.

Step 6. Assemble the Items in to a Test: The last step is to assemble the items in to a test paper or test booklet. This includes ordering the items, determining the layout of items within the booklet and establishing instructions to be placed at the beginning of the test.

7. Performance Evaluation

Written tests cannot measure a number of skills directly or indirectly. Such skills are speaking, laboratory work, playing dramas and social skills etc. These skills can be evaluated by direct observation of student performance. Such observations are called performance evaluation.

Characteristics of Performance Evaluation

1. It can measure both a process as well as product resulting from a process.
2. The evaluation can be done in natural or structured settings. In structured setting like that of the laboratory, the student is asked to perform the experiment before the evaluator.
3. The student's specific problem with respect to skill learning can be diagnosed with the help of performance evaluation.

Limitations of Performance Evaluation

1. It is usually inefficient and time-consuming to administer.
2. In scoring it, the subjective factor i.e. the evaluator's attitude towards the examinee plays an important role.
3. Performance evaluation pertains to recording and judging the adequacy of student's actions.
4. There is need of efficient evaluator.

Techniques of Performance Evaluation

1. Check-List: A check-list is listing of actions or descriptions that a participant or rater checks off as the given behaviour or outcomes as observed. It can be used by the teacher or by the pupil himself for evaluating progress. It is used to record the presence or absence or frequency of occurrence of the phenomenon.

In the words of Wrightstone, Justman and Robbins, "Check-list may be defined as a prepared list of items that may relate to a person, procedure, institution, building or similar objects."

In the check-list, after each item a space is provided for the subjects to indicate the presence or absence of the incident or item by checking 'Yes' or 'No'. It is helpful in evaluating performance skills. The data collected with the help of check-list helps the teacher/evaluator to evaluate the progress of the students in commerce.

It tells about the children who are making successful growth in some skills and habits. It is also helpful in diagnosing strengths and weaknesses of the students. It also tells us about the students who have difficulty in cooperating with others, who have special skill in organising a group for work, who knows how to use many kinds of materials and equipments. The teacher indicates the student's sequence of performance by numbering them in the order in which they occur. In this procedure, the teacher has to observe one student at a time and to record the performance as it occurs.

Examples

Like to study in the library.	Yes/No
Like to know about current events.	Yes/No
Participate in group discussion.	Yes/No
Cooperate with the students.	Yes/No

Thus, the check-list requires the checking of specific item.

2. Rating Scales: Rating scales are much like check-lists. However, they provide a scale or range of response for each items. They record opinions or judgement and indicate the degree or amount. By rating means the judgement of one person by another. It is the most commonly used technique for evaluating the students. An individual may be rated with respect to various aspects of efficiency. Opinions are usually expressed in a scale of values.

In the words of Wrightstone, Justman et. al. "A rating scale consists of a set of characteristics or qualities to be judged and some type of scale for indicating the degree to which, each attribute is present."

Rating techniques are devices by which such judgements may be quantified.

According to Good and Hatt, the design of rating technique must always take into account the existence of three elements:

(*i*) The judge who will do the ratings,
(*ii*) The phenomenon to be rated and
(*iii*) The continuum along which they will be rated.

These can be of five categories:

(*a*) Descriptive Rating Scale
(*b*) Numerical Rating Scale
(*c*) The Graphic Rating Scale
(*d*) The Percentage of Group Rating Scale
(*e*) Ordinal Rating Scale.

For example qualities associated with delivering speech may be rated on a scale as follows:

5. Outstanding.
4. Very Good
3. Good
2. Acceptable, meets class standards
1. Below class standards.

Rating scale is very useful technique because it takes less time than other techniques. It helps the rater to be a better judge of man. The teacher who has little training for the purpose can also use it. But on the other hand it suffers from halo-effect, logical error and the proximity error.

3. Anecdotal Records: They are important methods of collecting information about the individual. It is an objective amount of pupil's behaviour and personality observed by the teacher. This record is the result of incidental observation. Hence this is called informal observation. These records may be used to obtain regarding a number of learning outcomes and other aspects of social development.

In the words of Strang, "Anecdotal record is a specialised form of incidental observation. It is a description of the child's conduct and personality pattern in terms of frequent, brief, concrete observation of the pupil made and recorded by the teacher."

It also makes possible to diagnose the problems of the students. The students can use it for self-appraisal also. It provides an explanation of actual behaviour in natural settings. It provides a variety of descriptions concerning the behaviour of the pupil in diverse situations. It contributes to understanding of changing personality pattern.

Purposes of Anecdotal Records

- To know student's interests.
- To know change in attitudes.
- To provide evidence of progress of learning in commerce.
- To describe social adjustment.
- To mention clearly the situations which provide anti-social behaviour.

Thus, anecdotal records are very useful to know about pupil's progress but the teacher should take care while preparing it.

The performance can be tested in the form of product preparation, model construction, enactment of role play, etc. by applying the techniques of rating scale, cumulative records, check-lists etc., while working as well as after the finishing of the work.

8. Continuous and Comprehensive Evaluation (CCE)

National policy of education, 1986 mentioned about continuous and comprehensive evaluation of pupils which covers both scholastic and co-scholastic aspects of their development, and suggested for elimination of excessive element of chance and subjectivity, de-emphasizing memorization.

The evaluation process ascertain the workability of learning experiences and change of behaviour of the students while evaluating the learning of the students it has to be assessed continuously. The learner is to be assessed throughout the year. Evaluation is a continuous process as it starts from the day a child is admitted in the institution. We are to observe the working of the students continuously and assessing whether the educational process is successful or not and whether the desired changes are taking place in the students or not.

Evaluation is comprehensive in the sense that the overall personality of the child is assessed in all spheres of life.

Comprehensive Evaluation: The process used to know the achievement of the objectives related to scholastic and non-scholastic aspects of the students is known as comprehensive evaluation process. The traditional examination system was focussed on scholastic area where student was tested on due basis of his knowledge and understanding about the terms, concepts, principles related to the subject only. It never focussed on non-scholastic areas i.e. development his personality, interest, attitudes, aptitude values, participation in extra- curricular activities etc. Thus the objective of harmonious development of the child remains unfulfilled. The evaluation of scholastic and non-scholastic areas should be included to make the evaluation comprehensive. The National Education Policy 1986 and its modified from 1992 stated that evaluation process should include all the learning experiences related to scholastic and non- scholastic areas.

Since abilities, attitudes and aptitudes can manifest themselves in forms other than the written word, the term refers to application of a variety of tools and techniques and aims at assessing a learner's development in higher order thinking skills such as analysing, evaluating and creating. Assessment during the course of studies or formative assessment, must be based on a variety of evidence and lend to diagnosis of learning gaps and their remediation.

Comprehensive

Scholastic aspects including curricular areas of subject specific areas	Co-scholastic aspects include skills, co-curricular activities, attitudes and values

Features

Some of the important features of comprehensive evaluation are as follows:

1. The overall personality of the child is assessed.
2. It is not limited to the bookish knowledge only.
3. It includes the evaluation of attitude and aptitude also.
4. It refers to the scholastic and non-scholastic areas of evaluation of pupil's growth.
5. The function of the school is not limited to build up the cognitive capacities but also to develop his non-cognitive abilities.
6. Several work experiences are included in the curriculum for the development of the children.

Continuous Evaluation: Continuity of assessment refers to the periodicity and frequency of assessment. It means integrations of assessment with teaching-learning process. It demand unit teaching and testing approach, and requires continual diagnosis of learning gaps to provide basis for remedial action. It focuses on regular feedback to teachers and students for improving teaching and learning process. Therefore, continuity of assessment leads to growth, development, improvement and adaptation of teaching-learning strategies.

Continuous

Spread over the entire span of academic session	Regularity of assessment with feedback

The important features of continuous evaluation are as follows:

1. It means regularity in assessment and testing the student's achievements throughout the year.
2. It helps in giving proper guidance regularly.

3. It is likely to obtain the valuable data about the strengths and weaknesses of the children.
4. The feedback helps the teacher in improving the level of achievement by adopting remedial strategies.
5. It also helps in comprehensive evaluation.
6. It covers mainly the scholastic areas.
7. It includes testing of teacher's own teaching.

Thus the achievement of objectives of the subject and topic can be tested through continuous evaluation.

Advantages and Importance of Continuous and Comprehensive Evaluation

Evaluation plays a significant role in the field of education. The merits of CCE are as follows:

1. *Development of study habits:* It develops the study habits i.e. library consultation because without that they can't get the detailed knowledge of the subject matter & the others.
2. *Self-confidence:* It helps in increasing the self-confidence among students.
3. *More valid:* It provides more valid information about the child growth.
4. *Provides opportunities for discussion:* It helps in providing men and more opportunities for discussion to the students.
5. *Develop holistically:* It helps the child in the holistic development because no aspect is ignored.
6. *Prediction:* On the basis of CCE, the prediction regarding the success of the student in future can be made effectively.
7. *Punctuality and regularity:* The students become regular and punctual. They remain regular in doing their homework, class work and other assignments.
8. *Reduce stress:* It aims to help reduce stress in students because they work alongside the students individually and guide them depending on their specific strengths and ability. In addition, they refrain from using negative language of a student can't complete a project or understand something.
9. *Holistic education:* The CCE system focuses on holistic education which aims to develop various aspects of a student's personality which ultimately helps them identify what they are better at and stronger at in terms of academics.
10. *No pressure:* There is no pressure for students to become highly academic because they aim to encourage individuals to choose subjects based on their interests while retaining the importance of academia. They aim to make the students feel more relaxed so that they can improve on their academic ability without feeling under pressure.
11. Identify learning progress of students at regular time intervals on small portion of content.
12. Employing a variety of remedial measures of teaching based on learning needs and potential of different students.
13. Encourage learning through employment of a variety of teaching aids and

techniques.

14. Involve learners' activity in the learning process.
15. Recognise and encourage specific abilities the students, who do not excel in academic but perform well in other co-curricular areas.
16. It helps the child make informed choice of subjects in class XI based on his aptitude, interests, liking and academic performance.
17. Due to acquisition of additional life skills like thinking and emotional skills, students are expected to meet different life situations with greater maturity.
18. It helps the learner to develop holistically in terms of personality i.e. physically fit, mentally alert and emotionally balanced.
19. The students have more time with them to develop their interests, hobbies and personalities.
20. It is more valid than external examinations as it covers all the topics of the syllabus through assessment on daily as well as periodic basis.
21. The problem of indiscipline remains subsided because students remain busy throughout the time.
22. It is more reliable than external examination.
23. It motivates the pupils to work regularly and thoroughly.
24. It enables school authorities to diagnose pupils' difficulties in learning and provide opportunities to find out needs, interests, abilities and aptitudes of the learners.
25. It aims at finding out what the child knows, what she can do and what intelligence she possesses rather than finding out that she does not know what she can't do and what intelligence she does not possess.
26. It helps in grading the students at the end of the academic session.

Disadvantages or Limitation of Continuous and Comprehensive Evaluation

1. *Wide bracket of grading system:* A downside of CCE is the grading system. That is because the bracket is very wide. For example, students that score 90 and 100 will get 'A' grade. You may see this as a position scheme because it gives the chance for more student to receive a higher grade, however a student that score 8 more points that someone else, but doesn't receive a better grade may be unfair.

2. *More stress:* Despite the system using to lessen stress, the grading system may in fact cause more stress for the students. For example, a student may feel more pressure to get a higher grade because the grade margin is substantially large than you would expect.

3. *Time constraints:* It requires teachers to spend more time evaluating individual students. While the advantages of this include a broader view of the child's progress and more interactions with the child's parents, it can put additional strain on teachers that negatively influences their ability to assess students. Student conferences are more frequent under this system, requiring teachers to add more hours to their week day.

4. *Potential for inconsistencies:* CCE requires all teachers to be trained and adhere to the same assessment methods. However, the system is liable to suffer from many inconsistencies. Teachers are charged with assessing cognitive abilities

as well as health habits, work habits, cleanliness and cooperation. Training teachers in assessing these values may not provide any more consistent results than standardised testing.

5. *Potential for prejudice:* It aimed at grooming students as well as shaping their attitudes, beliefs and values. The potential for prejudice against minority groups or sectarian religious groups is a great risk in a system based on teacher-only assessment. Standardised tests allow students whose grades may be negatively influenced by teacher prejudice to prove their capability outside of the classroom.

6. *The ghost of classroom past:* Traditionally, students have started every new school year without any known pre-determined expectations by teachers. This can be liberating for students who wish to leave their poor performance behind and apply themselves a new. However, under CCE, carrying records of poor performance in elementary through high school may engender in students a low expectations of their ability to overcome that history of performance. A teacher's ability to read student's entire history may unintentionally establish expectations of poor performance that prevents teachers from applying different methods of teaching subjects to struggling students.

7. *Shirkers of work:* Shirkers of work in the teaching profession may not work and the standards of teaching-learning may go down.

8. *Incomplete without external examination:* In the absence of external examination/a public examination at the end of the year it would be incomplete.

9. *Insecurity for students:* Sometimes some teachers threaten their students about the evaluation and make them insecure.

10. *Lack of devoted teachers:* CCE can be effective only with the true and devoted teachers, which are lacking.

In spite of above said disadvantages and limitations of CCE, it is very important. Its effectiveness depends upon the capability of teacher also. It not only checks the cognitive abilities of the student but also help in improving them. The teacher should utilise it in an effective way, so that its purpose can be fulfilled.

Steps/Procedure of CCE

The CCE shall be carried out in four areas of students' progress in all the elementary classes. These are as follows:

1. Curricular areas
2. Other curricular areas
3. Curricular activities
4. Personal social qualities

1. Curricular areas: These includes all subjects of study as languages, maths, general science, social studies and predominantly covers the cognitive domain aiming at the intellectual development of children. The evaluation of curricular areas required more inputs to make it more systematic. Evaluation in curricular areas has to be continuous from the beginning of the academic session. A session is divided in two phases: April to September and October to March. In each phase there shall be three assessments at an interval of two months. Each assessment shall cover the portions covered within that period only.

In curricular areas there shall be both formal and informal evaluation as a part of CCE. Assessment of students learning in these areas shall be done through teacher made unit tests. A variety of tools/techniques shall be used as written, oral, assignment, projects, etc.

2. Other Curricular Areas: Subjects like art education, health and physical education, peace education, school education come under this area. The students should be observed and assessed by the teachers. Evaluation shall be made through project and performance etc. However, students' learning and progress on the above areas are to be evaluated internally by the teacher in and outside the classroom. The results of evaluation shall be shared with student and parents through report card.

3. Curricular Activities: Every school organises a variety of curricular activities to provide students with opportunities for participation, exposure, experiences and building his/her capabilities/skills to promote various dimensions of personality.

Prior to NCF 2005 the activities such as debates, recitation, creative writing, music, drama, dance, painting, drawing, games, sports and other outdoor and indoor activities were termed as non-scholastic, co-scholastic or co-curricular activities and were mostly neglected in schools. However, NCF 2005 has considered that all activities being organised in schools are essentially a part of curriculum and should be considered as curricular activities.

4. Evaluation of personal and social qualities (PSQ): Students through interaction with their peers, teachers and school environment develop many personal and social qualities. All such traits contribute to student's personality PSQ as suggested in NCF 2005 should be an integral part of curricular areas and curricular activities in each and every class; and as an element of affective domain. Keeping in mind the maturity level of the students, the teacher shall observe the direction of development rather than its status. The teacher will observe and record PSQ, using behaviour indicators with the help of 5-point scale so as to eliminate unhealthy competition.

The Continuous and Comprehensive Evaluation Scheme indicated by the National Policy has following dimensions:

Scholastic Aspects

Curricular Areas

- Knowledge
- Understanding
- Application
- Skills

Techniques of Evaluation

1. Written examinations
2. Oral examinations
3. Practice examinations

Tools of Evaluation

1. Question papers
2. Unit tests
3. Project works
4. Surveys
5. Assignments
6. Home work

Periodicity of Evaluation

Twice in an academic session.

	Coverage For all students
Non-Scholastic Aspects *Health status* – Height in relation to age – Weight in relation is height – Chest Expansion – Eye sight	*Techniques of Evaluation* – Medical check-up – Observation by the teacher. *Tools of Assessment* – Height and weight chart, – weighing machine – Measuring tapes. *Periodicity of Assessment* – Twice in an academic year *Coverage* – All students
Personal and social qualities – Regularity – Discipline – Punctuality – Habit of cleanliness – Initiative – Civil consciousness sense of responsibility – Diligence – Sprit of social service	*Techniques of Evaluation* – Observation *Tools of Evaluation* – Anecdotal Records – Rating Scales *Coverage* – The first four to be assessed in respect of all students and the rest only when evidences are available.
Interests	
1. Literary Interests – Recitation – Debates – Creative writing – Extra Reading 2. *Scientific Interests* – Exploration – Experimentation – Commerce club activities 3. *Cultural Interests* – Dramatics 4. *Artistic Interests* – Drawing – Painting	*Technique of Evaluation* – Observation – Standardised objective tests – Interest Inventory *Tools of Evaluation* – Daily Dairy – Socio-metric Scale – Rating scale
Attitudes – Towards teachers – Towards School mates – Towards School Programmes – Towards School Property	– Attitude scales

Values

- Dignity of labour
- Honesty
- Courage

– A student will be evaluated only when evidences are available.

Thus, continuous and comprehensive evaluation of students is possible through cumulative Record Cards maintained in the school for each child. It has also been written in the modified curriculum framework given by NCERT, in 2005 that continuous and comprehensive evaluation is the only meaningful technique of evaluation. The main thing is to be keep in mind that how this can be used effectively.

In this way the journey of student's assessment gone a long way passing through oral testing, written testing, public examination, internal and external assessment, continuous and comprehensive evaluation and competency-based assessment.

Tools and Techniques of Evaluation

The tools and techniques of evaluation may be classified as follows:

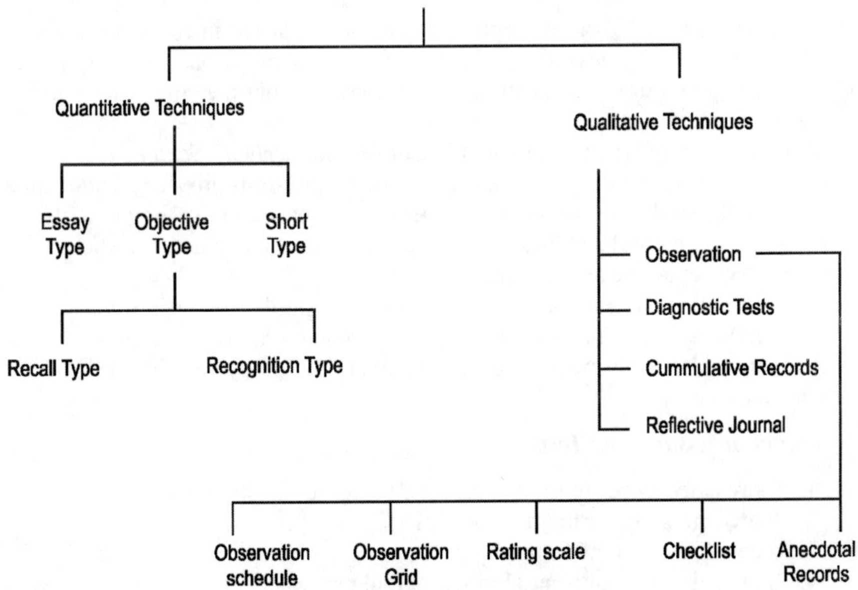

QUANTITATIVE TECHNIQUES

1. Essay Type Tests

Generally essay type tests are teacher-made tests used to measure the outcomes of the commerce instructions. These are the tests in which the students have to write answers of some questions in a fixed time. It is widely used to estimate the ability to remember, to organise and to synthesize. The construction of these questions is of such type that their answers take the forms of essay. It has more effect on expression, good handwriting, way of writing, and language, etc. In these tests the temperament of the examiner, personal views etc. are dominating.

These tests have been greatly appreciated because of freedom of response it allows. It is the test of an inductive approach to a problem and application of the knowledge obtained and how the student is able to relate one branch of knowledge with the other.

According to Dewey "Children have natural liking to exchange views. For satisfying that liking, the knowledge of language is necessary. This examination is very helpful in satisfy their liking."

It usually places emphasis on a larger segment of the subject or an integrated total unit. In this type of tests, the pupil must produce something than guessing or recognizing the answer. These tests may be used for measuring those learning outcomes that cannot be measured by objective type tests. These tests are introduced in India with the outgrowth of the British pattern of education and its acceptance by a number of Indian educational institutions.

Type of Questions

The questions under Essay Type Tests can be classified in two categories:

(a) Restricted Response Questions: This type of questions tend to restrict both the context and the form of students' response. Sometimes the space and the words are restricted. e.g.

Q. Make a list of six private companies of Indian Private Sector.

(b) Extended Response Questions: This type of questions provide a wide range of freedom to the students to express their views. They can organise their knowledge according to their mental capability. This freedom helps the students to show their ability to select, organise and integrate the matter, e.g.

Q. Write a detailed note on the changing role of public sector in India.

It is needless to emphasise that essay type, when planned carefully, serve a useful function. It is the most used kind of examination system because of the following advantages.

Advantages of Essay Type Tests

1. It provides freedom to express their views to the students.
2. It measures higher mental abilities.
3. It encourages creative thinking.
4. It provokes thoughts and higher mental process.
5. These are economical.
6. It is widely accepted.
7. It measures originality and initiations.
8. It develops power of concentration.
9. A large number of students can be examined simultaneously.
10. It encourages composition and thus helps to stimulate imagination and association.
11. It minimizes cheating.
12. It helps in examining the critical power of the students.
13. It improves the language and expression power of the students.

14. It provides qualitative interpretations.
15. It is easy to construct and to apply.

Thus, essay type tests are helpful in testing the student's abilities to organise and summarize ideas; describe events, persons and places; interpret data, apply principles, think creatively and critically. It forms the basis for the appraisal of skill in organising and summarizing the information.

Demerits and Limitations of Essay Type Tests

Though the essay type test is the means of measuring the verbal fluency, style of expression and organisation of thoughts and the attitude of experience towards problems and subjects considered in the class, yet it lacks most of the qualities of a good measuring device. These are said to be good servants but bad masters. It has following demerits and limitations:

1. Not Valid: Essay type test is not valid because it includes many irrelevant factors such as quality of the spellings, handwriting and language used, as well as bluffing for which there is no formula for correction.

2. Less Comprehensive: It is less comprehensive because it is a general complaint among the students that the question did not suit them. It is inadequate to test examinee's knowledge and ability through particular set of questions. The limited number of questions (generally ten) cannot cover the complete syllabus. The students, who know the art of examinations or guessing the question are branded as intelligent, hard working, possessing a fertile brain, etc.

3. Time Consuming: Essay type test is time consuming for students to attempt as well as for teachers to evaluate.

4. Includes Subjectivity: Essay type test is subjective because the marking is influenced by the whims of the examiner.

5. Less Reliability: It has less reliability. The same teacher if re-examine a set of essay test after an interval of two or three weeks will differ markedly in the second scoring. Studies have also shown that the teachers cannot agree with each other as to the marks to be assigned to the essay type examination answer sheet.

6. Emphasis on Expression: An important demerit of the essay test is that an outside examiner does not possess knowledge of the pupil's average work. His expression affects the achievement of marks.

7. Emphasis on Writing and Speed: In essay type test the examinee has to write a lot. Taking an examination becomes an art. Speed of writing is also an important factor in this test.

8. Emphasis on Cramming: It stimulates an unhealthy competitive spirit among children and encourage cramming of subject matter rather than reflective thinking.

9. Difficult to Discriminate: Essay type test does not help in discriminating the students according to their abilities and knowledge.

10. Variability in the standards of Paper Setting: The preparation of essay type test is easy but subjective. Some examiners set it very difficult, while others set it very easy. The difficulty level varies from year to year, institution to institution, university to university.

Realising the drawbacks of essay type test a controversy arose among the educationists whether to mend or end such type of tests and the milder view has had the upper hand. A number of committees were set up by the Government of India to find out the ways of improving the system of examination.

Suggestions for Improvement in Essay Type Test

Essay type test can be much improved with the help of the following suggestions:

1. Before the examination, the students may understand the difference between terms like discuss, define, explain, describe and other similar terms.
2. The questions in the test should preferably put minimum stress on the recall of isolated factual knowledge and the listing of the memorized information. The emphasis should be given on the coverage of learning objectives rather than context coverage.
3. The language of the questions should be simple and clear.
4. The questions should be specified so that it can require a definite answer.
5. The difficulty level of the questions should be according to the level of the students.
6. The instructions in the question paper should be clear cut.
7. Advantages of well planned answer, instead of haphazard ones, may be emphasized and explained.
8. The instructions for evaluation should be given in simple and clear language.
9. The question in the test should be specified so that an answer key may be prepared in advance and provided to the examiners.
10. The marks should be assigned for each part of a question separately.
11. The students may be guided to write the answers systematically in an organised manner and to give a clear and lucid interpretation of their ideas.

Thus, by including all these suggestions in an essay type test this can probably be used with reasonable success by almost any teacher who is willing to read patiently.

2. Objective Type Test

Objective type tests have been developed to meet two basic short comings of the essay type test – subjectivity in scoring and practically eliminating the possibility of bluffing on the part of the students. A student cannot misrepresent himself on whatever behaviour is being measured by the test. These tests require the students to develop creative and original thoughts, the basis for choice among the alternatives. On the one hand, they control the behaviour of the students and, on the other hand, they also control the behaviour of the teacher by providing less freedom in evaluation process.

Type of Questions in Objective Type Test

It can be classified in various ways according to their purpose, the mental process involved in answering them or their form. The questions should be suited to the purpose and to the type of material involved. The teacher should not decide in advance that he would construct a test of 20 completions, 40 true–false, etc. He should firstly decide the understanding and skill to be measured then decide whatever type seems best suited.

The following are the important types:

1. Recall Type: In this test the students are requested to supply missing items of information usually words, numbers or phrases and to complete the sentences.

(a) Short answer: While writing such items it should be kept in mind that the question require a definite and restricted answer.

Example:

(*i*) What is tele-banking?

(*ii*) Name the parties of insurance contract.

(b) Controlled completion: In these items, the space should be provided to respond the question but many spaces should not be in one sentence.

Examples:

(*i*) Fidelity insurance contract is between some employer and _________.

(*ii*) Communication means transmitting facts and ideas from _________.

(*c*) Listing: This type of item is used to test the ability to classify facts.

Examples:

(*i*) List the following modes of communication in traditional period and modern period
Courier service, Telephone, Fax, Telegram, e-mail, correspondence through post offices.

(*ii*) List the primary and secondary functions of bank from the following:
Accepting of Deposits, Purchase and sale of securities, Letter of Reference, Overdraft, Term loan, Locker facilities.

Thus we say that recall type tests are useful to develop problem solving skills and help to develop the general mental ability of the students.

2. Recognition Type: Recognition type questions try to test the knowledge, understanding and application ability of the students. It also tests the recognition ability of the child because in these students are to recognise the correct answers.

1. Constant Alternative Items: The format of items that represent true/false and allied varieties requires examinees to select the answer from two alternatives, which remain the same for the whole series of items. These items are usually in the form of statements (sometimes in question form) and examinees are to make judgement both their truth or falsity. These items may also take the form of Yes-No, agree-disagree, synonyms-antonyms, correct-wrong, etc.

(a) True-false

(*i*) ATM is an automatic machine which operates for all the 24 hours. (T/F)

(*ii*) Ford Motors is not the MNC of U.S.A. (T/F)

(*b*) Right-Wrong.

(*i*) State bank of India is a commercialised bank. (R/W)

(*ii*) Equity shareholders are called the owners of company. (R/W)

(*c*) Agree, Disagree.

(*i*) Trade credit is the example of long-term finance. (A/D)

(*ii*) E-commerce includes interactions among the geographically dispersed units of the business. (A/D)

(*d*) Yes/No

(*i*) Is customer participation necessary to buy a service? (Y/N)

(*ii*) Does the state government issue 'Certificate of Registration' to a firm? (Y/N)

(*e*) Correction Variety

Underline the false part of the statement and write the correction in the brackets provided.

(*i*) A partner whose association with the firm is unknown to the general public is called sleeping partner. ()

(*ii*) Warehousing is a technique which distributes the risk of one person among many. ()

While writing these items it should be kept in mind that we should not use trivial statements which includes many aspects to be judged and the words like usually, mostly, etc. should not be utilised. Care may be taken that length of true and false statements should approximately be the same. Moreover, number of false statements should be more, because of their better discrimination power.

3. *Multiple-choice*: The most potential and useable form of objective test is the MCQ. These items are either used exclusively as in some selection tests or in combination with other forms of questions as in most of the examinations conducted by the examination board of other agencies. These type of items are based on response-directed stimulus, in which responses or options may be arranged in different ways. When the purpose of examination is to rank the candidates for selection or awarding scholarships as in national talent search examination conducted by NCERT, these items may be used exclusively to ensure complete objectivity in scoring. In these type of items, the responses are usually lettered, A, B, C, D, E, and the student is required to choose the correct alternative that represents the correct answer, i.e., key.

(I) Which of the following is not covered under General Insurance?

A. Life Insurance Key

B. Theft Insurance Distributors

C. Fire Insurance options or responses

D. Marine Insurance

(II) Which of the following devices is needed for internet?

A. Computer Systems

B. Modem

C. Telephone Connection

D. All of the above

A common multiple choice item is usually written in verbal form, but it may be based on a diagram, picture, graph, table or a map. The items can be in different forms as:

- Single response variety
- Multiple response variety
- Best least or worst variety
- All or none variety
- Multiple completion or Multiple selections

- Combined response variety
- Classification variety
- Negative response variety
- Sequenced response variety
- Cause and effect variety
- Analogy type items
- Assertion reasoning variety

Thus, one can use any form of MCQ depending on the nature of competency to be tested and the scope of content cluster in a topic. However, ensuring good quality items demands:

- Knowledge of criteria of a good MCQ.
- Understanding of criteria of a good MCQ.
- Choosing the most relevant form of MCQ.
- Homogeneity of distracters as far as possible.
- Use of not less than three options.

4. Matching Type: Matching type items are prescribed as set of terms, events, phrases, definition etc. called the premises, which are written on the left hand side, say column I. Another set of names, pictures, statements etc. called the responses, are placed on the right hand side under columns II. Students are asked to match each items with the corresponding response, which is considered as one test item. Relationship may be between a term and definition, object and its functions, inventors and inventions, author and work, dates and events, problems and solutions, etc.

Example:

Directions – for each term in column I, select the statement from column II that defines it best, and write its serial number in the parentheses provided on the left against each item.

Column I	Column II
( ) Insurance	A. Through which raw material is converted in to finished product.
( ) Industry	B. Relates with reconstruction of sick public sector units.
( ) Bank	C. A technique which distributes the risk of one person among many.
( ) BIFR	D. Relates with transactions of money.

Such items are good for testing the students' ability to establish relationship between two sets of objects, concepts, events, etc. Major criticism about these items is that they measure lower level of learning outcomes involving ability to recall date, events, etc. But this is not true.

If the teacher is well trained to develop these items, he can use them effectively. Common errors found in such items are vague direction, vaguely stated premises, long responses, lack of homogeneity in responses, difficulty for students to respond or key the items etc.

5. Rearranging Type Items: In these type of items students are required to re-arrange the randomly presented material into some specified order. Material may be presented in the form of a series of statements one after the other or responses may be given of the multiple choice type. Direction is to be provided whether the responses are to be rearranged by writing them in specified order, to serial them in particular order, or indicate the serial number of each, etc.

(i) Functional Order: Rearrange the following steps involved in the import trade by an importer, giving the serial number, in the bracket provided against each:

1. Placing an indent or order. ( )
2. Trade enquiry. ( )
3. Sending letter of credit. ( )
4. Obtaining foreign exchange. ( )
5. Obtaining import licence. ( )

(ii) Chronological Order: In it, certain items/things/activities are to be arranged in chronological order:

Example: ICICI, NABARD, SFCs, IDBI.

(iii) Logical Order: Rearrange the following steps in correct order for creating an effective strategic control for an organisation, indicating the correct order by the serial number against each step in the given parentheses.

No.	Steps	Correct order
1.	Compare Actual Performance	( )
2.	Establish standards and Targets	( )
3.	Initiate Corrective Actions	( )
4.	Create measuring and monitoring system.	( )

Thus, there are different type of test items which can be prepared for objective type test. The most frequently used format of objective questions are the multiple choice question, which form a significant part of most of our achievement and selection tests, having the greatest potential of all the types of questions. A teacher, however, must be clear whether and when it is advisable to use these items.

Advantages of Objective Type Tests

1. They are more valid.
2. They are more reliable.
3. Time saver for examiner and students.
4. Helpful for making score quick and easy.
5. More comprehensive and make a wider range of questions possible.
6. No need for cramming.
7. Free from complications, hence saves the students from misleading.
8. Values to knowledge not efficiency and expertise in use of words.
9. Reduces the role of luck or chance.
10. Easy to administer.
11. Varying standards among the examiners can be eliminated.
12. Examiner cannot be bluffed.
13. Helpful in providing guidance for further teaching programme.
14. Provides self satisfaction to pupils after getting marks as expected.

15. Only knowledge is tested not the language.
16. Not affected by the personal business of the teacher.
17. Possibility of classification of students in different categories.
18. No place for irrelevant factors.
19. Help in development of wholesome personality.
20. Style and handwriting is useless, only real answer is needed.

Demerits and Limitations of Objectives type tests

1. Extraordinary traits cannot be exhibited.
2. Encourage guess work in answering.
3. More scope for using unfair means.
4. Imagination and reasoning power falls down due to short writing.
5. Children fall victim of psychological effects.
6. Difficult to frame.
7. Measurement of higher mental process is not possible.
8. Costlier than essay type tests.
9. Ignore the writing capability of the students.
10. Not able to test the ability to present the subject matter in an organised way.
11. Complete and reliable assessment is not possible due to incomplete information of the subject matter by students.
12. Continuously dropping in thinking, discussion and rationalisation.
13. Not helpful in testing the critical power of the students.
14. Only marks gaining becomes a question, creeping new ideas is totally distorted.
15. Capabilities and talents of student cannot be identified due to mechanical process of student mind.

But inspite of these disadvantages and limitations, objective type tests are very useful for the evaluation of the students. These should be used with essay type and short answer type tests.

3. Short Answer Type Test

In this type of tests, short questions are set to which pointed answers have to be given by the students. The purpose of these tests is to test a large amount of knowledge, ability and understanding within a short time. The scoring of short answer type questions can be tedious and somewhat subjective. It is almost impossible to write good short answer questions that require the student to exhibit synthesis and interpretation. Very short answer type questions are also used in commerce which require a pin-pointed answer.

QUALITATIVE TECHNIQUES

1. Observation

Assessment of pupils through observing their behaviours comes very naturally. All of us observe others and draw conclusion about them. This is a popular technique in guidance also. The observation may be structured, where the students may be asked to do certain activity, or unstructured where observations are made about the students in their normal routines.

It is important to note here that drawing conclusion through observing a person during one incident is not appropriate. It is necessary to make observations over a longer period in varying situations and circumstances with varying groups. The locality of the situation should also be kept in mind. For example, if a person is showing aggressive behaviour, the situations where he is aggressive should be analysed properly before aiming at any definite conclusion.

There are many ways to record classroom observations as:

(*i*) *Observation Schedule:* Observation schedule is a device consisting of questions. It is better or rather essential to work and a well structured observation schedule to observe the intended behaviours systematically in the form of a proforma to indicate the criterion behaviours under observations, the evidence to be looked for judging the criteria applied and the rating on the effectiveness of the criteria used, which could be a three point or five point rating (numerical, letter grades or in qualitative description, depending upon the nature of behaviour observed). It can be used by a single observer or more than one observer who rates the individual on the scale provided.

(*ii*) *Observation Grid or Sheet:* Observations of student performances can also be recorded on class grids or sheets. These can be used for a particular period of time or a particular task. The grids can also be pasted inside a folder for privacy. They can also be put on the classroom wall / or board, so that students can see the outcomes being assessed.

(*iii*) *Rating Scales:* A rating scale is a device for obtaining judgements of the degree to which an individual possesses certain behavioural traits and attributes. These may be desired for evaluating a great variety of traits as generosity, leadership, cooperativeness, resourcefulness, discipline, interests and other personal and social qualities which involve qualitative assessment.

(*iv*) *Checklists:* A checklist is similar in appearance and use to a rating scale. The basic difference between them is in the types of judgement called for. For instance, a rating scale provides an opportunity to indicate the degree to which a particular characteristic, or a trait is present in an individual, the checklist on the other hand, calls for a simple 'yes-no' judgement.

(*v*) *Anecdotal Records:* One of the important observation tool that can be used to evaluate the non-cognitive behavioural aspects of students is an anecdotal record. It is a verbal snap shot of a single but significant event recorded in its setting to describe observation made by the observer. Descriptors are factual records and not interpretation of what happened.

Example (Record of students A)

- Does not participate in the classroom discussion.
- Seldoms completes the home assignments in commerce.
- Never responds to teacher's questions.
- Does not show concern for improvement in learning.
- Feels nervous to speak to the teacher, and avoids the teacher as for as possible.

An anecdotal record is a factual description of meaningful events, which a teacher has observed of her pupils in everyday in and out of classrooms situation.

Suggestions for writing Anecdotal Record

- Make a record soon after the incident is observed.
- Limit each anecdote to a brief description of a single specific incident.
- Record the factual description of the incident and not its interpretation.
- Make the description of the incident as objective as possible.
- Collect a number of anecdotes on a pupil before drawing inference concerning a typical behaviour.
- Record both possible and negative behavioural incidents in proper setting.

How anecdotal records help teachers?

Anecdotal records help teachers to understand pupils to–

- Understand the child's personality,
- Identify the child's needs and help in proper development of the child.
- Help in improving and adopting teacher's approaches and attitudes towards the child.
- Avoid unwanted inferences about children caused by lack of knowledge.
- Undertake necessary steps to solve the problems of the child.
- Understand more about child's behaviour and to establish congenial atmosphere for children to develop healthy personality.

An anecdotal record not only provides the concrete evidence about a child to the teacher, but also to other school personnel interested in a particular child's adjustments. A systematic record to which one can refer for an accurate account of the child's behaviour is certainly preferable to memory.

Where can the children be observed?

Observation for anecdotal records should be made in a variety of situations as pupils show different behaviour under different circumstances. If the record is really to reflect the pupil's individuality, most observations should be made on situation in which he has freedom to display a variety of reactions, where he chooses his companions freely and his social relations.

(*vi*) *Systematic Case Study:* Under this method, the major activity is to collate all the information collected from various sources and techniques. This can be the information from the school record, from achievement records, the psychological tests, or informations collected by the teacher. Allport says that, "It provides a framework within which the psychologist can place all her observations gathered by other methods."

Thus for structured observation of any pupil, these techniques can be used effectively to evaluate.

2. Diagnostic Test

Just as a doctor diagnoses a patient to find the nature, type and extent of his/her disease before prescribing medicine, a teacher of commerce applies diagnostic test to diagnose the particular strength and weaknesses of the student. Generally, we find that students have difficulties in understanding and learning certain concepts. The difficulties may vary from individual to individual and class to class. In order to make the teaching-learning process effective, it is essential to find the learning difficulties of students during instruction. The diagnostic tests consist of items based on a detailed analysis of the specific skills involved in successful performance and a study of the most common errors made by students.

Diagnosis of persistent learning difficulties involves much more than diagnostic testing, but such tests are useful in the total process. The diagnostic test takes place where the formative test leaves off. If pupils do not respond to the feedback – corrective prescriptions of formative testing they need for a more detailed search for the source of learning error is indicated. Such tests are also commonly called learning tests, quizzes, unit tests and the like.

Since our focus is on the pupil's learning difficulties, diagnostic tests must be constructed in the light of the most common sources of error encountered by the students. Such tests are typically confirmed to a limited area of instruction, and the test items tend to have relatively low level of difficulty.

Types of Diagnostic Tests

Diagnostic test are mainly classified into two categories:

1. Educational Diagnostic Tests: Educational diagnostic tests are related to study material designed for specific level or standard of education. These tests diagnose disorder of material according to the level of class.

2. Physical or Clinical Diagnostic Tests: Physical or clinical diagnostic tests are related to hearing, vision and other things that cause hindrance in the course of child's learning.

Characteristics of Diagnostic Tests

1. It is a qualitative test.
2. It finds out weaknesses or deficiencies of a child in learning of the content.
3. It is an effective tool for teachers that helps in planning and organizing remedial teaching.
4. It arranges the items in learning sequence in order of positive transfer of learning.
5. It adopts objective type test only.
6. It fully emphasizes on all learning and teaching points.
7. In diagnostic test no scores are assigned for correct answer but wrong responses are considered in view of the sequence of the content identify the cause for the wrong answer.
8. It needs an expert to identify the causes for wrong answers.
9. In diagnostic test no learning point is omitted or ignored.
10. The purpose of diagnostic test is the remedial teaching and instruction.

Uses/Functions of Diagnostic Test

1. Diagnostic tests are useful in finding out the strength and weaknesses of the individuals.

2. These are helpful in finding out the causes of those problems which remain unchecked and unremedied by formative evaluation.
3. These are helpful in locating the areas in which additional instruction is required or in which teaching method have to be improved.
4. These are helpful in identifying the use of faulty, roundabout or incorrect procedures.
5. The tests are useful to both the attainment as well as difficulties of pupils whose achievements are not up to the mark.
6. They help in dividing pupils in the groups for special coaching or remedial teaching as the case may be.
7. It provides useful feedback to the students.
8. It helps in designing course and curricula according to the capabilities of the learner to help him overcome his deficiencies in knowledge, skills and abilities and to assist him in making the best use of his potentialities.

Steps for the Construction of Diagnostic Test

The following are the steps used for preparing the diagnostic test–

- Formulate the objective
- Analyse the content in to sub-topics.
- Identify the difficulties in the order of sub-topics.
- Analyse the items and modify them.
- Final draft of the test is prepared.
- Prepare manual to the test.
- Remedial devices and measures.

Thus, diagnostic test results will reveal in a comprehensive way, the exact level reached by pupil and the precise nature of difficulties. These tests will help to find out the specific kind of instruction and practice that will be required to bring achievement up to the desired level.

3. Cumulative Records

As the result of evaluation is of great importance for deciding about educational and vocational destiny of the students, the testing results should be recorded in an organised form. This record of testing must be conveniently available for various users.

The cumulative records include the scholastic test results and other type of information on pupils like non-scholastic achievement, essential for describing her personality, guidance provided, etc. Testing programmes in various scholastic and non-scholastic learning activities and their methods of recording is a local matter and differs from school to school or in the schools of one area to schools of other area. The important thing about the records is not what is put in to them, but how much is extracted out of them. How the records are being used for all round development of personality of the children is most essential. According to *Wrightstone* and others *"Cumulative Record is a method for recording, filling and using informations essential to the guidance of the students."*

There are much information to be included systematically in the records as:

(*i*) Personal Identification Data (*ii*) Family Background
(*iii*) Health and Physical growth (*iv*) School history
(*v*) Abilities (*vi*) Leisure time activities, Hobbies
(*vii*) Co-curricular activities (*viii*) Educational vocational plans
(*ix*) Problem areas (*x*) Report from teachers, parents, peer group
(*xi*) Reading habits (*xii*) Periodical follow up
(*xiii*) Scholastic achievements (*xiv*) Character building values

The information to fill up the format has to be collected and compiled through various sources such as school records, teachers, the child himself, the report cards, psychological tests, etc.

Features of a Good Record Card

Hahn and Mcclean has listed the following features of a good CRC:

1. A comprehensive and detailed system of cumulative personnel records is indispensable for the proper functioning of the modern school.
2. The record system should be simple enough and well enough organised so that the essential facts about the pupil will be brought together on one central record card in such a way that they may be easily studied by teachers and counsellors.
3. An attempt should be made to keep the records high in reliability and comparability by basing them as far as possible on objective data.
4. The record system should provide for a minimum of repetition of items.
5. There is a natural and logical relationship between the information on reports made to parents and the information recorded for the purpose of permanent record.
6. It must be revised frequently as a school's theory of education changes.

Merits/Advantages of Cumulative Records

1. It provides a sound data base which can help in understanding the student, his academic performance, his family background, his behaviour, his assets, his relationship with others, etc.
2. It helps in improving the methods of teaching by revealing the needs of the students.
3. This can serve as a tool for discussion with the employees.
4. It can help in diagnosing the problem and plan remedial measures.
5. It can serve as an aid for parent-teacher counselling.
6. It is an aid in the search of talent.
7. It helps in the classification of pupils.
8. On the basis of this data base, group and individual guidance activities can be planned.
9. It provides data for objective evaluations.

Thus, as a general principle any information useful for effective implementation of educational objectives and presentation of a true picture of the pupil should be included in the records. However, we should take care that the system does not become too burdensome for teachers. Record keeping is not an end in itself. Using the record for guidance, improvement of teaching strategies, economical use of the available resources in the school and true assessment of pupil should be one major outcomes of the records.

National Education Policy 2020 lay great emphasis on the multidimensional report card which will include the reporting of everything done by the student in different areas as:

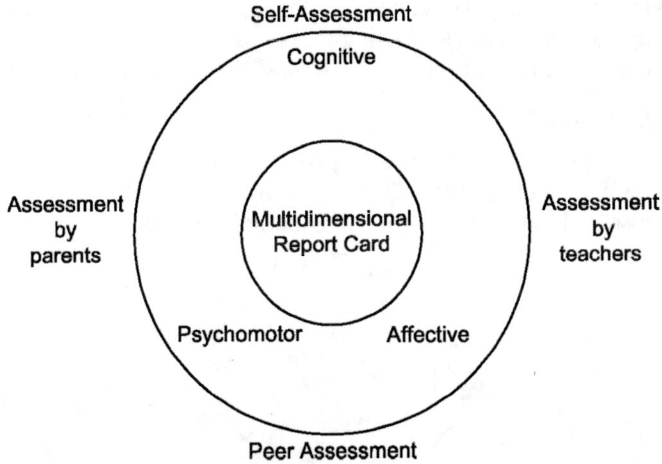

The report card should be multilayered and compile the assessment from different sources. It will be completely redesigned by states/UTs under the guidance from PARAKH, NCERT as well as SCERT. It will include progress of the child in inquiry-based learning as well as experienced learning. It will provide important information on how to support in and out of the classroom. Thus, the report card will be a holistic, 360 degree, multi-dimensional that reflects in detail the progress as well as the uniqueness of each learner in all domains.

4. Reflective Journal

John Dewey believed that education should serve not only as a means of acquiring information but also as a way to bring learning in our everyday action and behaviour. Most successful learners know how to identify questions and problems as they reflect on what-they already know, what they want and need to know and how they will proceed to increase their understanding.

Zemelmen, Daniels and Hyde (1993) believe that the most powerful learning happens when students monitor self or reflect. As learners continue to distinguish what they know from what they need to reevaluate or relearn, they begin to translate discoveries they have made about their own learning into plans for improvement.

Reflective journal is a personal record of students' learning experiences. It is the perfect place to jot down some of life's biggest thoughts. In it a person can write about a positive or negative event that he/she experienced, what it means or meant to him/her, and what he/she may have learned from that experience. For example, who was there, what was the purpose of the event, what do you think about it, how does it make you feel, etc. while writing a reflection journal, you are simply documenting something that has happened in your life that requires you to make a change or consider the impact of your decision. In many ways, your journal is a dialogue that you are having with yourself. You are forcing your brain to think critically about something and to write the words accordingly. It is used to explore situations from personal perspective, but generally within the context of learning from student's own experiences. They are:

- What happened ? (Reflecting on actions)
- Why did it happen? (Reflecting in actions)
- What can be learnt from this for future actions? (Reflecting for actions)

Purpose/Importance

A well written journal can be an effective tool. Writing in your journal can be an incredibly useful to help you better understand yourself and the world you operate in. The purposes behind writing a reflective journal are as follows:

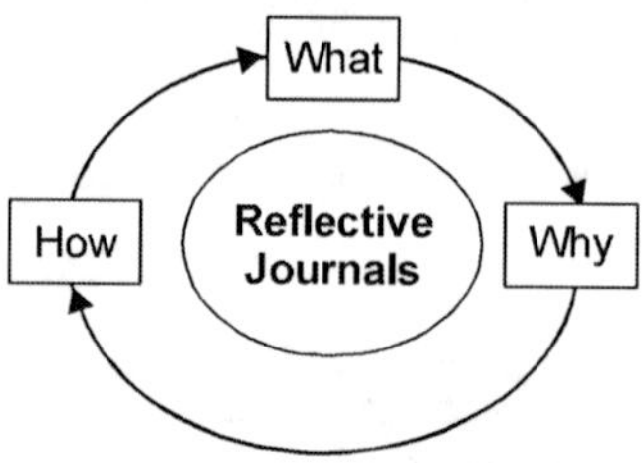

- *To make sense of things what happened:* When we are seeing the happening in front of us, then act of writing down the details of what happened may give you perspective that you may not have otherwise. It will sound as if you are describing the details to someone who was not there. You may start thinking about that.
- *To speculate as to why something is the way:* What you think or do can come from your own sense or from something, you have heard at a lecture or read in a book. It can be a very useful exercise in reasoning while speculating, why something is the way. You can reason out in your mind or your can discuss with others.
- *To get thoughts and ideas out of your mind:* Sometimes you may be in a stress, then writing down your thoughts can help resolve pressure or help resolve problems. This will also help you to focus on the task at hand.
- *To force the brain to think critically:* In many ways, your journal is a dialogue that you are having with yourself. It will help you in forcing your brain to think critically about something and to give them words in writing.
- *To start criticism of your own:* Reflective journal allows you to make a mistake and keep going. Who cares if you don't phrase that exactly how you should have or you did not spell that word right. Nobody will criticize you and you can do your own criticism.
- *To share your ideas and thoughts with others:* You can get opinions of others about what you wrote. This can help you clarify your feelings and you can understand yourself more deeply.

• *To align future actions with your reflected values and experiences:* It also helps you to think that whether you want to stick to your original views or you want to make changes on the basis of your speculations. You can decide about your future actions and make changes to your entries at any time.

Thus, in a reflective journal, you can write about a positive or negative event that you experienced. Firstly, it means forcing yourself to write, but after a while it will become the second nature. One of the most commonly used and therapeutic ways to utilize your journal is to reflect upon your experiences you deem profound or that had an impact on your life. It will give you a completely different perspective on things. It is a personal account of educational experiences that offers a variety of benefits, from enhancing your writing skills and helping you retain information to allowing you to express your thought on new ideas and theories.

Guidelines for writing a Reflection Journal

Writing a reflective journal requires not only that you describe a learning experience, but also feelings and opinions about the subject matter. There is no set structure for writing a reflective journal because it is of you, written by you and for you. However, there are certain guidelines that will make you more successful:

1. Always keep the journal nearby: The first step is that whenever any thought or idea is coming in your mind, strikes in you mind, or you are seeing some event or happening and an insightful observation is there, prepare to jot down your thoughts and opinions on something you are learning anytime. Always keep your journal with you, it may be in the form of diary or on mobile phone.

2. Make Regular entries: It is your journal and you are free to write in any form and style, so, it is important to write regular entries. This ensures you are reviewing content and actively thinking about what you have learned. It will help in developing your writing, keen observational and critical thinking skills. In the end you can analyse yourself.

3. Participate observe, summarize and contemplate: While writing the reflective diary, the foremost part is reflection, but it is also important that you first participate in a learning activity, make observation and summarize facts and experiences. For example, when the pupil-teachers are going for school observation and are writing about a cultural event, be sure to first cover what you did, what was the goal, what is the outcome prior to elaborating on your ideas, experiences, and opinion. So, first participate, observe and then write the reflection.

4. Review regularly: This step is of much importance. Take time to read over previous journal entries and see how new experiences, additional readings, new knowledge and time have altered your thinking and feeling about the material you have been analyzing and contemplating. It will make the journal more valuable to you personally.

Reflective journal allow students to practice their writing skills in an open-minded format that encourage the same thought process that is used in analytical process. It can be supported in classrooms by creating opportunities that allows students to think about their learning, their own lives, and the world around them. The process often illuminates problems, misunderstanding, confusions and helps determine new growth, independence and responsibility for learning.

Just as reflective journal open the windows of a student's mind, they also allow teachers to look in. Thus, it can become a useful assessment tool that can give teachers additional insight into how students value their own learning and progress. Encourage students to extend, defend, debate and question their own ideas. The teacher can help the students by observing the progression of their thought and understanding by setting them rewrite or comment on earlier entries.

GRADING SYSTEM

Realising the lacunae in our examination system, a lot of thinking with deliberate efforts to bring about examination reforms has been the features of post-independence Indian education. National Curriculum Framework for School Education published by NCERT (2005) also reiterated the need for declaring results in terms of grades in place of marks. In recent years the most widely debated aspect of our innovation in evaluation is the grading system.

Grading implies classification of students into a few ability groups or categories according to their level of achievement in the examinations. The achievement can be in the form of numerical (1, 2, 3 etc.) or letter grades (A, B, C etc.). While developing the grading system, it is of utmost significance that the meaning of each grading symbol be clearly spelt out.

In education, grade is standardised evaluation of a students work. In some countries, evaluation can be expressed quantifiably, and calculated into a numeric grade point average (GPA), which is used as a metric by employees and others to assess and compare students.

The grading system in India varies somewhat as a result of being a large country. The most predominant form of grading is the percentage system. An examination consists of a number of questions each of which gives credit. The sum of credit for all questions generally counts up to 100. The grade awarded to a student is the percentage of all subjects taken in an examination awarded at the end of the year. The percentage system is used at both the levels i.e. school and university. Some universities also use the grading system and a CGPA on a 4 to 10 point scale. Notably, all the IITs, IT - BHU, NITs, IIITs, BIT Mesra, BITS Pilani (Pilani, Goa Campuses), Jawaharlal Nehru University and in most of the states technical universities follow this system. DA-IICT, Gandhinagar uses a 4 point scale, but they too have switched to a 10 point system while Symbiosis Institute of Technology still uses it. However, the grades themselves may be absolute (as in NIT, Rourkela, Durgapur, BIT Mesra), exclusively relative (as in BITS Pilani, NITS at Surathkal, NIT Warangal, NIT Calicut, NIT Trichy, Surat and Manipal University), or a combination of absolute, relative and historic, as in some NITs, ITTs, DA-IICT and IIIT-Hyderabad.

There are several recognised school boards in India which makes an objective comparison of percentage grade awards by one examination difficult with those for another, even for an examination at the same level. In recent years the system of grading has become quite popular in many Indian universities and schools. The grading system is in vogue in the United States and Canada and has now been adopted to suit the Indian conditions.

In grading system, grades instead of marks are assigned to the examinee on the basis of quality of his answer. Various grades referring to various qualities are predetermined. The overall assessment of the students is indicated in terms of O, A, B, C, D, E, F. An example will illustrate this point in which Various grades ranging from excellent to very poor are given.

	Quality	*Grades*
1.	Excellent	O
2.	Very Good	A
3.	Good	B
4.	Average	C
5.	Satisfactory/Below Average	D
6.	Poor	E
7.	Very Poor	F

From the proper evaluation of a grading system to evaluate the performance of students a number of factors or issues will have to be taken to consideration. In the first place, the question arises as to the levels of grading that will have to be used for reporting the performance of students; in the second place, the important consideration is to fix and evolve an objective and scientific criteria for awarding grades. Generally, the criteria for assigning the grades is developed around a statistical cut off point usually on the basis of numerical marking.

Performance, and due to mathematical precision, the reliability of the measure often gets lost. To overcome this shortcoming of marking system, it is suggested that students may be placed in ability bands that represent ranges of scores. Each ability band may be designated with a letter, which is called a 'grade'.

The process is as follows:

Marks → Percentage → Grade → GPA

Variations in the Grading System

- *Variation in Different Eras:* Like all prototypes, the A-F system admits many variations. These often take the form of plusses and minuses, thereby producing a scale having the possibility of fifteen distinct units: A+, A, A-, B+, B..., F-. In actual practice, the grade of A+ is scarcely ever used and the same is true for D+ and D- and F+ and F-, thereby yielding a scale of between eight to ten units. Generally speaking, the greater the number of units in the grading system the more precisely does it hope to quantify student performance. What is interesting in this regard, are fluctuations in the actual number of units used in different historical eras. Without going too deeply into the relevant historical facts, it is clear that certain historical periods, such as the 1960s, reduced the grading system to two or so units-Pass, No Credit (P/NC)-whereas other periods, such as the 1980s, expanded it to ten, eleven or twelve units.
- *Variations in Breadth:* Variations in the breadth of the grading system

would seem to have significant educational implications. At a minimum, these differences may be taken to imply that scales having a large number of units indicate a relative comfort in making precise distinctions, whereas those having fewer units suggest a relative discomfort in making such distinctions. In the case of more differentiated systems, distinctions and rankings are significant, and individual achievement is emphasised; in the case of less differentiated systems, distinctions and rankings are de-emphasised and inter-student competition is minimised. To some degree, it is possible to view fluctuations in American grading systems as reflecting a more general ambivalence the society has in regard to competition and cooperation, between individual recognition and social equity. Educational institutions sometimes emphasise strict evaluation, competition, and individual achievement, whereas at other times they emphasise less precise evaluation, cooperation, and sympathetic understanding for students of all achievement levels.

- *GPA Scale:* Another property of grading system is that individual class grades often are combined to produce an overall metric called the grade point average or GPA. Unlike its constituent values, which usually are carried to only one (or no numerically significant places), the GPA presents a metric of 400 units yielding the possibility that a GPA of 3.00 will locate the student in the category of "good" whereas a value of 2.99 will exclude him or her from this category. In the same way, however, admission to graduate school, preliminary selection for interviews by a desirable company, and so forth, may be defined by a single point difference on the GPA scale (e.g. 3.50 versus 3.49 for Phi Beta Kappa etc.).
- *Variation on the Basis of Different Courses:* Because GPAs are significant in categorising student performance, a number of evaluations have been made of their reliability and validity. One issue to be addressed here concerns field of study, where it is well documented that classes in the natural sciences and business produce lower overall grades than those in the humanities or social sciences. What this means is that it is unreasonable to equate grade values across disciplines. It also suggests that the GPA is composed of unequal components and that students may be able to secure a higher GPA by a judicious selection of courses.

Although other factors may be mentioned aside from academic discipline (such as SAT level of school, quality and nature of tests, etc.) the conclusion must be that the GPA is a poor measure and should not be used by itself in coming to significant decisions about the quality of student performance or differences between departments and/or educational institutions. The GPA is also a relatively poor basis on which to predict future performance, which perhaps explains why such attempts are never very impressive. In fact, a number of meta-analyses of this relationship, conducted every ten years or so since 1965 reveals that the median correlation between GPA and future performance is 0.18; a value that is neither very useful nor impressive. The strongest relationship between GPA and future achievement is usually found between undergraduate GPA and first-year performance in graduate or professional school.

- *Grade Inflation and Deflation:* Despite such difficulties in understanding the exact meanings of grades and the GPA, they remain important social metrics and sometimes yield heated discussions over issues such as grade inflation. Although grade inflation has many different meanings, it usually is defined by an increase in the absolute number of As and Bs over some period of years. The tacit assumption here seems to be that any continuing increase in the overall percentage of "good grades" or in the overall GPA implies a corresponding decline in academic standards. Although historically there have been periods in which the number of good grades decreased (so-called grade deflation), significant social concerns usually only accompany the grade inflation pattern. This one-sided emphasis suggests that grade inflation is as much a socio-political issue as an educational one and depends upon the dubious equating of grades with money. What really seems of concern here is a value issue, not a cogent analogy that reveals anything significant about grades or money.

Scheme of Grading in India at School Level

As a matter of fact the Board has been preparing itself and all the stakeholders for a change to move over from numerical marking systems to grading system during the past few years by creating a climate of acceptance. The Board has already in a phased manner, introduced the grading system based on absolute marks up to class VIII. Now, therefore, the CBSE, in consultation with the Ministry of Human Resource Development, Government of India has decided to introduce nine point grading system.

In this system, student's performance will be assessed using conventional numerical marking mode, and the same will be later converted into the grades on the basis of the pre-determined marks ranges as detailed below:

Students are assessed according to the following grades

Scholastic-A			*Scholastic~B*
Marks Range	*Grade*	*Grade Point*	*Grade*
91-100	A1	10.0	A+
81-90	A2	9.0	A
71-80	Bl	8.0	B+
61-70	B2	7.0	B

The Board decided to introduce the grading scheme at Secondary level for classes IX & X from the academic year 2009-10. Accordingly, the "Statement of subject-wise Performance" to be issued by the Board w.e.f. the Class X Examination 2010 will have only grades. Similarly, the schools were also directed to introduce the Grading Scheme in the evaluation of their students in Class IX under the scheme of CCE as detailed in the Circular No. 39 dated 20th September, 2009.

Methods of Grading System

There are basically two methods of grading system.

1. Direct Grading

In this method grades are allotted to questions directly on the basis of their quality. If answer written by the examine is of very fine quality almost incomparable to any other answer, it will be considered excellent and grade 'O' will be assigned to it. If the quality of the answer is very poor, F grade will be assigned to it on a seven-point scale.

If there are more than one question in a question paper say seven and each question is graded differently by the examiner, than final grade of the examinee will be calculated by using the following formula:

$$\text{Overall Grade} = \frac{\Sigma \text{ Grades}}{\text{No. of questions}}$$

An example will illustrate this point. Suppose seven questions were graded by an examiner in the following manner on a seven point scale "Find the overall grade of the examinee".

Grades allotted to different questions from first to seventh

= A, C, C, D, O, F, C

Solution.

Step-1. Numerals are assigned to different grades from 1 -7 in the following manner:

Grades	O	A	B	C	D	E	F
Numerals	7	6	5	4	3	2	1

Step II. These numbers are put below the grades in the following manner:

Assigned Grade	A	C	C	D	O	F	C
Assigned Numerals	6	4	4	3	7	1	4

Step III. These numerals are summed up and total is divided by the number of questions in the following way:

$$\frac{29}{7} \quad 4.14$$

Overall Grade = C

Merits

- It minimise the inter examiner variability.
- It is easier to use when compared with other methods of grading.

Demerits of Direct Grading

- Determination of quality of an answer is a subjective phenomenon. It lies in the mind of examiner which varies from examiner to examiner. Thus different process will grade the examinee differently.
- Even the same examiner cannot grade the same examinee in the same way because criteria of quality may change over a period of time.
- An examiner cannot judge the quality of a question with evaluating at least some considerable number of answer books of different examinees. It will take much time.
- If all the examines in the group are very poor, the exact quality of a question cannot be determined.
- The examiner compares the quality of the examinee with his own quality, if he has a high quality of response in his mind, he will evaluate the

examinee at low grade.

Thus, direct grading lacks objectivity and precisions and also diagnostic value.

2. Grading by Score Conversion

It is a mid-way approach between grading and making and thus it can remove some of the defects of both the system that is:

- It classifies the students into less number of categories and thus creates less confusion.
- Qualitative assessment which is advocated by philosophers is possible here.

In this method, answer sheets of students are first scored in usual manner, than these scores are converted into grades on the basis of the two criteria given below:

(a) Determining of Grade by Fixing Range of Scores

In this method different grades are allotted to students on the basis of range of scores for example seven point scale can be prepared in the following manner:

Grade	*Scores*
0	Above 91%
A	81%-90%
B	61%-80%
C	51%-60%
D	41%-50%
E	33%-40%
F	Below-33%

(b) Determination of Grade by Preparing Merit List of All the Students This method has been exactly adopted by CBSE in India. Answer sheets of all the students evaluated in usual manner. Then subject wise merit list of all the students are evaluated in usual manner, the students wise merit list of all students is prepared. Those students who score less than 33% in a particular subject are considered failed in that subject and they are allotted grade E. The remaining pass students in the subject are equally divided into eight sections. 12% passed students who are on the top of the merit list are allotted grade A1, next 12% students are allotted grade A2, next 12% students are allotted grade Bl and at last bottom 12% are allotted grade D2 and in this way a nine point scale, Al, A2, Bl, B2, CI, C2, Dl, D2 and E are prepared.

Types of Grading

Grading is of two types:

1. Absolute Grading
2. Comparative/Relative Grading

1. Absolute Grading: In simple words, students in different subjects, irrespective of the fact whether there is scope for higher scores, for example, in mathematics in which several students can score 100 per cent marks and in English scores are comparatively lower, students are given grades in accordance with the same yardstick. In both the subjects grading is based on the same cut-off point.

Merits

1. Negative effects of pass/fail eliminated.
2. Meaning of each grade is distinctively understandable.
3. Easy for teachers to award grades as per pre-determined range of marks.
4. No complications.
5. Students have the freedom to strive for highest possible grades.
6. Simple and straightforward.
7. Difficulties of test affect the distribution of grades.

Demerits

1. Grades may not be comparable.
2. Different categories are arbitrarily decided.
3. Distribution of marks is taken on its face value.
4. Number of students placed in different categories will differ from subject to subject and year to year.

2. Comparative Grading: Sometimes the grades awarded may be compared within and between groups. Grades are given on the basis of rank order or percentiles. For example, top 5 per cent students may be given Grade A. Grade A in one subject would be quite different from Grade B in another subject. Comparing grades awarded by a single teacher (intra-group) and by different teachers (inter-group) with reference to a larger group is considered as norm-referenced. For example, in mathematics students scoring 94 or more marks may be given Grade A in English students scoring marks between 80 and 90 may be placed in Grade A. Thus, comparative grading is preferred. It provides better comparability of scores irrespective of the scoring possibility i.e. whether a subject is scoring or non-scoring.

Merits

1. Negative effects of pass/fail eliminated.
2. It provides a more meaningful profile of the performance/achievement of a student or group.
3. The gap between scoring or non-scoring subjects is done away with for grading is not based on absolute marks but is based on rank order or percentiles.
4. Undue significance attached to marks is reduced.
5. Comparability even across auricular areas.
6. Grades can be added.
7. Difficulty of test does not affect the distribution of grades.

Demerits

1. The procedures of awarding grades is complicated.
2. Award of grades to students is not determined by their individual performance but by the performance of the group.

3. Difficult to use for teachers.

To conclude, there are various tools and techniques of evaluation which can be used by the teachers as well as other school authorities to evaluate the performance of the students in various fields. It depends on the teachers to decide about the technique according to the situation. NEP 2020 proposes to set up a National Assessment Centre, the PARAKH (Performance Assessment, Review, and Analysis of knowledge for Holistic Development), as a standard body under the Ministry of Education. Its focus on assessment and board examination reform is a step in the right direction as they play a major role in ensuring students improve academically. It recognizes the need to evaluate higher order skills indicating a shift in the focus of assessment. By emphasizing the need to redesign progress cards and board exams, it encourages testing of core competencies. The NEP'S move to prioritize assessment can make India globally competitive in education, encouraging our students to be out of box as well as in front to lead the way for the rest of the world.

15

Lesson-Planning

'Lesson must be prepared for there is nothing so fatal to a teacher's progress as unpreparedness."

Planning is undoubtedly an important aspect in all the spheres of life. If we talk about teaching then all depends on the efficiency and intelligence of the teacher how she/he plans. Teaching involves careful planning. Lesson plan is actually a plan of actions. It is the core, the heart of effective teaching. The teacher should know beforehand what to teach and how to teach. A teacher may know his subject well, may be acquainted with all methods necessary for successful teaching, may have a dynamic personality and yet may fail because he has neglected to map out the road towards the goal for which he is striving. If the teacher wants successful results in the form of all round development of personality of the child, then his teaching needs greater planning and deeper thinking.

The word 'Lesson Plan' consists of two words: 'Lesson' and 'Plan'. 'Lesson' means the subject matter which is to be taught by the teacher and 'Plan' means a set of decisions about how to do. Thus, lesson plan means outline of the important points of a lesson arranged in the systematic order in which they are to be presented to the students by the teacher. Thus, lesson planning is a plan of actions which includes the objectives, strategies, subject matter, methods of teaching and tactics for achieving the objectives of the lesson.

In the words of Bossing, "Lesson-plan is the title given to the statement of the objectives to be realised and the specific means by which these are attained as a result of activities engaged during the period."

According to Department of Education, NCERT (1974), "A lesson plan is a verbal statement of the utilizations of education theory content and techniques or devices of teaching to achieve the state purpose of schooling, both general and specific. It is a device to help children learn creatively and thoroughly.

In the words of Bining and Bining, "Daily lesson planning involves defining the objectives, selecting and arranging the subject matter and determining the methods and procedure."

Thus, we can say that lesson plan:

- is a blue print
- is guide map for action
- is a comprehensive chart of classroom teaching
- is a creative piece of work
- is the teacher's mental and emotional visualisation of the classroom experiences

- is the means for evaluating the results of teaching
- is the sum of procedures and activities to be done by students and teacher.

Importance/Merits/Advantages of Lesson Planning

1. It makes lesson interesting and simple through selecting the relevant methods, devices and strategies in advance.
2. It delimits the field of work of the teacher as well as of the students and provides a definite objective for each day's work.
3. It helps in managing teaching material in a proper manner.
4. It helps in developing reasoning power and imagination power in the evaluation in the form of feedback.
5. It enables the teacher to prepare pivotal questions and illustration.
6. It provides opportunities for an adequate checking of the outcomes of instructions.
7. It ensures a proper connection of new lesson with the previous lesson.
8. It makes the teacher more competent in dealing with various difficulties and problems of students in the class.
9. It helps the teacher to correlate various aspects of the subject matter in the class.
10. It helps to save time and energy of both teacher and students.
11. It develops confidence among the teachers to face the class.
12. It helps to avoid needless repetition.
13. In enables the teacher to know how to establish the situation with reinforcement.
14. It helps in developing certain possibilities of the students and particularly in terms of their desired behavioural outcomes.
15. It helps to motivate the students systematically because the teacher keeps in mind the individual differences of the pupils.

Precautions while Preparing the Lesson-Plan

A commerce teacher should keep in mind the following points while preparing a successful lesson plan:

1. A lesson plan should preferably be written.
2. It should clearly state the objectives, general and specific, to be achieved.
3. The commerce teacher should have proficiency or mastery over the subject matter.
4. The teacher should plan his teaching work according to the needs, interests, aptitude and attitude of the pupils.
5. The teacher should frame thought-provoking questions, which will stimulate the students to think independently and develop habits of critical thinking.
6. The teacher should try to coordinate between the time duration of the lesson and the subject matter to be taught.
7. It should be linked with the previous knowledge of the students.
8. There must be enough place of assignments in the lesson plan.

9. It should be flexible because it is a means not an and.
10. The pupils must be given enough space to be active.
11. It should refer to the reference material because this will motivate the bright students to do extra reading.

Types of Lesson

Human personality has three distinctive features i.e., head, heart and hand. For all round development of personality these aspects are to be given foremost importance in commerce. For this purpose the curriculum has to be developed to provide such activities which are related to head, heart and hand.

The functions of head relates with mind, the heart's function with feeling and the hand's function is action. Hence, head gains knowledge, heart deals with emotions and feeling and the function is appreciation and hands are always involved in activity.

The following diagram given below explains the idea:

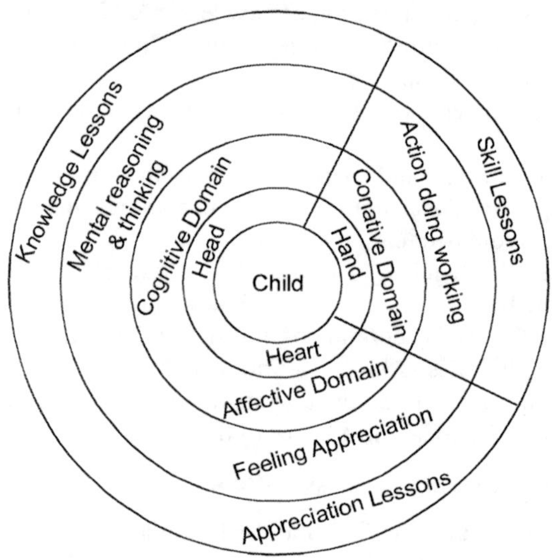

Fig. 14.1: Types of Lessons

There are three type of lessons:

(*a*) *Knowledge Lesson:* Lessons where acquisition of information is required for example learning of business studies, taxation, banking, etc.

(*b*) *Skill Lesson:* A lesson which provides an opportunity of specific activity e.g. writing, drawing of maps and diagrams, etc.

(*c*) *Appreciation Lesson:* Lesson in which the child gets training in aesthetics or development of taste e.g. learning poetry, enjoying music, etc.

Procedure in Planning the Lesson

Many elaborate plans have been set up but they all have these three procedures essential as a basis:

1. Defining and stating the aims and objectives.

2. Selecting and arranging the subject matter.
3. Determining the methods of teaching.

1. Aims and Objectives: In all planning, the dominate note must be objectives. The teacher must bear in mind that there is a hiearchy of objectives, among which there must be no contradiction. This hierachy extends from the generals and proceeds to the specific. It includes:

(*a*) The general objectives of the educational process.
(*b*) The subject objectives.
(*c*) The unit objectives.
(*d*) The specific/behavioural objectives for the daily lesson.

(*a*) *General Objectives:* The general objectives of education have been recommended by different commissions and committees in their reports. The commerce teacher must formulate all his objectives in harmony with these general objectives of education because commerce is a part of education which leads to social, economic and civic development of the child.

(*b*) *Subject Objectives:* These are of vital concern to the teacher. He needs to find out why he is teaching commerce. With the general goal of education in mind, the teacher may well ask himself at the close of the year what advancement his pupils have made towards these goals by learning the subject.

(*c*) *Unit Objectives:* The teacher is more vitally concerned with unit objectives, because it is he who must formulate the objectives for the units of subject matter. The teacher must know his purpose in teaching the unit. He must see that his purpose is in harmony with the objectives of the subject.

(*d*) *The Specific Objectives of the Daily Lesson:* The specific teaching objectives concerns with what the teacher expects to achieve during the class period. He should have a definite end in view as to what he expects to accomplish each day. For example, he may set up the objectives to have the pupils understand the chief causes of nationalising the banks in India. All his efforts then been bent to the task that the pupils may, at the close of the lesson, have an understanding of these causes. These objective should be in harmony with the objectives of the unit. Now a days it has been felt that these objectives should be framed in behavioural terms as suggested by Bloom, Mason and Simpson. In this relation Atkin suggested that, "Higher order objectives are best pursued whenever the opportunity arises rather than according lead to the discussion of some significant problem or issue, the teacher may see the opportunity for pursuing objectives whose introduction might have second artificial or non-productive if the teacher initiated them."

The pupil's aim is a matter of motivation. It is unwise for a teacher to think that he can set up aim for the pupils without motivation and then expect the pupil to accept it as his own. It is the teacher's task to motivate the work and develop interest, so that the pupils will desire to take up the problem as their own. Such motivation is the greatest objective, on the part of the teacher to accomplish in the art of teaching.

Thus, there should be harmony between all these objectives and a teacher can't get success and unable to evaluate his teaching without proper aims and objectives.

2. Selecting and Arranging the Subject Matter: Selection of material requires careful discrimination in all the branches related to commerce. The material should not be included in the lesson that does not contribute to the aim. On the other hand, teacher must take care in the use of text book. The material of the text book must be regarded as subject matter to be used in the light of specific aims, not as something to be closely followed. Regarding the arranging of subject matter, much has been said by many writers about the psychological order as opposed to the logical. It means that the material should be arranged in terms of the learner's experience, rather in terms of the subject itself. This idea was advocated as early as in the eighteenth century by Rousseau in his Emile. But later on Herbart favours logical order. It is therefore essential while teaching commerce not to ignore the logical arrangements of subject matter, but it is necessary to base that arrangement on the experience of the pupil.

3. Determining the Methods of Teaching: To accomplish the aims of topic it is essential to select the proper method and device of teaching. The teacher may use the combination of different methods as lecture method, discussion method, etc., and device as blackboard, map making, illustrations while teaching. It is essential that the teacher should know how he is going to proceed during the class teaching, but if the actual situation demands the deviations from the set plan, he should also be prepared for that with possible disastrous results.

The other steps to be followed in general/daily lesson plans are:

(i) Teaching Aids: Different teaching aids are to be utilized to make the subject matter interesting and learnable.

(ii) Previous Knowledge of the Child: Before starting the topic teacher should know about the previous knowledge of the students so that he/she may correlate it with the new knowledge or topic of the lesson.

(iii) Introduction: In this step, the pervious knowledge of the students is tested with the help of different questions.

(iv) Statement of Aim: The teacher gives statement related to the topic i.e., today we shall study............... (the name of the topic). After it, the topic is written on the chalkboard.

(v) Presentation: Different formats may be used but the most popular one is:

Teaching Points	*Teaching-Learning Activities*		*Chalk Board Work*
	Teacher's Activities	*Pupils' Activities*	

The format can be different from the point of view of the organisation of content, the steps remains the same:

Teaching Points: The content of the topic is divided into small parts and each part is treated as teaching point.

Teacher's Activities: These refer to the teacher's statements, developmental questions, demonstrations, experiments, illustrations, narration and other activities performed by the teacher.

Student's Activities: These refer to the activities as listening, writing watching, giving responses, etc., performed by the student in the classroom.

Chalkboard Work: It is to be developed with the help of the students. The teacher writes the main points, definitions and draw diagrams.

(vi) Evaluation: After completing the topic, the teacher evaluates the knowledge gained by the students. It may be in the form of written or oral. Short answer questions should be asked and objective type questions are best for the evaluation.

(vii) Generalization: After completing the topic, teacher generalise the subject matter in three to four lines what they have studied today.

(viii) Home Work: It should be based on the knowledge, understanding, skill and application.

Sufficient margin should be provided for supervisor's remarks.

Approaches to Lesson Planning

1. Herbartian Approach

German philosopher and educationist John Fredrick Herbart (1776-1841) developed a psychological procedure in the field of lesson planning. He and his disciples Ziller, Ryan and others have emphasized the following five steps for planning a lesson which are still preferred by many:

(*a*) *Preparation:* According to Herbart, the mind of the child must be prepared to receive new knowledge. During this step, the teacher tried to arouse curiosity in the students by asking the questions based on knowledge previously acquired. It is just like preparing the land before sowing the seed.

Content: The content of the preparation is previous knowledge and so it would contain no new knowledge. It might be recapitulation or a previous lesson's salient points. It may be on correlated topics from other subjects. It may belong to the pupil's interest of a homely nature. It may be concerned with daily life affairs.

Form: The form of the preparation is by questions and answers. It should be completely of pupil's work and so he must be guided to bring out his apperception masses by well directed questions from the teacher.

Time: The time spent on this step should be very brief. In a nutshell, preparation has two parts:

(*i*) Testing the previous knowledge of the students.

(*ii*) Announcement of the aim of the lesson in hand to the students.

In the words of J. Welkon we can say, "To know where the pupils are and where they should try to be are the first two essentials of good teaching."

(*b*) *Presentation:* This step involves a great deal of mental activity on the part of the students as well as teachers. The teacher wants that the students should grasp and understand the new knowledge fully and intelligently. New knowledge is to be joined to the old. This step is characterised by vividness, emphasis, repetition and interest. There are varieties of presentation *i.e.* telling, lecturing, narration, demonstration etc. The teacher should keep in mind the following principles:

(*i*) *Principle of successive clearness:* Sequential and successive clearness must be strictly adhered to. All sections of presentation should be well connected.

(*ii*) *Principle of Absorption and Integration:* Each section or item of new knowledge or material at first should be exclusively attended to.

(*iii*) *Principle of Selection and Division:* The teacher should give priority to two questions: they are:

1. What is to be presented?
2. How much is to be presented?

The students and teacher participation is to be decided by the teacher.

(*c*) *Association and Comparison:* At this stage, the new ideas or knowledge to be learnt is to be compared and associated with already known ideas and facts. The mind does not stag in details. It wants to make uniformities out of variety and thus to arrive at law, principles, generalizations or universal truth.

The teacher's part at this step is to arouse interest, afford the people with opportunities for gaining experiences and associating new facts with old knowledge. It is felt that knowledge is not like piling up bricks. It is like a tree that grows. Through the creative process something new is made or discovered by the pupils themselves.

Association or comparison is sometimes not considered as a separate step, but a part of presentation. Its significance is in making correlation between the old and new.

(*d*) *Generalization:* In this step, the teacher further involves the student to understand the learning of material properly. The teacher uses the inductive process to come to the generalization. The teacher should not be impatient to save children from the trouble of thinking. The formulation should be the work of the students, the teacher is only to make it exact.

Generalization is of little value to the children if it is not the product of their own thinking, reflection or experience. Therefore, the teacher is to remain in the background at this step.

(*e*) *Application:* The mind moves from particular to general, from general back to particular. We have at this step, reached to the universal from the individual, now we shall have to apply the universal again to individuals if we want to make it clear to our mind and be in a position to use it. It is always the desire of the pupils to make use of generalization because unless a general truth had been earned it does not become permanent possession, unless it is applied it never becomes part of our intellectual store.

Knowledge is for use and this step puts it into vital connection with the needs of daily life. Here knowledge becomes clear and meaningful. In commerce, the question of application arises only in those cases where the pupils are required to prepare an income tax chart, enquiry into the ethics of running business through questionnaire, etc.

Hence, by application we secure the activity of the pupils and we know that knowledge is power only when it is put to use. It consolidates the knowledge psychologically, because the knowledge learnt is applied to similar situations.

Application is a means of ensuring knowledge and understanding, knowledge becomes a part and parcel of the mental make-up when it is put to use and verified.

Merits of Herbart Approach of Lesson-Planning

The Herbartian approach is utillized in making lesson plans because of the following merits:

1. It is useful for achieving the cognitive objectives of teaching.
2. It employs the synthesis of inductive and deductive methods of teaching.
3. It is the simplest and easy approach of lesson-planning.
4. It uses the previous knowledge of the students for imparting new knowledge.
5. It is logical and psychological. It incorporates principles of learning in a psychological way.
6. It is useful in teaching all the branches of commerce.

Demerits/Limitations of Herbart Approach of Lesson-Planning

Although it is the most popular approach of lesson planning, yet, it has certain demerits and limitations as follows:

1. It is highly loaded by *cognitive objectives* and ignores *affective* and *psychomotor objectives*. It is suitable only for knowledge lessons and not for skill and appreciation. Comparison and generalization are not needed in it.
2. It does not consider the *learning structure* in organizing teaching activities. It does not provide opportunities to the students for self-motivation, initiation and discussion while teaching.
3. The teaching activities are less *meaningful*. The lesson becomes stereotyped, students get bored and lose their interest.
4. It confines the teaching up to *memory level* only. It speaks of passivity on the part of the learning process.
5. It is *highly structured* and does not provide opportunities for teacher's creativity and originality.
6. It deals with comparison or association as a separate step, whereas it is throughout in the presentation stage. It is mere repetition.
7. It is teacher-centered approach.
8. It is very difficult to establish generalistions.
9. It is not applicable to all lessons.

A.E. Griffin matter evaluate this approach as, "Herbartian techniques are quite enough to convert a highly motivated youngsters into a first class technician, book keeper, accountant, secretary or minor executive, carrying out with skill and intelligence the plans or instructions. But they are not good enough to develop real scientist or map policy making executive or anything else that requires the independent judgement of a free and inquiring mind."

2. Morrison's Approach of Lesson Planning (Unit Planning)

Dr. H.C. Morrison (1871-1945) of Chicago University is the exponent of this approach. It is known as unit approach because this approach is based on the unit method for planning the teaching-learning process.

In the words of Morrison, "Unit is a comprehension and significant aspect of the environment of an organised science and art."

Dr. Morrison provides five steps for the lesson planning as follows:

1. Exploration
2. Presentation
3. Assimilation
4. Organisation
5. Recitation

1. Exploration: This step is concerned with exploring the entering behaviour of the students. The teacher is required to establish the behaviour repertoire by linking the new knowledge with the previous knowledge of the students through questioning or discussion, etc.

2. Presentation: This step is concerned with providing new experiences to the learners. It includes an analysis and presentation of the learning material in a logical sequence by encouraging students' participation in teaching.

3. Assimilation: This step is concerned with the creation of motivational situation to facilitate learning. It provides an opportunity to the students for practice which enables them to retain longer what is learnt.

4. Organisation: This step involves giving assignments to the students to organise the subject matter in a logical and systematic order at their own which will show the understanding of the unit.

5. Recitation: In this step, the teacher gives the time to the students to recite the learned material *i.e.* to test that to what extent student have grasped the content and developed meaningful behaviours.

Merit of the Unit Approach

The advantage of unit approach of lesson planning are as follows:

1. It facilitates the management of learning. It aims at the complete mastery over the learning material presented in a particular unit.
2. The content of the syllabus is divided into units and sub-units, so it is based on psychological approach.
3. The teaching learning process becomes easy, simple and interesting.
4. It encourages the habit of self-study among students.
5. It provides opportunities for healthy interaction between teacher and students.
6. It does not confine the teaching up to memory level but it also incorporates understanding level.
7. The assimilation, understanding and mastery of a unit motivates the students to learn the next teaching or learning units.
8. As the sequence of learning activities, and the related learning materials to be used, is listed in the unit, so, it simplifies the lesson planning also.

Limitations of Unit Approach

1. Preparation/planning of unit is not an easy task.
2. There is lack of freshness.
3. Over burdening of teacher with written work.
4. It is time consuming process.

5. Teaching becomes mechanical.

In daily lesson planning, the students may not have a sense of accomplishment in terms of true learning as the same can't be tested, but at the end of an instructional unit in teaching of commerce, the students can judge the accomplishment.

A unit plan is similar to a daily lesson-plan in many ways. Objectives give direction to its organisation and sequence. A unit plan has five sections namely – *Introduction, objectives, contents, hints for teachers* and *evaluation.*

It is different from daily lesson plan because it is more extensive. Its objectives have a wider scope.

Essential Features of Unit Plan

A good unit should answer some questions like:

- Why i.e. objectives.
- What i.e. content.
- How i.e. methods, techniques of teaching.
- With what i.e. Material needed.
- How will i.e. Evaluation Process.

Format of Unit Plan

Class ____________

Subject ____________

Name of the Unit ____________

No. of Periods required for the unit ____________

Sub Units	*Teaching Points*	*Behavioural Objectives*	*Teaching Learning Situations*	*Teaching Aids*	*Evaluation*	*Home Assignments*

3. Evaluation Approach of Lesson Planning

Dr. Benjamin S. Bloom believes that education is a tripolar process which involves educational objectives, learning experiences and change in behaviour as:

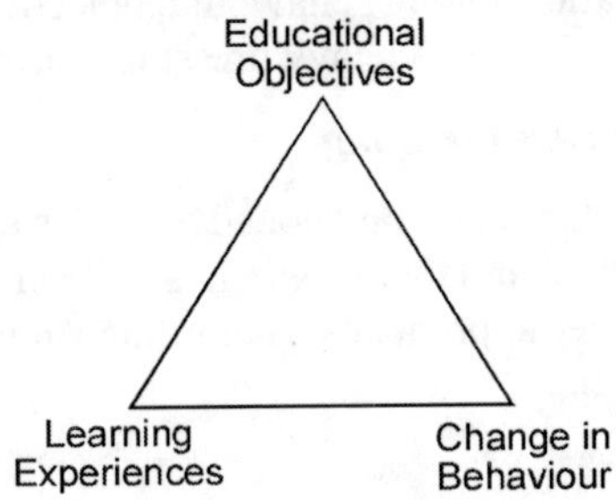

This approach includes all the activities of teaching and evaluates the performance of pupils in the terms of learning objectives. This approach is called 'objective centred' rather than 'content centred' because it includes learning outcomes in terms of cognitive, affective and psychomotor objectives.

It involves three steps for the lesson planning as:

Step I – Formulation of Objectives

The first step is to formulate the objectives in relation to the entering behaviour, desired behavioural changes and learning experiences to be presented to the pupils.

Step II – Providing Learning Experiences

This step is concerned with provision to generate suitable learning environment, so that, objectives can be achieved easily. It includes teacher's activities as lecturing, demonstration (knowledge objective), question-answer, discussion (understanding objective), interaction, tutorial, project (Application objective), problem solving method (creativity / skill objective) and pupils' activities.

Step III – Evaluation

In this step the teacher uses different evaluation techniques or devices to find out the extent to which stipulated objectives have been realised and the effectiveness of the learning experiences.

Merits

1. It is based on psychological principles of teaching and learning.
2. It lays stress on the evaluation of the desired behavioural changes.
3. It is helpful to modify and improve the student' and teacher's activities.
4. It is based on providing purposeful teaching.
5. It is objective centred.

Limitations

1. It is a highly structured approach and dominated by the role of the teacher in the teaching learning process or we may say it is teacher centred approach.
2. It provides no freedom to teacher and students.
3. Lesson plan work is more rigid and mechanical.
4. The task of integration among behavioural objectives, learning experiences and evaluation devices puts heavy pressure on teachers and the students.

4. RCEM Approach of Lesson Planning

RCEM approach of lesson planning is developed by Indian educationists at Regional College of Education, Mysore and that is why it is called RCEM approach. It is an improvement over the earlier approaches. According to this approach, the lesson plan consists of three aspects:

1. Input
2. Process

3. Output

1. Input: It includes the identification and specification of objectives. They are known as Expected Behavioural Outcomes. These are classified into four broad categories as explained in the chapter of writing instructional objectives in behavioural terms as – knowledge, under-standing, application and creativity. These objectives are written in behavioural terms by employing 17 mental abilities. The entering behaviour of the learners are also identified. The instructional process is determined by these objectives.

2. Process: The process is concerned with the presentation of the subject matter. Different strategies and methods are used for the effective presentations. It also includes the interaction of teacher and students. The opportunities are provided for the maximum participation of the students. It includes use of audio-visual aids, techniques of motivation, ways of securing suitable classroom interaction, etc. for the attainment of stipulated objectives.

3. Output: This aspect includes the *Real Learning outcome* (RLO). In the aspect of process, learning experiences are provided for the desirable behavioural change among the students. That change in behaviour is known as real learning outcome. That can be known with the help of various devices of evaluation as objective test, oral test, essay type test, etc. It is an evaluation phase of the lesson plan.

5. Constructivist Lesson Plan

Constructivist lesson plan is based on the theory of constructivism, which was originated by Jean Piaget. He believed young children learn by doing, constructing knowledge from experiences rather by telling them by an adult about their world. In this the teacher provides learning experiences for students and give students the opportunities to think through problems and find solutions.

Features

- The teacher and the students interact.
- The focus shifts from teacher to students in an effort to enhance thinking.
- The students can work in groups as well as individually.
- Learning is not set on specified time frame.
- The format is one that goes beyond structure and more hands on approach.
- The teacher is the leader but the students also remain as active participants.
- Student's mistakes are seen as opportunities to tailor learning.

Thus, the purpose of a constructivist learning is for the students to acquire knowledge and create an understanding on their own, with the guidance of the teacher.

Elements: The constructivist lesson plan uses six basic elements to come up with a strategy of how the learning process will occur:

Situation: In this plan the teacher tries to create a situation in front of the students. There must be a title, problem solving, answering of questions, conclusion drawing, and goal setting, all centered around how the student is going to come up with their own understanding.

Grouping: In this phase, the students can be grouped in teams, or they can work individually or with their peer group. The other part deals with the material and how the groups will use the material for explanation and event.

Bridge: The teacher is to form a bridge between the prior understanding of the students and the new knowledge which is required to provide them. For this teacher can plan any activity like game etc.

Question: In this the teacher is to engage the student in teaching learning process. The questioning can be used as prompts to continue engaging.

Exhibit: In this phase the students are to exhibit themselves. It is similar to a show and tell the students to remain active in the phase.

Reflection: In the last phase, reflection will be there where thinking and thoughts are emphasized. The students can look back on what was learned and the teacher can look back on what was taught.

Thus, in this plan the role of the student and the teacher are always changing to bring about learning. Encouragement, engagement, and active participation are all essential in the constructivist lesson plan. Active sharing of information is involved during the teaching learning process. The teacher is merely guiding the thoughts of the student to bring about learning and understanding.

5E's Model of Constructivist Lesson Plan

Today, all over the world, while teaching commerce, it is targeting to have student's gain the qualification as creativity, team work, cooperation, criticism, time management and introducing an idea. Today, modern teaching approaches are fictionalized on how students get information and how these are utilized practically by them.

5E model is compatible with constructive learning approach based on educational theorists John Dewey and Jean Piaget. Picture young children in a sand box. As they scoop and shovel sand in a bucket, they are learning how much sand it takes to fill the bucket. Compare that to a teacher telling students, 'seven scoops of sand will fill the bucket. Which do you think will be long lasting and more important?

5E's model of constructivism is given by Roger W. Bybee and Joseph A. Taylor. It helps in enriching the curiosity of the learners. The levels of the model are as follows:

1. *Engage:* It is the first level. During this level the teacher will not provide any information to the students. This level provides opportunity for the teacher to discover what student's know or what they think they know. The teacher creates interest, generates curiosity, raises questions and elicit responses that uncover what the students know or think about the topic/concept with the help of brainstorming, demonstration, reading, analyzing a graphic organizer etc. The student make connections between past and present learning experiences, lay the organizational ground work for the activities ahead and stimulate their involvement in the anticipation of these activities.

2. *Explore:* The purpose of this level is to provide common set of experiences as well as a broad range of experiences. The teacher acts as a facilitator, encourage the students to work together without any direct instruction, observes and listens to

the students as they interact, asks probing questions to redirect the students' investigations when necessary, and provides time to the students to puzzle through problems. The students can be involved in different activities to explore as read authentic resources to collect information, solve a problem, construct a model etc. They think freely but within the limits of the activity, records observation and ideas, suspend judgement, test predictions and hypotheses. They can try alternative and discuss them with others. Thus, the students inquiry process drives the instruction during an exploration.

3. *Explain:* This level provides opportunities for students to connect their previous experiences and to begin to make conceptual sense of the main idea within the unit of study. The teacher encourages the students to explain concepts and definitions in their own words, and asks for justification and clarification from students. This level also provides opportunities for teachers to demonstrate formal terms, definition and explanations for concepts, processes, skills or behaviour. The teacher uses students' previous experiences as basis for explaining concepts. While working in groups, learners support each other's understanding as they articulate their observations, ideas, questions and hypotheses. Created works as writing, drawing, videos, are communication that provide recorded evidence of the learner's development, progress and growth. Language enhances the sharing and communication between facilitator and students.

4. *Extend/Elaborate:* In this level, students apply or extend the concepts in new situations and relate their previous experience with new ones. This level allows the student to practice skill and behaviour. Through new experience, the learners develop deeper understanding of major concepts, obtain more information about areas of interest and refine their skills. The teacher expects the students to use formal labels, definitions and explanations provided previously, encourages the students to apply or to defend the concepts and skills in new situations, reminds them of alternative explanation, refers them to existing date and evidences and asks what do you already know? What do you think....? On the other hand, students use previous information to ask questions, propose solutions, make decisions and design experiments. They can draw reasonable conclusions from evidences.

5. *Evaluate:* The fifth 'E' is an ongoing diagnostic process that allows the teacher to determine whether the learner has attained understanding of concepts and knowledge. Evaluation of students' conceptual understanding and ability to use skills begins at the first level. The teacher observes the students as they apply new skills and concepts, assesses students' knowledge and skills, looks for evidence that the students have changed their thinking or behaviour, allows students to assess their learning and group-process skills and asks open-ended questions as why do you think......? What evidence do you have? Different tools for assessment can be used as rubric, performance assessment, observation, product evaluation, formal entry portfolio, etc.

After evaluation, the teacher can fill the gaps in information and make everything clear. Thus with the help of this model the students are prevented to memorize the subject matter. It can be called a value added model also.

6. NTeQ Model of Lesson Planning

The i**N**tegrating **T**echnology for in**Q**uiry (NTeQ) mode provides a framework for creating an environment for students to use computers as tools to build a study educational background while solving meaningful problems. It was developed by Morrison and Lowther in 2010. By using the computer, students not only learn lesson objectives, but also develop real-life knowledge and skills. In the modern age classroom teachers are bombarded with technological advances that can complement or inhibit instructions. Educators should have an understanding of technology supports higher order thinking which includes Bloom's taxonomy, critical thinking, creative thinking and metacognition. This higher order thinking is the backstory for the NTeQ lesson design. The instructor design is student oriented means that students are empowered and take on the role of a researcher whereas the teachers assume the role of designer, manager and facilitator. It includes the following steps:

Specific objectives → Computer functions → Specify problems → Date manipulations → Results presentation
↓
Assessment ← Support activity ← Activities after computer use ← Activities before computer use ← Activities during computer use

Fig.: NTeQ Lesson Plan Model Ten Step Approach

(a) *Specific Objectives:* While framing the objectives we should cover all the constructions for the unit or lesson. It should not include only the information related to the computer components. Example:

The students will produce a power point presentation explaining various elements of an industry. It will include information on the industry's production function, produce, administrative process etc.

(b) *Computer functions:* If we are to create a successful integrated computer lesson, we must find a match between the lesson's objectives and one or more computer functions as use industry.

We can include power point, microsoft publishers as computer functions.

(c) *Specify problems:* In this step the teacher will specify the problems that the students will investigate solve as part of the educational process. Thinking skills of the students will be developed and the students will gain the knowledge specified in the objectives as well students this week, we are going to research different industries producing cars in India. You will need to discover different elements of the industries. You will create a Power Point presentation to present in the class the elements of different industries.

(d) *Data Manipulation:* In this step the students will learn to manipulate the data. It is directly related to the computer functions and the objectives. For example: The students will use appropriate search engines, print information, save pictures, create slides, insert pictures and sound, use clip art etc.

(e) *Results Presentation:* The students will decide about the type of product they will use to illustrate the achieved objectives as written report presentation, poster, artwork. The students will present report in front of the other students.

(f) *Activities during computer use:* The teacher will determine what the students will do while doing work at the computer. Firstly, we should identify the activities in which the students will remain engaged while using the computer as for the project you must use at least two websites, find graphs for Power Point, create informational Power Point.

(g) *Activities before computer use:* One the teacher decides about the activities the students will do while using the computer then he/she can focus on the activities they must complete before using the computer. For example: Use print resources to locate as much information as possible about assigned industries, write the information for each slide on Power Point.

(h) *Activities after Computer Use:* In this step, the activities showed focus on exploring the results obtained while using the computer. If the students have analysed the results of a study, their neat focus should be on interpreting or explaining the results. For example: Interpret the articles in a written report, present the report in front of the students, listen and evaluate the report of other students.

(i) *Supporting Activities:* After the decision about the computer activities, the teacher should also focus on the supporting activities that will help the students in the achivement of objectives, but however computer independent. For example: create a model of the assigned industry; bring in something that relates to the industry to be used during the presentation, bring videotapes.

(j) *Assessment:* The final step of this model is the development of assessment strategies for the assigned task. However, assessment to be meaningful has to be related with stated objectives and has to go beyond paper and pencil type test, emphasizing authenticity in the form of portfolio and rubric. A portfolio shows overt evidence of knowledge acquired because it can be seen and felt. In the same way, a rubric provides criteria for measuring outcomes and proving feedback. In this model the assessment should not encourage role memorization and perhaps guess work.

Thus NTeQ model is a technology driven model as the users of the model have to be computer literate. It can be adjudged as providing ICT integration in our school system. We cannot be lagging behind in basic ICT competencies in an era that ICT ifself has revolutionised the world and her operation. The teacher and the learner should be ICT savry or fluent to be able to tap into the rich potential of the model. The model is student centred, goal oriented, focus on meaningful performance, measurement of outcomes in reliable and valid ways, interactive, self-correcting and advocate team effort.

7. Eclectic Approach of Lesson Planning

It should be remembered that planning cannot be a stereotyped affair in commerce. What has been said is suggestive rather than final. It might become monotonous to follow a similar play day after day. Herbartian approach is limited to the realisation of the cognitive objectives and is hardly feasible in skill and appreciation objectives. Evaluation (RCEM) approach has a wider scope. But both the approaches are teacher centred. Evaluation approach is based upon psychological principles of learning but it is very difficult to follow in the normal classroom set up. It needs expert teachers. However, in school careful and detailed daily lesson planning is necessary for every teacher. The teacher should follow the harmonious blending of all the approaches as far as possible. The important and fruitful point that a teacher should keep in mind that he should follow an approach in which her/his students become active participants in the teaching learning process.

8. Lesson Planning Based on Skills (Micro Plan)

Micro teaching is one of the most important development in the field of teaching practice. It is like a simulated social skill teaching to provide the feedback to teacher trainee for the modification of teacher behaviour. It provides training regarding different teaching skill in which the normal complexities of classroom are reduced and in which the teacher gets feedback on the performance. In it teacher teaches a small unit to a group of 5 to 10 students for a small period of 5 to 10 minutes and one teaching skill is practised during the teaching. It is completely different from daily lesson plan. It provides an opportunity to practise one teaching skill at a time and with information about their performance immediately after completion of their lesson. Its focus is to develop certain teaching skill and not the development of pupils abilities. It is highly individualized plan. These lesson plans are very small in comparison to daily lesson plan. Following points should be kept in mind while preparing the micro lesson plan.

1. Specific Objectives: The objective of micro lesson plan is not to teach the subject matter, but a coordinated practice of one or two skills at a time. Its focus is to develop certain teaching skill.

2. Selection of the Subject Matter: The subject matter is selected on the basis of the skill, which is to be practised. An example of the skill of illustration with examples is to be used then such type of matter will be selected in which there will be maximum use of illustration, so that it can be practised completely. Inspite of this it also has to be kept in mind that so much subject matter should be selected that will be completed in time as well as all the components should be used.

3. Planning for Re-practice: After the teaching of micro-lesson, the observer gives his feedback and keeping in mind that the same skill is to be re-planned for different subject matter. The suggestions given in the feedback find place in it and as a result the pupil teacher will gain mastery in one skill.

4. Simulated Conditions: In micro teaching peers should act as pupils. There is no need of school students.

Thus, micro teaching helps in build up confidence step by step, provides continuous reinforcement to the teacher trainee performance and improves his teaching behaviour. A good micro lesson plan prepares the way for a good mega lesson plan. The main limitation of this type of practice is that the main emphasis is on learning teaching skills – the content which forms the most important component of the teaching learning process, is not paid adequate attention.

MICRO LESSON PLAN – 1

Name	:	Roll No.	:
Subject	: Commerce	Class	: XI
Topic	: Communication and Its Process	Skill	: Narration

Teaching Aids: Chalklboard, chalk, duster, charts.

Introductory Statements:

Pupil Teacher: What is important to establish proper relation among the works of various individuals.

Pupil: Exchange of ideas.

Pupil Teacher: How is it possible?

Pupil: By telling, listening and understanding.

Pupil Teacher: Well students, placing our ideas before others by telling, listening and understanding is called communication. Today we shall study about communication. (Write down in your notebook). The word communication has been derived from latin word 'communis' which means 'common' (use of chalkboard) meaning there by common among to or more than two people, in equal measure. (Change in voice). In this way communication means sharing thoughts among two or more than two people (movement). Thus, under communication the sharing of thought among different people is done in such a manner that the listener is receiving them in the same spirit with which they are being told. (Change in form of speech)

Now write down (Narrate), In the words of Newman and Summer, "communication is an exchange of facts, ideas, opinions or emotions by two or more persons." Two things come out about communication (change in gesture). Firstly the exchange of facts, ideas, opinions or emotions and secondly the receiver should receive in the same spirit with which they are being communicated to him (movement). Communication is a circular process which means that there are various steps one after the other (showing on the chart)

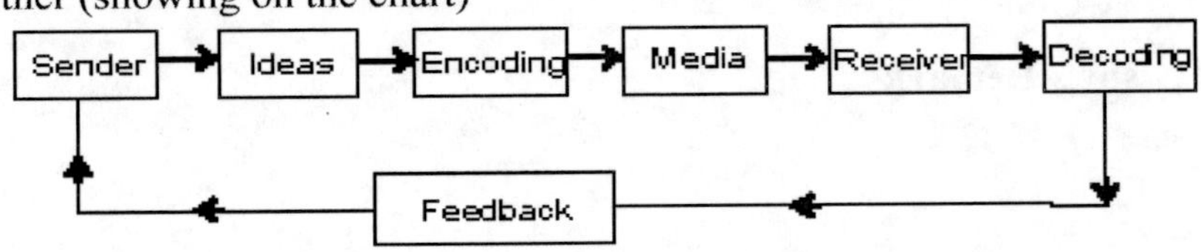

For example—manager acts as a sender. He wants to convey information of ordering to supply some material. This is an idea. When idea is expressed in words, is known as encoding. If message is sent by using telephone then telephone is a media. Call attandent is receiver when the receiver try to understand the message in detail, his effort is called decoding, whether message received correctly or not, the sender wants to confrm. This effort to know is called feedback. It is business organisation, no work can be accomplished without completing the process of communication (change in voice)

The above process makes it clear that communication is a process of imparting ideas and making one self clear understood by others. Now, I ask some questions:

Pupil Teacher's Activities	**Pupils' Activities**
What does the word 'communis' mean?	The word 'communis' mean 'common'.
What is communication?	Communication is a circular process of exchanging ideas, facts and information.
What is Encoding?	Expressing ideas, facts and information in words is called encoding.

Observation Schedule:

Components	**Rating scale**				
Use of Introductory statement	0	1	2	3	4
Use of suitable language	0	1	2	3	4
Change in form of speech	0	1	2	3	4
Change in Voice	0	1	2	3	4
Use of gesture	0	1	2	3	4
Continuity in narration	0	1	2	3	4
Movement in the class	0	1	2	3	4
Use of visual technique	0	1	2	3	4

Rating Scale:

0 → Not Satisfactory
1 → Satisfactory
2 → Average
3 → Good
4 → V-Good

Supervisor's Remarks

MICRO LESSON PLAN – 2

Name :
Subject : Commerce
Topic : Social Responsibility of Business
Roll No.:
Class : XI
Skill : Probing Questions

Teaching Aids: Chalkboard, Chalk, Duster

Pupil Teacher's Activities	Pupils' Activities	Components
What is Responsibility?	Doing One's duty.	Prompting
What is social Responsibility?	It means responsibility towards society.	Seeking further information
What is social responsibility of business?	It means the satisfaction of various groups along with the owner.	Seeking futher information
What are the various groups of society?	Owners, employees consumers, suppliers competitors, Government, community, world.	Seeking furher information
What are the social responsibility towards Government?	To pay taxes and observe government rules.	Seeking further information
Was there any other responsibility towards Government?		Prompting
Tell seema	To establish new industries and help the government in economic development.	Redirecting
Why is it necessary to take care of social responsibility towards govt?	It is necessary to avoid excessive Govt. Interference.	Increasing critical awareness
Tell me, what happens when business is not responsible for employees?	Employees are not satisfed and create problem of industrial disputes.	Prompting
In what way, they are satisfed?	To pay proper salary to give a share of profit to provide clean work atmosphere to fulfll their needs.	Refocusing
What should a business do to increase its proft?	To make available good quality goods at cheaprates to bring out reality in advertisement etc.	Prompting
What should be done by a businessman to satisfy customers?	No response	Refocusing
What are the responsibilities of a business towards world? Sanjana!	To contribute to the international peaces, to observe the rules of international market, to trade with honest, to help in the devolpment of economi-	Redirection

Pupil Teacher's Activities	Pupils' Activities	Components
How can you say that social responsibilities can not be ignored?	cally backward countries. Business is a part of society so they must have positive attitude towards the needs of society to ensure the success of the organisation in future.	Increasing critical Awareness

In simple words, social responsibilities means the performance of those functions which are inaccordance with the feeling, wishes and expectations of society.

Observation Schedule :

Components	Rating scale				
Prompting	0	1	2	3	4
Seeking further information	0	1	2	3	4
Refocusing	0	1	2	3	4
Redirecting	0	1 2		3	4
Critical awareness	0	1	2	3	4

Rating Scale:

0 → Not satisfactory
1 → Satisfactory
2 → Average
3 → Good
4 → V-Good

Supervisor's Remarks

MICRO LESSON PLAN – 3

Name : Roll No.:
Subject : Commerce Class : XI
Topic : Communication Skill : Probing Questions

Teaching Aids: Chalkboard, Chalk, Duster

Pupil Teacher's Activities	Pupils' Activities	Components
What is communication? I am talking to you, is it a communication?	Yes, communication is the passing of information or message.	Prompting
What are the elements of communication?	(1) Receiver (2) Message	Seeking futher information
Is there any other element of communication?	No response	
How do we come to know that the receiver had understood the message of communication?	By feedback	Refocussing
How many types of communication are there?	(*i*) Formal (*ii*) Informal	Seeking further information
What is formal communication?	Offcial communication which follows the chain of demand.	Seeking further information
What is informal communication?	Communication through informal contracts among the people.	Seeking futher information
Is there any advantage of formal communication?	No response	
Sanjana, you tell is there any advantage?	Reliability and orderly fow of information.	Redirecting
Is there any advantage of informal communication?	Speed is very fast.	
How many types of communication is there?	(1) Downward (2) Upward (3) Horizontal	Seeking futher information
How many types of methods of communication are there?	(1) Oral (2) Written	
It there any other method?	No response	
If a person can't speak and write then how will he communicate his message?	By gesture and by actions	Refocussing
What is oral communication?	Exchange messages with the help of spoken words.	Seeking futher information
Can you explain that in an organisation which method of communication should be used?		Critical awareness

Thus communication is the passing of information or message in oral or written form, formally or informally.

Observation Schedule:

Components	**Rating scale**				
Prompting	0	1	2	3	4
Seeking further information	0	1	2	3	4
Refocussing	0	1	2	3	4
Redirecting	0	1 2		3	4
Critical awareness	0	1	2	3	4

Rating Scale:

0 → Not Satisfactory
1 → Satisfactory
2 → Average
3 → Good
4 → V-Good

Supervisor's Remarks

MICRO LESSON PLAN – 4

Name :
Subject : Commerce
Topic : Recruitment & Selection

Roll No.:
Class : XI
Skill : Stimulus Variation

Criteria of the Skill

(1) Getting pupil's attention.
(2) Clarifcation of the content.
(3) Creating interest among the students.
(4) Maximum involvement of the students.

Opening Statement

Dear students! Today, we shall study about recruitment and selection.

Pupil Teacher's Activities	Pupils' Activities	Components
What is Recruitment?	Recruitment is the process of searching prospective employee and stimulate them to apply for job.	Students involvement
Recruitment process involves: (1) Identifcation of source (2) Assess their validity (3) Invites application from condidates who are suitable?		Change in interacting style
What are the sources of recruitment (pointing to a students)	(1) Internal sources (2) External sources	Use of gesture student involvement
Now, internal source of recruitment means sources of labour supply exist within organisation.		Verbal focus
What are the types of internal sources of recruitment. (Writing on the board?)	(1) Transfer (2) Promotion	Verbal visual focus
What is the merit of recruitment?		
Good, Is there any demerit of Internal sources?	Other employees get motivation.	Students involvement
	(1) More competition (2) Fresh talent will not come.	Students involvement
And, external source means recruitment of employees from outside the organisation.		Change in interacting style.
What is selection? Can you tell what is selection? (Pointing to a students) (movement)		Pause
	It involves a series of steps by which candidates are screened for choosing the most	Use of gesture

Pupil Teacher's Activities	Pupils' Activities	Components
What are the steps involved in selection process?	suitable candidate for vacant job. (1) Obtaining information about the candidates. (2) Choosing the right person.	Student involvement

Thus recruitment is the process of searching prospective employee and stimulate them to apply for job. The source for it can be interval as well as external.

Observation Schedule:

Components	Rating scale				
Movement	0	1	2	3	4
Use of Gestures	0	1	2	3	4
Change in speech pattern	0	1	2	3	4
Focussing	0	1	2	3	4
Change in interaction style	0	1	2	3	4
Oral Visual switching	0	1	2	3	4
Pausing	0	1	2	3	4
Physical involvement of Pupils.	0	1	2	3	4

Rating Scale:

0 → Not satisfactory
1 → Satisfactory
2 → Average
3 → Good
4 → Very Good.

Supervisor's Remarks

MICRO LESSON PLAN – 5

Name :
Subject : Commerce
Topic : Communication

Roll No.:
Class : XI
Skill : Explaining

Criteria of skill:

1. Introducing an idea or concept to the students.
2. Establishing structural relationship in language for fow of ideas.
3. Covering main ideas of the concept.
4. Keeping normal speed in explanation.
5. Attending completeness of idea.

Opening statement:

Dear students! Today, we shall study the meaning and types of communication.

Pupil Teacher's Activities	Pupils' Activities	Components
Communication is an important requirement of every business. "Communication is an exchange of facts, ideas, opinions or emotions by two or more persons".	Pupils are listening and noting down in their note books.	Covering essential points
There are four aspects of communication: (*a*) message (*b*) sender (*c*) receiver (*d*) feedback	Students are understanding.	Covering essential points
There are two basic forms of communication: (*a*) Non-verbal communication (*b*) Verbal communication	Students are taking interest.	Explaining the points
Verbal communication is further divided into two: (*a*) Oral (*b*) Written	Pupils are listening very carefully and noting down in their notebooks.	Covering essential points
The term 'non verbal' means "without words" for example: (1) Our ancestors communicated with one another by using body language (2) Red and green traffc lights, road pictographs are examples of non verbal communication	Students are listening and understanding.	Use of relevant examples
Verbal communication involves the use of symbols that have universal meaning for all who are taking part in the process. It may be oral or written. P.T. : What is communication?	Students are understanding	Covering the essential points

Student : It is an exchange of facts, ideas, opinions or emotions by two or more persons.

P.T.: Which are basic forms of communication?

Student: Verbal and Non-verbal.

Thus the traders and businessmen communicate verbally and non-verbally with their customers.

Observation Schedule:

Components			**Rating scale**		
Desirable Behaviours					
(1) Use of introductory statement	0	1	2	3	4
(2) Use of concluding statement	0	1	2	3	4
(3) Use of explaining links	0	1	2	3	4
(4) Use of visual techniques	0	1	2	3	4
(5) Defning technical words	0	1	2	3	4
(6) Covering essential points	0	1	2	3	4
(7) Testing pupil's understanding	0	1	2	3	4
(8) Interesting to pupils	0	1	2	3	4
Undersirable Behaviours	0	1	2	3	4
(9) Use of irrelevant statements	0	1	2	3	4
(10) Lack of continuity in statements	0	1	2	3	4
(11) Lack of fuency is explaining	0	1	2	3	4
(12) Use of vague words and phrases	0	1	2	3	4

Rating Scale:

0 → Not satisfactory
1 → Satisfactory
2 → Average
3 → Good
4 → Very Good

Supervisor's Remarks

Bibliography

Aggarwal, J.C., *Teaching of Commerce, A Practical Approach*

Ahuwalia, S.L., *Audio Visual Handbook*

All India Council of Secondary Education, *Draft Syllabus in Commerce for Higher Secondary School*

Bhaba Kamla and B.D. Bhaba, *The Principles and Method of Teaching*.

Bhall, C.L., *Audio-Visual Aids in Education.*

Bhatnagar, Suresh, *Technology of Teaching.*

Bhatt, B.D. and Sharma, S.R., *Modern Educational Series: Educational Technology.*

Bhorali, D., *Commerce Education in India.*

Bloom, Begamin, S., *Taxonomy of Educational Objectives.*

Bossing, N.L., *Teaching in Secondary Schools.*

Braskamp, L.A., *Evaluating teaching effectiveness.*

Dahiya, S.S., *Educational Technology: Towards Better Teacher Performance* .

Daughtrey, A.S., *Methods of Basic Business and Economic Education.*

Dhand, *Techniques of teaching.*

Dile, David, D., *What Teachers Need to know of the Knowledge, Skills and Values Essential for Good Teaching.*

Enterline, H.C., *Trends of thought in Business Education.*

Gratz, J.E., *Future Curriculum in Business Education.*

Gupta, S. and Narta, S.S., *Commerce Education in the New Millennium.*

Harms and Stach, *Methods in Vocational Business Education.*

Husain, Noushad, *Computer Assisted Learning: Theory and Practice.*

Khan, M.S., *Commerce Education.*

Locoman, S., *Mastering the Techniques of Teaching.*

Mehra,V., *Educational Technology.*

NCERT, *Audio-Visual Hand Book.*

Pal, Hansraj, *Teaching of Commerce (Hindi).*

Popham, Schag and Blockhuss, *A Teaching and Learning System for Business Education.*

Rao Seema, *Teaching of Commerce.*

Remmere, N.H. and Cage, N.L., *Educational Measurement and Evaluation.*

Robert, Molenda, Michael and Ressel, Heinich, J.D., *Instructional Media and the New Technologies of Instruction.*

Sands Lester, B., *Audio-Visual Procedures in teaching.*

Satlow, I.D., *Teaching Business subjects Effectively.*

Sharma R.A., *Curriculum Development.*

Shilt, B.A., *Business education a Retrospection.*
Siddiqui Nasim and Poonam Gaur, *Educational Technology and Teaching Skills.*
Singh L.C. and Sharma R.D., *Micro Teaching-Theory and Practices.*
Singh, R. and Singh, P., *Teaching of Commerce.*
Srivastva, H.S. *Curriculum and Methods of Teaching.*
Sterling G. Callahan, Calhown, C.C., *Successful Teaching in Secondary School Managing and learning Process in Business Education.*
Taiwo, A. A., *Foundations of Classroom Testing.*
Tonee, H.A., *Principles of Business Education.*
Tripathi, S., *Techniques of Teaching* .
UGC, Report of the Curriculum Development Centre in Commerce.

Exercise

Chapter 1. Meaning, Nature and Scope of Commerce

1. Defne commerce.
2. Discuss the nature and scope of commerce.
3. Defne commerce and give its scope and limitation.
4. What do you mean by commerce? Is it science or an art or both? Discuss in detail.
5. Mention the signifcance of commerce in school curriculum.
6. Why students should be taught the subject of commerce at senior secondary level? Explain. Give concrete examples to support your answer.
7. Describe briefy the objectives of teaching commerce at secondary stage by ICSE.
8. What is the theoretical value of learning commerce?
9. Write practical values of teaching commerce.
10. Why should commerce be taught at the school stage?
11. What is the importance of commerce in life?

Chapter 2. Understanding Business Studies and Accountancy

1. Explain the meaning and characteristics of Business.
2. What are the types of utilities created by a business?
3. Explain the classifcation of Business Activities on the basis of their function.
4. Describe the concept of Business.
5. Defne Business.
6. Describe nature and scope of Business Studies.
7. Accountancy is science or an art or both. Explain.
8. Defne Accountancy
9. Describe limitations of accountancy.
10. What do you understand by Accountancy? Describe its nature and scope.
11. Describe the importance of teaching accountancy.
12. How business studies plays an important role for the students of commerce?

Chapter 3. Aims and Objectives of Teaching Commerce

1. Discuss the aims of teaching commerce.
2. Enlist the desirable outcomes of commerce education.
3. Enumerate the aims of teaching commerce at higher secondary stage of education.
4. "Commerce education should be vocation based." Explain the purpose of commerce education in the light of this statement.
5. What are the main objectives of teaching commerce?
6. What are the aims of teaching commerce? How far these aims realized in our schools?
7. What should be the aims of teaching commerce in democratic set-up of India?

Describe.

8. Explain the objectives of accountancy.
9. State the objectives of Business Studies.
10. Explain Bloom's taxonomy of instructional objectives.
11. Explain psychomotor objectives as given by different educationists.
12. Explain cognitive objectives in detail.
13. Explain the affective objectives with example from commerce.
14. Whether psychomotor objectives of commerce can be measured? If yes, how?
15. Describe revised taxonomy of Bloom given by Krathwohl and Anderson. Illustrate with examples.
16. Differentiate between Bloom's taxonomy and the taxonomy given by Anderson and Krathwohl.
17. Describe digital taxonomy of Bloom.
18. How digital taxonomy is different from the revised Bloom's taxonomy given by the Krathwohl and Anderson? Explain with examples.
19. Frame behavioural objectives related to any topic of business studies based on digital taxonomy.

Chapter 4. Writing Instructional Objectives in Behavioural Terms

1. What is the need of writing instructional objectives in behavioural terms?
2. Give at least three objectives from cognitive domain, two from affective domain and one from psychomotor domain with their behavioural changes.
3. What do you think of a student completely absorb himself in solving accounts problems? Answer in terms of objectives.
4. Which type of speed, accuracy and practice come under behavioural aspect? Answer with examples.
5. Describe Mager's approach of writing instructional objectives in behavioural terms with the help of examples.
6. Describe Miller's approach of writing instructional objectives in behavioural terms with the help of examples.
7. Illustrate with suitable examples the RCEM approach of writing objectives in behavioural terms.
8. What do you mean by writing instructional objectives in behavioural terms? Describe various plans of writing objectives in behavioural terms.
9. Frame behavioural objectives on any topic of Accountancy on the basis of revised Bloom's Taxonomy.
10. Illustrate with example related to any topic of Business studies, the Bloom's digital taxonomy of objectives.

Chapter 5. Curriculum and Textbook of Commerce

1. What considerations should be kept in mind while constructing the commerce curriculum?
2. Evaluate the prevailing commerce curriculum in your state. What suggestions would you like to make it more effective and meaningful?
3. What type of activities will you suggest in commerce curriculum at higher secondary stage?
4. What do you mean by curriculum? Describe the process of developing the commerce curriculum.
5. How will you select material for commerce curriculum?
6. Why should the commece curriculum be frequently revised?

7. List the major defects of commerce curriculum prescribed for higher secondary classes in your state.
8. What are the suggestions given by New Education Policy 2020 regarding curriculum? What changes should be done in the curriculum of commerce while following the suggestions given by NEP 2020.
9. Explain the essential qualities of good commerce text book.
10. Examine critically the business studies text-books prescribed for XI class in your state.
11. Describe the importance of a text-book in teaching commerce.
12. What factors should be kept in mind while selecting a text-book for accounts for class XI ?
13. Explain the role of library in teaching commerce.
14. Suggest a few important ways for effcient and proper use of commerce library.
15. What should be the content of a commerce library?
16. "A text-book should be used as a servant and not master." Explain this statement.
17. Explain the criteria usually used for the evaluation of the text-book of commerce.
18. "Text-book is the basic instrument of teaching ." Elaborate the statement.
19. What are the suggestions given by New Education Policy 2020 regarding the textbook?

Chapter 6. Self Instructional Modules and Materials in Teaching Commerce

1. What are self instructional modules? Discuss their importance in the teaching of commerce.
2. What are different types of programmed instruction? Explain.
3. Describe the procedure of developing programmed instructions.
4. What are the instructional values of group directed instruction in teaching of commerce?
5. Explain the basic steps in writing commerce programme.
6. What are the advantages of computer assisted instruction in teaching of commerece?
7. What steps will you follow while utilizing group directed instructions in your class of commerce?
8. What are the different group directed instructional modules in commerce?
9. Explain the developments in the feld of ICT and CAI.
10. What are the limitations of Computer Assisted Instructions? How these can be controlled?
11. Prepare an instructional module on any topic of Business studies based on CAI.
12. How will you teach accounts with the help of ICT? Illustrate with example.
13. What is the meaning of On line Banking?
14. What are the advantages of Internet in business activities?
15. Explain the importance of instruction material in teaching of commerce.
16. What is the procedure for selection of instructional material for commerce teaching?
17. As a teacher what type of material will you use for teaching commerce at

senior secondary level? Give examples.

18. What type of equipment and aids should be used to make the teaching of commerce effective? Explain.

19. Discuss the teaching learning situation in which you would like to use chart.

20. What precautions should be kept in mind while using graph and tables in the class?

21. How will you utilize television programme to teach Business studies is an effective way?

22. Prepare a power point presentation on any topic of Business studies. How will you make it effective?

23. What is social networking? How will you use it to make teaching and learning of commerce effective? Explain with examples.

24. In the period of digitalization, as a teacher how will you enhance learning of commerce with blogs?

Chapter 7. Effective Skills and Methods of Teaching Commerce

1. How to make the chalkboard work neat and clean?

2. How can you secure and sustain pupil's attention?

3. What are the components of classroom management?

4. Defne the skill of explaining? Describe its various components.

5. How can you bring clarity and understanding of abstract concept?

6. What are the components of skill of stimulus variation?

7. Describe the components of skill of illustration with examples.

8. Classify the following reinforcess in different categories.

(*i*) Writing pupils' answer on the chalkboard.
(*ii*) Say Um, aha.
(*iii*) Smiling on pupils' response.
(*iv*) Use ideas of pupil for the development of lesson.
(*v*) Carry on, think again.
(*vi*) Frowning at the incorrect response of the pupil.

9. Match the following:

Column I	**Column II**
Techniques	**Statements**
Prompting	Ask related question
Seeking further information	Direct question to many pupils
Redirection	Get more information
Refocussing	Give reasons for the response
Increasing critical awareness	Give hints to pupils

10. What is problem solving method in teaching? How does it differ from project method? Explain its merits and demerits.

11. What do you mean by project method? How will you use it for teaching commerce?

12. Describe the various methods of teaching commerce. Which method is best and why?

13. Describe in detail the uses of discussion method in teaching commerce.

14. How would you use 'Socialized Recitation' method to teach commerce?

15. What do you mean by supervised study? How can it be used in teaching commerce? Describe its merits and demerits.

16. What do you mean by lecture method in teaching commerce? Describe its merits and demerits.

17. In what situation lecture-cum-discussion method can be used in commerce teaching?
18. "Lecture-cum-discussion method is an improvised form of lecture method". Elaborate.
19. What do you mean by role play? Describe its merits and limitations.

Chapter 8. Specifc Approaches of Teaching Book Keeping

1. Describe the journal approach of teaching book-keeping.
2. Write a short note on Balance sheet approach of teaching book-keeping.
3. What do you mean by book keeping? Explain the principles of teaching book keeping.
4. Explain the ledger approach of teaching book-keeping.
5. What is the meaning of book keeping? What are its instructional objectives?

Chapter 9. Active Learning Strategies

1. What do you mean by active learning?
2. How a teacher can utilize brainstorming in the class? Illustrate with example.
3. What are the different active learning strategies? Explain any three.
4. What is the responsibility of the teacher while utilising active learning strategies in the classroom?
5. Create an active learning strategy to teach any topic of commerce in your class.
6. Will problem based learning encourage your students to discuss a topic with one another? Clarify the statement with example.
7. What do you mean by experimental learning activity as explained by New Education Policy 2020? How active learning strategies will help in getting experimental learning?
8. Whether collaborative learning strategy help in producing deeper understanding of the students? If yes, How?
9. Peer teaching activities help boost vital skills and behaviours including student interaction accountability and group processing. Comment on this statement.
10. As a teacher, what is your role in the active learning classroom?
11. How will you provide your students the opportunities to refect on the learning process?
12. Will brain storming help your students to think deeply and critically about a topic or lesson or will it be simply a comprehension exercise?

Chapter 10. Co-Curricular Activities in Commerce

1. What do you mean by co-curricular activities? Discuss their need and importance in teaching of Commerce.
2. What are the different principles of organising co-curricular activities related to Commerce?
3. Write down the values of co-curricular activities in the feld of Commerce. Explain some important activities that can be undertaken by Commerce students.
4. Discuss the need and importance of feld trip in the teaching of Commerce.
5. Discuss the importance of debate in the teaching of Commerce. State the steps for organising debates.

6. How will you create commerce club? Explain its merits.

Chapter 11. Commerce Teacher

1. "In the hands of an inspired teacher, commerce can become a means of real education." Discuss.
2. Describe the role of teacher in teaching commerce.
3. Describe the qualities should a teacher of commerce possess in order to be a successful and popular teacher.
4. Go over the list of qualities and characteristics that enter into the personality and write down those which you think could easily be improved in your own life and those which would be diffcult.
5. Discuss the slogan: "We are teaching pupils, not subject matter."
6. Why do the commerce require the highest type of teachers?
7. How can the teacher can cultivate better relationships with his pupils and colleagues?

Chapter 12. Construction of Tests in Commerce

1. What do you mean by achievement test? Explain its purposes.
2. Defne achievement test. What is its importance?
3. Describe in detail the construction process of achievement test.
4. Construct an achievement test related to Business Studies in Commerce for 11th class of 100 marks.
5. In what situations the objective type questions are preferred to essay type and why?
6. If a teacher does not prepare a blueprint what are the likely consequences in terms of its impact on quality of the achievement test?
7. If more essay type questions are included in an achievement test it may lower the reliability of the test. If ETQ are totally excluded from a test it may affect validity of the test, justify.
8. What do you mean by item analysis? Discuss the methods of calculating diffculty value of items.
9. What do you mean by diffculty value of an item? Describe different methods of calculating diffculty value of an item.
10. Describe the meaning of discriminating index. Discuss the major steps in calculating discriminating index of an ability test.
11. Discuss the major problems of item analysis and cite examples.
12. Distinguish between diffculty value and validity index of an item.
13. Write short notes on:
    - (i) Purpose of item analysis
    - (ii) Item validity
    - (iii) Relationship between item validity and discriminating power.
    - (iv) Problem related to dichotomised items.
14. How the problem of controlling unwanted factors can be solved?
15. An achievement test consists of multiple choice item, each having from alternatives. It was administered to 125 students. If the item no. 40 was solved correctly by 65 students, 26 students did not reach to it and the rest gave incorrect answer, then calculate the diffculty level of this item.
16. What do you mean by unit test? Describe its uses.

17. What are the criteria of a good unit test?
18. Formulate a test on the unit 'Management' for the duration of 40 minutes.
19. Describe the different steps for preparing a unit test.
20. Discuss the purposes of a unit test.
21. What is the procedure of preparing a blue-print for the unit test? Illustrate with example.

Chapter 13. Pedagogical Analysis in Commerce

1. What do you mean by 'Pedagogical Analysis'?
2. How the pedagogical analysis can be useful for a commerce teacher?
3. What are the different steps of pedagogical analysis?
4. Describe them in detail with example. Give pedagogical analysis of the following unit keeping in mind the steps of it:
   (*i*) Final Accounts
   (*ii*) Offce Management
   (*iii*) Double Entry System.

Chapter 14. Assessment, Evaluation and Grading in Commerce

1. What do you understand by assessment?
2. What do you understand by Evaluation? Explain its functions.
3. What is the importance of evaluation in commerce?
4. Knowledge of evaluation is essential for effective teaching. Critically examine this statement.
5. What are the various techniques of evaluation? Discuss the advantages of essay type tests.
6. What do you mean by objective type test in commerce? Describe various types of objective type question with suitable examples.
7. What improvement do you suggest in the existing pattern of examination in commerce? Explain.
8. What is diagnostic test? Explain its needs and importance.
9. For the beneft of different users of cumulative record what information about a student would you like to record?
10. Describe the non-scholastic areas you would like to evaluate for students of commerce.
11. What do you mean by continuous and comprehensive evaluation? In what ways it is helpful for better teaching and better learning?
12. How observation tool can be helpful for the evaluation of students in commerce?
13. What are the different techniques of observation? Explain in details.
14. How the records can be helpful in the evaluation of a student in commerce?
15. What are the different characteristics of a good test in commerce?
16. Assess the uses of essay type examination in commerce. Give suggestions for its improvement.
17. Give two examples of each type of objective type question from business studies.
18. Prepare an effective question paper for XI class in Accountancy.
19. 'Knowledge of evaluation techniques is essential for effective teaching'.

Critically examine this statement.

20. 'The summative and formative evaluation are complementary to each other'. Justify.

21. How performance of students in commerce can be evaluated? Illustrate with examples.

22. What improvements are suggested by Education Policy 2020 is the process of evaluation?

23. Explain different ways to access student learning in commerce.

24. What issues a teacher should consider while assigning test grades?

25. Give suggestions to help students do better in exams.

26. Describe the ways to write effective multiple choice questions in commerce with examples.

27. Explain different approaches of assigning grades.

28. As a teacher, how will you encourage your students for improvement after every test?

29. On what basis you would like to assign grade to your students?

30. Compare between criterion-referenced grading and norm-referenced grading.

31. How refective journal will help in assessing the students themselves?

32. Explain qualitative techniques of evaluation.

Chapter 15. Lesson Planning

1. What do you understand by lesson plan? Throw light on its merits and demerits.

2. Explain the Herbart steps of lesson planning.

3. Write in detail Morrison's approach of lesson planning.

4. Prepare a lesson plan for +1 commerce class on any topic of your choice.

5. What is lesson plan? Describe the various steps of lesson planning.

6. What precaution does a teacher exercise while preparing the lesson plan in commerce?

7. What do you understand by Evaluation approach of lesson planning? Describe in detail.

8. What are the different approaches of lesson planning? Describe one of them in detail.

9. Describe the need and importance of lesson planning.

10. Why should a teacher prepare his/her lesson plan? What main points should be considered in this regarded?

11. What guidelines should a teacher use for better teaching practice?

12. What is NTeQ model of lesson planning?

13. Describe steps of lesson planning in NTeQ model.

14. Prepare a lesson plan for teaching business studies based on NTeQ model.

15. Describe the steps of lesson planning based on 5Es.

16. What are 5Es in lesson planning? Explain with example from commerce.

17. What is the 5Es model of commerce teaching?

18. 'Teachers who can incorporate 5Es model in their classroom help students to build a strong foundation of knowledge through active participation.' Justify.

19. Describe the application and effectiveness of 5Es model of teaching in commerce.